taste of home

Best Church Supper
RECIPES

taste of home

REIMAN MEDIA GROUP, INC. · GREENDALE, WISCONSIN

taste of home

Reader's Digest

A TASTE OF HOME/READER'S DIGEST BOOK

© 2009 Reiman Media Group, Inc.
5400 S. 60th St., Greendale WI 53129
All rights reserved.
Taste of Home and Reader's Digest are registered
trademarks of The Reader's Digest Association, Inc.

Editors: Heidi Reuter Lloyd, Mark Hagen
Art Director: Edwin Robles, Jr.
Layout Designers: Emma Acevedo,
Catherine Fletcher
Proofreader: Julie Schnittka
Editorial Assistant: Barb Czysz
Recipe Asset Management System:
Coleen Martin, manager;
Sue A. Jurack, specialist
Food Director: Diane Werner RD
Recipe Testing and Editing: Taste of Home Test Kitchen
Food Photography: Reiman Photo Studio
Cover Photo Photographer: Dan Roberts
Cover Photo Food Stylist: Diane Armstrong
Cover Photo Food Set Stylist: Jennifer Bradley Vent
Photography Coordinator: Trudi Bellin
Additional Photography: Mark Derse
Additional Cover Photography: Ken Dequaine

Senior Editor, Books: Mark Hagen
Creative Director: Ardyth Cope
Chief Marketing Officer: Lisa Karpinski
Vice President, Executive Editor/Books: Heidi Reuter Lloyd
Senior Vice President, Editor in Chief: Catherine Cassidy

The Reader's Digest Association, Inc.
President and Chief Executive Officer: Mary G. Berner
President, U.S. Affinities: Suzanne M. Grimes
SVP, Chief Marketing Officer: Amy J. Radin
President, Global Consumer Marketing: Dawn M. Zier

International Standard Book Number (10): 0-89821-776-8
International Standard Book Number (13): 978-0-89821-776-6
Library of Congress Control Number: 2008934688

For other Taste of Home books and products,
visit www.tasteofhome.com.
For more Reader's Digest products and information,
visit www.rd.com (in the United States)
www.rd.ca (in Canada)

Printed in China
7 9 10 8

Special thanks to
St. James Catholic Church,
Franklin, Wisconsin

St. Charles Borromeo Parish,
Milwaukee, Wisconsin

Pictured on front cover (clockwise from bottom):
Asparagus Pasta Salad (p. 107), Crispy Fried Chicken (p. 6),
Four-Fruit Compote (p. 120) and Chocolate Mint Brownies
(p. 192).

Table of Contents

Church Supper Classics 5

Appetizers & Snacks 23

Comforting Casseroles 41

Slow Cooker Favorites 63

Breakfast & Brunch 85

Salads & Side Dishes 103

Hearty Main Dishes 131

Soups & Sandwiches 153

Delightful Desserts 169

Seasonal Fare 193

Quick & Easy 215

Feeding a Crowd 231

Index 249

Nourish the body as well as the soul with 506 Potluck Dishes

Fellowship, friends, fun and of course, great food. These are the heartwarming traits that draw folks to church suppers time and again.

From coast to coast, hundreds of thousands of people gather regularly to share a spirit of camaraderie over delicious dinners, brunches and picnics, featuring foods that are prepared by fellow patrons.

That's why we have created this collection of 506 all-time favorite potluck dishes. With *Best Church Supper Recipes,* you'll never have to worry about what you're going take to a carry-in meal again. That's because each of the items shared here has been taste-tested and approved by family cooks just like you!

From appetizers and side dishes to entrees and desserts, each of this book's specialties serves eight guests or more, travels well and offers the sort of must-try flavor that will have everyone at the potluck talking about your delightful contribution.

The next time you sign up to bring a main course, consider a comforting classic such as Ham 'n' Cheese Potato Bake (page 10) or Make-Ahead Sloppy Joes (page 156). You might also want to try Cheesy Shell Lasagna (page 60) from the chapter "Comforting Casseroles" or hearty Chicken Stew (page 74) from "Slow Cooker Favorites."

You'll never be at a loss when it comes to finding the perfect side dish either. Ideal for family reunions, holiday menus and church suppers alike, specialties such as Deluxe German Potato Salad (page 124) and Patchwork Rice Pilaf (page 130) complement nearly any entree. If you'd rather contribute a baked good, see the recipes for Angel Rolls (page 19), Lemon Poppy Seed Bread (page 87) and Butter-Dipped Biscuit Squares (page 228). They're sure to stand out on the buffet table.

What church supper would be complete without a trip (or two) to the dessert table? Heavenly cakes, old-fashioned cookies, fudgy brownies and those oh-so-tasty pies make every potluck a surefire success.

There are plenty of sweet sensations from which to choose. Dazzle friends with Maple-Mocha Brownie Torte (page 170), Deep-Dish Cherry Pie (page 175) or Black Forest Trifle (page 189). No matter what after-dinner delicacy you prepare, it's bound to become your signature creation at get-togethers.

Not sure you will have time to cook for an upcoming covered-dish dinner? With the satisfying recipes in the "Quick & Easy" chapter, you'll discover how quickly you can whip up a memorable item. And thanks to the dishes in "Feeding a Crowd," you can serve 50, 75 or even 100 folks. This book has you covered for all your holiday- and season-themed meals, too. Just turn to page 198 and take a look at Christmas Fruit Salad or see page 212 for Easter Egg Bread.

Regardless of what recipes you try first, you will find that every dish in *Taste of Home Best Church Supper Recipes* is made to be enjoyed with friends and family in the spirit of fellowship with which it is shared.

Pictured below: Marinated Vegetable Salad (p. 18), Grilled Picnic Chicken (p. 9), Southwestern Pasta Salad (p. 8), Summer Sub Sandwich (p. 10), Brownies in a Cone (p. 21) and Root Beer Cookies (p. 20).

Church Supper Classics

Crispy Fried Chicken

(pictured below)
Donna Kuhaupt, Slinger, Wisconsin
Well-seasoned with oregano and sage, this classic is sure to satisfy guests at church potlucks. The Sunday dinner staple is first fried and then baked to a crispy golden brown. I love fixing it for family and friends.

1-1/2 cups all-purpose flour
  1/2 cup cornmeal
  1/4 cup cornstarch
    3 teaspoons salt
    2 teaspoons paprika
    1 teaspoon dried oregano
    1 teaspoon rubbed sage
    1 teaspoon pepper
    2 eggs
  1/4 cup water
    2 broiler/fryer chickens (3 to 4 pounds *each*), cut up
Vegetable oil for frying

In a large resealable plastic bag, combine the flour, cornmeal, cornstarch, salt, paprika, oregano, sage and pepper. In a shallow bowl, beat eggs and water. Dip chicken in egg mixture; place in the bag, a few pieces at a time, and shake until coated.

In an electric skillet, heat 1 in. of oil to 375°. Fry chicken, a few pieces at a time, for 3-5 minutes on each side or until golden and crispy.

Place in two ungreased 15-in. x 10-in. x 1-in. baking pans. Bake, uncovered, at 350° for 25-30 minutes or until chicken is tender and juices run clear.

Yield: 12 servings.

Herb-Buttered Corn

(pictured above)
Donna Smith, Victor, New York
My husband and I love fresh corn on the cob, and this is a mouth-watering way to serve it.

  1/2 cup butter, softened
    1 tablespoon minced fresh chives
    1 tablespoon minced fresh dill
    1 tablespoon minced fresh parsley
  1/2 teaspoon dried thyme
  1/4 teaspoon salt
Dash garlic powder
Dash cayenne pepper
  10 ears fresh corn, husked and cooked

In a bowl, combine first eight ingredients; mix well. Spread over each ear of corn.

Yield: 10 servings.

Seafood Delight

Sandra Pacak, Indianapolis, Indiana
Here's a simple crab spread that's sure to please no matter where it's served. Take it to your next get-together and watch folks gobble it up.

    1 package (8 ounces) cream cheese, softened
    1 can (6 ounces) crabmeat, drained, flaked and cartilage removed
  1/2 cup seafood sauce
  1/4 cup prepared horseradish
    1 teaspoon lemon juice
Assorted crackers

In a mixing bowl, beat cream cheese until smooth. Spread onto a 10-in. serving plate. Combine the crab, seafood sauce, horseradish and lemon juice; mix well. Spread over cream cheese. Serve with crackers.

Yield: about 2 cups.

Church Coleslaw

Marjorie Force, Boonton, New Jersey
After enjoying this coleslaw for years at many church functions, I finally asked for the recipe. I'm so glad I did! It can be put together in no time, so it's perfect when time is tight.

   1 cup mayonnaise
1/2 cup sugar
1/3 cup cider vinegar
   1 teaspoon salt
1/8 teaspoon pepper
1/8 teaspoon paprika
1/2 medium head cabbage, shredded
   2 medium carrots, shredded
   1 celery rib, shredded

Place the first six ingredients in a blender or food processor. Cover and process on high until the sugar is dissolved, about 30 seconds. In a large bowl, combine cabbage, carrots, celery and dressing; toss to coat.
Yield: 8-10 servings.

Seven-Fruit Salad

(pictured below)
Martha Cutler, Willard, Missouri
This refreshing fruit medley, lightly coated with cherry pie filling, makes a great potluck or picnic dish. You can substitute other fruits, such as red grapes or bananas, and use strawberry pie filling instead of cherry.

   2 cans (15 ounces *each*) reduced-sugar sliced peaches, drained
   2 cans (11 ounces *each*) mandarin oranges, drained
   1 can (20 ounces) unsweetened pineapple chunks, drained
   1 cup reduced-sugar cherry pie filling
   1 cup halved fresh strawberries
   1 cup green grapes
1/2 cup fresh *or* frozen blueberries

In a large bowl, combine the peaches, oranges, pineapple and pie filling. Add the strawberries, grapes and blueberries; stir gently. Refrigerate leftovers.
Yield: 10 servings.

Double Chip Bars

(pictured above)
Victoria Lowe, Lititz, Pennsylvania
Peanut butter and chocolate make these dessert bars perfect for charity bake sales and school treats. The bars go together so quickly that I can even make them on my busiest days.

    1/2 cup butter
1-1/2 cups graham cracker crumbs
      1 can (14 ounces) sweetened condensed
          milk
      2 cups (12 ounces *each*) semisweet
          chocolate chips
      1 cup peanut butter chips

Place butter in a 13-in. x 9-in. x 2-in. baking pan; place in a 350° oven until melted. Remove baking pan from the oven. Sprinkle the cracker crumbs evenly over butter. Pour the milk evenly over crumbs. Sprinkle with chips; press down firmly.

Bake at 350° for 25-30 minutes or until golden brown. Cool on a wire rack before cutting.

Yield: 3 dozen.

Potluck Pointer

Don't be afraid to mix up the ingredients in Double Chip Bars. Try replacing the peanut butter chips with butterscotch chips or eliminate a cup of chocolate chips and use chopped peanuts and shredded coconut in its place.

Southwestern Pasta Salad

(pictured below)
Ann Brown, Bolivar, Missouri
This satisfying salad has a nice blend of textures and flavors. I really appreciate its make-ahead convenience.

      1 package (1 pound) small shell pasta
    2/3 cup cider vinegar
      2 celery ribs, chopped
      6 green onions, thinly sliced
    1/2 cup chopped green pepper
      1 can (15-1/2 ounces) black-eyed peas,
          rinsed and drained
      1 can (11 ounces) whole kernel corn,
          drained
      1 can (2-1/4 ounces) sliced ripe olives,
          drained
    1/2 cup sliced stuffed olives
      3 tablespoons diced pimientos
    1/3 cup mayonnaise
    1/4 cup vegetable oil
      1 to 2 teaspoons chili powder
      1 teaspoon salt
    1/4 teaspoon Worcestershire sauce
    1/8 to 1/4 teaspoon hot pepper sauce

Cook pasta according to package directions; drain and rinse with cold water. Place in a large bowl; add the vinegar and toss to combine.

Stir in the celery, onions, green pepper, peas, corn, olives and pimientos. In a small bowl, combine the remaining ingredients; stir into pasta mixture. Cover and refrigerate overnight.

Yield: 10-12 servings.

Grilled Picnic Chicken

(pictured above)
Cindy DeRoos, Iroquois, Ontario
*This chicken marinates overnight so it's ready to grill
the following day. Try it the next time you are in charge of
preparing the main course.*

1-1/2 cups white vinegar
  3/4 cup vegetable oil
    6 tablespoons water
4-1/2 teaspoons salt
1-1/2 teaspoons poultry seasoning
  3/4 teaspoon garlic powder
  3/4 teaspoon pepper
    3 broiler/fryer chicken (3 to 4 pounds *each*),
      quartered or cut up

In a bowl, combine the first seven ingredients. Remove 1 cup marinade for basting; cover and refrigerate.

Pour the remaining marinade into a gallon-size resealable plastic bag; add chicken. Seal the bag and turn to coat; refrigerate for 4 hours or overnight, turning once or twice.

Drain and discard marinade. Grill chicken, uncovered, over medium heat for 30 minutes, turning once. Baste with the reserved marinade. Grill 10-20 minutes longer or until the juices run clear, turning and basting several times.

Yield: 12 servings.

Ham 'n' Cheese Potato Bake

(pictured below)
Barbara Larson, Rosemount, Minnesota
This hearty ham and hash brown casserole is frequently requested at large gatherings with family members. I often include it on my brunch buffets.

   1 package (24 ounces) frozen O'Brien hash brown potatoes
   2 cups cubed fully cooked ham
3/4 cup shredded cheddar cheese, *divided*
   1 small onion, chopped
   2 cups (16 ounces) sour cream
   1 can (10-3/4 ounces) condensed cheddar cheese soup, undiluted
   1 can (10-3/4 ounces) condensed cream of potato soup, undiluted
1/4 teaspoon pepper

In a large bowl, combine potatoes, ham, 1/2 cup cheese and onion. In another bowl, combine sour cream, soups and pepper; add to potato mixture and mix well.

   Transfer to a greased 3-qt. baking dish. Sprinkle with remaining cheese. Bake, uncovered, at 350° for 60-65 minutes or until bubbly and potatoes are tender. Let stand for 10 minutes before serving.
Yield: 10-12 servings.

Summer Sub Sandwich

(pictured above)
Laverne Renneber, Chelan, Saskatchewan
When I need to feed a large group, I turn to this super, ham-and-cheese sandwich. It can be assembled in mere minutes.

 1 package (3 ounces) cream cheese, softened
 1 loaf (20 inches) unsliced French bread, halved lengthwise
 6 slices deli ham
 6 slices provolone cheese
 1 jar (4-1/2 ounces) sliced mushrooms, drained
 2 medium tomatoes, thinly sliced, optional
 1 small onion, thinly sliced
 2 banana peppers, thinly sliced
 2 cups shredded lettuce

Spread cream cheese on bottom half of bread. Layer with the ham, cheese, mushrooms, tomatoes if desired, onion, peppers and lettuce. Replace the top. Cut into 1-1/2-in. slices.
Yield: 10-15 servings.

Deli-Style Pasta Salad

(pictured above)
Joyce McLennan, Algonac, Michigan
Pasta provides a base for this tongue-tingling, make-ahead salad. It has lots of fresh and satisfying ingredients topped with a flavorful dressing. It's terrific to take to a potluck or serve to company.

- 1 package (12 ounces) uncooked tricolor spiral pasta
- 6 ounces thinly sliced hard salami, julienned
- 6 ounces provolone cheese, cubed
- 1 can (2-1/4 ounces) sliced ripe olives, drained
- 1 small red onion, thinly sliced
- 1 small zucchini, halved and thinly sliced
- 1/2 cup chopped green pepper
- 1/2 cup chopped sweet red pepper
- 1/4 cup minced fresh parsley
- 1/4 cup grated Parmesan cheese
- 1/2 cup olive oil
- 1/4 cup cider vinegar
- 1 garlic clove, minced
- 1-1/2 teaspoons ground mustard
- 1 teaspoon dried basil
- 1 teaspoon dried oregano
- 1/4 teaspoon salt
- Dash pepper
- 2 medium tomatoes, cut into wedges

Cook the pasta according to package directions; rinse in cold water and drain. Place in a large bowl; add the next nine ingredients.

In a jar with tight-fitting lid, combine oil, vinegar, garlic, mustard, basil, oregano, salt and pepper; shake well. Pour over salad; toss to coat.

Cover and chill for 8 hours or overnight. Toss before serving. Garnish with tomatoes.

Yield: 10-12 servings.

Green Bean Casserole

(pictured below)
Anna Baker, Blaine, Washington
This has always been one of my favorite "convenience dishes" because it can be prepared ahead and refrigerated until ready to bake. It's a long-time classic that people never tire of.

 2 cans (10-3/4 ounces *each*) condensed
    cream of mushroom soup, undiluted
 1 cup milk
 2 teaspoons soy sauce
 1/8 teaspoon pepper
 2 packages (16 ounces *each*) frozen whole *or*
    cut green beans, cooked and drained
 1 can (6 ounces) french-fried onions, *divided*

In a mixing bowl, combine soup, milk, soy sauce and pepper. Gently stir in beans. Spoon half of the mixture into a 12-in. x 8-in. x 2-in. baking dish. Sprinkle with half of the onions. Spoon remaining bean mixture over the top.

Bake at 350° for 30 minutes or until heated through. Sprinkle with remaining onions. Return to oven for 5 minutes or until the onions are brown and crispy.

Yield: 10 servings.

Three-Bean Casserole

(pictured above)
Jane Bone, Cape Coral, Florida
This is an old Mennonite recipe. I often take a big pot of these tangy beans to pitch-in suppers or large gatherings, and everyone enjoys them.

 2 bacon strips, chopped
 1 large green pepper, chopped
 1 medium onion, chopped
 1 can (28 ounces) pork and beans
 1 can (16 ounces) kidney beans, rinsed and
    drained
 1 can (15-1/4 ounces) lima beans, rinsed
    and drained
 1/2 cup ketchup
 1 jar (4 ounces) diced pimientos
 1/4 cup packed brown sugar
 1 tablespoon Worcestershire sauce
 1 teaspoon ground mustard

In a large nonstick skillet, cook bacon over medium heat until crisp. Remove to paper towels; drain, reserving 1 tablespoon drippings. In the drippings, saute green pepper and onion until tender.

Combine the beans in a large bowl. Gently stir in pepper mixture and bacon. Stir in the ketchup, pimientos, brown sugar, Worcestershire sauce and mustard until combined.

Transfer to a 2-qt. baking dish coated with nonstick cooking spray. Cover and bake at 350° for 50-60 minutes or until bubbly.

Yield: 9 servings.

Slow-Cooked Spaghetti and Meatballs

Jackie Grant, Vanderhoof, British Columbia
When I had this sauce at my sister-in-law's, I had to have the recipe. After all these years, I still think it's the best I've tasted. Served from the slow cooker, the zesty entree is ideal for bring-a-dish suppers.

 3 pounds ground beef
 1 cup finely chopped onion, *divided*
 1 teaspoon salt
 1/2 teaspoon pepper
 1 can (46 ounces) tomato juice
 1 can (28 ounces) diced tomatoes, drained
 1 can (15 ounces) tomato sauce
 2 celery ribs, chopped
 3 bay leaves
 2 garlic cloves, minced

In a bowl, combine the beef, 1/2 cup onion, salt and pepper; mix well. Shape into 1-in. balls. In a large skillet over medium heat, brown meatballs with remaining onion.

Transfer to a 5-qt. slow cooker; add the remaining ingredients. Cover and cook on low for 8-10 hours or until heated through, stirring occasionally. Remove and discard bay leaves.

Yield: 20 servings (about 4-1/2 quarts).

Best Deviled Eggs

Jesse and Anne Foust, Bluefield, West Virginia
Dill weed, garlic powder and ground mustard make these the best deviled eggs we've ever tasted.

 12 hard-cooked eggs
 1/2 cup mayonnaise
 1 teaspoon dried parsley flakes
 1/2 teaspoon minced chives
 1/2 teaspoon ground mustard
 1/2 teaspoon dill weed
 1/4 teaspoon salt
 1/4 teaspoon paprika
 1/8 teaspoon pepper
 1/8 teaspoon garlic powder
 2 tablespoons milk
Fresh parsley
Additional paprika

Slice eggs in half lengthwise; remove yolks and set whites aside. In a small bowl, mash yolks. Add the next 10 ingredients; mix well. Evenly fill the whites. Garnish with parsley and paprika.

Yield: 2 dozen.

Deluxe Macaroni 'n' Cheese

(pictured above)
Bertha Johnson, Indianapolis, Indiana
Here's an all-time classic that folks can't get enough of. Made creamy with cheddar cheese and sour cream, the casserole is a welcome addition to any party.

 2 cups small-curd cottage cheese
 1 cup (8 ounces) sour cream
 1 egg, lightly beaten
 3/4 teaspoon salt
Garlic salt and pepper to taste
 2 cups (8 ounces) shredded sharp cheddar cheese
 1 package (7 ounces) elbow macaroni, cooked and drained
Paprika, optional

In a large bowl, combine the cottage cheese, sour cream, egg, salt, garlic salt and pepper. Add cheddar cheese; mix well. Add macaroni and stir until coated.

Transfer to a greased 2-1/2-qt. baking dish. Bake, uncovered, at 350° for 25-30 minutes or until heated through. Sprinkle with paprika if desired.

Yield: 8-10 servings.

Pizza by the Yard

(pictured above)
Jean Johnson, La Veta, Colorado
These unique pizzas are always a hit. They're equally as good after the party; I enjoy them when I raid the fridge in the middle of the night...if there's any leftover, that is!

      1 pound lean ground beef
    1/2 cup sliced ripe olives
    1/2 cup chopped onion
    1/2 cup grated Parmesan cheese
      1 can (6 ounces) tomato paste
      1 teaspoon dried oregano
      1 teaspoon salt
    1/8 teaspoon pepper
      1 loaf French bread (20 inches), halved
         lengthwise
      3 medium tomatoes, sliced
      2 cups (8 ounces) shredded part-skim
         mozzarella cheese

In a bowl, combine the beef, olives, onion, Parmesan cheese, tomato paste, oregano, salt and pepper. Spread to the edges of the cut surface of the bread.

Broil 6 in. from the heat for 8-10 minutes or until the meat is fully cooked. Top with tomatoes and cheese. Broil 2-3 minutes more or until cheese is melted.

Yield: 8 servings.

Potluck Pointer

Sprigs of fresh herbs such as parsley and basil make eye-catching and fragrant garnishes for platters at covered-dish events. Dress up a serving dish of meat, pasta or fruit with the bright, leafy greens.

Apple Cherry Cobbler

(pictured below)
Eleanore Hill, Fresno, California
With an out-of-the-ordinary combination of fruits, this recipe gives a tasty twist to traditional desserts. Topped with whipped cream, it's old-fashioned comfort food updated to tempt folks of all ages.

        1 egg, beaten
      1/2 cup sugar
      1/2 cup milk
        2 tablespoons vegetable oil
        1 cup all-purpose flour
    2-1/4 teaspoons baking powder
        1 can (21 ounces) apple pie filling
        1 can (21 ounces) cherry pie filling
        1 tablespoon lemon juice
        1 teaspoon vanilla extract

TOPPING:
      1/3 cup packed brown sugar
        3 tablespoons all-purpose flour
        1 teaspoon ground cinnamon
        2 tablespoons butter, softened

In a bowl, combine first four ingredients. Combine flour and baking powder; add to egg mixture and blend well.

Pour into a greased 13-in. x 9-in. x 2-in. baking pan. Combine pie fillings, lemon juice and vanilla; spoon over batter.

For topping, combine all ingredients; sprinkle over filling. Bake at 350° for 40-45 minutes or until bubbly and cake tests done. If necessary, cover edges with foil to prevent over browning.

Yield: 12-16 servings.

Hearty Chicken Vegetable Soup

(pictured above)
Bertha Vogt, Tribune, Kansas
I experimented with various ingredients to create a heart-warming soup, and this is the result. It's especially good to take to potlucks or share with friends. Leftovers are wonderful reheated for a fast lunch the next day.

          1 roasting chicken (about 5 pounds), cut up
             and skin removed
          2 celery ribs, sliced
          1 large onion, chopped
    2-1/2 quarts water
          1 can (14-1/2 ounces) stewed tomatoes
          4 medium carrots, sliced
          2 medium potatoes, peeled and cubed
          1 medium turnip, peeled and cubed
          2 tablespoons chicken bouillon granules
        1/2 teaspoon minced fresh parsley
        3/4 teaspoon *each* dried basil, oregano and
             tarragon
        3/4 teaspoon salt
        3/4 teaspoon pepper
        1/2 teaspoon garlic powder
          2 cups fresh broccoli florets
          2 cups frozen peas, optional

Place the chicken, celery, onion and water in a Dutch oven or soup kettle; bring to a boil. Skim fat. Reduce heat; cover and simmer for 1-1/2 to 2 hours or until chicken is tender. Remove chicken; cool.

Remove meat from bones and cut into bite-size pieces; return to pan. Add tomatoes, carrots, potatoes, turnip, bouillon and seasonings; bring to a boil. Reduce heat; cover and simmer for 20 minutes. Add broccoli and peas if desired; simmer 15-20 minutes longer or until vegetables are tender.
Yield: 16 servings (about 4 quarts).

Potluck Chicken Casserole

(pictured below)
Faye Hintz, Springfield, Missouri
This may be a basic chicken casserole, but I never bring home leftovers whenever I take it to a potluck. The stick-to-your-ribs dish has lots of appeal, and I like that the golden crumb topping adds a little crunch to each serving.

          8 cups cubed cooked chicken
          2 cans (10-3/4 ounces *each*) condensed
             cream of chicken soup, undiluted
          1 cup (8 ounces) sour cream
          1 cup crushed butter-flavored crackers
             (about 25 crackers)
          2 tablespoons butter, melted
          1 teaspoon celery seed
    Fresh parsley and sweet red pepper rings, optional

Combine chicken, soup and sour cream; spread into a greased 13-in. x 9-in. x 2-in. baking dish. Combine crumbs, butter and celery seed; sprinkle over chicken mixture.

Bake, uncovered, at 350° for 30-35 minutes or until bubbly. Garnish with parsley and red pepper if desired.
Yield: 10-12 servings.

Chunky Beef Chili

(pictured below)
Vicki Flowers, Knoxville, Tennessee
When I first tasted this chili that my brother created, I couldn't wait to share it. It's the best I've ever had.

1/2 cup all-purpose flour
1-1/2 teaspoons *each* dried thyme and rosemary, crushed
1-1/2 pounds beef stew meat, cut into 1-inch cubes
1/2 pound ground beef
1 can (14-1/2 ounces) beef broth
1 large onion, finely chopped
1/2 cup chopped green pepper
1 garlic clove, minced
1 can (4 ounces) chopped green chilies
1 to 2 jalapeno peppers, seeded and minced
1 can (15 ounces) crushed tomatoes
2 cans (15-1/2 ounces *each*) chili beans, undrained
1 can (15-1/2 ounces) pinto beans, rinsed and drained
1 can (15 ounces) white kidney *or* cannellini beans, rinsed and drained
1 can (6 ounces) tomato paste
2 tablespoons ground cumin
1 teaspoon dried oregano
1/2 teaspoon *each* pepper, white pepper and cayenne pepper
3 to 4 drops hot pepper sauce
Shredded cheddar cheese, optional

In a plastic bag, combine flour, thyme and rosemary; add beef cubes and shake to coat.

In a 4-qt. kettle or Dutch oven, brown ground beef and the beef cubes; drain. Add remaining ingredients except cheese. Cover and simmer for 5 hours. Garnish with cheese if desired.

Yield: 10-12 servings (3 quarts).

Editor's Note: When cutting or seeding hot peppers, use rubber or plastic gloves to protect your hands. Avoid touching your face.

Potluck Strawberry Trifle

Celia Clark, New Tazewell, Tennessee
This recipe is a great way to serve dessert to a crowd. Frozen pound cake, strawberries and whipped topping add to the ease of preparation for this trifle, which is made in a jelly roll pan.

>   2 packages (3 ounces *each*) cook-and-serve vanilla pudding mix
>   2 packages (3 ounces *each*) strawberry gelatin
>   1 package (10-3/4 ounces) frozen pound cake, thawed
>   1 package (20 ounces) unsweetened frozen strawberries, thawed and halved
>   1 carton (8 ounces) frozen whipped topping, thawed

Prepare pudding according to package directions; cool. Prepare gelatin according to package directions; refrigerate until partially set. Meanwhile, slice the pound cake into 26 pieces. Place in an ungreased 15-in. x 10-in. x 1-in. baking pan. Top with strawberries. Spoon gelatin over strawberries. Refrigerate until set.

Carefully spread cooled pudding over gelatin (pan will be full). Carefully spread with whipped topping. Refrigerate until serving.

Yield: 24-30 servings.

Chocolate-Covered Crispies

Patricia Carmichael, Gibsons, British Columbia
Candy bars are the secret behind these treats. They are a fun change from the classic snack, plus they're so quick to make.

>   4 Milky Way candy bars (2.05 ounces *each*), cut up
>   3/4 cup butter, cubed, *divided*
>   3 cups crisp rice cereal
>   1 cup (6 ounces) semisweet chocolate chips

In a saucepan over low heat or in a microwave-safe bowl, melt candy bars and 1/2 cup butter; stir until blended. Stir in cereal. Pat into a greased 11-in. x 7-in. x 2-in. pan.

In another saucepan or microwave-safe bowl, melt the chocolate chips and remaining butter; stir until smooth. Spread over cereal mixture. Refrigerate until firm.

Yield: 2 to 2-1/2 dozen.

Editor's Note: In Canada, substitute Mars Bars for Milky Way bars.

Creamy Hash Brown Bake

(pictured above)
Yvonne Nave, Lyons, Kansas
This cheesy casserole couldn't be much easier to toss together. I just mix up the ingredients and sprinkle crushed potato chips on top. The result is so rich and satisfying that some people even enjoy it as a meatless entree.

>   1 can (10-3/4 ounces) condensed cream of mushroom soup, undiluted
>   1 can (10-3/4 ounces) condensed cheddar cheese soup, undiluted
>   1 cup (8 ounces) sour cream
>   1/2 cup butter, softened
>   1/4 cup chopped onion
>   1/2 teaspoon salt
>   1 package (28 ounces) frozen O'Brien hash brown potatoes
>   3/4 cup crushed potato chips

In a large bowl, combine the soups, sour cream, butter, onion and salt. Add potatoes; mix well.

Pour into a greased 13-in. x 9-in. x 2-in. baking dish. Sprinkle with potato chips. Bake, uncovered, at 350° for 55-60 minutes or until the potatoes are tender.

Yield: 10-12 servings.

Marinated Vegetable Salad

(pictured below)
Rita Wagers, Emporia, Kansas
This recipe is so versatile because you can use whatever vegetables you prefer. It's a nice change from typical mayonnaise-based salads.

  3 cups fresh broccoli florets
  2 cups fresh cauliflowerets
1-1/2 cups fresh baby carrots
  2 celery ribs, cut into 1/2-inch pieces
  1 medium zucchini, sliced
  1 can (14 ounces) water-packed artichoke hearts, rinsed, drained and quartered
  1 can (6 ounces) pitted ripe olives, drained
  1 jar (4-1/2 ounces) whole mushrooms, drained

DRESSING:
  3/4 cup vegetable oil
  1/3 cup cider vinegar
    1 teaspoon garlic salt
  3/4 teaspoon sugar
  1/2 teaspoon salt
  1/2 teaspoon lemon-pepper seasoning

In a large salad bowl, combine the first eight ingredients. In a jar with a tight-fitting lid, combine the dressing ingredients; shake well. Pour over the vegetable mixture and toss to coat.

Cover and refrigerate for 8 hours or overnight, stirring occasionally.

Yield: 14 servings.

Pecan-Filled Coffee Rings

Charlotte Schoening, Waterford, Wisconsin
This favorite family recipe was handed down to me by my great-grandmother. The easy-to-handle sweet dough produces two tempting rings that look lovely drizzled with a powdered sugar glaze.

  1 package (1/4 ounce) active dry yeast
  2 teaspoons plus 1/2 cup sugar, *divided*
  1 cup warm milk (110° to 115°)
  1 cup butter, softened
  3 egg yolks, beaten
  1 teaspoon vanilla extract
  1/2 teaspoon salt
  4 to 4-1/2 cups all-purpose flour

FILLING:
1-1/2 cups ground pecans
  1/2 cup sugar
    1 egg
    3 tablespoons butter, softened
    1 teaspoon vanilla extract

GLAZE:
    1 cup confectioners' sugar
    1 tablespoon lemon juice
    1 tablespoon milk

In a bowl, dissolve yeast and 2 teaspoons sugar in warm milk; let stand for 5 minutes. In a mixing bowl, cream butter and remaining sugar.

Beat in the egg yolks, vanilla and salt. Add yeast mixture and 1 cup flour; beat until smooth. Stir in enough remaining flour to form a soft dough. Turn onto a floured surface; knead until smooth and elastic, about 6-8 minutes. Place in a greased bowl, turning once to grease top. Cover and let rise in a warm place until doubled, about 1-1/4 hours.

Punch dough down. Turn onto a lightly floured surface; divide in half. Roll each portion into a 16-in. x 9-in. rectangle. Combine filling ingredients; spread over dough to within 1 in. of edges. Roll up jelly-roll style, starting with a long side; pinch seam to seal.

Place seam side down on greased baking sheets; pinch ends together to form a ring. With kitchen scissors, cut from the outside edge two-thirds of the way toward center of ring at 1-in. intervals. Separate strips slightly and twist to allow filling to show. Cover and let rise until doubled, about 45 minutes.

Bake at 350° for 30-35 minutes or until golden brown. Remove from pans to wire racks; cool for 20 minutes. Combine glaze ingredients; drizzle over warm rings.

Yield: 2 rings.

Apple Broccoli Salad

Brenda Sue Huntington, Clemons, New York
I came up with this recipe in an attempt to combine the flavors of Waldorf salad and my favorite broccoli salad. It really appeals to my family and friends.

     6 medium tart apples, chopped
     3 cups broccoli florets
     1 small onion, chopped
   1/2 cup raisins
 1-1/2 cups mayonnaise
     2 tablespoons white vinegar
 1-1/2 teaspoons sugar
   1/2 teaspoon lemon juice
   1/2 teaspoon salt
    10 bacon strips, cooked and crumbled
   1/2 cup coarsely chopped walnuts

In a large bowl, combine the apples, broccoli, onion and raisins. In a small bowl, combine the mayonnaise, vinegar, sugar, lemon juice and salt; pour over apple mixture and toss to coat. Cover and chill for at least 2 hours. Just before serving, stir in the bacon and walnuts.

Yield: 10-12 servings.

Candy Snack Mix

Mary Newsom, Grand Ridge, Florida
Chock-full of raisins, peanuts and M&M's, this crunchy, salty-sweet mix stays fresh for weeks. I keep it on hand to serve to unexpected guests or contribute to last-minute gatherings with friends.

     1 package (24 ounces) roasted peanuts
     1 package (18 ounces) Golden Grahams cereal
     1 package (15 ounces) raisins
   1/2 cup butter
    12 ounces white candy coating
     2 cups creamy peanut butter
     1 package (2 pounds) confectioners' sugar
     1 package (15 ounces) red and green milk chocolate M&M's

In a large bowl, combine the peanuts, cereal and raisins. In a heavy saucepan over low heat, melt butter, candy coating and peanut butter; stir until smooth. Pour over peanut mixture and toss to coat. Place sugar in a large bag; add coated mixture. Close bag and shake to coat. Spread onto baking sheets; sprinkle with M&M's. When cool, store in airtight containers.

Yield: 25 cups.

Angel Rolls

(pictured above)
Debbie Graber, Eureka, Nevada
Folks will delight in these soft, tender yeast rolls. The crowd-pleasers are ready in a jiffy, thanks to a package of quick-rise yeast. I love the down-home flair they add to meals and how well they go with anything found on a buffet table.

 3-1/2 cups bread flour, *divided*
     2 tablespoons sugar
     1 package (1/4 ounce) quick-rise yeast
 1-1/4 teaspoons salt
     1 teaspoon baking powder
   1/2 teaspoon baking soda
     1 cup warm buttermilk (120° to 130°)
   1/2 cup vegetable oil
   1/3 cup warm water (120° to 130°)
Melted butter

In a mixing bowl, combine 1-1/2 cups flour, sugar, yeast, salt, baking powder and baking soda. Add the buttermilk, oil and water; beat until moistened. Stir in enough remaining flour to form a soft dough.

Turn onto a floured surface and knead until smooth and elastic, about 4-6 minutes. Cover and let rest for 10 minutes.

Roll out to 1/2-in. thickness; cut with a 2-1/2-in. biscuit cutter. Place on a greased baking sheet. Bake at 400° for 15-18 minutes or until golden brown. Brush tops with butter.

Yield: 14 rolls.

Editor's Note: Warmed buttermilk will appear curdled.

Root Beer Cookies

(pictured below)
Violette Bawden, West Valley City, Utah
Since it's too difficult to take root beer floats to a picnic, take these cookies instead! The only hard part will be convincing your family to wait until the event to sample them.

- 1 cup butter, softened
- 2 cups packed brown sugar
- 2 eggs
- 1 cup buttermilk
- 3/4 teaspoon root beer concentrate *or* extract
- 4 cups all-purpose flour
- 1 teaspoon baking soda
- 1 teaspoon salt
- 1-1/2 cups chopped pecans

FROSTING:
- 3-1/2 cups confectioners' sugar
- 3/4 cup butter, softened
- 3 tablespoons water
- 1-1/4 teaspoons root beer concentrate *or* extract

In a large mixing bowl, cream butter and brown sugar. Add eggs, one at a time, beating well after each addition. Beat in buttermilk and root beer concentrate. Combine the flour, baking soda and salt; gradually add to creamed mixture. Stir in pecans.

Drop by tablespoonfuls 3 in. apart onto ungreased baking sheets. Bake at 375° for 10-12 minutes or until lightly browned. Remove to wire racks to cool. In a mixing bowl, combine frosting ingredients; beat until smooth. Frost cooled cookies.
Yield: about 6 dozen.

Orange Lemonade

(pictured above)
Tracie Loyd, Powell, Tennessee
This lemonade is a wonderful thirst quencher for a picnic or after a hot day of yard work or sports activities. It's truly a family favorite.

- 2 quarts water
- 1 cup sugar
- 1 can (12 ounces) frozen orange juice concentrate, thawed
- 1 can (12 ounces) frozen lemonade concentrate, thawed

In a saucepan, heat water and sugar until sugar is dissolved, stirring occasionally. Cool. Transfer to a large pitcher or container; stir in concentrates. Chill.
Yield: 12 servings.

Brownies in a Cone

(pictured above)
Mitzi Sentiff, Greenville, North Carolina
These brownie-filled ice cream cones are a fun addition to any summer get-together. They appeal to the child in everyone.

> 1 package fudge brownie mix (13-inch x 9-inch pan size)
> 17 ice cream cake cones (about 2-3/4 inches tall)
> 1 cup (6 ounces) semisweet chocolate chips
> 1 tablespoon shortening
> Colored sprinkles

Prepare brownie batter according to package directions, using 3 eggs. Place the ice cream cones in muffin cups; spoon about 3 tablespoons batter into each cone.

Bake at 350° for 25-30 minutes or until a toothpick comes out clean and top is dry (do not overbake). Cool completely.

In a microwave, melt chocolate chips and shortening; stir until smooth.

Dip tops of brownies in melted chocolate; decorate with sprinkles.

Yield: 17 servings.

Potluck Pointer

If you just don't have time to cook for the church supper, ask if you can contribute paper plates, napkins or plastic eating utensils. Or, volunteer to set up the dinner tables or promise to help clean up after the event.

Church Supper Sloppy Joes

(pictured below)
Rose Thompson, Colorado Springs, Colorado
My family loves these sandwiches. I prepared them when I worked in a school lunchroom and heard nothing but compliments.

> 7 pounds lean ground beef
> 1-1/2 cups chopped onion
> 1-1/2 cups chopped celery
> 1/2 cup packed brown sugar
> 2 tablespoons prepared mustard
> 6 cups tomato sauce
> 1/2 cup white vinegar
> 2 to 3 teaspoons minced garlic
> Salt and pepper to taste
> 1-1/2 cups (6 ounces) shredded sharp cheddar cheese
> Hamburger buns

In a large skillet, brown beef, onion and celery. Cook in batches if necessary. Drain any fat. Add all remaining ingredients except last two; cook 10 minutes.

Stir in cheese; cook until melted. Serve on buns.

Yield: 50 servings.

Mostaccioli

(pictured above)
Nancy Mundhenke, Kinsley, Kansas
Even though we're not Italian, this rich pasta dish is a family tradition at special occasions. I was delighted the first time I tried the recipe—it has all the flavor of lasagna without the work.

   1 pound uncooked mostaccioli
1-1/2 pounds bulk Italian sausage
   1 jar (28 ounces) meatless spaghetti sauce
   1 egg, beaten
   1 carton (15 ounces) ricotta cheese
   2 cups (8 ounces) shredded part-skim
      mozzarella cheese
1/2 cup grated Romano cheese

Cook pasta according to package directions; drain. Crumble sausage into a Dutch oven. Cook over medium heat until no longer pink; drain. Stir in the spaghetti sauce and pasta. In a bowl, combine the egg, ricotta cheese and mozzarella cheese.

Spoon half of the pasta mixture into a greased shallow 3-qt. baking dish; layer with cheese mixture and remaining pasta mixture. Cover and bake at 375° for 40 minutes. Uncover; top with Romano cheese. Bake 5 minutes longer or until heated through.

Yield: 10-12 servings.

Potluck Pointer

Taking a toddler to a potluck? They can be picky eaters, so you may want to contribute a dish you know your tyke enjoys. Or, take along some crackers, sliced veggies and a few slices of deli meat so they're sure to eat something once dinner is served.

Double-Decker Brownies

Heather Hooker, Belmont, Ontario
With two taste-tempting layers and a heavenly frosting, these decadent brownies beckon folks to enjoy them. You'll find yourself making them for birthday treats as well as charity bake sales, work snacks and more.

CHOCOLATE LAYER:
   2 eggs, lightly beaten
   1 cup sugar
3/4 cup all-purpose flour
1/2 cup chopped walnuts
Pinch salt
1/2 cup butter, melted
1/4 cup baking cocoa

BUTTERSCOTCH LAYER:
1-1/2 cups packed brown sugar
1/2 cup butter, softened
   2 eggs
   2 teaspoons vanilla extract
1-1/2 cups all-purpose flour
1/4 teaspoon salt
1/2 cup chopped walnuts

FROSTING:
1/2 cup packed brown sugar
1/4 cup butter, cubed
   3 tablespoons milk
1-1/2 cups confectioners' sugar, sifted
1/3 cup semisweet chocolate chips
1/3 cup butterscotch chips
   1 tablespoon shortening

In a bowl, combine eggs, sugar, flour, walnuts and salt. In another bowl, stir butter and cocoa until smooth; add to egg mixture and blend well with a wooden spoon. Pour into a greased 13-in. x 9-in. x 2-in. baking pan; set aside.

For butterscotch layer, cream brown sugar and butter in a mixing bowl. Beat in eggs and vanilla. Stir in flour, salt and walnuts. Spoon over the chocolate layer. Bake at 350° for 30-35 minutes or until brownies begin to pull away from sides of pan; cool.

For frosting, combine brown sugar, butter and milk in a small saucepan; bring to a boil and boil for 2 minutes. Remove from the heat; stir in confectioners' sugar until smooth. Quickly spread over brownies.

In a small saucepan over low heat, melt chocolate chips, butterscotch chips and shortening, stirring frequently. Drizzle over frosting.

Yield: 3 dozen.

Pictured below: Chicken-Pesto Pan Pizza (p. 28) and Ricotta Pepperoni Dip (p. 29).

Appetizers & Snacks!

Mini Chicken Turnovers

(pictured above)
Mary Detweiler, West Farmington, Ohio
I've been making these hearty hors d'oeuvres for several years. They take a little extra time to assemble, but it's worth it since they taste so special.

FILLING:
- 3 tablespoons chopped onion
- 3 tablespoons butter
- 1-3/4 cups shredded cooked chicken
- 3 tablespoons chicken broth
- 1/4 teaspoon *each* garlic salt, poultry seasoning and pepper
- 1 package (3 ounces) cream cheese, cubed

PASTRY:
- 1-1/2 cups all-purpose flour
- 1/2 teaspoon salt
- 1/2 teaspoon paprika
- 1/2 cup cold butter, cubed
- 4 to 5 tablespoons cold water

In a large skillet, saute onion in butter until tender. Stir in chicken, broth, seasonings and cream cheese; set aside.

In a large bowl, combine flour, salt and paprika; cut in butter until mixture resembles coarse crumbs. Gradually add water, tossing with a fork until a ball forms.

On a floured surface, roll out pastry to 1/16-in. thickness. Cut with a 2-1/2-in. round cookie cutter. Reroll scraps and cut more circles. Mound a heaping teaspoon of filling on half of each circle. Moisten edges with water; fold pastry over filling and press edges with a fork to seal.

Place on ungreased baking sheets. Repeat with remaining pastry and filling. Prick tops with a fork. Bake at 375° for 15-20 minutes or until golden brown.

Yield: about 2-1/2 dozen.

Colorful Crab Appetizer Pizza

(pictured below)
Diane Caron, Des Moines, Iowa
If you're looking for an easy yet special appetizer, this dish really stands out. It's a fresh-tasting and lovely variation on chilled veggie pizza. I make it for get-togethers.

- 1 tube (8 ounces) refrigerated crescent rolls
- 1 package (8 ounces) cream cheese, softened
- 1-1/2 cups coarsely chopped fresh spinach, *divided*
- 1 green onion, thinly sliced
- 1-1/2 teaspoons minced fresh dill *or* 1/2 teaspoon dill weed
- 1 teaspoon grated lemon peel, *divided*
- 1/2 teaspoon lemon juice
- 1/8 teaspoon pepper
- 1-1/4 cups chopped imitation crabmeat
- 1/4 cup chopped ripe olives

Unroll crescent roll dough and place on an ungreased 12-in. pizza pan. Flatten dough, sealing seams and perforations. Bake at 350° for 8-10 minutes or until lightly browned; cool.

In a small mixing bowl, beat cream cheese until smooth. Stir in 1 cup spinach, onion, dill, 1/2 teaspoon lemon peel, lemon juice and pepper. Spread over the crust. Top with crab, olives and remaining spinach and lemon peel. Cut into bite-size squares.

Yield: 8-10 servings.

Party Pitas

Janette Root, Ellensburg, Washington
Whenever the ladies of our church host a bridal shower, these mini sandwiches appear on the menu. Not only are they fast and delicious, but they look so pretty.

  1 package (8 ounces) cream cheese, softened
1/2 cup mayonnaise
1/2 teaspoon dill weed
1/4 teaspoon garlic salt
  8 mini pita breads (4 inches)
16 fresh spinach leaves
3/4 pound shaved fully cooked ham
1/2 pound thinly sliced Monterey Jack cheese

In a large mixing bowl, beat the cream cheese, mayonnaise, dill and garlic salt until blended.

Cut each pita in half horizontally; spread 1 tablespoon cream cheese mixture on each cut surface. On eight pita halves, layer spinach, ham and cheese. Top with remaining pita halves. Cut each pita into four wedges; secure with toothpicks.

Yield: 32 pieces.

Asparagus Snack Squares

Judy Wagner, Chicago, Illinois
Cut into bite-sized pieces, this simple, pizza-like dish makes for sensational appetizers. Sometimes, I even serve it as a main course at luncheons.

  1 cup chopped sweet onion
  2 garlic cloves, minced
  3 tablespoons butter
  1 pound fresh asparagus, trimmed
1/4 teaspoon pepper
  2 tubes (8 ounces *each*) refrigerated crescent rolls
  1 cup (4 ounces) shredded part-skim mozzarella cheese
  1 cup (4 ounces) shredded Swiss cheese

In a large skillet, saute onion and garlic in butter over medium heat until tender.

Cut asparagus into 1-in. pieces; set the tips aside. Add remaining asparagus to skillet; saute until crisp-tender, about 4-6 minutes. Add asparagus tips and pepper; saute 1-2 minutes longer or until asparagus is tender.

Press dough into an ungreased 15-in. x 10-in. x 1-in. baking pan; seal seams and perforations. Bake at 375° for 6-8 minutes or until lightly browned. Top with asparagus mixture; sprinkle with cheeses. Bake 6-8 minutes longer or until cheese is melted. Cut into squares.

Yield: 3 dozen.

Rainbow Gelatin Cubes

(pictured above)
Deanna Pietrowicz, Bridgeport, Connecticut
These perky gelatin cubes are fun to serve and to eat! I vary the colors to match the occasion…pink and blue for a baby shower, school colors for a graduation party, etc. Kids of all ages snap them up.

    4 packages (3 ounces *each*) assorted flavored gelatin
    6 envelopes unflavored gelatin, *divided*
5-3/4 cups boiling water, *divided*
    1 can (14 ounces) sweetened condensed milk
  1/4 cup cold water

In a bowl, combine one package flavored gelatin and one envelope unflavored gelatin. Stir in 1 cup boiling water until dissolved. Pour into a 13-in. x 9-in. x 2-in. dish coated with nonstick cooking spray; refrigerate until almost set but not firm, about 20 minutes.

In a bowl, combine the condensed milk and 1 cup boiling water. In another bowl, sprinkle two envelopes unflavored gelatin over cold water; let stand for 1 minute. Stir in 3/4 cup boiling water. Add to the milk mixture. Spoon 1-1/4 cups of the creamy gelatin mixture over the first flavored gelatin layer. Refrigerate until set but not firm, about 25 minutes.

Repeat from beginning of recipe twice, alternating flavored gelatin with creamy gelatin layers. Chill each layer until set but not firm before pouring next layer on top. Make final flavored gelatin; spoon over top. Refrigerate for at least 1 hour after completing last layer. Cut into 1-in. squares.

Yield: about 9 dozen.

Fried Cinnamon Strips

(pictured above)

Nancy Johnson, Laverne, Oklahoma
I first made these crispy strips for a special family night at our church. Most of them were snapped up before dinner! The change-of-pace snacks are irresistible.

  1   cup sugar
  1   teaspoon ground cinnamon
 1/4 teaspoon ground nutmeg
 10   flour tortillas (8 inches)
Vegetable oil

In a large resealable plastic bag, combine sugar, cinnamon and nutmeg; set aside.

Cut tortillas into 3-in. x 2-in. strips. Heat 1 in. of oil in a skillet or electric fry pan to 375°; fry 4-5 strips at a time for 30 seconds on each side or until golden brown. Drain on paper towels.

While still warm, place strips in bag with sugar mixture; shake gently to coat. Serve immediately or store in an airtight container.
Yield: 5 dozen.

Baked Sausage Wontons

Karen Rolfe, Dayton, Ohio
These savory appetizers offer an attractive change from the usual party fare. It takes a little effort to assemble them, but the shells can be made ahead and frozen to help streamline prep time.

 1/2 pound bulk pork sausage
 1/2 cup finely shredded carrot
 1/4 cup finely chopped water chestnuts
  2   teaspoons cornstarch
 1/2 teaspoon ground ginger
 1/3 cup chicken broth

  1   tablespoon sherry *or* additional chicken broth
  1   tablespoon reduced-sodium soy sauce
 40   wonton wrappers

In a large skillet, cook sausage over medium heat until no longer pink; drain. Stir in carrot and water chestnuts.

Meanwhile, in a bowl, combine cornstarch and ginger. Stir in the broth, sherry or additional broth and soy sauce until smooth. Stir into sausage mixture. Bring to a boil; cook and stir for 1-2 minutes or until thickened.

Gently press wonton wrappers into miniature muffin cups coated with nonstick cooking spray. Lightly coat wontons with nonstick cooking spray. Bake at 350° for 5 minutes.

Remove wontons from cups and arrange upside down on greased baking sheets. Bake 5 minutes longer or until lightly browned. Turn wontons; fill each with about 1 teaspoon sausage mixture. Bake for 2-3 minutes or until filling is heated through.
Yield: 40 wontons.

Hawaiian Roll-Ups

Ethel Lenters, Sioux Center, Iowa
Served at my baby shower luncheon many years ago, these roll-ups feature pineapple, ham and bacon for a tropical twist everyone loves.

 1/2   cup milk
  1   teaspoon prepared mustard
  3   drops Worcestershire sauce
  1   cup soft bread crumbs
 2/3   cup packed brown sugar
  1   teaspoon dried minced onion
  1   teaspoon salt
 1/4   teaspoon pepper
1-1/2 pounds lean ground beef
 14   thin slices deli ham
 14   bacon strips, halved widthwise
  1   can (8 ounces) pineapple tidbits, undrained

In a large bowl, combine the first eight ingredients. Crumble beef over mixture; mix well. Spread beef mixture over each ham slice. Roll up, starting with a short side. Cut in half widthwise; wrap a bacon slice around each. Secure with toothpicks.

Place in an ungreased 13-in. x 9-in. x 2-in. baking dish. Pour pineapple over roll-ups. Cover and bake at 375° for 30 minutes. Uncover; bake 30 minutes longer or until heated through.
Yield: 28 roll-ups.

Garden Focaccia

(pictured above)

Mary Ann Ludwig, Edwardsville, Illinois

Frozen bread dough is the convenient base for this herbed flat bread. The savory slices are popular at summertime gatherings, and they make a delicious way to use garden tomatoes and zucchini.

- 1 loaf (1 pound) frozen bread dough, thawed
- 1 tablespoon olive oil
- 1 tablespoon minced fresh rosemary *or* 1 teaspoon dried rosemary, crushed
- 1 tablespoon minced fresh thyme *or* 1 teaspoon dried thyme
- 1 package (8 ounces) cream cheese, softened
- 1/4 cup finely chopped onion
- 1 garlic clove, minced
- 4 large fresh mushrooms, sliced
- 3 medium tomatoes, sliced
- 1 small zucchini, thinly sliced
- 1/4 cup grated Parmesan cheese

On a lightly floured surface, roll dough into a 15-in. x 10-in. rectangle. Place in a greased 15-in. x 10-in. x 1-in. baking pan. Cover and let rise for 30 minutes.

Using your fingertips, press indentations in the dough. Brush with oil; sprinkle with rosemary and thyme. Bake at 400° for 12-15 minutes or until golden brown. Cool slightly.

In a mixing bowl, combine cream cheese, onion and garlic. Spread over crust. Top with mushrooms, tomatoes and zucchini; sprinkle with Parmesan cheese. Bake for 12-15 minutes or until lightly browned. Cool for 5 minutes before cutting.

Yield: 20 slices.

Potluck Pointer

Consider bringing a pizza cutter to your next church supper. In addition to cutting appetizer pizzas, they're great for slicing loaves of focaccia and other flat breads, as well as pans of brownies and bars.

Chicken-Pesto Pan Pizza

(pictured below)
Juanita Fleck, Bullhead City, Arizona
Packaged pesto mix makes an incredible replacement for tomato sauce in this tempting pizza. Cut it into small squares for a warm appetizer people will rave about throughout the night.

- 1 tube (13.8 ounces) refrigerated pizza crust
- 1/2 cup water
- 3 tablespoons olive oil
- 1 envelope pesto sauce mix
- 1 package (10 ounces) frozen chopped spinach, thawed and squeezed dry
- 1/2 cup ricotta cheese
- 1/4 cup chopped onion
- 2 cups shredded cooked chicken
- 1 jar (4-1/2 ounces) sliced mushrooms, drained
- 4 plum tomatoes, sliced
- 1 cup (4 ounces) shredded Swiss cheese
- 1/4 cup grated Romano cheese

Unroll pizza crust into an ungreased 15-in. x 10-in. x 1-in. baking pan; flatten dough and build up edges slightly. Prick dough several items with a fork. Bake at 425° for 7 minutes or until lightly browned.

Meanwhile, combine the water, oil and pesto sauce mix in a saucepan. Cook until heated through (do not boil). Add the spinach, ricotta and onion; mix well. Spread over crust. Top with the chicken, mushrooms, tomatoes and Swiss and Romano cheeses. Bake at 425° for 7 minutes or until crust is golden and cheese is melted.

Yield: 8 servings.

Chive-Cheese Corn Bread

(pictured above)
Sybil Eades, Gainesville, Georgia
Dressed up with cheddar cheese, this corn bread goes well with any main dish. The chives and sharp cheddar cheese give it a special flavor. Try cutting the moist bread into strips to feed a hungry crowd.

- 1 cup cornmeal
- 1 cup all-purpose flour
- 1/4 cup sugar
- 4 teaspoons baking powder
- 2 eggs
- 1 cup milk
- 1/4 cup butter, melted
- 1 cup (4 ounces) shredded sharp cheddar cheese
- 3 tablespoons minced chives

In a large bowl, combine cornmeal, flour, sugar and baking powder. In another bowl, whisk the eggs, milk and butter. Stir into dry ingredients just until moistened. Gently fold in cheese and chives.

Pour into a greased 13-in. x 9-in. x 2-in. baking pan. Bake at 400° for 18 minutes or until golden brown. Cut into strips; serve warm.

Yield: 12-15 servings.

Herbed Cheese Wafers

Mildred Sherrer, Fort Worth, Texas
Tarragon, oregano, garlic and two types of cheese combine to create these scrumptious, bun-like wafers. They make a perfect contribution to bring-a-dish dinners because they complement most other foods so well.

- 3/4 cup butter, softened
- 1/2 cup shredded cheddar cheese
- 1/3 cup crumbled blue cheese
- 1 tablespoon minced fresh tarragon *or* 1 teaspoon dried tarragon
- 1/2 teaspoon dried oregano
- 1 small garlic clove, minced
- 2 cups all-purpose flour

In a large, mixing bowl, beat butter, cheeses, tarragon, oregano and garlic until well mixed. Beat in flour (the dough will be crumbly). Shape into a 14-in. roll. Wrap tightly with plastic wrap. Refrigerate for 4 hours or overnight.

Cut into 1/4-in. slices; place on ungreased baking sheets. Bake at 375° for 10-12 minutes or until golden brown. Cool on wire racks.

Yield: about 4-1/2 dozen.

Crispy Cheese Twists

Mary Maxeiner, Lakewood, Colorado
My grown son enjoys these cheese twists so much that I'll often bake an extra batch as a special surprise just for him. They make a great anytime snack.

- 6 tablespoons butter, softened
- 1 garlic clove, minced
- 1/8 teaspoon pepper
- 1 cup (4 ounces) shredded cheddar cheese
- 2 tablespoons milk
- 1 tablespoon minced fresh parsley
- 1 tablespoon snipped fresh dill *or* 1 teaspoon dill weed
- 1 cup all-purpose flour

In a mixing bowl, combine the butter, garlic and pepper; beat until light and fluffy. Stir in cheese, milk, parsley and dill. Gradually add flour, mixing thoroughly.

Divide dough into 20 pieces. Roll each piece into a 10-in. log; cut each in half and twist halves together. Place 1 in. apart on an ungreased baking sheet. Bake at 375° for 10-12 minutes or until golden brown. Remove to wire racks.

Yield: 20 twists.

Ricotta Pepperoni Dip

(pictured above)
Barbara Carlucci, Orange Park, Florida
This warm dip gets its flavor from an herb soup mix and three kinds of cheese. The golden bread strips bake up easily with a tube of refrigerated pizza crust.

PIZZA STICKS:
- 1 tube (10 ounces) refrigerated pizza crust
- 1 tablespoon olive oil
- 2 tablespoons grated Parmesan cheese
- 1 tablespoon Italian seasoning
- 1/4 teaspoon garlic powder
- 1/8 teaspoon pepper

DIP:
- 1 cup (8 ounces) sour cream
- 1 cup ricotta cheese
- 1 tablespoon savory herb with garlic soup mix
- 1/4 cup chopped pepperoni
- 1 cup (4 ounces) shredded part-skim mozzarella cheese
- 1 tablespoon grated Parmesan cheese

On a lightly floured surface, roll out pizza crust to a 12-in. x 8-in. rectangle. Brush with oil. Combine the Parmesan cheese, Italian seasoning, garlic powder and pepper; sprinkle over dough. Cut into 3-in. x 1-in. strips; place on a greased baking sheet. Bake at 425° for 6-9 minutes or until golden brown.

Meanwhile, combine the sour cream, ricotta, soup mix and pepperoni in a saucepan; heat through. Stir in mozzarella and Parmesan cheese just until melted. Serve warm with pizza sticks.

Yield: about 2-1/2 dozen pizza sticks and 2 cups dip.

Fruit Kabobs

(pictured below)
Cheryl Ollis, Matthews, North Carolina
Here's a great way to bring something colorful, nutritious and fun to a buffet. Everyone likes fresh fruit, and these skewers are great served alongside the creamy coconut dip.

1 medium tart apple, cut into 1-inch chunks
1 medium pear, cut into 1-inch chunks
1 tablespoon lemon juice
1 can (8 ounces) unsweetened pineapple chunks, drained
24 grapes (about 1/4 pound)
24 fresh strawberries

COCONUT DIP:
1-1/2 cups fat-free vanilla yogurt
4-1/2 teaspoons flaked coconut
4-1/2 teaspoons reduced-sugar orange marmalade

Toss apple and pear with lemon juice. Divide fruit into 12 portions and thread onto wooden skewers. Combine dip ingredients in a small bowl; serve with the kabobs.

Yield: 12 kabobs.

Cheesy Onion Roll-Ups

Barbara Keith, Faucett, Missouri

These roll-ups are very fast to fix. You can make them ahead and keep them wrapped in the refrigerator until you're ready to leave for the event.

- 1 cup (8 ounces) sour cream
- 1 package (8 ounces) cream cheese, softened
- 1/2 cup finely shredded cheddar cheese
- 3/4 cup sliced green onions
- 1 tablespoon lime juice
- 1 tablespoon minced seeded jalapeno pepper
- 1 package (10 ounces) flour tortillas (6 inches), warmed

Picante sauce

In a bowl, combine the first six ingredients. Spread on one side of each tortilla and roll up tightly. Wrap and refrigerate for at least 1 hour. Slice into 1-in. pieces. Serve with picante sauce.

Yield: about 5 dozen.

Editor's Note: When cutting or seeding hot peppers, use rubber or plastic gloves to protect your hands. Avoid touching your face.

Ham and Cheese Puffs

Mrs. Marvin Buffington, Burlington, Iowa

These tasty, little bites always go over great. They're also delicious with soups and many of the items you'd expect to find on a buffet table.

- 1 package (2-1/2 ounces) thinly sliced deli ham, chopped
- 1 small onion, chopped
- 1/2 cup shredded Swiss cheese
- 1 egg
- 1-1/2 teaspoons Dijon mustard
- 1/8 teaspoon pepper
- 1 tube (8 ounces) refrigerated crescent rolls

In a large bowl, combine the first six ingredients; set aside. Divide crescent dough into 24 portions. Press into greased miniature muffin cups.

Spoon 1 tablespoon ham mixture into each cup. Bake at 350° for 13-15 minutes or until golden brown.

Yield: 2 dozen.

Baked Crab Dip

(pictured above)

Marie Shelley, Exeter, Missouri

This exquisite dip was one of the appetizers enjoyed at my grandson's wedding reception. It looks fancy but it's simple. You can fill the bread bowl early in the day, refrigerating it until serving. Just remove it from the refrigerator 30 minutes before baking it.

- 1 package (8 ounces) cream cheese, softened
- 2 cups (16 ounces) sour cream
- 2 cans (6 ounces *each*) crabmeat, drained, flaked and cartilage removed *or* 2 cups flaked imitation crabmeat
- 2 cups (8 ounces) shredded cheddar cheese
- 4 green onions, thinly sliced
- 2 round loaves (1 pound *each*) unsliced sourdough *or* Italian bread

Additional sliced green onions, optional

Assorted crackers

In a mixing bowl, beat cream cheese until smooth. Add sour cream; mix well. Fold in crab, cheese and onions. Cut the top third off each loaf of bread; carefully hollow out bottoms, leaving 1-in. shells. Cube removed bread and tops; set aside. Spoon crab mixture into bread bowls. Place on baking sheets. Place reserved bread cubes in a single layer around bread bowls. Bake, uncovered, at 350° for 45-50 minutes or until the dip is heated through. Garnish with green onions if desired. Serve with toasted bread cubes and crackers.

Yield: 5 cups.

Antipasto Platter

(pictured below)
Teri Lindquist, Gurnee, Illinois
Here's a wonderful change of pace from the selections you usually find on an appetizer buffet. It's one of our favorite party pleasers.

    1 jar (24 ounces) pepperoncinis, drained
    1 can (15 ounces) garbanzo beans *or*
         chickpeas, rinsed and drained
    2 cups halved fresh mushrooms
    2 cups halved cherry tomatoes
  1/2 pound provolone cheese, cubed
    1 can (6 ounces) pitted ripe olives, drained
    1 package (3-1/2 ounces) sliced pepperoni
    1 bottle (8 ounces) Italian vinaigrette
         dressing
Lettuce leaves

In a large bowl, combine the peppers, beans, mushrooms, tomatoes, cheese, olives and pepperoni. Pour vinaigrette over mixture; toss to coat. Refrigerate for at least 30 minutes or overnight. Arrange on a lettuce-lined platter. Serve with toothpicks.

Yield: 14-16 servings.

Hot Artichoke Spread

(pictured above)
Victoria Casey, Coeur d'Alene, Idaho
Green chilies add a bit of zip to this rich cracker spread. I serve it often at parties because it makes a lot, is quick to prepare and looks so pretty with the red tomatoes and green onions on top.

    1 can (14 ounces) water-packed artichoke
         hearts, drained and chopped
    1 cup mayonnaise
    1 cup grated Parmesan cheese
    1 can (4 ounces) chopped green chilies,
         drained
    1 garlic clove, minced
    1 cup chopped fresh tomatoes
    3 green onions, thinly sliced
Crackers *or* pita bread

In a large bowl, combine the first five ingredients. Spread into a 1-qt. baking dish or 9-in. pie plate.

   Bake, uncovered, at 350° for 20-25 minutes or until top is lightly browned. Sprinkle with tomatoes and onions. Serve with crackers or pita bread.

Yield: 4-1/2 cups.

Editor's Note: Reduced-fat or fat-free mayonnaise is not recommended for this recipe.

Sausage Sandwich Squares

Mary Merrill, Bloomingdale, Ohio
As Sunday school teachers, my husband and I often host youth groups, so I dreamed up this recipe to help feed bunches of hungry teenagers. They loved the pizza flavor of the meaty squares.

     3 to 3-1/2 cups all-purpose flour
     1 package (1/4 ounce) active dry yeast
   1/2 teaspoon salt
 1-1/3 cups warm water (120° to 130°)
     1 pound bulk Italian sausage
     1 sweet red pepper, diced
     1 green pepper, diced
     1 large onion, diced
     4 cups (16 ounces *each*) shredded part-skim
       mozzarella cheese
     1 egg
     1 tablespoon water
     2 tablespoons grated Parmesan cheese
     2 tablespoons minced fresh parsley
   1/2 teaspoon dried oregano
   1/8 teaspoon garlic powder

In a large bowl, combine 2 cups flour, yeast and salt. Add warm water; mix well. Add enough remaining flour to form a firm dough. Turn onto a floured surface; knead until smooth and elastic, about 6 minutes. Place in a greased bowl, turning once to grease top. Cover and let rise in a warm place until doubled, about 50 minutes.

In a large skillet, cook sausage until no longer pink; remove with a slotted spoon and set aside. In the drippings, saute peppers and onion until tender; drain.

Press half of the dough onto the bottom and 1/2 in. up the sides of a greased 15-in. x 10-in. x 1-in. baking pan. Spread sausage evenly over the crust. Top with peppers and onion. Sprinkle with mozzarella cheese. Roll out remaining dough to fit pan; place over cheese and seal the edges.

In a small bowl, beat egg and water. Add remaining ingredients; mix well. Brush over dough. Cut slits in top. Bake at 400° for 20-25 minutes or until golden brown. Cut into squares.

Yield: 12-15 servings.

Potluck Pointer

Feel free to experiment with the filling in Sausage Sandwich Squares. Because the recipe reflects pizza flavors, stir mushrooms, pepperoni or whatever other pizza toppings you enjoy into the sausage mixture.

Crispy Onion Wings

(pictured above)
Jonathan Hershey, Akron, Ohio
My wife, daughters and I always look forward to these buttery wings. The crisp coating of french-fried onions and potato chips is also great on chicken tenders that I make from cut-up chicken breasts.

    12 whole chicken wings (about 2-1/2
       pounds)
 2-1/2 cups crushed potato chips
     1 can (2.8 ounces) french-fried onions,
       crushed
   1/2 cup cornmeal
     2 teaspoons dried oregano
     1 teaspoon onion salt
     1 teaspoon garlic powder
     1 teaspoon paprika
     2 eggs, beaten
   1/4 cup butter, melted

Line a 15-in. x 10-in. x 1-in. baking pan with foil and grease the foil; set aside. Cut chicken wings into three sections; discard wing tip section.

In a large resealable plastic bag, combine the potato chips, onions, cornmeal and seasonings; mix well. Dip the chicken wings in eggs. Place in the bag, a few at a time; shake to coat and press crumb mixture onto chicken.

Place wings in prepared pan; drizzle with butter. Bake, uncovered, at 375° for 30-35 minutes or until chicken juices run clear and coating is crisp.

Yield: 2 dozen.

Editor's Note: This recipe was prepared with the first and second sections of the chicken wings.

Sweet-Sour Deviled Eggs

(pictured below)
Claudia Millhouse, Myersville, Maryland
My family doesn't like traditional deviled eggs, but they gobble these right up. The recipes yields 2 dozen, so I always have enough to take to a potluck or party.

       12   hard-cooked eggs
    1/3   cup plus 1 tablespoon mayonnaise
        5   teaspoons sugar
        5   teaspoons cider vinegar
        1   teaspoon prepared mustard
    1/2   teaspoon salt
    1/4   teaspoon pepper
Paprika and minced fresh parsley

Slice eggs in half lengthwise; remove yolks and set whites aside. In a small bowl, mash yolks with a fork. Add the mayonnaise, sugar, vinegar, mustard, salt and pepper. Stuff or pipe into egg whites. Garnish with paprika and parsley.
Yield: 24 servings.

Spinach Phyllo Bundles

(pictured above)
Eloise Olive, Greensboro, North Carolina
These golden triangles were inspired by spanakopita, a Greek spinach pie made with phyllo dough. The snacks are always winners.

        1   medium onion, chopped
        2   tablespoons plus 1/2 cup butter, *divided*
        1   package (10 ounces) frozen chopped
             spinach, thawed and squeezed dry
        1   cup (4 ounces) crumbled feta cheese
    3/4   cup small-curd cottage cheese
        3   eggs, lightly beaten
    1/4   cup dry bread crumbs
    3/4   teaspoon salt
    1/2   teaspoon dill weed
Pepper to taste
        1   package frozen phyllo dough, thawed (16
             ounces, 14-inches x 9-inches sheet size)

In a large skillet, saute onion in 2 tablespoons butter until tender. Remove from the heat. Stir in the spinach, feta cheese, cottage cheese, eggs, bread crumbs, salt, dill and pepper.

Melt remaining butter. Layer and brush five phyllo sheets with melted butter. Keep remaining phyllo covered to avoid drying out; save remaining sheets for another use.

Cut buttered sheets lengthwise into 2-in. strips; cut in half widthwise. Place 1 heaping tablespoon of filling at one end of each strip; fold into a triangle, as you would fold a flag.

Place on an ungreased baking sheet. Brush with butter. Bake at 400° for 15-20 minutes or until golden brown. Serve warm.
Yield: 28 appetizers.

Potluck Pointer

Don't have a storage container to easily transport a large number of deviled eggs? Drop by your local pizzeria and ask if you can have a new pizza box or two. The cardboard boxes are just the right depth for the eggs.

Spinach Squares

Patricia Kile, Greentown, Pennsylvania
Even people who don't care for spinach can't pass up these yummy appetizers when they're set on a buffet table.

- 2 tablespoons butter, *divided*
- 1 cup milk
- 3 eggs
- 1 cup all-purpose flour
- 1 teaspoon baking powder
- 3/4 teaspoon salt
- 1/2 teaspoon dried oregano
- 1/4 teaspoon pepper
- 1/4 teaspoon dried basil
- 1/4 teaspoon dried thyme
- 2 packages (10 ounces *each*) frozen chopped spinach, thawed and squeezed dry
- 2 cups (8 ounces) shredded cheddar cheese
- 2 cups (8 ounces) shredded Monterey Jack cheese
- 1 cup chopped onion

Sliced pimientos, optional

Brush the bottom and sides of a 13-in. x 9-in. x 2-in. baking dish with 1 tablespoon butter; set aside.

In a large mixing bowl, combine the remaining butter and the next nine ingredients. Stir in the spinach, cheeses and onion.

Spread in pan. Bake, uncovered, at 350° for 30-35 minutes or until a toothpick inserted near the center comes out clean and edges are lightly browned. Cut into squares. Garnish with pimientos if desired.

Yield: 32 appetizers.

Golden Chicken Nuggets

Karen Owen, Rising Sun, Indiana
I usually set a bowl of sweet-and-sour sauce near these herb-breaded bites for dipping.

- 1/2 cup dry bread crumbs
- 1/4 cup grated Parmesan cheese
- 2 teaspoons Italian seasoning
- 1 teaspoon salt
- 1/2 cup butter, melted
- 6 boneless skinless chicken breasts halves, cut into 1-inch cubes

In a shallow bowl, combine the first four ingredients. In another shallow bowl, add butter. Dip chicken in butter; roll in crumb mixture.

Place in a single layer on an ungreased 15-in. x 10-in. x 1-in. baking pan. Bake at 400° for 12-15 minutes or until juices run clear.

Yield: 4 dozen.

Broccoli-Chicken Cups

(pictured above)
Shirley Gerber, Roanoke, Illinois
I first sampled these savory, golden bites when my cousin made them for a bridal shower. All the ladies raved over the fantastic flavor of what they called "individual casseroles."

- 2 tubes (10 ounces *each*) refrigerated biscuit dough
- 2 cups (8 ounces) shredded cheddar cheese, *divided*
- 1-1/3 cups crisp rice cereal
- 1 cup cubed cooked chicken
- 1 can (10-3/4 ounces) condensed cream of mushroom soup, undiluted
- 1 package (10 ounces) frozen chopped broccoli, cooked and drained

Place biscuits in greased muffin cups, pressing dough over the bottom and up the sides. Add 1 tablespoon cheese and cereal to each cup.

In a large bowl, combine chicken, soup and broccoli; spoon into cups. Bake at 375° for 20-25 minutes or until bubbly. Sprinkle with remaining cheese.

Yield: 10-12 servings.

Potluck Pointer

Stack foil-lined muffin cups next to any dips, salsas or sauces you bring to potlucks. Each dinner guest can then fill a muffin cup without having the condiment run all over his or her plate.

Zippy Cheese Logs

Evangeline Rew, Manassas, Virginia
Due to popular demand, my ham-filled cheese logs have become tasty traditions at our women's Christmas brunch.

- 2 packages (8 ounces *each*) cream cheese, softened
- 1 cup small-curd cottage cheese
- 1 envelope (1 ounce) Parmesan Italian salad dressing mix
- 4 tablespoons minced fresh parsley, *divided*
- 1/2 cup minced fully cooked ham
- 1/2 cup chopped walnuts
Assorted crackers

In a large mixing bowl, beat cream cheese, cottage cheese and salad dressing mix until blended.

Line the bottom and sides of a 13-in. x 9-in. x 2-in. pan with waxed paper. Spread cheese mixture evenly in pan. Cover and refrigerate for 1 hour.

Remove waxed paper with cheese from pan. Sprinkle 2 tablespoons parsley in a 13-in. x 1-in. strip 1/2 in. from one long edge. Sprinkle ham over remaining cheese mixture.

Starting with parsley edge, carefully roll up jelly-roll style. Combine nuts and remaining parsley; roll log in parsley mixture. Cut log in half. Wrap; refrigerate at least 4 hours. Serve with crackers.

Yield: 2 cheese logs (about 1-3/4 cups each).

Olive Cheese Bread

Nancy McWhorter, Bridge City, Texas
The recipe for these cheesy squares was given to me by a co-worker's wife. With the addition of ripe olives and onions, they are the perfect complement to seafood, Italian food, barbecued fare or whatever you may find at a potluck.

- 1/2 cup butter, melted
- 1/2 cup mayonnaise
- 1 can (2-1/4 ounces) sliced ripe olives, drained
- 2 green onions, chopped
- 1-1/2 cups (6 ounces) shredded Monterey Jack cheese
- 1 loaf (1 pound) unsliced French bread

In a large bowl, combine the first five ingredients. Slice bread in half widthwise and lengthwise.

Place on an ungreased baking sheet. Spread cheese mixture over cut sides of bread. Bake at 350° for 15-20 minutes or until the cheese is melted.

Yield: 12-16 servings.

Editor's Note: Reduced-fat or fat-free mayonnaise may not be substituted for regular mayonnaise in this recipe.

Italian Bread Wedges

(pictured above)
Danielle McIntyre, Medicine Hat, Alberta
These savory wedges aren't hard to make, and they taste great alongside soups, salads, pasta dishes and other potluck staples.

> 3 teaspoons active dry yeast
> 1 cup warm water (110° to 115°), *divided*
> 1 teaspoon sugar
> 2 tablespoons canola oil
> 1 teaspoon salt
> 2-1/2 to 3 cups all-purpose flour

TOPPING:

> 1/3 cup Italian salad dressing
> 1/4 teaspoon garlic powder
> 1/4 teaspoon dried oregano
> 1/4 teaspoon dried thyme

Dash pepper

> 1 cup (4 ounces) shredded part-skim mozzarella cheese
> 1/4 cup grated Parmesan cheese

In a mixing bowl, dissolve yeast in 1/4 cup warm water. Add sugar; let stand for 5 minutes. Add the oil, salt, remaining water and 2 cups of flour; beat until smooth. Stir in enough remaining flour to form a soft dough. Turn onto a floured surface; knead until smooth and elastic, about 6-8 minutes. Place in a greased bowl, turning once to grease top. Cover and let rise in a warm place until doubled, about 40 minutes.

Punch dough down. Turn onto a lightly floured surface. Pat dough flat. Let rest for 5 minutes. Press into a greased 14-in. pizza pan. Spread with salad dressing. Combine the garlic powder, oregano, thyme and pepper; sprinkle over dough. Top with cheeses. Bake at 450° for 15-20 minutes or until golden brown. Serve warm.

Yield: 12 slices.

Tangy Mozzarella Bites

(pictured below)
Julie Wasem, Aurora, Nebraska
I adapted this recipe from one I found years ago, substituting ingredients most people have on hand. I like to serve it with crackers or small bread slices.

> 1/4 cup olive oil
> 1 to 2 teaspoons balsamic vinegar
> 1 garlic clove, minced
> 1 teaspoon dried basil
> 1 teaspoon coarsely ground pepper
> 1 pound part-skim mozzarella cheese, cut into 1/2-inch cubes

In a bowl, combine the oil, vinegar, garlic, basil and pepper. Add cheese; toss to coat. Cover and refrigerate for at least 1 hour.

Yield: about 3 cups.

Sunshine Chicken Wings

(pictured below)
Ami Miller, Plain City, Ohio
Casual get-togethers get a flavorful boost with these finger-licking-good wings. Add as much hot pepper sauce as you like, or omit it if you'd prefer a milder appetizer.

    2 jars (12 ounces *each*) orange marmalade
    3 cups ketchup
    1 cup packed brown sugar
    1 large onion, finely chopped
  1/2 cup butter, cubed
    3 tablespoons chili powder
    3 tablespoons vinegar
    1 tablespoon Worcestershire sauce
Hot pepper sauce to taste
    8 pounds whole chicken wings (about 40)

In a large saucepan, combine the first nine ingredients. Bring to a boil. Reduce heat; simmer, uncovered, for 15 minutes.

Meanwhile, cut chicken wings into three sections; discard wing tips. Dip wings into sauce and place on two foil-lined 15-in. x 10-in. x 1-in. baking pans.

Bake at 350° for 45 minutes, reversing pans once during baking. Serve immediately or cover and refrigerate for up to 2 days before serving. Reheat in the oven or electric roaster.

Yield: 15-20 servings.

Editor's Note: This recipe was prepared with the first and second sections of the chicken wings.

Roast Beef Roll-Ups

(pictured above)
Susan Scott, Asheville, North Carolina
You can't beat these flavorful roll-ups seasoned with salsa. They're a great addition to a buffet table and certainly offer a fun alternative to traditional potluck fare.

  1/2 cup sour cream
  1/4 cup mayonnaise
  1/4 cup salsa
   10 flour tortillas (8 inches), warmed
    1 pound thinly sliced cooked roast beef
   10 large lettuce leaves
Additional salsa

Combine sour cream, mayonnaise and salsa; spread over tortillas. Top with roast beef and lettuce. Roll up tightly and secure with toothpicks; cut in half. Serve with salsa.

Yield: 10 servings.

Potluck Pointer

When organizing a potluck, set out smaller platters of perishable foods. Storing the extras in a cooler or refrigerator and replenishing as needed keeps them at the proper temperature.

Sesame Cheese Ball

Brenda Baughman, Mansfield, Ohio
I came up with this cheese ball when I combined two favorite recipes. Unlike some cheese spreads that can be somewhat bland, this has a little zest. I make it for occasions throughout the year.

>   2 packages (8 ounces *each*) cream cheese,
>   softened
> 1-1/2 cups (6 ounces) finely shredded cheddar
>   cheese
>   1/2 cup finely chopped celery
>   1/3 cup finely chopped onion
>   1/2 teaspoon garlic salt
>   1/2 teaspoon seasoned salt
>   1/2 teaspoon hot pepper sauce
>   1/3 cup sesame seeds, toasted
> Assorted crackers

In a mixing bowl, combine the cream cheese, cheddar cheese, celery, onion, garlic salt, seasoned salt and hot pepper sauce; beat until well blended. Shape into a ball; roll in sesame seeds. Cover and refrigerate for 15 minutes. Serve with crackers.

Yield: about 20 servings.

Tortellini Nibblers

Stephanie Krienitz, Plainfield, Illinois
Looking for a unique appetizer idea? Try this pairing of cheese tortellini and a cool, creamy Parmesan sauce for dipping. Serve several tortellini on skewers or let guests pick out one or two with toothpicks.

>   1/2 cup fat-free milk
>   3 tablespoons nonfat dry milk powder
> 1-1/2 cups 1% cottage cheese
>   1/4 cup grated Parmesan cheese
>   1 tablespoon lemon juice
> 1-1/2 teaspoons minced fresh rosemary *or*
>   1/2 teaspoon dried rosemary, crushed
>   1/4 teaspoon salt
>   1/8 teaspoon pepper
>   1 package (9 ounces) refrigerated cheese
>   tortellini

In a blender or food processor, cover and process milk and milk powder until blended. Add the cottage cheese, Parmesan cheese, lemon juice, rosemary, salt and pepper; cover and process until smooth. Cover and refrigerate for 30 minutes. Cook tortellini according to package directions; drain. Serve with Parmesan sauce for dipping.

Yield: 20 servings.

Garlic Cheese Biscuits

(pictured below)
Gayle Becker, Mt. Clemens, Michigan
This is a savory variation on my favorite buttermilk biscuit recipe. Shredded cheddar cheese adds nice color, and the buttery garlic mixture I brush over the tops offers a burst of flavor to the little bites.

>   2 cups all-purpose flour
>   3 teaspoons garlic powder, *divided*
> 2-1/2 teaspoons baking powder
>   1/2 teaspoon baking soda
>   1 teaspoon chicken bouillon granules,
>   *divided*
>   1/2 cup butter-flavored shortening
>   3/4 cup shredded cheddar cheese
>   1 cup buttermilk
>   3 tablespoons butter, melted

In a large bowl, combine flour, 2 teaspoons garlic powder, baking powder, baking soda and 1/2 teaspoon bouillon; cut in shortening until mixture resembles coarse crumbs. Add cheese. Stir in buttermilk just until moistened.

Drop by heaping tablespoonfuls onto a greased baking sheet. Bake at 450° for 10 minutes.

Combine butter with remaining garlic powder and bouillon; brush over biscuits. Bake 4 minutes longer or until golden brown. Serve warm.

Yield: about 1 dozen.

Zesty Vegetable Dip

(pictured above)
Laura Mills, Liverpool, New York
My mother used to make this full-flavored dip for large gatherings, and it was so popular. Now I make it for the get-togethers I attend, and it's still well-received.

    1 cup mayonnaise
    1 cup (4 ounces) shredded sharp cheddar
        cheese
1/2 cup sour cream
    1 envelope Italian salad dressing mix
    1 tablespoon dried minced onion
    1 tablespoon dried parsley flakes
    1 tablespoon lemon juice
    1 teaspoon Worcestershire sauce
Assorted vegetables

In a large bowl, combine the first eight ingredients. Cover and refrigerate for 2 hours. Serve with vegetables.

Yield: 2 cups.

Wontons with Sweet-Sour Sauce

(pictured at right)
Korrin Grigg, Neenah, Wisconsin
This super-simple finger food makes an awesome appetizer and is perfect for potlucks. I serve the crispy pork rolls with a homemade sweet-and-sour sauce.

    1 can (14 ounces) pineapple tidbits
1/2 cup packed brown sugar
    1 tablespoon cornstarch
1/3 cup cider vinegar
    1 tablespoon soy sauce

1/2 cup chopped green pepper
1/2 pound ground pork
    2 cups finely shredded cabbage
3/4 cup finely chopped bean sprouts
    1 small onion, finely chopped
    2 eggs, lightly beaten
1/2 teaspoon salt
1/4 teaspoon pepper
    2 packages (12 ounces *each*) wonton
        wrappers
Oil for deep-fat frying

Drain pineapple, reserving juice. Set pineapple aside.

In a large saucepan, combine brown sugar and cornstarch; gradually stir in pineapple juice, vinegar and soy sauce until smooth. Bring to a boil; cook and stir for 2 minutes or until thickened. Reduce heat; stir in green pepper and pineapple. Cover and simmer for 5 minutes; set aside and keep warm.

In a large bowl, combine the pork, cabbage, sprouts, onion, eggs, salt and pepper. Place about 1 tablespoonful in the center of each wrapper. Moisten edges with water; fold opposite corners together over filling and press to seal.

In an electric skillet, heat 1 in. of oil to 375°. Fry wontons for 2-1/2 minutes or until golden, turning once. Drain on paper towels. Serve with sauce.

Yield: about 8-1/2 dozen (2-1/2 cups sauce).

Editor's Note: Fill wonton wrappers a few at a time, keeping the others covered with a damp paper towel until ready to use.

Pictured below:
Firecracker Casserole (p. 62).

Comforting Casseroles

Almond Celery Bake

(pictured above)
Judi Messina, Coeur d'Alene, Idaho
Whenever potluck guests sample this unique casserole, they're surprised at how delicious celery can be. I make the side dish with cream soup, cheddar cheese, bread crumbs and crunchy almonds but feel free to adjust the soup or cheese varieties to your liking.

       1 bunch celery, sliced (about 6 cups)
    3/4 cup shredded cheddar cheese
    1/2 teaspoon paprika
    1/8 teaspoon pepper
       1 can (10-3/4 ounces) condensed cream of
          celery soup, undiluted
       1 cup soft bread crumbs
    1/2 cup slivered almonds

Place the celery in a greased 2-qt. baking dish. Sprinkle with cheese, paprika and pepper. Top with the soup. Sprinkle with bread crumbs.

Cover and bake at 375° for 45 minutes. Uncover; sprinkle with the almonds. Bake 10-15 minutes longer or until golden brown.
Yield: 10-12 servings.

Popular Potluck Casserole

Debbi Smith, Crossett, Arkansas
Spice up the buffet line with this comforting main dish. Full of Tex-Mex taste, this crowd-pleasing ground beef and pasta bake is sure to disappear in a hurry.

       1 package (7 ounces) ring macaroni
       2 pounds ground beef
       1 medium onion, chopped
    1/4 cup chopped green pepper
    1/4 cup thinly sliced celery
       1 can (10-3/4 ounces) condensed cream of
          mushroom soup, undiluted
       1 can (10 ounces) diced tomatoes with
          green chilies
       1 can (8 ounces) tomato sauce
       1 to 2 tablespoons chili powder
       1 can (15-1/4 ounces) whole kernel corn,
          drained
       2 cups (8 ounces) shredded cheddar cheese,
          divided

Cook macaroni according to package directions. Meanwhile, in a large skillet, cook the beef, onion, green pepper and celery until meat is no longer pink and vegetables are tender; drain. Stir in the soup, tomatoes, tomato sauce and chili powder until combined.

Drain the macaroni; stir into beef mixture. Add the corn and 1-1/2 cups of cheese.

Transfer to a greased 13-in. x 9-in. x 2-in. baking dish. Sprinkle with remaining cheese. Bake, uncovered, at 350° for 25-30 minutes or until heated through.
Yield: 10-12 servings.

Pineapple Ham Bake

Patricia Throlson, Hawick, Minnesota
Five items are all you need for this tropical dish. Double the ingredients when attending an extra-large get-together.

       2 cans (8 ounces *each*) unsweetened crushed
          pineapple
    2/3 cup packed brown sugar
       1 tablespoon vinegar
       2 teaspoons ground mustard
       1 pound fully cooked ham, cut into 1/4-inch
          pieces

Combine the first four ingredients in an ungreased 2-qt. baking dish; mix well. Stir in ham.

Bake, uncovered, at 350° for 30-40 minutes or until heated through. Serve with a slotted spoon.
Yield: 8 servings.

Hamburger Casserole

(pictured below)

Helen Carmichall, Santee, California

This one-pot recipe is such a hit, it's traveled all over the country! My mother originated the recipe in Pennsylvania, I brought it to Texas when I married, I'm still making it in California, and my daughter treats her friends to this "oldie" in Colorado. Sliced potatoes make it hearty and lend a change of pace to pasta-based casseroles.

    2 pounds uncooked extra lean ground beef
       or ground round
    4 pounds potatoes, peeled and sliced 1/4
       inch thick
    1 large onion, sliced
    1 teaspoon salt, optional
  1/2 teaspoon pepper
    1 beef bouillon cube
    1 cup hot water
    1 can (28 ounces) tomatoes with liquid,
       cut up
Chopped fresh parsley, optional

In a Dutch oven, layer half of the meat, potatoes and onion. Sprinkle with half of the salt and pepper. Repeat layers. Dissolve bouillon in water; pour over all. Top with tomatoes. Cover and cook over medium heat for 45-50 minutes or until potatoes are tender. Garnish with parsley if desired.

Yield: 10 servings.

Four-Cheese Bow Ties

(pictured above)

Mary Farney, Normal, Illinois

My daughter-in-law shared this meatless favorite with me, and now it's popular in my house, too. With tomatoes and parsley, it's beautiful on a buffet table.

    2 cans (14-1/2 ounces *each*) diced tomatoes
    1 package (16 ounces) bow tie pasta
  1/4 cup butter, cubed
  1/4 cup all-purpose flour
  1/4 teaspoon salt
  1/4 teaspoon pepper
1-1/2 cups milk
1-1/2 cups (6 ounces) shredded part-skim
       mozzarella cheese
1-1/3 cups grated Romano cheese
  1/2 cup shredded Parmesan cheese
  1/4 cup crumbled blue cheese
  1/2 cup minced fresh parsley

Drain tomatoes, reserving 1-1/4 cups juice; set aside. Cook pasta according to package directions; drain.

In a saucepan, melt butter over medium heat. Stir in the flour, salt and pepper until smooth; gradually add milk and reserved tomato juice. Bring to a boil; cook and stir for 2 minutes or until thickened. Remove from the heat.

In a large bowl, combine the pasta, sauce and reserved tomatoes. Stir in the cheeses and parsley; toss gently. Place in a greased 3-1/2-qt. baking dish. Bake, uncovered, at 375° for 30-35 minutes or until golden and bubbly.

Yield: 12 servings.

Carrot Coin Casserole

(pictured below)
Linda Phillippi, Ronan, Montana
I carry this recipe when I attend a covered-dish dinner since someone always asks for it.

      12 medium carrots, sliced
       1 large onion, cut into 1/4-inch slices
       2 cups frozen peas
   1-1/2 cups (6 ounces) shredded cheddar cheese
       4 tablespoons butter, softened, *divided*
       2 tablespoons all-purpose flour
       1 teaspoon salt
     1/4 teaspoon pepper
     1/4 teaspoon ground nutmeg
   2-1/2 cups milk
       1 cup crushed butter-flavored crackers
          (about 25 crackers)

Place carrots and a small amount of water in a saucepan; cover and cook over medium heat until crisp-tender, about 6 minutes. Add onion; bring to a boil. Reduce heat; cover and simmer for 4-6 minutes or until onion is crisp-tender. Drain. Add peas and toss.

Place 4 cups in a greased shallow 3-qt. baking dish; sprinkle with cheese. Top with remaining vegetables. In a saucepan over medium heat, melt 1 tablespoon butter. Stir in flour, salt, pepper and nutmeg until smooth. Gradually add milk, stirring constantly. Bring to a boil; cook and stir for 2 minutes or until thickened. Pour over the vegetables.

In a small saucepan or skillet, combine cracker crumbs and remaining butter; cook and stir over medium heat until toasted. Sprinkle over casserole. Bake, uncovered, at 350° for 30-40 minutes or until bubbly.

Yield: 12 servings.

Greek Pasta and Beef

Dorothy Bateman, Carver, Massachusetts
This delightfully different casserole gives everyday macaroni and cheese an international flavor.

       1 package (16 ounces) elbow macaroni
       1 pound ground beef
       1 large onion, chopped
       1 garlic clove, minced
       1 can (8 ounces) tomato sauce
     1/2 cup water
       1 teaspoon salt
     1/2 teaspoon ground cinnamon
     1/4 teaspoon ground nutmeg
     1/4 teaspoon pepper
       1 egg, lightly beaten
     1/2 cup grated Parmesan cheese

SAUCE:
       1 cup butter
     1/4 cup all-purpose flour
     1/4 teaspoon ground cinnamon
       3 cups milk
       2 eggs, lightly beaten
     1/3 cup grated Parmesan cheese

Cook macaroni according to package directions. In a large skillet, cook beef, onion and garlic over medium heat until meat is no longer pink; drain. Stir in the tomato sauce, water and seasonings. Cover and simmer for 10 minutes, stirring occasionally. Drain macaroni.

In a large bowl, combine the macaroni, egg and Parmesan cheese; set aside. For sauce, in a large saucepan, melt butter; stir in flour and cinnamon until smooth. Gradually add milk. Bring to a boil over medium heat; cook and stir for 2 minutes or until slightly thickened. Remove from heat. Stir a small amount of hot mixture into eggs; return all to pan, stirring constantly. Stir in cheese.

In a greased 3-qt. baking dish, spread half of the macaroni mixture. Top with beef mixture and remaining macaroni mixture. Pour sauce over the top. Bake, uncovered, at 350° for 45-50 minutes or until bubbly and heated through. Let stand for 5 minutes before serving.

Yield: 12 servings.

Potluck Pointer

Don't forget about the utensils! Whether your casserole needs to be dished out with a slotted spoon, pasta fork or another serving tool, remember to pack it up before heading out the door.

Pepperoni Pizzazz

(pictured below)
Marge Unger, La Porte, Indiana

I've fixed this hearty main course for buffets, covered-dish dinners and even for company at my home. Keep the recipe handy, because you'll certainly be asked for it when you contribute it to an event.

8 ounces medium tube pasta
1 jar (28 ounces) spaghetti sauce, *divided*
1 jar (4-1/2 ounces) sliced mushrooms, drained
1 package (8 ounces) sliced pepperoni
1/2 cup chopped green pepper
1/2 cup chopped onion
1/2 cup grated Parmesan cheese
1/2 teaspoon garlic powder
1/2 teaspoon salt
1/8 teaspoon pepper
1/8 teaspoon crushed red pepper flakes
1 can (8 ounces) tomato sauce
2 cups (8 ounces) shredded part-skim mozzarella cheese

Cook pasta according to package directions. Meanwhile, combine 2-1/3 cups spaghetti sauce, mushrooms, pepperoni, green pepper, onion, Parmesan cheese, garlic powder, salt, pepper and red pepper flakes in a bowl.

Drain pasta; add to sauce mixture and mix well. Transfer to a greased 3-qt. baking dish. Combine the tomato sauce and remaining spaghetti sauce; pour over top. Cover and bake at 350° for 40-45 minutes or until bubbly. Sprinkle with mozzarella cheese. Bake, uncovered, 5-10 minutes longer or until cheese is melted. Let stand 5 minutes before serving.

Yield: 9 servings.

Spaghetti Goulash

(pictured below)
Jinger Newsome, Gainesville, Florida
My mother always made this delicious dish when we went to church dinners or had lots of company. Sometimes, she'd make two casseroles and save one in the freezer for the future.

> 1 package (16 ounces) thin spaghetti, broken in half
> 3/4 pound ground beef
> 3/4 pound bulk pork sausage
> 1 medium green pepper, chopped
> 1 medium onion, chopped
> 2 cans (14-1/2 ounces *each*) diced tomatoes
> 1 bottle (12 ounces) chili sauce
> 1 can (8 ounces) mushroom stems and pieces, drained
> 1 tablespoon Worcestershire sauce
> 1 teaspoon salt
> 1/4 teaspoon pepper
> 1 cup (4 ounces) shredded cheddar cheese, *divided*

Cook spaghetti according to package directions; drain. In a large skillet, cook the beef, sausage, green pepper and onion over medium heat until meat is no longer pink; drain. Add the tomatoes; cover and simmer for 45 minutes.

Remove from heat; stir in the chili sauce, mushrooms, Worcestershire sauce, salt, pepper and spaghetti.

Transfer to a greased 4-qt. baking dish or two greased 2-qt. baking dishes. Sprinkle with cheese. Cover and bake at 350° for 35-40 minutes or until heated through.

Yield: 12-16 servings.

Vegetable Bake

(pictured above)
Violet Klause, Onoway, Alberta
Even finicky eaters may change their minds about vegetables when they taste this cheesy casserole. It couldn't be easier to whip up, and it's so creamy and satisfying that no one suspects how nutritious it is. Best of all, it takes advantage of convenient frozen, canned and jarred vegetables.

> 1 package (16 ounces) frozen cauliflower, thawed
> 1 can (15-1/4 ounces) whole kernel corn, drained
> 1 package (10 ounces) frozen broccoli florets, thawed
> 1 can (14-3/4 ounces) cream-style corn
> 1 can (10-3/4 ounces) condensed cream of celery soup, undiluted
> 2 cups (8 ounces) shredded Swiss cheese
> 1 jar (4-1/2 ounces) sliced mushrooms, drained
> 1-1/2 cups soft rye bread crumbs (about 3 slices)
> 2 tablespoons butter, melted

In a bowl, combine the first seven ingredients. Pour into a greased 13-in. x 9-in. x 2-in. baking dish. Combine bread crumbs and butter; sprinkle over top.

Bake, uncovered, at 375° for 30-35 minutes or until bubbly. Let stand for 5 minutes before serving.

Yield: 8-10 servings.

Deluxe Potato Ham Bake

Diane Wilson Wing, Salt Lake City, Utah
A longtime favorite for potluck dinners is transformed from a side dish to a main course with the addition of cubed ham. This dish is always one of the first to go. In fact, people at the end of the line are disappointed if the pan is empty.

    2 cans (10-3/4 ounces *each*) condensed
       cream of chicken soup, undiluted
  1/4 cup butter, melted
    1 cup (8 ounces) sour cream
1-1/2 cups (6 ounces) shredded cheddar cheese
    1 medium onion, chopped
    2 cups cubed fully cooked ham
    1 bag (32 ounces) frozen Southern-style
       hash brown potatoes, thawed

TOPPING:
  1/4 cup butter, melted
  3/4 cup crushed cornflakes

In a large bowl, combine the first five ingredients. Stir in ham and potatoes. Spread into a greased 13-in. x 9-in. x 2-in. baking dish.

  For the topping, combine butter and cornflakes until crumbly. Sprinkle over top of ham mixture. Bake, uncovered, at 350° for 1 hour or until potatoes are tender.

Yield: 10-12 servings.

Hamburger Noodles

Alice Marie Caldera, Tuolumne, California
I first started making this in the 1950s when I needed to feed many mouths on a budget. Now my husband and I are empty nesters and I've had a hard time cutting back on serving sizes. It's a good thing my husband likes leftovers.

1-1/2 pounds ground beef
    1 medium onion, chopped
    2 teaspoons salt
    1 teaspoon chili powder
  1/4 teaspoon pepper
    1 package (16 ounces) elbow macaroni,
       cooked and drained
    1 package (10 ounces) frozen mixed
       vegetables, thawed
    2 cans (6 ounces *each*) tomato paste
    2 cups water
    1 cup (4 ounces) process cheese (Velveeta)

In a skillet, cook beef and onion over medium heat until meat is no longer pink; drain. Stir in salt, chili powder and pepper.

  Place macaroni in a greased 4-qt. baking dish; top with mixed vegetables and beef mixture. Combine tomato paste and water; pour over meat. Sprinkle with cheese.

  Bake, uncovered, at 400° for 20 minutes or until heated through.

Yield: 12 servings.

Colorful Veggie Bake

(pictured above)
Lisa Radelet, Boulder, Colorado
It's impossible to resist this cheesy casserole with its golden crumb topping sprinkled over bright vegetables. A versatile side that goes with any meat, it's a favorite to round out bring-a-dish meals.

    2 packages (16 ounces *each*) frozen
       California-blend vegetables
    8 ounces process cheese (Velveeta), cubed
    6 tablespoons butter, *divided*
  1/2 cup crushed butter-flavored crackers
       (about 13 crackers)

Prepare the vegetables according to package directions; drain. Place half in an ungreased 11-in. x 7-in. x 2-in. baking dish. In a small saucepan, combine cheese and 4 tablespoons butter; cook and stir over low heat until melted. Pour half over vegetables. Repeat layers.

  Melt the remaining butter; toss with cracker crumbs. Sprinkle over the top. Bake, uncovered, at 325° for 20-25 minutes or until golden brown.

Yield: 8-10 servings.

French Country Casserole

(pictured below)
Kim Lowe, Coralville, Iowa
A quick-to-fix version of a traditional French cassoulet, this hot dish was an instant hit with my husband, who enjoys smoked sausage. Just mix everything together and bake.

- 1 pound fully cooked kielbasa *or* Polish sausage, halved and cut into 1/4-inch slices
- 1 can (16 ounces) kidney beans, rinsed and drained
- 1 can (15-1/2 ounces) great northern beans, rinsed and drained
- 1 can (15 ounces) black beans, rinsed and drained
- 1 can (15 ounces) tomato sauce
- 3 medium carrots, thinly sliced
- 2 small onions, sliced into rings
- 1/2 cup dry red wine *or* beef broth
- 2 tablespoons brown sugar
- 2 garlic cloves, minced
- 1-1/2 teaspoons dried thyme

Combine all ingredients in a bowl; transfer to an ungreased 3-qt. baking dish. Cover and bake at 375° for 60-70 minutes or until the carrots are tender.

Yield: 9 servings.

Black Bean Tortilla Casserole

(pictured above)
Sue Briski, Appleton, Wisconsin
A cousin gave me this recipe because she knows my family loves southwestern fare. This is a delicious, meatless meal that most people really enjoy!

- 2 large onions, chopped
- 1-1/2 cups chopped green peppers
- 1 can (14-1/2 ounces) diced tomatoes, drained
- 3/4 cup picante sauce
- 2 garlic cloves, minced
- 2 teaspoons ground cumin
- 2 cans (15 ounces *each*) black beans, rinsed and drained
- 8 corn tortillas (6 inches)
- 2 cups (8 ounces) shredded Mexican cheese blend

TOPPINGS:
- 1-1/2 cups shredded lettuce
- 1 cup chopped fresh tomatoes
- 1/2 cup thinly sliced green onions
- 1/2 cup sliced ripe olives

In a large saucepan, combine the onions, peppers, tomatoes, picante sauce, garlic and cumin. Bring to a boil. Reduce heat; simmer, uncovered, for 10 minutes. Stir in the beans. Spread a third of the mixture in a 13-in. x 9-in. x 2-in. baking dish coated with nonstick cooking spray. Layer with four tortillas and 2/3 cup cheese. Repeat layers; top with remaining beans.

Cover and bake at 350° for 30-35 minutes or until heated through. Sprinkle with remaining cheese. Let stand for 5 minutes or until cheese is melted. Serve with toppings.

Yield: 9 servings.

Ham 'n' Tater Bake

Peggy Grieme, Pinehurst, North Carolina
I'm always asked for this casserole recipe because its flavor reminds friends of a loaded baked potato. It's just as good for company as it is for potlucks.

    1 package (28 ounces) frozen steak fries
    1 package (10 ounces) frozen chopped
        broccoli, thawed and drained
1-1/2 cups diced fully cooked ham
    1 can (10-3/4 ounces) condensed cream of
        broccoli soup, undiluted
  3/4 cup milk
  1/2 cup mayonnaise
    1 cup (4 ounces) shredded cheddar cheese

Arrange the fries in a greased 3-qt. baking dish; layer with broccoli and then ham. Combine the soup, milk and mayonnaise until smooth; pour over ham.

Cover and bake at 350° for 20 minutes. Sprinkle with cheese; bake, uncovered, 20-25 minutes longer or until bubbly.

Yield: 8 servings.

Editor's Note: Reduced-fat or fat-free mayonnaise is not recommended for this recipe.

Tuna Noodle Cups

Marlene Pugh, Fort McMurray, Alberta
For a fun take on tuna casserole, I mix up a handful of ingredients and pour everything into muffin cups. After baking, the comforting cups make individual servings that easily fit onto everyone's plate at a buffet.

  8 ounces medium egg noodles
  1 package (10 ounces) frozen peas and
     carrots, thawed
  1 small onion, finely chopped
  1 can (6-1/2 ounces) tuna, drained
  2 cups (8 ounces) shredded cheddar cheese
  3 eggs
  1 can (12 ounces) evaporated milk
  1/2 cup water

Cook noodles according to package directions drain and place in a large bowl. Add the peas and carrots, onion, tuna and cheese. In a small bowl, combine eggs, milk and water; stir into the noodle mixture. Spoon into greased muffin cups.

Bake at 350° for 30-35 minutes or until a knife comes out clean. Cool for 5 minutes; loosen edges with a knife to remove from cups.

Yield: about 1-1/2 dozen.

Pizza Pasta Casserole

(pictured below)
Nancy Scarlett, Graham, North Carolina
Pepperoni provides the zip in a pizza-flavored dish that kids of all ages will line up for. Best of all, the recipe makes two casseroles, so you can contribute one to a charity dinner and keep one in the freezer for your family.

  2 pounds ground beef
  1 large onion, chopped
  2 jars (28 ounces *each*) spaghetti sauce
  1 package (16 ounces) spiral pasta, cooked
     and drained
  4 cups (16 ounces) shredded part-skim
     mozzarella cheese
  8 ounces sliced pepperoni

In a large skillet, cook beef and onion until meat is no longer pink; drain. Stir in spaghetti sauce and pasta.

Transfer to two greased 13-in. x 9-in. x 2-in. baking dishes. Sprinkle with cheese. Arrange pepperoni over the top. Cover and freeze one casserole for up to 3 months.

Bake the second casserole, uncovered, at 350° for 25-30 minutes or until heated through.

To use frozen casserole: Thaw in the refrigerator overnight. Bake at 350° for 35-40 minutes or until heated through.

Yield: 2 casseroles (8-10 servings each).

Zucchini Ricotta Bake

(pictured above)
Eleanor Hauserman, Huntsville, Alabama
I have made this lasagna-like zucchini casserole frequently over the years and shared the recipe with many people. It's a little bit lighter than other layered casseroles.

    2 pounds zucchini
    1 carton (15 ounces) reduced-fat ricotta
       cheese
  1/2 cup egg substitute
  1/2 cup dry bread crumbs, *divided*
    5 tablespoons grated Parmesan cheese,
       divided
    1 tablespoon minced fresh parsley
  1/4 teaspoon dried oregano
  1/4 teaspoon dried basil
  1/8 teaspoon pepper
    1 jar (28 ounces) reduced-sodium meatless
       spaghetti sauce
1-1/2 cups (6 ounces) shredded part-skim
       mozzarella cheese

Cut zucchini lengthwise into 1/4-in. slices. Place in a basket over 1 in. of boiling water. Cover and steam for 5-6 minutes or until just tender. Drain; pat dry.

In a large bowl, combine ricotta, egg substitute, 3 tablespoons bread crumbs, 3 tablespoons Parme-san, parsley, oregano, basil and pepper; set aside.

Spread a third of the spaghetti sauce in a 13-in. x 9-in. x 2-in baking dish coated with non-stick cooking spray. Sprinkle with 2 tablespoons bread crumbs. Cover with half of the zucchini, ricotta mixture and mozzarella. Repeat layers of sauce, zucchini, ricotta mixture and mozzarella. Cover with remaining sauce.

Combine remaining crumbs and Parmesan; sprinkle over top. Cover and bake at 350° for 45 minutes. Uncover; bake 15 minutes longer. Let stand 15 minutes before cutting.
Yield: 12 servings.

Potluck Hot Dish

Dorothy Friez, McLaughlin, South Dakota
This beef and pork dish is my favorite item to take to bring-a-dish dinners. The down-home ingredients make it a guaranteed crowd-pleaser. The recipe is often requested, and I never hesitate to share it.

    1 pound ground pork
    1 pound ground beef
    1 large onion, chopped
    1 medium green pepper, chopped
    1 package (7 ounces) elbow *or* ring
       macaroni, cooked and drained
    2 cans (14-3/4 ounces *each*) cream-style
       corn
    2 cans (11-1/2 ounces *each*) condensed
       chicken with rice soup, undiluted
    1 can (10-3/4 ounces) condensed cream of
       mushroom soup, undiluted
    1 teaspoon salt
  1/2 teaspoon pepper
Seasoned salt to taste
  1/2 cup dry bread crumbs
    2 tablespoons butter, melted

In a large skillet, cook the meat, onion and green pepper over medium heat until meat is no longer pink; drain. Stir in macaroni, corn, soups and sea-sonings.

Transfer to a greased 13-in. x 9-in. x 2-in. baking dish. Toss bread crumbs and butter; sprinkle over top. Cover and bake at 350° for 45 minutes. Uncover and bake 15 minutes longer or until heated through.
Yield: 12 servings.

Veggie Noodle Ham Casserole

(pictured below)
Judy Moody, Wheatley, Ontario
This saucy main course is really quite versatile. Without the ham, it can be a vegetarian entree or a hearty side dish.

- 1 package (12 ounces) wide egg noodles
- 1 can (10-3/4 ounces) condensed cream of chicken soup, undiluted
- 1 can (10-3/4 ounces) condensed cream of broccoli soup, undiluted
- 1-1/2 cups milk
- 2 cups frozen corn, thawed
- 1-1/2 cups frozen California-blend vegetables, thawed
- 1-1/2 cups cubed fully cooked ham
- 2 tablespoons minced fresh parsley
- 1/2 teaspoon pepper
- 1/4 teaspoon salt
- 1 cup (4 ounces) shredded cheddar cheese, *divided*

Cook noodles according to package directions; drain. In a large bowl, combine soups and milk; stir in the noodles, corn, vegetables, ham, parsley, pepper, salt and 3/4 cup of cheese.

Transfer to a greased 13-in. x 9-in. x 2-in. baking dish. Cover and bake at 350° for 45 minutes. Uncover; sprinkle with remaining cheese. Bake 5-10 minutes longer or until bubbly and cheese is melted.

Yield: 8-10 servings.

Herbed Vegetable Medley

(pictured above)
Betty Blandford, Johns Island, South Carolina
Even those who resist eating vegetables will take to this piping-hot ground beef dish. Eggplant, zucchini, onion and yellow pepper are disguised by the bubbling tomato sauce.

- 2 pounds ground beef
- 1 medium eggplant, cubed
- 2 medium zucchini, cubed
- 1 medium onion, chopped
- 1 medium sweet yellow pepper
- 3 garlic cloves, minced
- 1 can (28 ounces) stewed tomatoes
- 1 cup cooked rice
- 1 cup (4 ounces) shredded cheddar cheese, *divided*
- 1/2 cup beef broth
- 1/2 teaspoon *each* oregano, savory and thyme
- 1/2 teaspoon salt
- 1/4 teaspoon pepper

In a Dutch oven, cook beef over medium heat until no longer pink; drain. Add the eggplant, zucchini, onion, yellow pepper and garlic; cook until tender. Add tomatoes, rice, 1/2 cup of cheese, broth and seasonings; mix well. Transfer to a greased 13-in. x 9-in. x 2-in. baking dish. Sprinkle with the remaining cheese. Bake, uncovered, at 350° for 30 minutes or until heated through.

Yield: 10 servings.

Black-Eyed Pea Casserole

(pictured above)
Kathy Rogers, Natchez, Mississippi
This group-size meal-in-one is quick and tasty, and its southern flair helps make it a great change-of-pace from dishes you normally find at potlucks. It's heartwarming to see so many people ask for seconds.

    2 packages (6 ounces *each*) long grain and
      wild rice mix
    2 pounds ground beef
    2 medium onions, chopped
    2 small green peppers, chopped
    4 cans (15-1/2 ounces *each*) black-eyed peas
      with jalapenos, rinsed and drained
    2 cans (10-3/4 ounces *each*) condensed
      cream of mushroom soup, undiluted
1-1/3 cups shredded cheddar cheese

In a large saucepan, cook the rice mixes according to package directions. Meanwhile, in a large skillet, cook the beef, onions and green peppers over medium heat until the meat is no longer pink; drain.

In a large bowl, combine the peas, soup, rice and beef mixture. Transfer to two greased 2-1/2-qt. baking dishes. Cover and bake at 350° for 20-25 minutes or until heated through. Uncover; sprinkle with cheese. Bake 5 minutes longer or until cheese is melted.

Yield: 2 casseroles (10-12 servings each).

Chili-Cheese Spoon Bread

Patricia Barkman, Riverton, Manitoba
Serve this versatile casserole as a snappy side dish or a meatless main course with plenty of mass appeal. My father raves about its green chilies, cheese and all of the corn flavor it has to offer.

1/2 cup egg substitute
  1 egg
  1 can (8-3/4 ounces) whole kernel corn,
    drained
  1 can (8-1/4 ounces) cream-style corn
  1 cup (8 ounces) reduced-fat sour cream
  1 cup (4 ounces) shredded reduced-fat
    cheddar cheese
  1 cup (4 ounces) shredded reduced-fat
    Mexican cheese blend *or* part-skim
    mozzarella cheese
  1 can (4 ounces) chopped green chilies,
    drained
1/2 cup cornmeal
  2 tablespoons butter, melted
1/2 teaspoon salt
1/2 teaspoon Worcestershire sauce
1/8 teaspoon cayenne pepper

In a large bowl, beat egg substitute and egg. Add the remaining ingredients; mix well. Pour into a 9-in. square baking dish coated with nonstick cooking spray. Bake at 350° for 35-40 minutes or until a knife inserted near the center comes out clean. Serve warm.

Yield: 9 servings.

Chicken 'n' Corn Bread Dressing

Pam West, Ernul, North Carolina
My nursing career keeps me busy, so easy recipes that taste great are important to me. I came up with this one by combining items I had on hand.

```
  2  celery ribs, chopped
  1  large onion, chopped
1/4  cup butter, cubed
  2  eggs
  2  cups buttermilk
  1  can (10-1/2 ounces) condensed chicken
     broth, undiluted
  2  packages (8-3/4 ounces each) corn
     bread/muffin mix
  1  can (8-3/4 ounces) cream-style corn
  2  teaspoons poultry seasoning
1/2  teaspoon salt
1/2  teaspoon pepper
  5  cups seasoned stuffing croutons
  3  cans (5 ounces each) white chicken,
     drained
  1  medium potato, peeled and diced
```

In a small saucepan, saute celery and onion in butter until tender; set aside. In a bowl, beat the eggs, buttermilk and broth. Stir in the muffin mixes, corn, poultry seasoning, salt and pepper; mix well. Add croutons, chicken, potato and celery mixture.

Transfer to a greased 13-in. x 9-in. x 2-in. baking dish. Bake, uncovered, at 375° for 30-35 minutes or until golden brown.
Yield: 10-12 servings.

Swiss 'n' Crab Supper Pie

(pictured above)
Kathy Crow, Cordova, Alaska
Crab is plentiful where we live, but canned crab makes a great "off-the-shelf" dish. I'm sure your friends will enjoy the delicious, easy-to-make pie as much as mine do.

```
  1  unbaked pastry shell (9 inches)
  1  can (7-1/2 ounces) crab, drained, flaked
     and cartilage removed
  1  cup shredded Swiss cheese
  2  green onions, sliced thin
  3  beaten eggs
  1  cup half-and-half cream
1/2  teaspoon salt
1/2  teaspoon grated lemon peel
1/4  teaspoon ground mustard
```
Dash mace
```
1/4  cup sliced unblanched almonds
```

Line a 9-inch tart pan with unpricked pastry shell; line pastry with heavy-duty foil. Bake at 450° for 5 minutes. Remove foil.

Arrange crab evenly over partially baked crust. Top with cheese and green onions. Combine remaining ingredients except almonds; pour over base. Top with almonds.

Bake at 325° for 45 minutes or until set. Remove from oven; let stand 10 minutes before serving.
Yield: 10 servings.

Potluck Pointer

Many cooks cover their casserole dishes with foil before driving to a church supper. All too often, however, they arrive to find that the casserole's top layer of cheese has stuck to the foil.

To help avoid this, spray the foil with nonstick cooking spray. Wrap the casserole with the foil, sprayed side down, and you're sure to find the hot dish intact when you arrive.

Wild Rice Harvest Casserole

(pictured below)
Julianne Johnson, Grove City, Minnesota
Winter is the ideal time to enjoy a big helping of my hearty casserole; it is packed with wild rice and chicken and topped with cashews.

    4 to 5 cups diced cooked chicken
    1 cup chopped celery
    2 tablespoons butter
    2 cans (10-3/4 ounces *each*) condensed
      cream of mushroom soup, undiluted
    2 cups chicken broth
    1 jar (4-1/2 ounces) sliced mushrooms,
      drained
    1 small onion, chopped
    1 cup uncooked wild rice, rinsed and
      drained
  1/4 teaspoon poultry seasoning
  3/4 cup cashew pieces
Chopped fresh parsley

In a skillet, brown chicken and celery in butter. In a large bowl, combine soup and broth until smooth. Add the mushrooms, onion, rice, poultry seasoning and chicken mixture.

    Pour into a greased 13-in. x 9-in. x 2-in. baking dish. Cover and bake at 350° for 1 hour. Uncover and bake for 30 minutes. Stir; sprinkle with cashews. Return to the oven for 15 minutes or until the rice is tender. Garnish with parsley.

Yield: 10-12 servings.

Hearty Rice Casserole

(pictured above)
Billie Bartlett, Monroe, Louisiana
Pork sausage and ground beef make this rice dish heartier than most, but canned soup makes it a snap to assemble.

    1 can (10-3/4 ounces) condensed cream of
      mushroom soup, undiluted
    1 can (10-3/4 ounces) condensed creamy
      onion soup, undiluted
    1 can (10-3/4 ounces) condensed cream of
      chicken soup, undiluted
    1 pound lean ground beef
    1 pound bulk pork sausage
    1 large onion, chopped
    1 large green pepper, chopped
    2 celery ribs, chopped
 1-1/2 cups uncooked long grain rice

Combine all of the ingredients in a greased 4-qt. baking dish; mix well. Cover tightly and bake at 350° for 60-70 minutes or until the rice is tender.

Yield: 12-16 servings.

Pierogi Casserole

Margaret Popou, Kaslo, British Columbia
Mashed potatoes and shredded cheddar cheese take center stage in this delicious take on lasagna. The layered entree comes together without much fuss, and people always line up for seconds.

        1   cup finely chopped onion
      1/4   cup butter
        2   cups small-curd cottage cheese, drained
        1   egg
      1/4   teaspoon onion salt
        2   cups mashed potatoes (with added milk and butter)
        1   cup (4 ounces) shredded cheddar cheese
      1/4   teaspoon salt
      1/8   teaspoon pepper
        9   lasagna noodles, cooked and drained

In a skillet, saute onion in butter until tender; set aside. In a bowl, combine cottage cheese, egg and onion salt. In another bowl, combine potatoes, cheddar cheese, salt and pepper. Place three noodles in a greased 13-in. x 9-in. x 2-in. baking dish. Top with cottage cheese mixture and three more noodles. Top with potato mixture, remaining noodles and sauteed onion. Cover and bake at 350° for 25-30 minutes or until heated through. Let stand 10 minutes before serving.
Yield: 12 servings.

Ground Beef Baked Beans

Louann Sherbach, Wantagh, New York
I serve this satisfying ground beef and bean bake with a tossed salad and some crusty bread.

        3   pounds ground beef
        4   cans (16 ounces *each*) pork and beans
        2   cups ketchup
        1   cup water
        2   envelopes onion soup mix
      1/4   cup packed brown sugar
      1/4   cup ground mustard
      1/4   cup molasses
        1   tablespoon white vinegar
        1   teaspoon garlic powder
      1/2   teaspoon ground cloves

In a Dutch oven, cook beef over medium heat until no longer pink; drain. Stir in the remaining ingredients; heat through. Transfer to two greased 2-qt. baking dishes. Cover and freeze one dish for up to 3 months. Cover and bake the second dish at 400° for 30 minutes. Uncover; bake 10-15 minutes longer or until bubbly.
Yield: 2 casseroles (10-12 servings each).

Meaty Spinach Manicotti

(pictured above)
Pat Schroeder, Elkhorn, Wisconsin
This hearty stuffed pasta dish feeds a crowd. Tangy tomato sauce tops manicotti filled with a mouth-watering blend of Italian sausage, chicken, spinach and mozzarella cheese.

        2   packages (8 ounces *each*) manicotti shells
      1/4   cup butter, cubed
      1/4   cup all-purpose flour
    2-1/2   cups milk
      3/4   cup grated Parmesan cheese
        1   pound bulk Italian sausage
        4   cups cubed cooked chicken *or* turkey
        2   packages (10 ounces *each*) frozen chopped spinach, thawed and squeezed dry
        2   eggs, beaten
        1   cup (4 ounces) shredded part-skim mozzarella cheese
        2   cans (26-1/2 ounces *each*) spaghetti sauce
      1/4   cup minced fresh parsley

Cook manicotti according to package directions. Meanwhile, melt butter in a saucepan. Stir in the flour until smooth. Gradually add milk. Bring to a boil; cook and stir for 2 minutes or until thickened. Stir in Parmesan cheese until melted; set aside. Drain manicotti; set aside.

In a large skillet, cook the sausage over medium heat until no longer pink; drain. Add the chicken, spinach, eggs, mozzarella cheese and 3/4 cup white sauce. Stuff into manicotti shells.

Spread 1/2 cup spaghetti sauce each in two ungreased 13-in. x 9-in. x 2-in. baking dishes. Top with manicotti. Pour remaining spaghetti sauce over the top.

Reheat the remaining white sauce, stirring constantly. Pour over spaghetti sauce. Bake, uncovered, at 350° for 45-50 minutes. Sprinkle with parsley.
Yield: 14-16 servings.

Turkey Noodle Casserole

(pictured below)
Georgia Hennings, Alliance, Nebraska
Celery, water chestnuts and mushrooms add texture and crunch to this hearty casserole that is full of ground turkey. I'll fix two and serve one with a salad to make a complete meal. I keep the second one in the freezer to bake when company's coming.

      2 pounds ground turkey
      2 cups chopped celery
  1/4 cup chopped green pepper
  1/4 cup chopped onion
      1 can (10-3/4 ounces) condensed cream of
         mushroom soup, undiluted
      1 can (8 ounces) sliced water chestnuts,
         drained
      1 jar (4-1/2 ounces) sliced mushrooms,
         drained
      1 jar (4 ounces) diced pimientos, drained
  1/4 cup soy sauce
  1/2 teaspoon salt
  1/2 teaspoon lemon-pepper seasoning
      1 cup (8 ounces) sour cream
      8 ounces wide egg noodles, cooked and
         drained

In a large skillet over medium heat, brown the turkey. Add celery, green pepper and onion; cook until tender. Stir in soup, water chestnuts, mushrooms, pimientos, soy sauce, salt and lemon-pepper. Reduce heat; simmer for 20 minutes.

Remove from the heat; add sour cream and noodles. Spoon half into a freezer container; cover and freeze for up to 3 months. Place remaining mixture in a greased 2-qt. baking dish. Cover and bake at 350° for 30-35 minutes or until heated through.

To use frozen casserole: Thaw in the refrigerator. Transfer to a greased 2-qt. baking dish and bake as directed.

Yield: 2 casseroles (6 servings each).

Apricot Barley Casserole

(pictured above)
Diane Swink, Signal Mountain, Tennessee
It doesn't take long to put together this pretty side dish dotted with dried apricots and golden raisins. Then just pop it into the oven and enjoy!

  2/3 cup pine nuts *or* slivered almonds
  1/4 cup butter, *divided*
      2 cups pearl barley
      1 cup sliced green onions
      7 cups chicken broth
  2/3 cup diced dried apricots
  1/2 cup golden raisins

In a large skillet, saute nuts in 2 tablespoons butter until lightly browned; remove and set aside. In the same skillet, saute the barley and onions in remaining butter until onions are tender. Add broth; bring to a boil. Stir in the apricots, raisins and reserved nuts.

Pour into a greased 13-in. x 9-in. x 2-in. baking dish. Bake, uncovered, at 325° for 1-1/4 hours or until barley is tender.

Yield: 8-10 servings.

Seafood Lasagna

Viola Walmer, Tequesta, Florida
Everyone seems to enjoy this dish. I like to prepare it the day before and refrigerate it overnight. Just take it out of the fridge 30 minutes before popping it in the oven.

- 3/4 cup chopped onion
- 2 tablespoons butter
- 1 package (8 ounces) cream cheese, cubed
- 1-1/2 cups (12 ounces) small-curd cottage cheese
- 1 egg, beaten
- 2 teaspoons dried basil
- 1 teaspoon salt
- 1/4 teaspoon pepper
- 1 can (10-3/4 ounces) condensed cream of shrimp soup, undiluted
- 1 can (10-3/4 ounces) condensed cream of mushroom soup, undiluted
- 1/2 cup white wine *or* chicken broth
- 1/2 cup milk
- 2 packages (8 ounces *each*) imitation crabmeat, flaked
- 1 can (6 ounces) small shrimp, rinsed and drained
- 9 lasagna noodles, cooked and drained
- 1/2 cup grated Parmesan cheese
- 3/4 cup shredded Monterey Jack cheese

In a large skillet, saute onion in butter until tender. Reduce heat. Add cream cheese; cook and stir until melted and smooth. Stir in cottage cheese, egg, basil, salt and pepper. Remove from the heat and set aside. In a bowl, combine the soups, wine or broth, milk, crab and shrimp.

Arrange three noodles in a greased 13-in. x 9-in. x 2-in. baking dish. Spread with a third of cottage cheese mixture and a third of the seafood mixture. Repeat layers twice. Sprinkle with Parmesan cheese.

Cover and bake at 350° for 40 minutes. Uncover; sprinkle with the Monterey Jack cheese. Bake 10 minutes longer or until cheese is melted and lasagna is bubbly. Let stand for 15 minutes before serving.

Yield: 12 servings.

Sausage Spaghetti Spirals

(pictured above)
Carol Carolton, Wheaton, Illinois
With hearty chunks of sausage and green pepper, this recipe makes a big pan, so it's nicely sized for a potluck.

- 1 pound bulk Italian sausage
- 1 medium green pepper, chopped
- 5 cups spiral pasta, cooked and drained
- 1 jar (28 ounces) meatless spaghetti sauce
- 1-1/2 cups (6 ounces) shredded part-skim mozzarella cheese

In a skillet, cook sausage and pepper until meat is no longer pink; drain. Stir in pasta and sauce. Transfer to a greased 13-in. x 9-in. x 2-in. baking dish. Cover and bake at 350° for 25 minutes. Uncover; sprinkle with cheese. Bake 5-10 minutes or until the cheese is melted.

Yield: 10 servings.

Potluck Pointer

It's a snap to reduce large-quantity casseroles that call for a 13-in. x 9-in. x 2-in. baking dish. Simply halve all of the ingredients and prepare the recipe in an 8-in. or 9-in. square dish. (Baking times may vary a bit.) You can enjoy your favorite potluck items at home, without worrying about leftovers.

Cheesy Zucchini Bake

(pictured above)
Sue Stanton, Linville, North Carolina
Ever since a friend shared this classic casserole with me, I look forward to our annual bounty of zucchini. The cheesy veggie bake makes a pretty entree or brunch item. I keep the recipe handy when I share it…I know I'll get requests!

4-1/2 cups sliced zucchini
   2 to 3 tablespoons olive oil
Salt and pepper to taste
   1 large onion, chopped
   2 tablespoons minced garlic
   1 can (10-3/4 ounces) tomato puree
   1 can (6 ounces) tomato paste
   3 tablespoons sugar
   1 teaspoon Italian seasoning
   1 teaspoon dried basil
   2 cans (2-1/4 ounces *each*) sliced ripe olives, drained
   3 cups (12 ounces) shredded part-skim mozzarella cheese
   6 eggs, lightly beaten
1-1/2 cups grated Parmesan cheese

In a large skillet, saute zucchini in oil until tender. Sprinkle with salt and pepper; stir. Transfer to an ungreased 13-in. x 9-in. x 2-in. baking dish.

In the same skillet, saute onion until crisp-tender. Add garlic; saute 3 minutes longer. Stir in tomato puree, tomato paste, sugar, Italian seasoning and basil. Bring to a boil. Reduce heat; simmer, uncovered, for 10-15 minutes or until slightly thickened. Stir in olives. Pour over zucchini. Sprinkle with mozzarella.

Combine the eggs and Parmesan cheese; pour over zucchini. Bake, uncovered, at 375° for 25-30 minutes or until a knife inserted near the center comes out clean. Let the dish stand for 15 minutes before serving.
Yield: 12-16 servings.

Pork Noodle Casserole

Bernice Morris, Marshfield, Missouri
Less expensive cuts of pork become tender and tasty in this creamy, meal-in-one delight.

   2 cups uncooked egg noodles
   2 pounds boneless pork, cut into 3/4-inch cubes
   2 medium onions, chopped
   2 cans (15-1/4 ounces *each*) whole kernel corn, drained
   2 cans (10-3/4 ounces *each*) condensed cream of mushroom soup, undiluted
1/2 teaspoon salt
1/2 teaspoon pepper

Cook noodles according to package directions. In a large skillet, cook pork and onions over medium heat until meat is no longer pink. Drain noodles. Stir the noodles, corn, soup, salt and pepper into pork mixture.

Transfer to a greased 3-qt. baking dish. Cover and bake at 350° for 30 minutes. Uncover; bake 15 minutes longer.
Yield: 8 servings.

Potluck Pointer

Don't flip your lid! To keep your dish's cover on while driving to the church supper, simply set a rubber band around the lid's knob and over one of the dish's handles. Pull another rubber band around the knob and over the other handle.

Neptune's Lasagna

Elena Hansen, Ruidoso, New Mexico
This comforting main course is loaded with scallops, shrimp and crab. The creamy sauce helps make it the "crown jewel" in my repertoire of recipes.

  1 green onion, finely chopped
  2 tablespoons vegetable oil
  2 tablespoons butter plus 1/2 cup butter, *divided*
1/2 cup chicken broth
  1 bottle (8 ounces) clam juice
  1 pound bay scallops
  1 pound uncooked small shrimp, peeled and deveined
  1 package (8 ounces) imitation crabmeat, chopped
1/4 teaspoon white pepper, *divided*
1/2 cup all-purpose flour
1-1/2 cups milk
1/2 teaspoon salt
  1 cup heavy whipping cream
1/2 cup shredded Parmesan cheese, *divided*
  9 lasagna noodles, cooked and drained

In a large skillet, saute onion in oil and 2 tablespoons butter until tender. Stir in broth and clam juice; bring to a boil. Add the scallops, shrimp, crab and 1/8 teaspoon pepper; return to a boil. Reduce heat; simmer, uncovered, for 4-5 minutes or until shrimp turn pink and scallops are firm and opaque, stirring gently. Drain, reserving cooking liquid; set seafood mixture aside.

In a saucepan, melt the remaining butter; stir in flour until smooth. Combine milk and reserved cooking liquid; gradually add to the saucepan. Add salt and remaining pepper. Bring to a boil; cook and stir for 2 minutes or until thickened. Remove from the heat; stir in cream and 1/4 cup Parmesan cheese. Stir 3/4 cup white sauce into the seafood mixture.

Spread 1/2 cup white sauce in a greased 13-in. x 9-in. x 2-in. baking dish. Top with three noodles; spread with half of the seafood mixture and 1-1/4 cups sauce. Repeat layers. Top with remaining noodles, sauce and Parmesan.

Bake, uncovered, at 350° for 35-40 minutes or until golden brown. Let stand for 15 minutes before cutting.

Yield: 12 servings.

Penne Sausage Bake

(pictured below)
Vicky Benscoter, Birmingham, Alabama
This comforting pasta dish was inspired by the delicious sausage rolls served at our favorite Italian restaurant. I serve it frequently for suppers and get-togethers since my husband thinks it's great...and it's easy to prepare!

  1 package (1 pound) penne pasta
  1 medium green pepper, chopped
  1 small onion, chopped
  1 tablespoon olive oil
  1 pound turkey Italian sausage links, casings removed
  3 cups fat-free meatless spaghetti sauce
1-1/2 cups (6 ounces) shredded part-skim mozzarella cheese
1/4 cup grated Parmesan cheese

Cook pasta according to package directions; drain. In a large skillet, saute green pepper and onion in oil for 6-7 minutes. Add sausage; cook and stir until sausage is no longer pink. Drain. Stir in the spaghetti sauce and pasta.

Transfer to a 3-qt. baking dish coated with nonstick cooking spray. Cover and bake at 350° for 15-20 minutes. Uncover; sprinkle with cheeses. Bake 5-10 minutes longer or until cheese is melted.

Yield: 9 servings.

Cheesy Shell Lasagna

(pictured below)
Mrs. Leo Merchant, Jackson, Mississippi
This zesty layered casserole is a real crowd-pleaser. It was one of our children's favorites when they were young...now our grandchildren love it! Plus, it's easier to make than traditional lasagna.

1-1/2 pounds lean ground beef
   2 medium onions, chopped
   1 garlic clove, minced
   1 can (14-1/2 ounces) diced tomatoes
   1 jar (14 ounces) meatless spaghetti sauce
   1 can (4 ounces) mushroom stems and pieces, undrained
   8 ounces uncooked small shell pasta
   2 cups (16 ounces) sour cream
 11 slices (8 ounces) provolone cheese
   1 cup (4 ounces) shredded part-skim mozzarella cheese

In a nonstick skillet, cook the beef, onions and garlic over medium heat until meat is no longer pink; drain. Stir in the tomatoes, spaghetti sauce and mushrooms. Bring to a boil. Reduce heat; simmer, uncovered, for 20 minutes. Meanwhile, cook pasta according to package directions; drain.

Place half of the pasta in an ungreased 13-in. x 9-in. x 2-in. baking dish. Top with half of the meat sauce, sour cream and provolone cheese. Repeat layers. Sprinkle with mozzarella cheese.

Cover and bake at 350° for 35-40 minutes longer or until the cheese begins to brown. Let stand for 10 minutes before cutting.

Yield: 12 servings.

Creamy Carrot Casserole

(pictured above)
Laurie Heward, Fillmore, Utah
My mom and I developed this recipe to see if there was a carrot dish that even people who don't like carrots would enjoy. So far, I haven't met anyone who hasn't cared for our creation.

1-1/2 pound carrots, peeled and sliced *or* 1 bag (20 ounces) frozen sliced carrots, thawed
   1 cup mayonnaise
   1 tablespoon grated onion
   1 tablespoon prepared horseradish
 1/4 cup shredded cheddar cheese
   2 tablespoons buttered bread crumbs

In a saucepan, cook carrots just until crisp-tender; drain, reserving 1/4 cup cooking liquid.

Place carrots in a 1-1/2 qt. baking dish. Combine mayonnaise, onion, horseradish and reserved cooking liquid; spread evenly over carrots. Sprinkle with cheese; top with bread crumbs.

Bake, uncovered, at 350° for 30 minutes.

Yield: 8-10 servings.

Oven Jambalaya

Pat Schroeder, Elkhorn, Wisconsin
If you're looking for a simple but delicious version of jambalaya, this is it!

2-1/4 cups water
1-1/2 cups uncooked long grain rice
   1 can (10-3/4 ounces) condensed cream of celery soup, undiluted
   1 can (10-3/4 ounces) condensed cream of onion soup, undiluted
   1 can (10 ounces) diced tomatoes and green chilies, undrained
   1 pound fully cooked smoked sausage, cut into 1/2-inch slices
   1 pound cooked medium shrimp, peeled and deveined

In a large bowl, combine the first five ingredients; mix well. Pour into a greased 13-in. x 9-in. x 2-in. baking dish.

Cover and bake at 350° for 40 minutes. Stir in sausage and shrimp. Cover and bake 20-30 minutes longer or until the rice is tender.
Yield: 8-10 servings.

Corn Bread Turkey Casserole

Michelle Flynn, Philadelphia, Pennsylvania
Folks who love turkey and stuffing will appreciate the flavor and convenience of my golden casserole.

   3 packages (6 ounces *each*) crushed corn bread stuffing mix
10 to 11 cups cubed cooked turkey *or* chicken
   2 cups (8 ounces) shredded cheddar cheese
   2 cans (10-3/4 ounces *each*) condensed cream of celery soup, undiluted
   2 cans (10-3/4 ounces *each*) condensed cream of chicken soup, undiluted
   1 can (10-3/4 ounces) condensed cream of mushroom soup, undiluted
   1 can (12 ounces) evaporated milk
1-1/2 cups (6 ounces) shredded Swiss cheese

Prepare stuffing mixes according to package directions. Add turkey and cheddar cheese. Combine the soups and milk. Pour 1 cup each into three greased 13-in. x 9-in. x 2-in. baking dishes. Top each with turkey mixture and remaining soup mixture. Sprinkle with Swiss cheese. Cover and bake the casseroles at 350° for 30-35 minutes or until bubbly. Let stand for 5-10 minutes before serving.
Yield: 3 casseroles (8-10 servings each).

Confetti Spaghetti

(pictured above)
Katherine Moss, Gaffney, South Carolina
It's not uncommon for folks to go back for second helpings of this hearty main dish when I share it at church carry-in suppers. The combination of ground beef, noodles, cheese and a zippy tomato sauce is a real people-pleaser.

   1 package (12 ounces) spaghetti
1-1/2 pounds ground beef
   1 medium green pepper, chopped
   1 medium onion, chopped
   1 can (14-1/2 ounces) diced tomatoes, undrained
   1 can (8 ounces) tomato sauce
   1 tablespoon brown sugar
   1 teaspoon salt
   1 teaspoon chili powder
1/2 teaspoon pepper
1/4 teaspoon garlic powder
1/8 teaspoon cayenne pepper
3/4 cup shredded cheddar cheese

Cook spaghetti according to package directions. Meanwhile, in a large skillet, cook beef, green pepper and onion over medium heat until meat is no longer pink; drain. Stir in tomatoes, tomato sauce, brown sugar, salt, chili powder, pepper, garlic powder and cayenne. Drain spaghetti; add to the beef mixture. Transfer to a greased 13-in. x 9-in. x 2-in. baking dish. Cover and bake at 350° for 30 minutes. Uncover; sprinkle with cheese. Bake 5 minutes longer or until cheese is melted.
Yield: 12 servings.

Butternut Squash Casserole

(pictured above)
Patricia Sheffer, Seneca, Pennsylvania
This scrumptious casserole goes with everything! It can be served hot today and cold tomorrow, as a main dish for meatless meals or as a side dish at a dinner party.

    5 cups shredded peeled butternut squash
Juice and grated peel of 1 lemon
    1 cup raisins
    6 to 8 dried apricots, chopped (about 1/3 cup)
    1 medium apple, cubed
    2 cups ricotta cheese
    1 egg, lightly beaten
    3 tablespoons plain yogurt
    1 teaspoon ground cinnamon
  1/8 teaspoon ground nutmeg
  1/2 cup chopped walnuts

In a large bowl, toss squash with lemon juice and peel. Place half in the bottom of a greased 11-in. x 7-in. x 2-in. baking dish.

Combine raisins, apricots and apple; sprinkle over squash. In a small bowl, mix cheese, egg, yogurt, cinnamon and nutmeg; spread over fruit mixture. Cover with remaining squash. Sprinkle with nuts. Cover with foil. Bake at 375° for 35-40 minutes or until done.

Yield: 10-12 servings.

Firecracker Casserole

(pictured on p. 41)
Teressa Eastman, El Dorado, Kansas
I loved this southwestern-style casserole when my mother made it years ago. Now my husband enjoys it when I prepare it. The flavor reminds me of enchiladas but without all of the work.

    2 pounds ground beef
    1 medium onion, chopped
    1 can (15 ounces) black beans, rinsed and drained
    1 to 2 tablespoons chili powder
    2 to 3 teaspoons ground cumin
  1/2 teaspoon salt
    4 flour tortillas (6 inches)
    1 can (10-3/4 ounces) condensed cream of mushroom soup, undiluted
    1 can (10 ounces) diced tomatoes and green chilies, undrained
    1 cup (4 ounces) shredded cheddar cheese

In a skillet, cook the beef and onion until the meat is no longer pink; drain. Add the beans, chili powder, cumin and salt.

Transfer to a greased 13-in. x 9-in. x 2-in. baking dish. Arrange tortillas over the top. Combine soup and tomatoes; pour over the tortillas. Sprinkle with cheese.

Bake, uncovered, at 350° for 25-30 minutes or until heated through.

Yield: 8 servings.

Grilled Cheese in a Pan

Mary Ann Wendt, Ada, Michigan
My cousin served this dish at a shower years ago, and my daughter and I immediately asked for the recipe. If you don't have all of the exact cheeses it calls for, you can switch a couple and it still tastes absolutely delicious.

    1 tube (8 ounces) refrigerated crescent rolls
    4 cups (1 cup *each*) shredded Muenster, Monterey Jack, Swiss and cheddar cheese
    1 package (8 ounces) cream cheese, sliced
    1 egg, lightly beaten
    1 tablespoon butter, melted
    1 tablespoon sesame seeds

Unroll crescent roll dough; divide in half. Seal perforations. Line an ungreased 8-in. square baking pan with half of the dough. Layer with the Muenster, Monterey Jack, Swiss, cheddar and cream cheese. Pour egg over all.

Top with remaining dough. Brush with butter; sprinkle with sesame seeds. Bake, uncovered, at 350° for 30-35 minutes or until golden brown.

Yield: 9 servings.

Pictured below:
Ham with Cherry Sauce (p. 71).

Slow Cooker
Favorites

Moist Poultry Dressing

(pictured above)
Ruth Ann Stelfox, Raymond, Alberta
Tasty mushrooms and onions complement the big herb flavor in this stuffing that stays nice and moist in the slow cooker.

- 2 jars (4-1/2 ounces *each*) sliced mushrooms, drained
- 4 celery ribs, chopped
- 2 medium onions, chopped
- 1/4 cup minced fresh parsley
- 3/4 cup butter, cubed
- 1-1/2 pounds day-old bread, crusts removed and cubed (about 13 cups)
- 1-1/2 teaspoons salt
- 1-1/2 teaspoons rubbed sage
- 1 teaspoon poultry seasoning
- 1 teaspoon dried thyme
- 1/2 teaspoon pepper
- 2 eggs
- 1 can (14-1/2 ounces) chicken broth

In a large skillet, saute the mushrooms, celery, onions and parsley in butter until the vegetables are tender. In a large bowl, toss the bread cubes with salt, sage, poultry seasoning, thyme and pepper. Add the mushroom mixture. Combine eggs and broth; add to the bread mixture and toss.

Transfer to 5-qt. slow cooker. Cover and cook on low for 4-5 hours or until a meat thermometer reads 160°.

Yield: 12-16 servings.

Slow-Simmered Kidney Beans

(pictured below)
Sheila Vail, Long Beach, California
My husband always nominates me to bring a side dish when we're invited to a potluck. Canned beans cut down on prep time yet get plenty of zip from bacon, apples, red peppers and onion. I like simmering this mixture in the slow cooker because it blends the flavors and I don't have to stand over the hot stove.

- 6 bacon strips, diced
- 1/2 pound smoked Polish sausage *or* kielbasa
- 4 cans (16 ounces *each*) kidney beans, rinsed and drained
- 1 can (28 ounces) diced tomatoes, drained
- 2 medium sweet red peppers, chopped
- 1 large onion, chopped
- 1 cup ketchup
- 1/2 cup packed brown sugar
- 1/4 cup honey
- 1/4 cup molasses
- 1 tablespoon Worcestershire sauce
- 1 teaspoon salt
- 1 teaspoon ground mustard
- 2 medium unpeeled red apples, cored and cut into 1/2-inch pieces

In a large skillet, cook bacon until crisp. Remove with a slotted spoon to paper towels. Add sausage to drippings; cook and stir for 5 minutes. Drain and set aside.

In a 5-qt. slow cooker, combine the beans, tomatoes, red peppers, onion, ketchup, brown sugar, honey, molasses, Worcestershire sauce, salt and mustard. Stir in the bacon and sausage. Cover and cook on low for 4-6 hours. Stir in apples. Cover and cook 2 hours longer or until bubbly.

Yield: 16 servings.

Minister's Delight

Mary Ann Potter, Blue Springs, Missouri
You'll need a can of cherry pie filling, a yellow cake mix and just two other ingredients to simmer up this warm dessert. A friend gave me the recipe several years ago, saying that a minister's wife fixed it every Sunday so she named it accordingly.

    1 can (21 ounces) cherry *or* apple pie filling
    1 package (18-1/4 ounces) yellow cake mix
1/2 cup butter, melted
1/3 cup chopped walnuts, optional

Place pie filling in a 1-1/2-qt. slow cooker. Combine dry cake mix and butter (mixture will be crumbly); sprinkle over filling. Sprinkle with walnuts if desired. Cover and cook on low for 2-3 hours. Serve in bowls.
Yield: 10-12 servings.

Pizza Casserole

Julie Sterchi, Harrisburg, Illinois
A friend from church gave me the recipe for this satisfying casserole for the slow cooker. It's always one of the first dishes emptied at potlucks, and it can easily be adapted to personal tastes.

    3 pounds ground beef
1/2 cup chopped onion
    1 jar (28 ounces) spaghetti sauce
    2 jars (4-1/2 ounces *each*) sliced
      mushrooms, drained
    1 teaspoon salt
1/2 teaspoon garlic powder
1/2 teaspoon dried oregano
Dash pepper
    1 package (16 ounces) wide egg noodles,
      cooked and drained
    2 packages (3-1/2 ounces *each*) sliced
      pepperoni
    2 cups (8 ounces) shredded cheddar cheese
    2 cups (8 ounces) shredded part-skim
      mozzarella cheese

In a Dutch oven, brown beef and onion over medium heat until meat is no longer pink; drain. Add spaghetti sauce, mushrooms, salt, garlic powder, oregano and pepper; heat through. Spoon 4 cups into a 6-qt. slow cooker. Top with half of the noodles, pepperoni and cheeses. Repeat layers. Cover and cook on high for 1 hour or until the cheese is melted.
Yield: 12 servings.

Barbecue Sausage Bites

(pictured above)
Rebekah Randolph, Greer, South Carolina
A sweet-and-tangy appetizer, this recipe pairs pineapple chunks with barbecue sauce and three kinds of sausage.

    1 package (1 pound) miniature smoked
      sausages
3/4 pound fully cooked bratwurst
3/4 pound smoked kielbasa *or* Polish sausage
    1 bottle (18 ounces) barbecue sauce
2/3 cup orange marmalade
1/2 teaspoon ground mustard
1/8 teaspoon ground allspice
    1 can (20 ounces) pineapple chunks, drained

In a 3-qt. slow cooker, combine the sausages. In a small bowl, whisk the barbecue sauce, marmalade, mustard and allspice. Pour over sausage mixture; stir to coat. Cover and cook on high for 2-1/2 to 3 hours or until heated through. Stir in pineapple.
Yield: 12-14 servings.

Chili Mac

(pictured above)
Marie Posavec, Berwyn, Illinois
This recipe has regularly appeared on my family menus for more than 40 years, and it's never failed to please at bring-a-dish gatherings.

- 1 pound ground beef, cooked and drained
- 2 cans (15 ounces *each*) hot chili beans
- 2 large green peppers, chopped
- 1 large onion, chopped
- 4 celery ribs, chopped
- 1 can (8 ounces) tomato sauce
- 1 envelope chili seasoning
- 2 garlic cloves, minced
- 1 package (7 ounces) elbow macaroni, cooked and drained

Salt and pepper to taste

In a 5-qt. slow cooker, combine the first eight ingredients. Cover and cook on low for 6 hours or until heated through. Stir in macaroni; mix well. Season with salt and pepper.
Yield: 12 servings.

Spice Coffee

Joanne Holt, Bowling Green, Ohio
Even those who usually don't drink coffee will find this special blend with a hint of chocolate appealing. I keep a big batch simmering at brunches and other parties.

- 8 cups brewed coffee
- 1/3 cup sugar
- 1/4 cup chocolate syrup

- 1/2 teaspoon anise extract
- 4 cinnamon sticks (3 inches)
- 1-1/2 teaspoons whole cloves

Additional cinnamon sticks, optional

In a 3-qt. slow cooker, combine the coffee, sugar, chocolate syrup and anise extract. Place cinnamon sticks and cloves in a double thickness of cheesecloth; bring up corners of cloth and tie with string to form a bag. Add to slow cooker. Cover and cook on low for 2-3 hours.

Discard spice bag. Ladle coffee into mugs; garnish each with a cinnamon stick if desired.
Yield: 8 cups.

Cranberry Apple Cider

(pictured below)
Jennifer Naboka, North Plainfield, New Jersey
Served warm from the slow cooker, this soothing beverage proves especially popular when it's cool outside. Cranberries and orange sections add a tangy twist to the spiced cider, making it ideal for Christmas gatherings.

- 4 cups water
- 4 cups apple juice
- 1 can (12 ounces) frozen apple juice concentrate, thawed
- 1 medium apple, peeled and sliced
- 1 cup fresh *or* frozen cranberries
- 1 medium orange, peeled and sectioned
- 1 cinnamon stick

In a 5-qt. slow cooker, combine all ingredients. Cover and cook on low for 2 hours or until cider reaches desired temperature. Discard cinnamon stick. If desired, remove fruit with a slotted spoon before serving.
Yield: 10 servings (about 2-1/2 quarts).

Slow-Cooked Broccoli

(pictured above)
Connie Slocum, Antioch, Tennessee
This crumb-topped side dish is quick to assemble and full of flavor. Since it simmers in a slow cooker, it frees up my oven for other things. This is a great help when I'm preparing several items for a big meal.

  2 packages (10 ounces *each*) frozen chopped broccoli, partially thawed
  1 can (10-3/4 ounces) condensed cream of celery soup, undiluted
1-1/2 cups (6 ounces) shredded sharp cheddar cheese, *divided*
  1/4 cup chopped onion
  1/2 teaspoon Worcestershire sauce
  1/4 teaspoon pepper
  1 cup crushed butter-flavored crackers (about 25)
  2 tablespoons butter

In a large bowl, combine broccoli, soup, 1 cup cheese, onion, Worcestershire sauce and pepper. Pour into a 3-qt. greased slow cooker. Sprinkle crackers on top; dot with butter. Cover and cook on high for 2-1/2 to 3 hours. Sprinkle with remaining cheese. Cook 10 minutes longer or until the cheese is melted.

Yield: 8-10 servings.

Potluck Pointer

Transporting more than one slow cooker to the church supper and can't find a cardboard box to carry them in? Try setting them in a sturdy laundry basket.

Hot Ham Sandwiches

(pictured below)
Susan Rehm, Grahamsville, New York
I came up with this crowd-pleasing recipe when trying to re-create a favorite sandwich from a restaurant near my hometown. Flavored with sweet relish, the ham sandwiches are oh-so-easy.

> 3 pounds thinly sliced deli ham (about 40 slices)
> 2 cups apple juice
> 2/3 cup packed brown sugar
> 1/2 cup sweet pickle relish
> 2 teaspoons prepared mustard
> 1 teaspoon paprika
> 12 kaiser rolls, split
> Additional sweet pickle relish, optional

Separate ham slices and place in a 3-qt. slow cooker. In a bowl, combine the apple juice, brown sugar, relish, mustard and paprika. Pour over ham.

Cover and cook on low for 4-5 hours or until heated through. Place 3-4 slices of ham on each roll. Serve with additional relish if desired.

Yield: 12 servings.

Slow-Cooked Short Ribs

(pictured above)
Pam Halfhill, Medina, Ohio
Smothered in a finger-licking barbecue sauce, these meaty ribs are a winner everywhere I take them. The recipe is great for a busy cook because once everything is combined, the slow cooker does all the work.

> 2/3 cup all-purpose flour
> 2 teaspoons salt
> 1/2 teaspoon pepper
> 4 to 4-1/2 pounds boneless beef short ribs
> 1/4 to 1/3 cup butter
> 1 large onion, chopped
> 1-1/2 cups beef broth
> 3/4 cup red wine vinegar
> 3/4 cup packed brown sugar
> 1/2 cup chili sauce
> 1/3 cup ketchup
> 1/3 cup Worcestershire sauce
> 5 garlic cloves, minced
> 1-1/2 teaspoons chili powder

In a large resealable plastic bag, combine the flour, salt and pepper. Add ribs in batches and shake to coat. In a large skillet, brown ribs in butter.

Transfer to a 6-qt. slow cooker. In the same skillet, combine the remaining ingredients. Cook and stir until mixture comes to a boil; pour over ribs. Cover and cook on low for 9-10 hours or until meat is tender.

Yield: 12 servings.

Turkey with Cranberry Sauce

Marie Ramsden, Fairgrove, Michigan
This is a very tasty and easy way to cook lots of turkey in slow cookers. Ideal for holiday potlucks, the sweet cranberry sauce complements the poultry nicely.

    2 boneless skinless turkey breast halves (4
       pounds *each*)
    1 can (14 ounces) jellied cranberry sauce
  1/2 cup plus 2 tablespoons water, *divided*
    1 envelope onion soup mix
    2 tablespoons cornstarch

Cut each turkey breast in half; place in two 5-qt. slow cookers. In a large bowl, combine the cranberry sauce, 1/2 cup water and soup mix; mix well. Pour half over each turkey. Cover and cook on low for 4-6 hours or until turkey is no longer pink and meat thermometer reads 170°. Remove turkey and keep warm.

   Transfer both cranberry mixtures to a large saucepan. Combine the cornstarch and remaining water until smooth. Bring cranberry mixture to a boil; gradually stir in cornstarch mixture until smooth. Cook and stir for 2 minutes or until thickened. Slice turkey; serve with cranberry sauce.

Yield: 20-25 servings.

Slow Cooker Mashed Potatoes

Trudy Vincent, Valles Mines, Missouri
Sour cream and cream cheese add richness to these smooth, make-ahead potatoes. They're wonderful when time is tight because they don't require any last-minute mashing.

    1 package (3 ounces) cream cheese,
       softened
  1/2 cup sour cream
  1/4 cup butter, softened
    1 envelope ranch salad dressing mix
    1 teaspoon dried parsley flakes
    6 cups warm mashed potatoes (without
       added milk and butter)

In a large bowl, combine the cream cheese, sour cream, butter, salad dressing mix and parsley; stir in potatoes. Transfer to a 3-qt. slow cooker. Cover and cook on low for 2-4 hours.

Yield: 8-10 servings.

Slow-Cooked Chicken and Stuffing

(pictured above)
Angie Marquart, New Washington, Ohio
This heavenly main dish has a flavorful blend of seasonings and the irresistible duo of tender chicken and moist dressing. It's nice enough for holiday celebrations but easy enough to fix year-round.

  2-1/2 cups chicken broth
      1 cup butter, cubed
    1/2 cup chopped onion
    1/2 cup chopped celery
      1 can (4 ounces) mushroom stems and
         pieces, drained
    1/4 cup dried parsley flakes
  1-1/2 teaspoons rubbed sage
      1 teaspoon poultry seasoning
      1 teaspoon salt
    1/2 teaspoon pepper
     12 cups day-old bread cubes (1/2-inch
         pieces)
      2 eggs
      1 can (10-3/4 ounces) condensed cream of
         chicken soup, undiluted
      5 to 6 cups cubed cooked chicken

In a large saucepan, combine the first 10 ingredients. Simmer for 10 minutes; remove from the heat. Place bread cubes in a large bowl. Combine eggs and soup; stir into broth mixture until smooth. Pour over bread and toss well.

   In a 5-qt. slow cooker, layer half of the stuffing and chicken; repeat layers. Cover and cook on low for 4-1/2 to 5 hours or until a meat thermometer inserted into the stuffing reads 160°.

Yield: 14-16 servings.

Tangy Beef and Vegetable Stew

(pictured below)
Amberleah Homlberg, Calgary, Alberta
This meal-in-one is sure to satisfy even the biggest of appetites. I combine chunks of beef with potatoes, carrots and plenty of other veggies. Mustard and horseradish add to the great flavor.

- 6 cups cubed peeled potatoes (1/2-inch pieces)
- 8 medium carrots, cut into 1/2-inch pieces
- 2 medium onions, cubed
- 4 pounds lean beef stew meat, cut into 1-inch pieces
- 1/3 cup vegetable oil
- 1/3 cup all-purpose flour
- 4 beef bouillon cubes
- 3 cups boiling water
- 1/3 cup white vinegar
- 1/3 cup ketchup
- 3 tablespoons prepared horseradish
- 3 tablespoons prepared mustard
- 2 tablespoons sugar
- 2 cups *each* frozen peas and corn
- 2 cups sliced fresh mushrooms

Place the potatoes, carrots and onions in a 6-qt. slow cooker.

In a large skillet, brown beef in oil, a single layer at a time; place over the vegetables. Sprinkle with flour.

Dissolve bouillon cubes in boiling water. Stir in vinegar, ketchup, horseradish, mustard and sugar; pour over meat and vegetables. Cover and cook on high for 5 hours. Add the peas, corn and mushrooms. Cover and cook on high for 45 minutes.

Yield: 12-16 servings.

Ham with Cherry Sauce

(pictured on p. 63)
Carol Lee Jones, Taylors, South Carolina
I often fix this delicious ham topped with a thick cherry sauce for church breakfasts. It's such a favorite that I've even served it at Easter dinners and at a friend's wedding brunch.

  1 boneless fully cooked ham (3 to 4 pounds)
1/2 cup apple jelly
  2 teaspoons prepared mustard
2/3 cup ginger ale, *divided*
  1 can (21 ounces) cherry pie filling
  2 tablespoons cornstarch

Score surface of ham, making diamond shapes 1/2 in. deep. In a small bowl, combine the jelly, mustard and 1 tablespoon ginger ale; rub over scored surface of ham. Cut ham in half; place in a 5-qt. slow cooker. Cover and cook on low for 4-5 hours or until a meat thermometer reads 140° and ham is heated through. Baste with cooking juices toward end of cooking time.

For sauce, place pie filling in a saucepan. Combine cornstarch and remaining ginger ale; stir into pie filling until blended. Bring to a boil; cook and stir for 2 minutes or until thickened. Serve over ham.

Yield: 10-12 servings.

Hot Fruit Salad

Barb Vande Voort, New Sharon, Iowa
This spicy fruit mixture is a breeze to make...just open the cans and empty them into the slow cooker. With its easy preparation and fantastic taste, the sweet side dish is ideal for celebrating any special occasion.

  1 jar (25 ounces) chunky applesauce
  1 can (21 ounces) cherry pie filling
  1 can (20 ounces) pineapple chunks, undrained
  1 can (15-1/4 ounces) sliced peaches, undrained
  1 can (15-1/4 ounces) apricot halves, undrained
  1 can (15 ounces) mandarin oranges, undrained
1/2 cup packed brown sugar
  1 teaspoon ground cinnamon

Place the first six ingredients in a 5-qt. slow cooker and stir gently. Combine brown sugar and cinnamon; sprinkle over fruit mixture. Cover and cook on low for 3-4 hours.

Yield: 16 servings.

Italian Turkey Sandwiches

(pictured above)
Carol Riley, Galva, Illinois
The recipe for these tasty turkey sandwiches makes plenty, so it's great for potlucks. I also make them for my family because whatever is left over is just as delicious the next day.

  1 bone-in turkey breast (5-1/2 pounds), skin removed
1/2 cup chopped green pepper
  1 medium onion, chopped
1/4 cup chili sauce
  3 tablespoons white vinegar
  2 tablespoons dried oregano *or* Italian seasoning
  4 teaspoons beef bouillon granules
11 kaiser *or* hard rolls, split

Cut turkey breast in half along the bone. Place the turkey breast, green pepper and onion in a 5-qt. slow cooker coated with nonstick cooking spray. Combine the chili sauce, vinegar, oregano and bouillon; pour over turkey and vegetables. Cover and cook on low for 5-6 hours or until meat juices run clear and vegetables are tender.

Remove turkey, reserving cooking liquid. Shred the turkey with two forks; return to cooking juices. Spoon 1/2 cup onto each roll.

Yield: 11 servings.

Old-World Sauerbraten

(pictured below)
Susan Garoutte, Georgetown, Texas
This German entree is phenomenal with potato pancakes and vegetables. Crushed gingersnaps, lemon and vinegar give the marinated beef and gravy an appetizing sweet-sour flavor that folks adore.

1-1/2 cups water, *divided*
1-1/4 cups cider vinegar, *divided*
   2 large onions, sliced, *divided*
   1 medium lemon, sliced
  15 whole cloves, *divided*
   6 bay leaves, *divided*
   6 whole peppercorns
   2 tablespoons sugar
   2 teaspoons salt
   1 boneless beef sirloin tip roast (3 pounds), cut in half
 1/4 teaspoon pepper
  12 gingersnap cookies, crumbled

In a large resealable plastic bag, combine 1 cup water, 1 cup vinegar, half of the onions, lemon, 10 cloves, four bay leaves, peppercorns, sugar and salt; mix well. Add roast. Seal bag and turn to coat; refrigerate overnight, turning occasionally.

Drain and discard marinade. Place roast in a 5-qt. slow cooker; add pepper and remaining water, vinegar, onions, cloves and bay leaves. Cover and cook on low for 6-8 hours or until meat is tender.

Remove roast and keep warm. Discard bay leaves. Stir in gingersnaps. Cover and cook on high for 10-15 minutes or until gravy is thickened. Slice roast; serve with gravy.

Yield: 12 servings.

Bandito Chili Dogs

(pictured above)
Marion Lowery, Medford, Oregon
I've brought these beefy chili dogs to family functions for years. Even the hot dogs cook in the slow cooker! Kids and adults alike love the cheesy chili sauce that comes together with canned items.

   1 package (1 pound) hot dogs
   2 cans (15 ounces *each*) chili without beans
   1 can (10-3/4 ounces) condensed cheddar cheese soup, undiluted
   1 can (4 ounces) chopped green chilies
  10 hot dog buns, split
   1 medium onion, chopped
   1 to 2 cups corn chips, coarsely crushed
   1 cup (4 ounces) shredded cheddar cheese

Place hot dogs in a 3-qt. slow cooker. In a large bowl, combine the chili, soup and green chilies; pour over hot dogs. Cover and cook on low for 4-5 hours. Serve hot dogs in buns; top with chili mixture, onion, corn chips and cheese.

Yield: 10 servings.

Ground Beef Stew

Sandra Castillo, Sun Prairie, Wisconsin
I created this chunky soup when looking for something inexpensive and easy to make. Bowls of the thick, comforting mixture are teaming with ground beef, potatoes and baby carrots.

- 1 pound ground beef
- 6 medium potatoes, peeled and cubed
- 1 package (16 ounces) baby carrots
- 3 cups water
- 2 tablespoons onion soup mix
- 1 garlic clove, minced
- 1 teaspoon Italian seasoning
- 1 to 1-1/2 teaspoons salt
- 1/4 teaspoon garlic powder
- 1/4 teaspoon pepper
- 1 can (10-3/4 ounces) condensed tomato soup, undiluted
- 1 can (6 ounces) Italian tomato paste

In a large skillet, cook beef over medium heat until no longer pink; drain. In a 5-qt. slow cooker, combine the next nine ingredients. Stir in the beef. Cover and cook on high for 4-5 hours. Stir in soup and tomato paste; cover and cook for 1 hour longer or until heated through.
Yield: 12 servings.

Chocolate-Raspberry Fondue

Heather Maxwell, Fort Riley, Kansas
You don't need a fancy fondue pot to make a melt-in-your-mouth sensation. I serve this dip in my small slow cooker. Folks of all ages love the chocolate-raspberry combination.

- 1 package (14 ounces) caramels
- 2 cups (12 ounces) semisweet chocolate chips
- 1 can (12 ounces) evaporated milk
- 1/2 cup butter
- 1/2 cup seedless raspberry jam
- Pound cake
- Assorted fresh fruit

In a large saucepan, combine the first five ingredients. Cook over low heat until caramels, chips and butter are melted, about 15 minutes. Stir until smooth. Transfer to a small slow cooker or fondue pot. Serve warm with pound cake or fruit.
Yield: 5 cups.

Hot Crab Dip

(pictured above)
Teri Rasey-Bolf, Cadillac, Michigan
I work full-time and coach soccer and football, so I appreciate recipes like this one that are easy to assemble. This warm and creamy seafood appetizer is perfect for large get-togethers.

- 1/2 cup milk
- 1/3 cup salsa
- 3 packages (8 ounces *each*) cream cheese, cubed
- 2 packages (8 ounces *each*) imitation crabmeat, flaked
- 1 cup thinly sliced green onions
- 1 can (4 ounces) chopped green chilies
- Assorted crackers

In a small bowl, combine milk and salsa. Transfer to a greased 3-qt. slow cooker. Stir in cream cheese, crab, onions and chilies. Cover and cook on low for 3-4 hours, stirring every 30 minutes. Serve with crackers.
Yield: about 5 cups.

Hot Bacon Cheese Dip

(pictured above)
Suzanne Whitaker, Knoxville, Tennessee
I've tried several appetizers before, but this one is a surefire people-pleaser. The dip has lots of bacon flavor and keeps friends happily munching. I serve it with tortilla chips or sliced French bread.

    2 packages (8 ounces *each*) cream cheese,
       cubed
    4 cups (16 ounces) shredded cheddar
       cheese
    1 cup half-and-half cream
    2 teaspoons Worcestershire sauce
    1 teaspoon dried minced onion
    1 teaspoon prepared mustard
   16 bacon strips, cooked and crumbled
Tortilla chips *or* French bread slices

In a 1-1/2-qt. slow cooker, combine the first six ingredients. Cover and cook for 2 hours or until cheeses are melted, stirring occasionally. Just before serving, stir in bacon. Serve warm with tortilla chips or bread.
Yield: 4 cups.

Chicken Stew

Linda Emery, Tuckerman, Arkansas
Try this slow cooker stew when you'd rather not be in the kitchen. Chicken, vegetables and seasonings give this specialty a great flavor, and it's even lower in fat than most stews.

    2 pounds boneless skinless chicken breasts,
       cut into 1-inch cubes
    2 cans (14-1/2 ounces *each*) fat-free chicken
       broth
    3 cups cubed peeled potatoes
    1 cup chopped onion
    1 cup sliced celery
    1 cup thinly sliced carrots
    1 teaspoon paprika
  1/2 teaspoon pepper
  1/2 teaspoon rubbed sage
  1/2 teaspoon dried thyme
    1 can (6 ounces) no-salt-added tomato paste
  1/4 cup cold water
    3 tablespoons cornstarch

In a 5-qt. slow cooker, combine the first 11 ingredients; cover and cook on high for 4 hours.
   Mix water and cornstarch until smooth; stir into stew. Cook, covered, 30 minutes more or until the vegetables are tender.
Yield: 10 servings.

Egg Noodle Lasagna

Mary Oberlin, Selinsgrove, Pennsylvania
I was lucky enough to receive this recipe from one of my friends. The perfect take-along for charity events and church potlucks, the comforting crowd-pleaser satisfies everyone who tries it.

  6-1/2 cups uncooked wide egg noodles
      3 tablespoons butter
  1-1/2 pounds ground beef
  2-1/4 cups spaghetti sauce
      6 ounces process cheese (Velveeta), cubed
      3 cups (12 ounces) shredded part-skim
         mozzarella cheese

Cook noodles according to package directions; drain. Add butter; toss to coat.
   In a large skillet, cook beef over medium heat until no longer pink; drain. Spread a fourth of the spaghetti sauce into an ungreased 5-qt. slow cooker. Layer with a third of the noodles, a third of the beef, a third of the remaining sauce and a third of the cheeses. Repeat layers twice.
   Cover and cook on low for 4 hours or until cheese is melted and lasagna is heated through.
Yield: 12-16 servings.

Shredded Beef Sandwiches

(pictured below)
Fran Frerichs, Gurley, Nebraska
Our family loves the mild barbecue flavor of these juicy sandwiches. The recipe makes a lot and the slow cooker keeps the meat warm, so it's a nice choice for parties.

     3 pounds beef stew meat, cut into 1-inch
       cubes
     3 medium green peppers, diced
     2 large onions, diced
     1 can (6 ounces) tomato paste
   1/2 cup packed brown sugar
   1/4 cup cider vinegar
     3 tablespoons chili powder
     2 teaspoons salt
     2 teaspoons Worcestershire sauce
     1 teaspoon ground mustard
    14 to 16 sandwich buns, split

In a 6-qt. slow cooker, combine the beef, peppers and onions. In a small bowl, combine tomato paste, brown sugar, vinegar, chili powder, salt, Worcestershire sauce and mustard. Stir into meat mixture. Cover and cook on high for 7-8 hours or until meat is tender. Skim fat from cooking juices. Shred beef, using two forks. With a slotted spoon, place 1/2 cup beef mixture on each bun.
Yield: 14-16 servings.

Potato Chowder

(pictured below)
Anna Mayer, Ft. Branch, Indiana
One of the ladies in our church quilting group brought this savory potato soup to a meeting, and everyone loved how the cream cheese and bacon made it so rich. It's easy to assemble in the morning, letting it simmer on its own all day.

     8 cups diced potatoes
   1/3 cup chopped onion
     3 cans (14-1/2 ounces *each*) chicken broth
     1 can (10-3/4 ounces) condensed cream of
       chicken soup, undiluted
   1/4 teaspoon pepper
     1 package (8 ounces) cream cheese, cubed
   1/2 pound sliced bacon, cooked and
       crumbled, optional
Minced chives, optional

In a 5-qt. slow cooker, combine the first five ingredients. Cover and cook on low for 8-10 hours or until potatoes are tender. Add cream cheese; stir until blended. Garnish with bacon and chives if desired.
Yield: 12 servings (3 quarts).

Place roast in a 3-qt. slow cooker; sprinkle with soup mix, browning sauce if desired, salt and pepper. Pour water over meat. Cover and cook on low for 8 hours.

Remove roast to a cutting board; let stand for 5 minutes. Add vegetables to slow cooker. Cube beef and return to slow cooker. Cover and cook on low for 1-1/2 hours or until vegetables are tender.

Combine cornstarch and cold water until smooth; stir into stew. Cover and cook on high for 30-45 minutes or until thickened.

Yield: 8-10 servings.

Beef and Barley

Linda Ronk, Melbourne, Florida
I've had the recipe for this country-style dish for years and rely on it when I'm hosting a large meal.

> 2 pounds ground beef, cooked and drained
> 1 can (15 ounces) diced carrots, undrained
> 1 can (14-1/2 ounces) diced tomatoes, undrained
> 1 can (10-3/4 ounces) condensed tomato soup, undiluted
> 2 celery ribs, finely chopped
> 1/2 cup water
> 1-1/2 to 2 teaspoons salt
> 1/2 teaspoon pepper
> 1/2 teaspoon chili powder
> 1 teaspoon Worcestershire sauce
> 1 bay leaf
> 1 cup quick-cooking barley
> 2 tablespoons butter
> 1 cup soft bread crumbs
> 1 cup (4 ounces) shredded cheddar cheese

In a 3-qt. slow cooker, combine the first 11 ingredients. In a skillet, lightly brown barley in butter. Add to the slow cooker; mix well. Sprinkle with bread crumbs and cheese. Cover and cook on high for 4 hours or until heated through. Discard bay leaf before serving.

Yield: 8 servings.

Busy Day Beef Stew

(pictured above)
Beth Wyatt, Paris, Kentucky
Here's a classic, old-fashioned beef stew that simmers for hours in the slow cooker. I call it my "lazy" stew because it feeds a lot of people, yet it's so easy to make.

> 1 boneless beef chuck roast (1 to 1-1/2 pounds)
> 1 envelope onion soup mix
> 2 teaspoons browning sauce, optional
> 1/2 teaspoon salt
> 1/2 teaspoon pepper
> 6 cups water
> 2 cups cubed peeled potatoes (1/2-inch pieces)
> 6 to 8 medium carrots, cut into chunks
> 1 medium onion, chopped
> 1 cup frozen peas, thawed
> 1 cup frozen corn, thawed, optional
> 5 tablespoons cornstarch
> 6 tablespoons cold water

Potluck Pointer

Unless you're preparing meat loaf, it's best to brown ground beef on the stovetop before adding it to your slow cooker. Not only will it be cooked through, but it will have a rich appearance, flavor and texture.

No-Fuss Pork and Sauerkraut

Joan Pereira, Avon, Massachusetts
A main course and a side dish all in one pot is what you get when you combine the following items in a slow cooker. I enjoy the mild apple flavor that this pork loin roast offers.

- 1 boneless whole pork loin roast (4 to 5 pounds), cut into quarters
- 1/3 cup Dijon mustard
- 1 teaspoon garlic powder
- 1 teaspoon rubbed sage
- 1 can (27 ounces) sauerkraut, rinsed and well drained
- 2 medium tart apples, sliced
- 1 cup apple juice

Rub sides of roast with mustard; sprinkle with garlic powder and sage. Place sauerkraut and half of the apples in a 6-qt. slow cooker. Top with the roast. Pour apple juice around roast; top with remaining apples.

Cover and cook on high for 4-5 hours or until a meat thermometer reads 160°.

Yield: 12-16 servings.

Two-Pot Dinner

Jean Roper, Palermo, California
My daughter received this recipe from a friend a while ago. Bacon gives it a wonderfully rich flavor, making it a much talked about dish at potlucks.

- 1 pound sliced bacon, cut into 2-inch pieces
- 1 large onion, chopped
- 1 pound ground beef
- 1 can (31 ounces) pork and beans
- 1 can (30 ounces) kidney beans, rinsed and drained
- 1 can (15 ounces) great northern beans, rinsed and drained
- 1 cup ketchup
- 1/3 cup packed brown sugar
- 3 tablespoons cider vinegar
- 1 tablespoon Liquid Smoke, optional

In a skillet, cook bacon over medium heat until crisp; remove with a slotted spoon to a 3-qt. slow cooker. Reserve 2 tablespoons drippings in the pan. Saute onion in drippings until browned; remove with a slotted spoon to slow cooker. In the same skillet, cook beef until no longer pink; drain and transfer to slow cooker. Add the remaining ingredients; mix well. Cover and cook on low for 4 hours or until heated through.

Yield: 10 servings.

Reuben Spread

(pictured above)
Rosalie Fuchs, Paynesville, Minnesota
I received the recipe for this hearty spread from my daughter. It tastes just like a Reuben sandwich. Serve it from a slow cooker set to low so that the spread stays warm.

1 jar (16 ounces) sauerkraut, rinsed and drained
1 package (8 ounces) cream cheese, cubed
2 cups (8 ounces) shredded Swiss cheese
1 package (3 ounces) deli corned beef, chopped
3 tablespoons prepared Thousand Island salad dressing
Snack rye bread *or* crackers

In a 1-1/2-qt. slow cooker, combine the first five ingredients. Cover and cook for 2 hours or until cheeses are melted; stir to blend. Serve warm with bread or crackers.

Yield: 3-1/2 cups.

Slow Cooker Cheese Dip

Marion Bartone, Conneaut, Ohio
I brought this spicy cheese dip to my guild, where it was a huge hit. It's a terrific take-along appetizer for large groups. Best of all, you can make it ahead of time and freeze it. Then all you have to do the day of your event is reheat it.

1 pound ground beef
1/2 pound bulk spicy pork sausage
2 pounds process American cheese, cubed
2 cans (10 ounces *each*) diced tomatoes and green chilies
Tortilla chips

In a large skillet, cook beef and sausage over medium heat until no longer pink; drain. Transfer to a 5-qt. slow cooker. Add cheese and tomatoes; mix well. Cover and cook on low for 4 hours or until the cheese is melted, stirring occasionally. Serve with tortilla chips.

Yield: 3 quarts.

Flavorful Beef in Gravy

Cheryl Sindergard, Plover, Iowa
Served over noodles, this fantastic supper showcases tender chunks of beef stew meat. The canned soups and onion soup mix make a mouth-watering gravy without much effort on your part.

- 1/3 cup all-purpose flour
- 3 pounds beef stew meat, cut into 1-inch cubes
- 3 tablespoons vegetable oil
- 2 cans (10-3/4 ounces *each*) condensed cream of mushroom soup, undiluted
- 1 can (10-3/4 ounces) condensed golden mushroom soup, undiluted
- 1 can (10-3/4 ounces) condensed cream of celery soup, undiluted
- 1-1/3 cups milk
- 1 envelope onion soup mix

Hot cooked noodles *or* mashed potatoes

Place flour in a large resealable plastic bag; add beef and toss to coat. In a skillet, brown beef in oil. Transfer beef to a 5-qt. slow cooker. Stir in the soups, milk and soup mix. Cover and cook on low for 7-8 hours or until the meat is tender. Serve over noodles or potatoes.
Yield: 10-12 servings.

Hearty Wild Rice

Mrs. Garnet Pettigrew, Columbia City, Indiana
My father-in-law used to make this casserole in the oven. I switched it to the slow cooker so I wouldn't need to keep an eye on it. This side dish complements many meals.

- 1 pound ground beef
- 1/2 pound bulk pork sausage
- 6 celery ribs, diced
- 2 cans (10-1/2 ounces *each*) condensed beef broth, undiluted
- 1-1/4 cups water
- 1 medium onion, chopped
- 1 cup uncooked wild rice
- 1 can (4 ounces) mushroom stems and pieces, drained
- 1/4 cup soy sauce

In a large skillet, cook beef and sausage over medium heat until no longer pink; drain.

Transfer to a 5-qt. slow cooker. Add the celery, broth, water, onion, rice, mushrooms and soy sauce; mix well. Cover and cook on high for 1 hour. Reduce heat to low; cover and cook for 4 hours or until the rice is tender.
Yield: 10-12 servings.

Marinated Pot Roast

(pictured above)
Marijane Rea, Milwaukie, Oregon
I've long used whole or ground cloves as my secret ingredient in cooking and baking. Added to an overnight marinade, they provide the gravy in this meaty main course with great flavor.

- 1 cup dry white wine *or* beef broth
- 1/3 cup reduced-sodium soy sauce
- 1 tablespoon olive oil
- 4 garlic cloves, minced
- 2 green onions, thinly sliced
- 1-1/2 teaspoons ground ginger
- 1/4 teaspoon pepper
- 4 whole cloves
- 1 boneless beef top round roast (4 pounds)
- 5 teaspoons cornstarch
- 5 teaspoons cold water

In a gallon-size resealable plastic bag, combine the first eight ingredients. Cut roast in half; add to marinade. Seal bag and turn to coat; refrigerate overnight.

Place roast and marinade in a 5-qt. slow cooker. Cover and cook on low for 8-10 hours or until meat is tender. Remove roast to a serving platter and keep warm. Pour cooking juices into a 2-cup measuring cup; discard whole cloves.

In a saucepan, combine cornstarch and cold water until smooth; stir in 1-1/2 cups cooking juices. Bring to a boil; cook and stir for 2 minutes or until thickened. Serve with the roast.
Yield: 12 servings.

Easy Chow Mein

(pictured above)
Kay Bade, Mitchell, South Dakota
My daughter gave me this simple recipe and it's one I turn to often. The exotic flavors make it a standout. I often make it for myself since the leftovers freeze so well.

  1 pound ground beef
  1 medium onion, chopped
  1 bunch celery, sliced
  2 cans (14 ounces *each*) Chinese vegetables, drained
  2 envelopes brown gravy mix
  2 tablespoons soy sauce
Hot cooked rice

In a skillet, cook beef and onion over medium heat until meat is no longer pink; drain. Transfer to a 3-qt. slow cooker. Stir in the celery, Chinese vegetables, gravy mix and soy sauce. Cover and cook on low for 4 hours or until celery is tender, stirring occasionally. Serve over rice.

Yield: 8 servings.

Hot Dogs 'n' Beans

June Formanek, Belle Plaine, Iowa
You'll please everyone with this tasty combination that's good for casual get-togethers. I frequently fix this when my whole family is home.

  3 cans (two 28 ounces, one 16 ounces) pork and beans
  1 package (1 pound) hot dogs, halved lengthwise and cut into 1-inch pieces
  1 large onion, chopped
1/2 cup packed brown sugar
  3 tablespoons prepared mustard
  4 bacon strips, cooked and crumbled

In a 5-qt. slow cooker, combine all ingredients. Cover and cook on low for 7-8 hours.

Yield: 10 servings.

Beef Barbecue

(pictured below)
Karen Walker, Sterling, Virginia
We like to keep our freezer stocked with plenty of beef roasts. When we're not in the mood for pot roast, however, I fix these satisfying sandwiches instead. The meat cooks in a tasty sauce while I'm at work. Then I just slice it thinly and serve it on rolls.

- 1 boneless chuck roast (3 pounds)
- 1 cup barbecue sauce
- 1/2 cup apricot preserves
- 1/3 cup chopped green *or* sweet red pepper
- 1 small onion, chopped
- 1 tablespoon Dijon mustard
- 2 teaspoons brown sugar
- 12 sandwich rolls, split

Cut the roast into quarters; place in a greased 5-qt. slow cooker. In a bowl, combine barbecue sauce, preserves, green pepper, onion, mustard and brown sugar; pour over roast. Cover and cook on low for 6-8 hours or until meat is tender.

Remove roast and thinly slice; return meat to slow cooker and stir gently. Cover and cook 20-30 minutes longer. Skim fat from sauce. Serve beef and sauce on rolls.

Yield: 12 servings.

Pork Chili

(pictured above)
Linda Temple, St. Joseph, Missouri
My husband usually tries to avoid spending time in the kitchen, but he'll frequently offer to prepare a big batch of this chili. Of course, he always eagerly serves as the taste-tester!

- 2-1/2 pounds boneless pork, cut into 1-inch cubes
- 2 tablespoons vegetable oil
- 1 can (28 ounce) diced tomatoes, undrained
- 1 can (15-1/2 ounces) chili beans, undrained
- 1 can (8 ounces) tomato sauce
- 1/4 cup salsa
- 1/4 cup chopped onion
- 1/4 cup chopped green pepper
- 1 tablespoon chili powder
- 1 teaspoon minced jalapeno pepper
- 1/4 teaspoon garlic powder
- 1/4 teaspoon cayenne powder
- 1/4 teaspoon pepper
- 1/4 teaspoon salt

In a large skillet over medium-high heat, brown pork in oil; drain. Place in a 5-qt. slow cooker; add remaining ingredients. Cover and cook on high for 2 hours. Reduce heat to low and cook 4 hours longer.

Yield: 10-12 servings.

Cheesy Creamed Corn

(pictured above)
Mary Ann Truitt, Wichita, Kansas
Even those who usually don't eat much corn will ask for a second helping of this side dish. People love the flavor, but I love how easy it is to make with items I usually have stocked in my kitchen.

    3 packages (16 ounces *each*) frozen corn
    2 packages (one 8 ounces, one 3 ounces)
       cream cheese, cubed
  1/4 cup butter, cubed
    3 tablespoons water
    3 tablespoons milk
    2 tablespoons sugar
    6 slices process American cheese, cut into
       small pieces

In a 3-qt. slow cooker, combine all the ingredients. Cover and cook on low for 4 hours or until heated through and the cheese is melted. Stir well before serving.

Yield: 12 servings.

Brisket for a Bunch

(pictured below)
Dawn Fagerstrom, Warren, Minnesota
This recipe makes tender slices of beef in a delicious au jus. To easily get very thin slices, chill the brisket before slicing then warm the slices in the juices.

    1 fresh beef brisket (2-1/2 pounds), cut in
       half
    1 tablespoon vegetable oil
  1/2 cup chopped celery
  1/2 cup chopped onion
  3/4 cup beef broth
  1/2 cup tomato sauce
  1/4 cup water
  1/4 cup sugar
    2 tablespoons onion soup mix
    1 tablespoon vinegar
   12 hamburger buns, split

In a large skillet, brown the brisket on each side in oil; transfer to a 3-qt. slow cooker. In the same skillet, saute celery and onion for 1 minute. Gradually add the broth, tomato sauce and water; stir to loosen the browned bits from pan. Add sugar, soup mix and vinegar; bring to a boil. Pour over brisket.

Cover and cook on low for 7-8 hours or until meat is tender. Let stand for 5 minutes before slicing. Skim fat from cooking juices. Serve meat in buns with cooking juices.

Yield: 10 servings.

Editor's Note: This is a fresh beef brisket, not corned beef. The meat comes from the first cut of the brisket.

Easy-Does-It Spaghetti

(pictured above)
Genevieve Hrabe, Plainville, Kansas
Combine cooked beef, pasta, canned mushrooms and a handful of other ingredients in your slow cooker for a yummy main course that will appeal to people of all ages. If you'd like, substitute 1/2 cup chopped onion for the dried minced onion.

- 2 pounds ground beef, cooked and drained
- 1 can (46 ounces) tomato juice
- 1 can (15 ounces) tomato sauce
- 1 can (8 ounces) mushroom stems and pieces, drained
- 2 tablespoons dried minced onion
- 2 teaspoon salt
- 1 teaspoon garlic powder
- 1 teaspoon ground mustard
- 1/2 teaspoon *each* ground allspice, mace and pepper
- 1 package (7 ounces) spaghetti, broken in half

In a 5-qt. slow cooker, combine beef, tomato juice, tomato sauce, mushrooms and seasonings. Cover and cook on high for 4 hours. Stir in spaghetti. Cover and cook on high 1 hour longer or until the spaghetti is tender.

Yield: 8-10 servings.

Potluck Pointer

It's a good idea to take an extension cord to the potluck with you. This way, you'll be able to plug in your slow cooker even if an outlet isn't directly behind the buffet. While you're at it, why not grab a second cord for anyone else who might bring a slow-cooked dish?

Creamy Hash Browns

(pictured above)
Donna Downes, Las Vegas, Nevada
My mother often took this comforting side dish to social dinners because it was such a hit. Now I get the same compliments when I make it. Bacon and onion jazz up a creamy mixture that takes advantage of convenient frozen hash browns and canned soups.

>   1 package (2 pounds) frozen cubed hash
>   brown potatoes
>   2 cups (8 ounces) cubed process cheese
>   (Velveeta)
>   2 cups (16 ounces) sour cream
>   1 can (10-3/4 ounces) condensed cream of
>   celery soup, undiluted
>   1 can (10-3/4 ounces) condensed cream of
>   chicken soup, undiluted
>   1 pound sliced bacon, cooked and crumbled
>   1 large onion, chopped
>   1/4 cup butter, melted
>   1/4 teaspoon pepper

Place potatoes in an ungreased 5-qt. slow cooker. In a large bowl, combine the remaining ingredients. Pour over the potatoes and mix well. Cover and cook on low for 4-5 hours or until potatoes are tender and heated through.

Yield: 14 servings.

Fruit Salsa

(pictured below)
Florence Buchkowsky, Prince Albert, Saskatchewan
Serve this fruity salsa anywhere you'd use ordinary salsa. My son and I experimented with different ingredients to find the combination we liked best. Preparing it in a slow cooker not only minimizes prep time but maximizes flavor.

>   1 can (11 ounces) mandarin oranges,
>   undrained
>   1 can (8-1/2 ounces) sliced peaches,
>   undrained
>   1 can (8 ounces) pineapple tidbits,
>   undrained
>   1 medium onion, chopped
>   1/2 *each* medium green, sweet red and yellow
>   pepper, chopped
>   3 garlic cloves, minced
>   3 tablespoons cornstarch
>   4 teaspoons white vinegar
>   Tortilla chips

In a 3-qt. slow cooker, combine the fruit, onion, peppers, garlic, cornstarch and vinegar; stir well. Cover and cook on high for 2 hours or until thickened and heated through, stirring occasionally. Serve with tortilla chips.

Yield: 4 cups.

Pictured below: Sausage Hash Brown
Bake (p. 86), Cream-Topped Grapes (p. 99)
and Apple Walnut Crescents (p. 93).

Breakfast &
Brunch

Sausage Hash Brown Bake

(pictured above)
Esther Wrinkles, Vanzant, Missouri
For this comforting, all-in-one breakfast casserole, I sand-wich pork sausage between layers of hash browns that are flavored with cream of chicken soup and French onion dip. Cheddar cheese completes the satisfying dish.

   2 pounds bulk pork sausage
   2 cups (8 ounces) shredded cheddar cheese,
      divided
   1 can (10-3/4 ounces) condensed cream of
      chicken soup, undiluted
   1 cup (8 ounces) sour cream
   1 carton (8 ounces) French onion dip
   1 cup chopped onion
1/4 cup chopped green pepper
1/4 cup chopped sweet red pepper
1/8 teaspoon pepper
   1 package (30 ounces) frozen shredded hash
      brown potatoes, thawed

In a large skillet, cook sausage over medium heat until no longer pink; drain on paper towels. In a large bowl, combine 1-3/4 cups cheese and the next seven ingredients; fold in potatoes.

    Spread half into a greased shallow 3-qt. baking dish. Top with sausage and remaining potato mixture. Sprinkle with remaining cheese. Cover and bake at 350° for 45 minutes. Uncover; bake 10 minutes longer or until heated through.

Yield: 10-12 servings.

Smoky Bacon Wraps

Cara Flora, Kokomo, Indiana
All you need are three ingredients to assemble these cute, little sausage-bacon bites. The simple breakfast item has a sweet and salty flavor, making the sausages great appetiz-ers as well.

   1 pound sliced bacon
   1 package (16 ounces) miniature smoked
      sausage links
   1 cup packed brown sugar

Cut each bacon strip in half widthwise. Wrap one piece of bacon around each sausage.

    Place in a foil-lined 15-in. x 10-in. x 1-in. bak-ing pan. Sprinkle with brown sugar. Bake, uncov-ered, at 400° for 30-40 minutes or until bacon is crisp and sausage is heated through.

Yield: about 3-1/2 dozen.

Ham 'n' Cheese Omelet Roll

(pictured below)
Nancy Daugherty, Cortland, Ohio
I love hosting brunch, and this special omelet roll is one of my favorite items to prepare and share. The dish has mouth-watering ingredients and an impressive look all rolled into one! A platter of these pretty swirled slices always disappears in no time.

    4 ounces cream cheese, softened
  3/4 cup milk
    2 tablespoons all-purpose flour
  1/4 teaspoon salt
   12 eggs
    2 tablespoons Dijon mustard
2-1/4 cups shredded cheddar cheese, *divided*
    2 cups finely chopped fully cooked ham
  1/2 cup thinly sliced green onions

Line the bottom and sides of a greased 15-in. x 10-in. x 1-in. baking pan with parchment paper; grease the paper and set aside.

In a small mixing bowl, beat cream cheese and milk until smooth. Add flour and salt; mix until combined. In a large mixing bowl, beat the eggs until blended. Add cream cheese mixture; mix well. Pour into prepared pan.

Bake at 375° for 30-35 minutes or until eggs are puffed and set. Remove from the oven. Immediately spread with mustard and sprinkle with 1 cup cheese. Sprinkle with ham, onions and 1 cup cheese.

Roll up from a short side, peeling parchment paper away while rolling. Sprinkle top of roll with the remaining cheese; bake 3-4 minutes longer or until cheese is melted.

Yield: 12 servings.

Lemon Poppy Seed Bread

(pictured above)
Karen Dougherty, Freeport, Illinois
The days I have time for baking are few and far between. That's why this extra-quick bread is perfect. In about an hour, I can make two loaves.

    1 package (18-1/4 ounces) white cake mix
    1 package (3.4 ounces) instant lemon pudding mix
    4 eggs
    1 cup warm water
  1/2 cup vegetable oil
    4 teaspoons poppy seeds

In a mixing bowl, combine the mixes, eggs, water and oil; beat until well mixed. Fold in poppy seeds.

Pour into two greased 9-in. x 5-in. x 3-in. loaf pans. Bake at 350° for 35-40 minutes or until bread tests done. Cool in pans for 10 minutes before removing to a wire rack.

Yield: 2 loaves.

Potluck Pointer

Impress fellow potluck guests by serving flavored butter alongside your bread. Simply soften the butter and stir in your favorite dried herbs to taste. Set the butter back in the refrigerator for a few hours to let the flavors blend a bit.

greased 10-in. springform pan. Place on a baking sheet. Pour egg mixture into pan.

Bake, uncovered, at 325° for 60-70 minutes or until a knife inserted near the center comes out clean. Let stand for 10 minutes before serving. Run a knife around edge of pan to loosen; remove sides. Cut into wedges.

Yield: 8-10 servings.

Mini Ham Quiches

Marilou Robinson, Portland, Oregon
These cute quiches are easy to fix for an after-church brunch when you don't want to fuss. Replace the ham with bacon, sausage, chicken or shrimp...or substitute chopped onion, red pepper or zucchini for the olives if you prefer.

  - 3/4 cup diced fully cooked ham
  - 1/2 cup shredded sharp cheddar cheese
  - 1/2 cup chopped ripe olives
  -   3 eggs, beaten
  -   1 cup half-and-half cream
  - 1/4 cup butter, melted
  -   3 drops hot pepper sauce
  - 1/2 cup biscuit/baking mix
  -   2 tablespoons grated Parmesan cheese
  - 1/2 teaspoon ground mustard

In a bowl, combine the ham, cheddar cheese and olives; divide among 12 greased muffin cups. In a mixing bowl, combine the remaining ingredients just until blended.

Pour over ham mixture. Bake at 375° for 20-25 minutes or until a knife inserted near the center comes out clean. Let stand for 5 minutes before serving.

Yield: 1 dozen.

Plum Sausage Bites

Heidi Fisher, Victoria, British Columbia
Packed with perky flavor, these links are a must at brunches and potlucks. Plum jelly, soy sauce and Dijon mustard create the thick, tangy sauce that clings to the sliced sausages.

  -   2 to 2-1/2 pounds uncooked pork sausage links, cut into 1-inch pieces
  -   1 cup plum, apple *or* grape jelly
  -   2 tablespoons soy sauce
  -   1 tablespoon Dijon mustard

In a large skillet, cook sausage over medium heat until no longer pink; drain and set sausage aside. In the same skillet, combine the jelly, soy sauce and mustard; mix well. Simmer, uncovered, for 5 minutes, stirring occasionally. Return sausage to the pan and heat through. Refrigerate any leftovers.

Yield: 18-22 servings.

Veggie-Packed Strata

(pictured above)
Jennifer Unsell, Tuscaloosa, Alabama
People are always eager to try this deliciously different casserole, featuring eggs and cheese. Baked in a spring-form pan, this colorful strata catches folks' attention no matter where it's served.

  -   2 medium sweet red peppers, julienned
  -   1 medium sweet yellow pepper, julienned
  -   1 large red onion, sliced
  -   3 garlic cloves, minced
  -   3 tablespoons olive oil, *divided*
  -   2 medium yellow summer squash, thinly sliced
  -   2 medium zucchini, thinly sliced
  - 1/2 pound fresh mushrooms, sliced
  -   1 package (8 ounces) cream cheese, softened
  - 1/4 cup heavy whipping cream
  -   2 teaspoons salt
  -   1 teaspoon pepper
  -   6 eggs
  -   8 slices bread, cubed, *divided*
  -   2 cups (8 ounces) shredded Swiss cheese

In a large skillet, saute the peppers, onion and garlic in 1 tablespoon oil until tender. Drain; pat dry and set aside. In the same skillet, saute yellow squash, zucchini and mushrooms in remaining oil until tender. Drain; pat dry and set aside.

In a large mixing bowl, beat the cream cheese, cream, salt and pepper until smooth. Beat in eggs. Stir in vegetables, half of the bread cubes and Swiss cheese. Arrange the remaining bread cubes in a

Overnight Pancakes

(pictured below)
Lisa Sammons, Cut Bank, Montana
These golden, fluffy pancakes are great for Sunday brunch-es with friends. The buttermilk batter is refrigerated overnight to help ease the morning rush.

- 1 package (1/4 ounce) active dry yeast
- 1/4 cup warm water (110° to 115°)
- 4 cups all-purpose flour
- 2 tablespoons baking powder
- 2 teaspoons baking soda
- 2 teaspoons sugar
- 1 teaspoon salt
- 6 eggs
- 1 quart buttermilk
- 1/4 cup vegetable oil

In a small bowl, dissolve yeast in water; let stand for 5 minutes.

Meanwhile, in a large bowl, combine the dry ingredients. Beat eggs, buttermilk and oil; stir into dry ingredients just until moistened. Stir in yeast mixture. Cover and refrigerate for 8 hours or overnight.

To make pancakes, pour batter by 1/4 cupfuls onto a greased hot griddle; turn when bubbles form on top of pancakes. Cook until second side is golden brown.

Yield: about 2-1/2 dozen.

Do-Ahead Brunch Bake

Joy Maynard, St. Ignatius, Montana
I wake up my clan with this convenient breakfast casserole that I assemble a night early. Loaded with hearty ham and hash browns, it's sure to start any day in a tasty way.

- 8 frozen hash brown patties
- 1 package (8 ounces) thinly sliced fully cooked ham, chopped
- 1-1/4 cups shredded reduced-fat cheddar cheese, *divided*
- 2 cups fat-free milk
- 1 can (10-3/4 ounces) reduced-fat reduced-sodium condensed cream of mushroom soup, undiluted
- 1 cup egg substitute
- 1 teaspoon ground mustard
- 1/4 teaspoon pepper

Place potato patties in a 13-in. x 9-in. x 2-in. baking dish coated with nonstick cooking spray. Top with ham and 1 cup cheese. Combine milk, soup, egg substitute, mustard and pepper; pour over cheese. Cover and refrigerate overnight.

Remove from the refrigerator 30 minutes before baking. Bake at 350° for 1 hour. Uncover and sprinkle with remaining cheese. Bake 20-25 minutes longer or until a knife inserted near the center comes out clean. Let stand 10 minutes before serving.

Yield: 12 servings.

Black Hills Golden Egg Bake

(pictured below)
Sandra Giardino, Rapid City, South Dakota
I developed this recipe when I was cooking for large groups of people. It's easy to make and gives you plenty of time to do other things while it's baking.

    1/2 cup sliced fresh mushrooms
    1/2 cup chopped green pepper
    1/4 cup butter, cubed
     10 eggs
    1/2 cup all-purpose flour
      1 teaspoon baking powder
    1/4 teaspoon salt, optional
      1 carton (16 ounces) small-curd cottage
         cheese
      2 cups (8 ounces) shredded cheddar cheese
      2 cups (8 ounces) shredded Monterey Jack
         cheese
    1/2 pound bulk pork sausage, cooked and
         drained
      6 bacon strips, cooked and crumbled
      1 can (2-1/4 ounces) sliced ripe olives,
         drained

In a skillet, saute mushrooms and green pepper in butter until tender. In a mixing bowl, combine eggs, flour, baking powder and salt if desired; mix well. Add mushroom mixture. Stir in remaining ingredients; mix well.

Pour into a greased 13-in. x 9-in. x 2-in. baking dish. Bake, uncovered, at 400° for 15 minutes. Reduce heat to 350°; bake 25-35 minutes longer or until a knife inserted near the center comes out clean.

Yield: 10-12 servings.

Brunch Enchiladas

(pictured above)
Gail Sykora, Menomonee Falls, Wisconsin
When I need a dish for a large brunch, I turn to this tried-and-true casserole. With ham, eggs and plenty of cheese, the enchiladas are flavorful, hearty and fun. Plus, they can be assembled the day before.

      2 cups cubed fully cooked ham
    1/2 cup chopped green onions
     10 flour tortillas (8 inches)
      2 cups (8 ounces) shredded cheddar cheese,
         divided
      1 tablespoon all-purpose flour
      2 cups half-and-half cream
      6 eggs, beaten
    1/4 teaspoon salt, optional

Combine ham and onions; place about 1/3 cup down the center of each tortilla. Top with 2 tablespoons cheese. Roll up and place seam side down in a greased 13-in. x 9-in. x 2-in. baking dish.

In a bowl, combine flour, cream, eggs and salt if desired until smooth. Pour over tortillas. Cover and refrigerate for 8 hours or overnight.

Remove from the refrigerator 30 minutes before baking. Cover and bake at 350° for 25 minutes. Uncover; bake for 10 minutes. Sprinkle with remaining cheese; bake 3 minutes longer or until the cheese is melted. Let stand for 10 minutes before serving.

Yield: 10 enchiladas.

Bacon Swiss Squares

Agarita Vaughan, Fairbury, Illinois
Not only does this recipe come together easily, but it's a cinch to double for a large event.

    2 cups biscuit/baking mix
  1/2 cup cold water
    8 ounces sliced Swiss cheese
    1 pound sliced bacon, cooked and crumbled
    4 eggs, lightly beaten
  1/4 cup milk
  1/2 teaspoon onion powder

In a bowl, combine the biscuit mix and water; stir 20 strokes. Turn onto a floured surface; knead 10 times. Roll into a 14-in. x 10-in. rectangle. Place on the bottom and 1/2 in. up the sides of a greased 13-in. x 9-in. x 2-in. baking dish. Arrange cheese over dough. Sprinkle with bacon. In a bowl, whisk eggs, milk and onion powder; pour over bacon.

Bake at 425° for 15-18 minutes or until a knife inserted near the center comes out clean. Cut into squares.

Yield: 12 servings.

Broccoli Quiche Muffins

Cindy Hrychuk, Gilbert Plains, Manitoba
These moist bites make great additions to brunch, but they're also tasty at lunch get-togethers or even for snacks. I keep a batch in the freezer—it's so handy to warm them in the microwave when time is short.

    1 package (10 ounces) frozen chopped
       broccoli, thawed and drained
    1 medium onion, chopped
  1/2 cup diced fully cooked ham
  1/2 cup grated Parmesan cheese
    6 eggs
  1/2 cup vegetable oil
1-1/4 cups all-purpose flour
    1 tablespoon baking powder
    1 teaspoon dried oregano
    1 teaspoon dried parsley flakes
  1/4 teaspoon garlic powder
  1/4 teaspoon salt
  1/4 teaspoon dried thyme

Combine the broccoli, onion, ham and cheese; set aside. In a mixing bowl, beat eggs until frothy. Add oil; mix well. Combine dry ingredients; add to the egg mixture just until moistened. Fold in broccoli mixture.

Fill greased muffin cups two-thirds full. Bake at 375° for 18-22 minutes or until muffins test done. Cool 10 minutes; remove from pan to a wire rack.

Yield: 1-1/2 dozen.

Strawberry Yogurt Crunch

(pictured above)
Becky Palac, Escondido, California
Yogurt is always a favorite at breakfast, but this recipe transforms it into something special. To change up the taste, just use a different flavor of yogurt.

  3/4 cup butter, softened
  1/3 cup packed brown sugar
  1/2 cup all-purpose flour
  1/2 teaspoon ground cinnamon
  1/4 teaspoon baking soda
    1 cup quick-cooking oats
    1 cup flaked coconut, toasted
  1/3 cup chopped nuts
    1 carton (8 ounces) frozen whipped
       topping, thawed
    2 cartons (6 ounces *each*) strawberry
       custard-style yogurt

In a large mixing bowl, cream butter and brown sugar. Combine the flour, cinnamon and baking soda; gradually add to creamed mixture. Stir in the oats, coconut and nuts. Remove 1 cup for topping.

Press remaining oat mixture into an ungreased 13-in. x 9-in. x 2-in. baking dish. Bake at 350° for 12-13 minutes or until light brown. Cool on a wire rack.

In a large bowl, fold whipped topping into yogurt. Spread over crust. Sprinkle with reserved oat mixture. Cover and refrigerate for 4 hours or overnight.

Yield: 12-15 servings.

Brunch Fruit Salad

(pictured below)
Millie Vickery, Lena, Illinois
This appealing fruit salad is a lovely addition to breakfast, lunch or even supper. Light and refreshing, it's perfect alongside egg bakes, sausages and the other hearty staples you find on breakfast buffets.

1	can (20 ounces) pineapple chunks
2	large firm bananas, cut into 1/4-inch chunks
1	cup green grapes
1	can (15 ounces) mandarin oranges, drained
1	Golden Delicious apple, sliced
1	Red Delicious apple, sliced
1/2	cup sugar
2	tablespoons cornstarch
1/3	cup orange juice
1	tablespoon lemon juice

Drain pineapple, reserving juice. Combine the pineapple, bananas, grapes, oranges and apples in a large bowl; set aside. In a small saucepan, combine sugar and cornstarch. Add the orange juice, lemon juice and reserved pineapple juice; stir until smooth.

Bring to a boil; reduce heat. Cook and stir for 2 minutes. Pour over fruit; mix gently. Cover and refrigerate until serving.

Yield: 10 servings.

Raspberry Cream Cheese Coffee Cake

(pictured above)
Susan Litwiller, Medford, Oregon
A cross between a coffee cake and cheesecake, this creation brings a touch of spring to any get-together. It's perfect for a brunch but it also makes a tasty dessert after dinner.

2-1/4	cups all-purpose flour
3/4	cup sugar
3/4	cup cold butter
1/2	teaspoon baking powder
1/2	teaspoon baking soda
1/2	teaspoon salt
3/4	cup sour cream
1	egg, beaten
1-1/2	teaspoons almond extract

FILLING:

1	package (8 ounces) cream cheese, softened
1/2	cup sugar
1	egg
1/2	cup raspberry jam
1/2	cup slivered almonds

In a large mixing bowl, combine flour and sugar. Cut in butter until mixture is crumbly. Remove 1 cup and set aside. To the remaining crumbs, add baking powder, baking soda and salt. Add the sour cream, egg and almond extract; mix well. Spread in the bottom and 2 in. up the sides of a greased 9-in. springform pan.

For the filling, in a small bowl, beat cream cheese, sugar and egg in a small bowl until blended. Pour over batter; spoon raspberry jam on top. Sprinkle with almonds and reserved crumbs.

Bake at 350° for 55-60 minutes. Let stand for 15 minutes. Carefully run a knife around the edge of pan to loosen; remove sides from pan.

Yield: 12 servings.

Melon Fruit Bowl

Edie DeSpain, Logan, Utah
This medley of strawberries, melon and pineapple gets its sweet taste from a creamy banana dressing.

> 1 medium cantaloupe, cut into chunks
> 1 medium honeydew, cut into chunks
> 3 cups fresh pineapple chunks
> 1 cup halved strawberries

BANANA DRESSING:
> 1 medium ripe banana, cut into chunks
> 1/2 cup sour cream
> 2 tablespoons brown sugar
> 1-1/2 teaspoons lemon juice

In a large bowl, combine the melons, pineapple and strawberries; set aside. Place the dressing ingredients in a blender; cover and process until smooth. Serve with fruit salad.

Yield: 12 servings.

Grits 'n' Sausage Casserole

Marie Poppenhager, Old Town, Florida
You could call this the "So Good Casserole," because that's what people say when they try it. It's a Southern specialty. It can even be assembled, covered and refrigerated overnight. Just remove the casserole from the refrigerator 30 minutes before baking and bake as directed.

> 3 cups water
> 1 cup quick-cooking grits
> 3/4 teaspoon salt, *divided*
> 2 pounds bulk pork sausage, cooked and drained
> 2 cups (8 ounces) shredded cheddar cheese, *divided*
> 3 eggs
> 1-1/2 cups milk
> 2 tablespoons butter, melted
> Pepper to taste

In a saucepan, bring water to a boil. Slowly whisk in the grits and 1/2 teaspoon salt. Reduce heat; cover and simmer for 5 minutes, stirring occasionally.

In a bowl, combine grits, sausage and 1-1/2 cups cheese. Beat eggs and milk; stir into grits mixture. Add butter, pepper and remaining salt.

Transfer to a greased 13-in. x 9-in. x 2-in. baking dish. Bake, uncovered, at 350° for 1 hour or until a knife inserted near the center comes out clean. Sprinkle with remaining cheese; bake 15 minutes longer or until cheese is melted. Let stand for 5 minutes before cutting.

Yield: 10-12 servings.

Apple Walnut Crescents

(pictured below)
Karen Petzold, Vassar, Michigan
A local apple orchard had a cook-off that I wanted to enter, so I created these golden cinnamon treats. They're a snap to assemble with convenient crescent roll dough.

> 2 packages (8 ounces *each*) refrigerated crescent rolls
> 1/4 cup sugar
> 1 tablespoon ground cinnamon
> 4 medium tart apples, peeled, cored and quartered
> 1/4 cup chopped walnuts
> 1/4 cup raisins, optional
> 1/4 cup butter, melted

Unroll crescent roll dough and separate into 16 triangles. Combine sugar and cinnamon; sprinkle about 1/2 teaspoon on each triangle. Place an apple quarter near the short side and roll up. Place in a lightly greased 15-in. x 10-in. x 1-in. baking pan.

Press walnuts and raisins if desired into top of dough. Drizzle with butter. Sprinkle with the remaining cinnamon-sugar. Bake at 375° for 20-24 minutes or until golden brown. Serve warm.

Yield: 16 servings.

Strawberry Fruit Dip

(pictured above)
Lydia Graf, Norton, Ohio
If you're thinking about taking a fruit tray to a breakfast social, consider bringing this creamy dip, too. Not only does it come together fast in a blender, but the dip calls for only five ingredients.

      1   cup sliced fresh strawberries
   1/4   cup sour cream
      1   tablespoon sugar
   1/4   teaspoon vanilla extract
   1/2   cup heavy whipping cream
Assorted fresh fruit

In a blender, combine the strawberries, sour cream, sugar and vanilla. Cover and process until smooth.

   In a small mixing bowl, beat cream until stiff peaks form. Fold into strawberry mixture. Cover and refrigerate for at least 1 hour. Serve with fruit.

Yield: 1-1/2 cups.

Ham-Swiss Strudel

Sally Coffey, Hilton, New York
You just can't beat this strudel stuffed with ham, cheese and rice when you want to serve a special breakfast or brunch.

   1-1/2   cups chicken broth
      3/4   cup uncooked long grain rice
         1   cup finely chopped onion
         1   tablespoon butter plus 1/2 cup butter, *divided*
       12   sheets phyllo dough (18 inches x 14 inches)
         4   ounces thinly sliced deli ham, julienned
         2   cups (8 ounces) shredded Swiss cheese
         1   teaspoon paprika

In a saucepan, bring broth to a boil; add rice. Reduce heat; cover and simmer for 15 minutes or until rice is tender. In another saucepan, saute onion in 1 tablespoon butter until tender; add to rice.

   Melt remaining butter. Place one sheet of phyllo dough on a work surface; brush with butter. Layer with remaining phyllo and butter (keep dough covered with waxed paper until ready to use). Spoon rice mixture over dough to within 1 in. of edges. Sprinkle with ham, cheese and paprika.

   Fold short sides 1 in. over filling. Roll up jelly-roll style, starting with a long side. Brush with remaining butter. Place seam side down on a greased baking sheet. Bake at 375° for 25-30 minutes or until golden. Cool 5 minutes; slice.

Yield: 10-12 servings.

Bacon Cheddar Pinwheels

Marlene Wyatt, New Franklin, Missouri
These fast, flaky rolls are perfect any time of the day, but they're especially tasty at brunch with scrambled eggs.

      2   cups all-purpose flour
      3   teaspoons baking powder
   1/4   teaspoon salt
   1/3   cup shortening
   3/4   cup milk
   1/2   pound sliced bacon, cooked and crumbled
   3/4   cup shredded cheddar cheese

In a bowl, combine flour, baking powder and salt; cut in shortening. Add milk; mix well. Turn onto a floured surface; knead 6-8 times. Roll into a 16-in. x 10-in. rectangle. Sprinkle with bacon and cheese. Roll up from a long side. Cut into 15 slices; place cut side down in greased muffin cups. Bake at 450° for 12-15 minutes or until golden. Serve warm. Refrigerate leftovers.

Yield: 15 rolls.

Blueberry Kuchen

(pictured below)
Anne Krueger, Richmond, British Columbia
Not only is this always a crowd-pleaser at church suppers, but I can prepare it in a wink. Our local peat bogs are known around the world for their beautiful blueberries, and this is the perfect recipe to showcase them.

1-1/2 cups all-purpose flour
  3/4 cup sugar
    2 teaspoons baking powder
1-1/2 teaspoons grated lemon peel
  1/2 teaspoon ground nutmeg
  1/4 teaspoon salt
  2/3 cup milk
  1/4 cup butter, melted
    1 egg, beaten
    1 teaspoon vanilla extract
    2 cups fresh *or* frozen blueberries

TOPPING:
  3/4 cup sugar
  1/2 cup all-purpose flour
  1/4 cup butter, melted

In a mixing bowl, combine the first six ingredients. Add the milk, butter, egg and vanilla. Beat for 2 minutes or until well blended.

Pour into a greased 13-in. x 9-in. x 2-in. baking pan. Sprinkle with blueberries. In a bowl, combine sugar and flour; add butter. Toss with a fork until crumbly; sprinkle over blueberries. Bake at 350° for 40 minutes or until lightly browned.

Yield: 12 servings.

Bacon 'n' Egg Lasagna

(pictured above)
Dianne Meyer, Graniteville, Vermont
My sister-in-law served this special dish for Easter one year, and our whole family loved the mix of bacon, eggs, noodles and cheese. Now I sometimes assemble it the night before and bake it in the morning for a terrific, hassle-free breakfast.

    1 pound sliced bacon, diced
    1 large onion, chopped
  1/3 cup all-purpose flour
  1/2 to 1 teaspoon salt
  1/4 teaspoon pepper
    4 cups milk
  12 lasagna noodles, cooked and drained
  12 hard-cooked eggs, sliced
    2 cups (8 ounces) shredded Swiss cheese
  1/3 cup grated Parmesan cheese
    2 tablespoons minced fresh parsley

In a skillet, cook bacon until crisp. Remove with a slotted spoon to paper towels. Drain, reserving 1/3 cup drippings. In the drippings, saute onion until tender. Stir in flour, salt and pepper until blended. Gradually stir in milk. Bring to a boil; cook and stir for 2 minutes. Remove from the heat.

Spread 1/2 cup sauce in a greased 13-in. x 9-in. x 2-in. baking dish. Layer with four noodles, a third of the eggs and bacon, Swiss cheese and white sauce. Repeat layers twice. Sprinkle with Parmesan cheese.

Bake, uncovered, at 350° for 35-40 minutes or until bubbly. Sprinkle with parsley. Let stand 15 minutes before cutting.

Yield: 12 servings.

Southwest Sausage Bake

(pictured below)
Barbara Waddel, Lincoln, Nebraska
This layered dish is not only delicious, but it's a real cinch to prepare. The tomato slices provide a nice touch of color. I always serve the crowd-pleasing casserole with sour cream and salsa.

      6 flour tortillas (10 inches), cut into
         1/2-inch strips
      4 cans (4 ounces *each*) chopped green
         chilies, drained
      1 pound bulk pork sausage, cooked and
         drained
      2 cups (8 ounces) shredded Monterey Jack
         cheese
     10 eggs
    1/2 cup milk
    1/2 teaspoon *each* salt, garlic salt, onion salt,
         pepper and ground cumin
Paprika
      2 medium tomatoes, sliced
Sour cream and salsa

In a greased 13-in. x 9-in. x 2-in. baking dish, layer half of the tortilla strips, chilies, sausage and cheese. Repeat layers. In a bowl, beat the eggs, milk and seasonings; pour over cheese. Sprinkle with paprika. Cover and refrigerate overnight.

Remove from the refrigerator 30 minutes before baking. Bake, uncovered, at 350° for 50 minutes. Arrange tomato slices over the top. Bake 10-15 minutes longer or until a knife inserted near the center comes out clean. Let stand for 10 minutes before cutting. Serve with sour cream and salsa.

Yield: 12 servings.

Blueberry Oat Muffins

(pictured above)
Mildred Mummau, Mt. Joy, Pennsylvania
Bursting with blueberries and hearty oats, these treats never last long on a brunch buffet. I enjoy the touch of spice they offer as well as the sweetness from the cinnamon-sugar topping.

  1-1/4 cups all-purpose flour
      1 cup quick-cooking oats
    1/2 cup sugar
      1 teaspoon baking powder
    1/2 teaspoon baking soda
    1/4 teaspoon salt
      2 egg whites
    1/2 cup water
    1/3 cup vegetable oil
      1 cup fresh *or* frozen blueberries

TOPPING:
      2 tablespoons sugar
    1/4 teaspoon ground cinnamon

In a bowl, combine the first six ingredients. In another bowl, beat egg whites, water and oil. Stir into dry ingredients just until moistened. Fold in blueberries.

Fill paper-lined muffin cups or muffin cups coated with nonstick cooking spray three-fourths full. Combine sugar and cinnamon; sprinkle over muffins.

Bake at 400° for 18-22 minutes or until a toothpick comes out clean. Cool for 5 minutes before removing from pan to a wire rack.

Yield: 1 dozen.

Editor's Note: If using frozen blueberries, do not thaw before adding to batter.

Cheesy Egg Puffs

Amy Soto, Winfield, Kansas
My father loves to entertain, and these buttery egg delights are one of his favorite items to serve at brunch. The leftovers are perfect to reheat in the microwave on busy mornings, so Dad always stashes a few aside for me to take home once the party is over.

- 1/2 pound fresh mushrooms, sliced
- 4 green onions, chopped
- 1 tablespoon butter plus 1/2 cup butter, cubed, *divided*
- 1/2 cup all-purpose flour
- 1 teaspoon baking powder
- 1/2 teaspoon salt
- 10 eggs, lightly beaten
- 4 cups (16 ounces) shredded Monterey Jack cheese
- 2 cups (16 ounces) small-curd cottage cheese

In a skillet, saute the mushrooms and onions in 1 tablespoon butter until tender. In a large bowl, combine the flour, baking powder and salt.

In another bowl, combine eggs and cheeses. Melt remaining butter; add to egg mixture. Stir into dry ingredients along with mushroom mixture.

Fill greased muffin cups three-fourths full. Bake at 350° for 35-40 minutes or until a knife inserted near the center comes out clean. Carefully run the knife around edge of muffin cups before removing.
Yield: 2-1/2 dozen.

Mini Sausage Pizzas

Janice Garvert, Plainville, Kansas
Dressed with sausage and cheese, these English muffins make a fun addition to any breakfast. My husband and son particularly enjoy them.

- 1 pound bulk pork sausage
- 2 jars (5 ounces *each*) sharp American cheese spread
- 1/4 cup butter, softened
- 1/8 to 1/4 teaspoon cayenne pepper
- 12 English muffins, split

In a large skillet, cook sausage over medium heat until no longer pink; drain well. In a small mixing bowl, beat the cheese, butter and pepper. Stir in the sausage. Spread on cut sides of muffins.

Wrap individually and freeze for up to 2 months. Or place on a baking sheet and bake at 425° for 8-10 minutes or until golden brown.
Yield: 2 dozen.

Citrus Grove Punch

(pictured above)
Susan West, North Grafton, Massachusetts
This pretty, sparkling punch blends orange, grapefruit and lime juices with ginger ale.

- 3 cups sugar
- 2 cups water
- 6 cups orange juice, chilled
- 6 cups grapefruit juice, chilled
- 1-1/2 cups lime juice, chilled
- 1 liter ginger ale, chilled

In a saucepan, bring sugar and water to a boil; cook for 5 minutes. Cover and refrigerate until cool.

Combine juices and sugar mixture; mix well. Just before serving, stir in ginger ale. Serve over ice.
Yield: 6 quarts.

Almond Fruit Squares

(pictured above)
Iola Egle, McCook, Nebraska
These sweet squares are a breeze to fix, thanks to the refrigerated crescent roll dough that serves as the crust. With a layer of cream cheese, berries, grapes and kiwifruit, they can be served for breakfast or as a summer dessert.

> 2 tubes (8 ounces *each*) refrigerated crescent rolls
> 3 tablespoons sugar, *divided*
> 1 package (8 ounces) cream cheese, softened
> 1/3 cup almond paste
> 1/2 teaspoon almond extract
> 2 cups halved fresh strawberries
> 1 can (11 ounces) mandarin oranges, drained
> 1 cup fresh raspberries
> 1 cup halved green grapes
> 2 kiwifruit, peeled, quartered and sliced
> 1/2 cup apricot preserves, warmed
> 1/2 cup slivered almonds, toasted

Unroll crescent dough and separate into eight rectangles. Place in an ungreased 15-in. x 10-in. x 1-in. baking pan. Press onto bottom and up sides; seal seams and perforations. Sprinkle with 1 tablespoon sugar.

Bake at 375° for 14-16 minutes or until golden brown. Cool. In a mixing bowl, beat cream cheese, almond paste, extract and remaining sugar until smooth. Spread over crust. Top with fruit. Brush with preserves; sprinkle with almonds.

Yield: 16 servings.

Hearty Hotcakes

Nancy Horsburgh, Everett, Ontario
I blend buttermilk with cornmeal and two kinds of flour for these filling pancakes that truly wake up the taste buds. Oats give the golden hotcakes a unique crunch.

> 1 cup all-purpose flour
> 1/2 cup whole wheat flour
> 1/2 cup cornmeal
> 1/2 cup quick-cooking oats
> 2 tablespoons sugar
> 1/2 teaspoon baking powder
> 1/2 teaspoon baking soda
> 1/2 teaspoon salt
> 1 egg
> 2-1/2 cups buttermilk
> 3 tablespoons butter, melted
> Maple syrup *or* topping of your choice

In a bowl, combine the dry ingredients. In a small bowl, beat egg, buttermilk and butter; stir into dry ingredients just until moistened. Pour batter by 1/4 cupfuls onto a lightly greased hot griddle; turn when bubbles form on top. Cook until second side is golden brown. Serve with syrup or topping of your choice.

Yield: 16 hotcakes.

Homemade Sage Sausage Patties

Diane Hixon, Niceville, Florida
Oregano, garlic and sage add zippy flavor to these quick-to-fix ground pork patties. I've had this Pennsylvania Dutch recipe for years, and it always brings compliments.

> 3/4 cup shredded cheddar cheese
> 1/4 cup buttermilk
> 1 tablespoon finely chopped onion
> 2 teaspoons rubbed sage
> 3/4 teaspoon salt
> 3/4 teaspoon pepper
> 1/8 teaspoon garlic powder
> 1/8 teaspoon dried oregano
> 1 pound ground pork

In a bowl, combine the first eight ingredients. Crumble pork over mixture and mix well. Shape into eight 1/2-in. patties. Refrigerate for 1 hour. In a nonstick skillet over medium heat, fry patties for 6-8 minutes on each side or until meat is no longer pink.

Yield: 8 servings.

Glazed Bacon

Janet Nolan, Navesink, New Jersey

Everyone agrees that this bacon is just as sweet as candy due to its brown sugar and orange juice glaze. My mom would make it for special-occasion breakfasts. Now I serve it often.

    1   pound sliced bacon
    1   cup packed brown sugar
    1/4 cup orange juice
    2   tablespoons Dijon mustard

Place bacon on a rack in an ungreased 15-in. x 10-in. x 1-in. baking pan. Bake at 350° for 10 minutes; drain. Combine the brown sugar, orange juice and mustard; pour half over bacon. Bake for 10 minutes. Turn bacon and drizzle with remaining glaze. Bake 15 minutes longer or until golden brown. Place bacon on waxed paper until set. Serve warm.

Yield: 8 servings.

Cream-Topped Grapes

(pictured below)
Viola Geyer, Uhrichsville, Ohio

I like to dollop this heavenly, four-ingredient sauce over refreshing red and green grapes.

    4   ounces cream cheese, softened
    1/4 cup sugar
    1/2 teaspoon vanilla extract
    1/2 cup sour cream
    3   cups seedless green grapes
    3   cups seedless red grapes

In a small mixing bowl, beat the cream cheese, sugar and vanilla. Add the sour cream; mix well. Divide grapes among individual serving bowls; dollop with topping.

Yield: 8 servings.

Scrambled Egg Muffins

(pictured above)
Cathy Larkins, Marshfield, Missouri

After enjoying Scrambled Egg Muffins at a local restaurant, I came up with this savory version that my husband likes even better.

    1/2 pound bulk pork sausage
    12 eggs
    1/2 cup chopped onion
    1/4 cup chopped green pepper
    1/2 teaspoon salt
    1/4 teaspoon pepper
    1/4 teaspoon garlic powder
    1/2 cup shredded cheddar cheese

In a skillet, cook the sausage over medium heat until no longer pink; drain. In a bowl, beat the eggs. Add onion, green pepper, salt, pepper and garlic powder. Stir in sausage and cheese.

Spoon by 1/3 cupfuls into greased muffin cups. Bake at 350° for 20-25 minutes or until a knife inserted near the center comes out clean.

Yield: 1 dozen.

Potluck Pointer

Pork sausage gives Scrambled Egg Muffins a down-home flavor that's ideal for rise-and-shine potlucks. If you only have ground beef on hand, feel free to use that instead. Add a dash of fennel seed to the beef as it cooks for extra flair.

Brunch Berry Pizza

(pictured above)
Maria Schuster, Wolf Point, Montana
This beautiful, berry-topped pizza tastes as good as it looks! It's impossible to resist the pecan shortbread crust, rich cream cheese layer, glossy topping and sprinkling of luscious fresh berries. It's convenient to make the night before.

    1   cup all-purpose flour
  1/4   cup confectioners' sugar
  1/2   cup cold butter
  1/2   cup chopped pecans
    1   package (8 ounces) cream cheese,
        softened
    1   egg
  1/3   cup sugar
TOPPING:
1-3/4   cups frozen mixed berries, thawed
  1/2   cup sugar
    2   tablespoons cornstarch
  1/4   cup water
2-1/2   cups fresh strawberries, sliced
    2   cups fresh blackberries
    2   cups fresh raspberries
    1   cup fresh blueberries

In a bowl, combine flour and confectioners' sugar. Cut in butter until crumbly. Stir in pecans. Press into an ungreased 12-in. pizza pan. Bake at 350° for 12-14 minutes or until crust is set and edges are lightly browned.

Meanwhile, in a mixing bowl, beat cream cheese, egg and sugar until smooth. Spread over crust. Bake 8-10 minutes longer or until set. Cool to room temperature.

For topping, process berries and sugar in a blender or food processor until blended. In a saucepan, combine cornstarch and water until smooth. Add berry mixture. Bring to a boil; cook and stir 2 minutes or until thickened. Set saucepan in ice water 15 minutes, stirring several times.

Spread berry mixture over the cream cheese layer. Arrange fresh fruit on top. Refrigerate for at least 2 hours before slicing.
Yield: 10-12 servings.

Ham 'n' Cheese Strata

(pictured below)
Marilyn Kroeker, Steinbach, Manitoba
My family wouldn't mind if I made this every weekend! A comforting combination of popular breakfast ingredients, this layered casserole is a guaranteed hit at morning potlucks.

   12   slices white bread, crusts removed
    1   pound fully cooked ham, diced
    2   cups (8 ounces) shredded cheddar cheese
    6   eggs
    3   cups milk
    2   teaspoons Worcestershire sauce
    1   teaspoon ground mustard
  1/2   teaspoon salt
  1/4   teaspoon pepper
Dash cayenne pepper
  1/4   cup finely chopped onion
  1/4   cup finely chopped green pepper
  1/4   cup butter, melted
    1   cup crushed cornflakes

Arrange six slices of bread in the bottom of a greased 13-in. x 9-in. x 2-in. baking dish. Top with ham and cheese. Cover with remaining bread.

In a bowl, beat eggs, milk, Worcestershire sauce, mustard, salt, pepper and cayenne. Stir in onion and green pepper; pour over all. Cover and refrigerate overnight.

Remove from the refrigerator 30 minutes before baking. Pour butter over bread; sprinkle with cornflakes. Bake, uncovered, at 350° for 50-60 minutes or until a knife inserted near the center comes out clean. Let stand 10 minutes before serving.
Yield: 8-10 servings.

Black Forest Crepes

(pictured above)
Lisa Tanner, Warner Robins, Georgia
These fancy-looking crepes are a sweet ending to special get-togethers. I fill them with cherry pie filling and top them with chocolate sauce, whipped cream and a sprinkling of baking cocoa.

- 1-1/2 cups buttermilk
- 3 eggs
- 3 tablespoons butter, melted
- 1 cup all-purpose flour
- 2 tablespoons sugar
- 2 tablespoons baking cocoa

CHOCOLATE SAUCE:
- 3/4 cup sugar
- 1/3 cup baking cocoa
- 1 can (5 ounces) evaporated milk
- 1/4 cup butter
- 1 teaspoon vanilla extract
- 1 can (21 ounces) cherry pie filling

In a small mixing bowl, combine the buttermilk, eggs and butter. Combine the flour, sugar and baking cocoa; add to milk mixture and mix well. Cover and refrigerate for 1 hour.

Heat a lightly greased 8-in. nonstick skillet; pour 2 tablespoons batter into the center of skillet. Lift and tilt pan to evenly coat bottom. Cook until top appears dry; turn and cook 15-20 seconds longer. Remove to a wire rack. Repeat with remaining batter, greasing skillet as needed. When cool, stack crepes with waxed paper or paper towels in between.

For sauce, in a small saucepan, combine sugar and cocoa. Whisk in milk; add butter. Bring to a boil over medium heat, stirring constantly. Remove from the heat; stir in vanilla.

To serve, spoon about 2 tablespoons pie filling down the center of each crepe. Fold sides of crepe over filling; place in a greased 13-in. x 9-in. x 2-in. baking pan. Bake, uncovered, at 225° for 15 minutes. Transfer to serving plates; drizzle with warm chocolate sauce.

Yield: 10 servings (20 crepes).

Amish Breakfast Casserole

Beth Notaro, Kokomo, Indiana
We enjoyed a hearty breakfast bake during a visit to an Amish inn. When I asked for the recipe, one of the ladies told me the ingredients right off the top of her head. I modified it a bit to create this particular version. You can also try breakfast sausage in place of bacon.

- 1 pound sliced bacon, diced
- 1 medium sweet onion, chopped
- 6 eggs, lightly beaten
- 4 cups frozen shredded hash brown potatoes, thawed
- 2 cups (8 ounces) shredded cheddar cheese
- 1-1/2 cups (12 ounces) small-curd cottage cheese
- 1-1/4 cups shredded Swiss cheese

In a large skillet, cook bacon and onion until bacon is crisp; drain. In a bowl, combine the remaining ingredients; stir in bacon mixture. Transfer to a greased 13-in. x 9-in. x 2-in. baking dish.

Bake, uncovered, at 350° for 35-40 minutes or until set and bubbly. Let stand for 10 minutes before cutting.

Yield: 12 servings.

Meaty Apple Skillet

(pictured above)
Sharon Berry, Henderson, Nevada
I love having family over for breakfast, and they all look forward to this down-home specialty. Cinnamon, nutmeg and apple slices help combine the flavors of the four different meats in this robust dish.

   1 large tart apple, peeled and thinly sliced
   2 tablespoons butter
   1 teaspoon ground cinnamon
 1/8 teaspoon ground nutmeg
   2 teaspoons cornstarch
 2/3 cup cranberry-apple juice
   1 pound smoked kielbasa *or* Polish sausage
 3/4 pound bulk pork sausage, cooked and drained
 3/4 pound pork sausage links, cooked and sliced
1-1/2 cups cubed fully cooked ham

In a skillet, saute apple slices in butter; sprinkle with cinnamon and nutmeg. Cover and cook for 5 minutes or until apples are tender. Combine cornstarch and juice until smooth; stir into apple mixture. Bring to a boil; cook and stir for 2 minutes or until thickened. Add the sausage and ham; heat through.
Yield: 12-16 servings.

Hearty French Toast

(pictured below)
Page Alexander, Baldwin City, Kansas
Since you make it ahead, this dish and fruity sauce is wonderful to bring to a daytime get-together.

 24 slices day-old French bread (3/4 inch thick)
 12 thin slices fully cooked ham
 12 thin slices cooked turkey
  1 to 2 medium tart apples, peeled and thinly sliced
 12 thin slices provolone cheese
  4 eggs
  1 cup milk
 1/4 teaspoon ground nutmeg

APPLE CRANBERRY SAUCE:
1-1/2 cups cranberry juice
  2 tablespoons cornstarch
  1 tablespoon brown sugar
  1 teaspoon grated orange peel
 1/8 teaspoon ground cinnamon
  1 medium tart apple, peeled and finely chopped

Place half of the bread in a greased 13-in. x 9-in. x 2-in. baking dish; top each with a slice of ham, turkey, two to three apple slices and a piece of cheese (cut or fold meat and cheese to fit). Top with remaining bread.

In a bowl, beat the eggs, milk and nutmeg; pour over the bread. Cover and chill 6 hours or overnight. Remove from the refrigerator 30 minutes before baking.

Bake, uncovered, at 350° for 30 minutes or until a knife inserted near the center comes out clean. Let stand for 10 minutes.

Meanwhile, in a saucepan, combine the first five sauce ingredients; cook and stir over medium heat until thickened. Cook and stir 2 minutes longer. Stir in apple. Serve warm over French toast.
Yield: 12 servings.

Pictured below:
Parsley Tortellini Toss (p. 113).

Salads &
Side Dishes

Beans 'n' Greens

(pictured above)
Dorothy Pritchett, Wills Point, Texas
Tasty and a snap to make, this side dish is a guaranteed salad-bar star. The snappy marinade dresses up green beans, spinach and lettuce nicely. I keep the recipe at the front of my easy-to-make file.

1	cup olive oil
1/4	cup white vinegar
1-1/2	teaspoons salt
1-1/2	teaspoons sugar
1/2	teaspoon celery seed
1/2	teaspoon paprika
2	cans (14-1/2 ounces *each*) cut green beans, drained
8	cups torn lettuce
4	cups torn fresh spinach
2	cups (8 ounces) shredded Swiss cheese

In a jar with tight-fitting lid, combine the first six ingredients; shake well. Pour over green beans; let stand for 15 minutes. Just before serving, drain beans, reserving the marinade.

In a salad bowl, combine the beans, lettuce, spinach and Swiss cheese. Drizzle with the reserved marinade and toss to coat.

Yield: 14-18 servings.

Rhubarb Berry Delight Salad

(pictured at right)
Joan Sieck, Rensselaer, New York
Rhubarb, strawberries and raspberry flavors steal the show in this sweet gelatin. The treat also features a creamy vanilla layer.

4	cups diced rhubarb
2	cups fresh *or* frozen strawberries
1-1/2	cups sugar, *divided*
1	package (6 ounces) raspberry-flavored gelatin
2	cups boiling water
1	cup milk
1	envelope unflavored gelatin
1/4	cup cold water
1-1/2	teaspoons vanilla extract
2	cups (16 ounces) sour cream

In a saucepan, cook rhubarb, strawberries and 1 cup sugar until fruit is tender. In a large bowl, dissolve raspberry gelatin in boiling water. Stir in fruit; set aside.

In another pan, heat milk and remaining sugar over low until sugar is dissolved. In a small bowl, soften unflavored gelatin in cold water; add to hot milk mixture and stir until gelatin is dissolved. Remove from the heat; add vanilla. Cool to lukewarm; blend in sour cream. Set aside and cool to room temperature.

Pour a third of the fruit mixture into a 3-qt. bowl; chill until almost set. Spoon a third of the sour cream mixture over fruit; chill until almost set. Repeat layers twice, chilling between layers if necessary. Refrigerate until firm, at least 3 hours.

Yield: 12 servings.

Pizza Salad

Debbie Jones, California, Maryland
A fun summer dish, this unique pasta salad tastes as good as it looks. I love to take it to parties. The zesty flavor really rounds out barbecues.

  1 pound spiral macaroni, cooked and drained
  3 medium tomatoes, diced and seeded
16 ounces cheddar cheese, cubed
  1 to 2 bunches green onions, sliced
  3 ounces sliced pepperoni
3/4 cup vegetable oil
2/3 cup grated Parmesan cheese
1/2 cup red wine vinegar
  2 teaspoons dried oregano
  1 teaspoon garlic powder
  1 teaspoon salt
1/4 teaspoon pepper
Croutons, optional

In a large bowl, combine macaroni, tomatoes, cheddar cheese, green onions and pepperoni. In a small bowl, combine oil, Parmesan cheese, vinegar and seasonings; pour over macaroni mixture. Cover and refrigerate for several hours. Top with croutons just before serving if desired.

Yield: 16 servings.

Tossed Spinach Salad

Myra Innes, Auburn, Kansas
From-scratch French-style dressing is a bold topping that suits the ingredients in this salad. When I make it to share at a get-together, there's never any to bring home.

  1 package (10 ounces) fresh spinach, torn
  1 pound fresh mushrooms, sliced
1/2 pound sliced bacon, cooked and crumbled
  3 celery ribs, sliced
  1 cup (4 ounces) shredded cheddar cheese
  3 hard-cooked eggs, chopped
  3 green onions, sliced
  1 cup ketchup
3/4 cup white vinegar
3/4 cup vegetable oil
1/2 cup sugar
  1 teaspoon salt
  1 teaspoon Worcestershire sauce

In a large salad bowl, combine the first seven ingredients. In a jar with a tight-fitting lid, combine the remaining ingredients; shake until sugar is dissolved. Drizzle over salad and toss to coat. Serve immediately.

Yield: 12 servings.

Italian Potato Salad

(pictured above)
Ardis Kohnen, Rudolph, Wisconsin
With six grown daughters who visit frequently, I have plenty of chances to serve this family favorite. It's wonderful with everything from pork chops to burgers.

  3 pounds potatoes
1/3 cup Italian salad dressing
  4 hard-cooked eggs, chopped
3/4 cup chopped celery
1/3 cup chopped onion
1/4 cup chopped cucumber
1/4 cup chopped green pepper
1/2 cup mayonnaise
1/4 cup sour cream
  1 teaspoon prepared horseradish
Chopped fresh tomatoes

Place potatoes in a saucepan; cover with water. Bring to a boil and cook until tender; drain and cool. Peel and cube potatoes; place in a large bowl. Add dressing and toss to coat. Cover and chill for 2 hours. Add eggs, celery, onion, cucumber and green pepper; mix well. In a small bowl, combine mayonnaise, sour cream and horseradish; mix well. Pour over potato mixture and toss to coat. Chill for at least 1 hour. Top with tomatoes.

Yield: 8-10 servings.

Calico Potato Salad

(pictured below)
Christine Hartry, Emo, Ontario
One of the nice things about this salad is how versatile it is. It goes well with a variety of meats and offers a little kick from chili powder and hot pepper sauce. I've taken it to potlucks and even square dances.

DRESSING:
- 1/2 cup olive oil
- 1/4 cup vinegar
- 1 tablespoon sugar
- 1-1/2 teaspoons chili powder
- 1 teaspoon salt, optional
- Dash hot pepper sauce

SALAD:
- 4 large red potatoes (about 2 pounds), peeled and cooked
- 1-1/2 cups cooked whole kernel corn
- 1 cup shredded carrot
- 1/2 cup chopped red onion
- 1/2 cup diced green pepper
- 1/2 cup diced sweet red pepper
- 1/2 cup sliced pitted ripe olives

In a small bowl or jar, combine all dressing ingredients; cover and chill. Cube potatoes; combine with corn, carrot, onion, peppers and olives in a salad bowl. Add dressing; toss lightly. Cover and chill until serving.
Yield: 14 servings.

Country Rice Salad

Arlyn Kramer, El Campo, Texas
We enjoy rice, and this refreshing salad is a delicious way to prepare it. This recipe makes a nice change from potato salad and goes especially well with grilled hamburgers.

DRESSING:
- 1/2 cup mayonnaise
- 1/4 cup prepared mustard
- 2 tablespoons sugar
- 1 teaspoon white vinegar
- 1/4 teaspoon salt
- 1/8 teaspoon pepper

SALAD:
- 3 cups cooked rice, chilled
- 1/4 cup sweet pickle relish
- 1 jar (2 ounces) chopped pimientos, drained
- 1/3 cup finely chopped green onions (including tops)
- 1/4 cup finely chopped green pepper
- 1/4 cup finely chopped celery
- 3 hard-cooked eggs, diced
- 1 to 2 tablespoons milk, optional
- Fresh parsley
- Cherry tomatoes

In a small bowl, combine the dressing ingredients. Set aside. In a large salad bowl, combine all salad ingredients. Pour dressing over rice mixture; stir gently. Add milk to achieve desired consistency. Chill several hours before serving. Garnish with parsley and cherry tomatoes.
Yield: 10 servings.

Tangy Cauliflower Salad

Sharon Skildum, Maple Grove, Minnesota
Grapes are the surprising ingredient in this crunchy vegetable salad. Honey and prepared mustard give the dressing just the right taste.

- 1 large head cauliflower, broken into florets (about 6 cups)
- 1 cup halved green grapes
- 1 cup coarsely chopped walnuts
- 1 cup mayonnaise
- 1/3 cup honey
- 1 tablespoon prepared mustard

In a large bowl, toss cauliflower, grapes and walnuts. Combine the mayonnaise, honey and mustard; pour over cauliflower mixture and stir to coat.
Yield: 10 servings.

Asparagus Pasta Salad

(pictured below)

Jean Nelson, Tallulah, Louisiana

I got this recipe from my sister-in-law while visiting her in Texas. Because it's loaded with chicken and ham, I usually prepare it in the summer as a light evening meal for my family or as an extra-special lunch for friends.

    1   pound fresh asparagus, cut into 1-1/2-
        inch pieces
    1   package (16 ounces) multicolored
        corkscrew pasta, cooked and drained
    1   cup diced cooked chicken
    1   cup diced fully cooked ham
    2   medium tomatoes, seeded and diced
  1/2   cup sliced ripe olives
1-1/2   cups prepared zesty Italian salad dressing
1-1/2   teaspoons dill weed

Place asparagus in a large saucepan with enough water to cover; cook until crisp-tender. Drain and cool. In a large bowl, combine asparagus and remaining ingredients; toss to coat. Cover and refrigerate 3-4 hours or overnight.

Yield: 12 servings.

Potluck Pointer

While you can enjoy a pasta, rice or potato salad right after tossing it together, you'll find tastier results if it chills a bit in the refrigerator and the flavors have blended.

Almond Mandarin Salad

(pictured below)
Jacquelyn Smith, Soperton, Georgia
After my daughters-in-law and I enjoyed a similar salad at a restaurant, I decided to come up with my own version. It has quickly become an all-time favorite.

   1/2 cup sliced almonds
     1 tablespoon sugar

DRESSING:
   1/4 cup vegetable oil
     2 tablespoons orange juice
     1 tablespoon lemon juice
     1 tablespoon cider vinegar
     1 teaspoon sugar
   1/4 teaspoon salt
   1/4 teaspoon grated orange peel

SALAD:
     8 cups torn mixed salad greens
     1 can (11 ounces) mandarin oranges, drained
     2 celery ribs, chopped
   1/4 cup chopped green onions

In a small skillet, heat the almonds and sugar over low heat. Cook and stir until almonds are coated with sugar glaze; remove and cool. In a jar with a tight-fitting lid, combine the dressing ingredients; shake well. In a bowl, combine greens, oranges, celery and onions. Add dressing and almonds; toss to coat.

Yield: 10-12 servings.

Kielbasa Summer Salad

(pictured above)
Sara Primarolo, Sanquoit, New York
The unexpected combination of flavors and textures in this cool salad sparks taste buds. It can be a main course for a luncheon or a side dish at a dinner or a barbecue. I received many requests for the recipe when I shared it at a potluck.

     1 pound fully cooked smoked kielbasa *or* Polish sausage
     1 can (15-1/2 ounces) black-eyed peas, rinsed and drained
     2 medium tart apples, cut into 1/2-inch chunks
     1 medium green pepper, chopped
     4 large green onions, thinly sliced

DRESSING:
   1/3 cup vegetable oil
     3 tablespoons cider vinegar
     1 tablespoon Dijon mustard
     2 teaspoons sugar
   1/2 to 1 teaspoon pepper

Halve sausage lengthwise and cut into 1/4-in. slices. In a nonstick skillet, brown sausage. Drain on paper towels. In a bowl, combine peas, apples, green pepper, onions and sausage. In small bowl, combine the dressing ingredients; mix well. Pour over sausage mixture and toss to coat. Cover and refrigerate for 4 hours or overnight.

Yield: 10 servings.

Artichoke-Red Pepper Tossed Salad

Rachel Hinz, St. James, Minnesota
I lived in France during college, and I learned to make an incredible vinaigrette. My host family served the dressing with artichoke hearts.

- 1 head iceberg lettuce, torn
- 1 bunch romaine, torn
- 1 can (14 ounces) water-packed artichoke hearts, rinsed, drained and chopped
- 2 medium sweet red peppers, julienned
- 1/2 cup thinly sliced red onion
- 1/2 cup olive oil
- 1/2 cup red wine vinegar *or* cider vinegar
- 2 tablespoons Dijon mustard
- 2 teaspoons sugar
- 1 teaspoon seasoned salt
- 1/2 cup shredded Parmesan cheese

In a large bowl, combine the first five ingredients. In a jar with a tight-fitting lid, combine oil, vinegar, mustard, sugar and seasoned salt; shake well. Drizzle over salad and toss to coat. Sprinkle with Parmesan cheese.
Yield: 20-25 servings.

Ham & Turkey Pasta Salad

Lori Cole, Broken Arrow, Oklahoma
When a potluck's coming up, people always ask me to bring what they call "that noodle salad you make." Based on the raves it's received, I know folks are referring to this meaty dish.

- 3-3/4 cups uncooked bow tie pasta
- 1 cup chopped fully cooked lean ham
- 1 cup chopped cooked turkey breast
- 1 cup (4 ounces) shredded reduced-fat cheddar cheese
- 1/4 cup chopped onion
- 1/4 cup chopped celery
- 1 hard-cooked egg, chopped
- 1 cup fat-free mayonnaise
- 1/4 cup picante sauce
- 1 teaspoon salt
- 1/4 teaspoon pepper
- 1/4 teaspoon sugar

Cook pasta according to package directions; drain and rinse with cold water. In a large bowl, combine the pasta, ham, turkey, cheese, onion, celery and egg. In a small bowl, combine the remaining ingredients. Pour over salad and gently toss to coat. Cover and refrigerate for 2 hours before serving.
Yield: 10 servings.

Fluffy Fruit Salad

(pictured above)
Ann Heinonen, Howell, Michigan
I like to bring my mom's fruit salad to covered-dish suppers. The sweet, creamy sauce combined with all the colorful fruit makes it a hit with everyone who attends.

- 2 cans (20 ounces *each*) unsweetened crushed pineapple
- 2/3 cup sugar
- 2 tablespoons all-purpose flour
- 2 eggs, lightly beaten
- 1/4 cup orange juice
- 3 tablespoons lemon juice
- 1 tablespoon vegetable oil
- 2 cans (15 ounces *each*) fruit cocktail, drained
- 2 cans (11 ounces *each*) mandarin oranges, drained
- 2 bananas, sliced
- 1 cup heavy whipping cream, whipped

Drain pineapple, reserving 1 cup juice in a small saucepan. Set pineapple aside. To saucepan, add sugar, flour, eggs, orange juice, lemon juice and oil. Bring to a boil, stirring constantly. Boil for 1 minute; remove from the heat and let cool. In a salad bowl, combine the pineapple, fruit cocktail, oranges and bananas. Fold in whipped cream and cooled sauce. Chill for several hours before serving.
Yield: 12-16 servings.

Ham 'n' Cheese Potato Salad

(pictured below)
Tamara Sellman, Barrington, Illinois
This is one potato salad that's hearty enough to be a main course. My family likes to take it along when we go on picnics, but I found that it's ideal for just about any affair where you're asked to contribute a tasty dish.

2-1/2 to 3 pounds red potatoes
    1 cup mayonnaise
  1/2 cup sour cream
    2 tablespoons Dijon mustard
    1 teaspoon celery seed
  1/2 teaspoon salt
  1/4 teaspoon pepper
    8 ounces Monterey Jack cheese, cubed
    2 cups diced fully cooked ham
  3/4 cup chopped fresh tomatoes
  1/4 cup sliced green onions
  1/4 cup minced fresh parsley

In a saucepan, cook potatoes in boiling salted water until tender; drain and cool.

Meanwhile, in a large salad bowl, combine mayonnaise, sour cream, mustard, celery seed, salt and pepper; mix well. Cut potatoes into cubes. Add to mayonnaise mixture and toss to coat. Add remaining ingredients; mix well. Cover and refrigerate for at least 2 hours.

Yield: 16-20 servings.

Layered Fresh Fruit Salad

(pictured above)
Page Alexander, Baldwin City, Kansas
People always pass the compliments when I take this lovely salad to bring-a-dish suppers. It's nice on a hot day… with a winter meal…or as a dessert!

CITRUS SAUCE:
  2/3 cup orange juice
  1/3 cup fresh lemon juice
  1/3 cup packed brown sugar
    1 cinnamon stick
  1/2 teaspoon grated orange peel
  1/2 teaspoon grated lemon peel

FRUIT SALAD:
    2 cups cubed fresh pineapple
    1 pint fresh strawberries, hulled and sliced
    2 kiwifruit, peeled and sliced
    3 medium bananas, sliced
    2 oranges, peeled and sectioned
    1 red grapefruit, peeled and sectioned
    1 cup seedless red grapes

In a saucepan, bring all sauce ingredients to a boil; simmer 5 minutes. Cool.

Meanwhile, in a large bowl, layer the pineapple, strawberries, kiwifruit, bananas, oranges, grapefruit and grapes. Remove cinnamon stick from the sauce and pour sauce over fruit. Cover and refrigerate for several hours.

Yield: 10-12 servings.

Overnight Coleslaw

Fern Hammock, Garland, Texas
This has been a well-used salad from my recipe box for a long time. When my office had covered-dish get-togethers, I was always asked to bring my tangy coleslaw.

  12 cups shredded cabbage (1 medium head)
   1 green pepper, chopped
   1 medium red onion, chopped
   2 carrots, shredded
   1 cup sugar

DRESSING:
   1 cup white vinegar
 3/4 cup vegetable oil
   2 teaspoons sugar
   1 teaspoon ground mustard
   1 teaspoon celery seed
   1 teaspoon salt

In a large bowl, combine first four ingredients. Sprinkle with sugar; set aside. In a saucepan, combine dressing ingredients; bring to a boil. Remove from the heat and pour over vegetables, stirring to cover evenly. Cover and refrigerate overnight. Stir well before serving.

Yield: 12-16 servings.

Pasta Crab Salad

Carol Blauw, Holland, Michigan
When it comes to cooking, I believe the simpler the better. A few years ago, a co-worker told me about this tasty, easy-to-prepare salad and it's been a favorite ever since.

4-1/2 cups uncooked tricolor spiral pasta
     1 package (16 ounces) imitation crabmeat, flaked
   1/3 cup *each* chopped celery, green pepper and onion
   1/2 cup reduced-fat mayonnaise
   1/2 cup reduced-fat ranch salad dressing
     1 teaspoon dill weed

Cook pasta according to package directions; drain and rinse in cold water. Place in large bowl; add the crab, celery, green pepper and onion. In a small bowl, combine the mayonnaise, salad dressing and dill weed. Pour over pasta mixture and toss to coat. Cover and refrigerate for at least 2 hours before serving.

Yield: 10 servings.

Crunchy Corn Medley

(pictured below)
Meredith Cecil, Plattsburg, Missouri
This recipe came from my husband's aunt, who's an excellent cook. It's crunchy, colorful and combined with a light, tasty dressing. I've shared the dish at many events and people quickly add it to their recipe collections.

   2 cups frozen peas, thawed
   1 can (15-1/4 ounces) whole kernel corn, drained
   1 can (15-1/4 ounces) white *or* shoepeg corn, drained
   1 can (8 ounces) water chestnuts, drained and chopped
   1 jar (4 ounces) diced pimientos, drained
   8 green onions, thinly sliced
   2 celery ribs, chopped
   1 medium green pepper, chopped
 1/2 cup vinegar
 1/2 cup sugar
 1/4 cup vegetable oil
   1 teaspoon salt
 1/4 teaspoon pepper

In a large bowl, combine the first eight ingredients. In a small bowl, combine vinegar, sugar, oil, salt and pepper; whisk until sugar is dissolved. Pour over corn mixture; mix well. Cover and refrigerate for at least 3 hours. Stir just before serving; serve with a slotted spoon.

Yield: 10 servings.

Sally's Vegetable Salad

(pictured above)
Sally Payne, Fruitland, Idaho
I came up with this recipe one summer evening when we had unexpected company drop by. I raided the vegetable bin and combined everything I had. Now we enjoy this salad whenever there's a crowd to feed.

  1 medium head cauliflower, broken into florets
  1 medium bunch broccoli, broken into florets
  1 cup diagonally sliced celery
  1 cup fresh *or* frozen peas
1/2 pound sliced bacon, cooked and drained
  2 teaspoons chopped green onion tops
  1 can (8 ounces) water chestnuts, sliced and drained

DRESSING:
  2 cups mayonnaise
1/4 cup sugar
1/4 cup Parmesan cheese
  2 teaspoons white vinegar
1/4 teaspoon salt
  1 teaspoon finely chopped white onion

In a large salad bowl, mix together the first seven ingredients; cover. Let stand in refrigerator while mixing dressing. Combine dressing ingredients; pour over vegetables at least 1 hour before serving.
Yield: 10-12 servings.

Potluck Pointer

Perishable foods such as mayonnaise-based salads should be stored below 45° for food safety concerns. These items should never be left at room temperature for more than 2 hours. One way to keep salads cold is to nestle the serving dish in a larger bowl filled with ice cubes. Sealing the cubes in storage bags prevents a mess as the ice melts.

Parsley Tortellini Toss

(pictured on p. 103)
Jacqueline Graves, Lawrenceville, Georgia
Here's a pasta salad that's sure to keep folks coming back for seconds. Tortellini, cheese, ham, turkey and a harvest of veggies make the pasta toss satisfying enough for a main dish.

  1 package (16 ounces) frozen cheese tortellini
1-1/2 cups cubed provolone cheese
1-1/2 cups cubed part-skim mozzarella cheese
  1 cup cubed fully cooked ham
  1 cup cubed cooked turkey
  1 cup frozen peas, thawed
  2 medium carrots, shredded
1/2 medium sweet red pepper, diced
1/2 medium green pepper, diced
  1 cup minced fresh parsley
1/2 cup olive oil
  3 tablespoons cider *or* red wine vinegar
  2 tablespoons grated Parmesan cheese
  2 garlic cloves, minced

Cook tortellini according to package directions; rinse in cold water and drain. Place in a large bowl; add the next eight ingredients. In a jar with a tight-fitting lid, combine the remaining ingredients and shake well. Pour over salad and toss to coat. Cover and refrigerate until serving.

Yield: 12-15 servings.

Four Bean Salad

Hope Huggins, Santa Cruz, California
My mother gave me this recipe, but I added garbanzo beans to it. It's not too sweet and not too sour.

  1 can (14-1/2 ounces) green beans, drained
  1 can (14-1/2 ounces) wax beans, drained
  1 can (15 ounces) garbanzo beans, rinsed and drained
  1 can (16 ounces) kidney beans, rinsed and drained
1/4 cup green pepper, julienned
  8 green onions, sliced
3/4 cup sugar
1/2 cup cider vinegar
1/4 cup vegetable oil
1/2 teaspoon salt

In a large salad bowl, combine all of the beans, green pepper and onions. In a small bowl, combine remaining ingredients; stir until sugar is dissolved. Pour over bean mixture. Cover and refrigerate overnight, stirring several times.

Yield: 10-12 servings.

Layered Spinach Salad

(pictured above)
Lori Cumberledge, Pasadena, Maryland
Here's a real eye-catcher with bright and pretty layers. People enjoy the unique addition of cheese tortellini, so the salad always goes fast!

  1 package (9 ounces) refrigerated cheese tortellini
  2 cups shredded red cabbage
  6 cups torn fresh spinach
  2 cups cherry tomatoes, halved
1/2 cup sliced green onions
  1 bottle (8 ounces) ranch salad dressing
  8 bacon strips, cooked and crumbled, optional

Cook tortellini according to package directions. Drain and rinse with cold water; set aside. In a large glass bowl, layer cabbage, spinach, tortellini, tomatoes and onions. Pour dressing over top; sprinkle with bacon if desired. Cover and refrigerate for at least 1 hour.

Yield: 10 servings.

Southwestern Salad

(pictured above)
Carolyn Oler, Gilbert, Arizona
My mother gave me this recipe several years ago, and I've prepared it often ever since. It can be a meal in itself or served with a big Mexican dinner.

1 can (15 ounces) pinto beans, rinsed and drained
1 bunch green onions with tops, sliced
1 large tomato, seeded and chopped
1 medium ripe avocado, chopped
1 bottle (8 ounces) Catalina salad dressing, *divided*
2 cups (8 ounces) shredded cheddar cheese
1 medium head lettuce, torn into bite-size pieces
4 cups corn chips

In a large salad bowl, toss together the beans, green onions, tomato, avocado and half of the Catalina dressing. Top with cheese and then lettuce. Refrigerate. Just before serving, add corn chips to salad and toss. Serve with remaining dressing.
Yield: 8-10 servings.

California Pasta Salad

Jeanette Krembas, Laguna Niguel, California
Not only does this make-ahead salad travel well to get-togethers such as picnics, but people absolutely love it when it gets there.

1 pound thin spaghetti *or* vermicelli, broken into 1-inch pieces, cooked
3 large tomatoes, diced
2 medium zucchini, diced
1 large cucumber, diced

1 medium green pepper, diced
1 sweet red pepper, diced
1 large red onion, diced
2 cans (2-1/2 ounces *each*) sliced ripe olives, drained
1 bottle (16 ounces) Italian salad dressing
1/4 cup grated Parmesan *or* Romano cheese
1 tablespoon sesame seeds
2 teaspoons poppy seeds
1 teaspoon paprika
1/2 teaspoon celery seed
1/4 teaspoon garlic powder

Combine all ingredients in a large bowl; cover and refrigerate 8 hours or overnight.
Yield: 10-15 servings.

Marinated Veggie Salad

(pictured below)
Lynn Grate, South Bend, Indiana
This is my favorite potluck salad. I get compliments every time I make it. It's also an ideal make-ahead item since it needs to marinate overnight.

1 pint cherry tomatoes, halved
1 medium zucchini, cubed
1 medium yellow summer squash, cubed
1 medium cucumber, cubed
1 *each* medium sweet yellow, red and green pepper, cut into 1-inch pieces
1 can (6 ounces) pitted ripe olives, drained
1 small red onion, chopped
1/2 to 3/4 cup Italian salad dressing

In a serving bowl, combine all ingredients. Cover and refrigerate overnight.
Yield: 12 servings.

Mostaccioli Veggie Salad

(pictured below)
Julie Sterchi, Harrisburg, Illinois
I first sampled this refreshing salad at a church supper several years ago. The mix of pasta, zucchini, cucumber and black olives is coated with a light vinaigrette. Any pasta can be substituted for the mostaccioli.

  3 cups uncooked mostaccioli
  1 medium cucumber, thinly sliced
  1 small yellow summer squash, quartered and sliced
  1 small zucchini, halved and sliced
1/2 cup diced sweet red pepper
1/2 cup diced green pepper
1/2 cup sliced ripe olives
  3 to 4 green onions, chopped

DRESSING:
1/3 cup sugar
1/3 cup white wine vinegar
1/3 cup vegetable oil
1-1/2 teaspoons prepared mustard
3/4 teaspoon dried minced onion
3/4 teaspoon garlic powder
1/2 teaspoon salt
1/2 teaspoon pepper

Cook pasta according to package directions. Drain and rinse in cold water. Place in a large bowl; add the cucumber, summer squash, zucchini, peppers, olives and onions.

In a jar with a tight-fitting lid, combine the dressing ingredients; shake well. Pour over pasta mixture and toss to coat. Cover and refrigerate for 8 hours or overnight. Toss again before serving.
Yield: 10 servings.

Garden Bean Salad

(pictured above)
Bernice McFadden, Dayton, Ohio
My mother gave me this crunchy bean salad recipe many years ago, and I often take it to covered-dish dinners. It looks especially attractive served in a glass bowl, showing off the colorful vegetables.

  1 can (15-1/2 ounces) cut green beans, rinsed and drained
  2 cans (15-1/4 ounces *each*) lima beans, rinsed and drained
  1 can (16 ounces) kidney beans, rinsed and drained
  1 can (14-1/2 ounces) wax beans, rinsed and drained
  1 can (15 ounces) garbanzo beans, rinsed and drained
  1 large green pepper, chopped
  3 celery ribs, chopped
  1 jar (2 ounces) sliced pimientos, drained
  1 bunch green onions, sliced
  2 cups vinegar
  2 cups sugar
1/2 cup water
  1 teaspoon salt

Place beans in a large bowl. Add green pepper, celery, pimientos and green onions; set aside. Combine remaining ingredients in a heavy saucepan; bring to a boil. Boil for 5 minutes. Remove from heat and immediately pour over vegetables. Refrigerate several hours or overnight before serving.
Yield: 12-16 servings.

Shrimp Pasta Salad

Sherri Gentry, Dallas, Oregon
This tasty and refreshing salad stirs up quickly yet looks elegant, so it's an easy way to impress guests.

    12   ounces spiral pasta, cooked and
         drained
     1   package (10 ounces) frozen cooked
         shrimp, thawed
    1/4 cup sliced green onions
    1/4 cup Parmesan cheese
    1/3 cup vegetable oil
    1/3 cup red wine vinegar
  2-1/2 teaspoons dill weed
     2   teaspoons salt
    3/4 teaspoon garlic powder
    1/2 teaspoon pepper

In a large bowl, combine pasta, shrimp, onions and Parmesan cheese. In a small bowl, combine remaining ingredients. Pour over pasta mixture and toss. Cover and chill for 1-2 hours.
Yield: 10 servings.

Tomato Parmesan Salad

Michele Bently, Niceville, Florida
This homemade dressing jazzes up romaine and iceberg lettuce with terrific results. Red onions, tomatoes and shredded Parmesan add a splash of interest.

  1-1/3 cups vegetable oil
     1   cup red wine vinegar
     2   garlic cloves, minced
Salt and pepper to taste
     2   bunches romaine lettuce, torn
     1   head iceberg lettuce, torn
     2   small red onions, thinly sliced
     2   large tomatoes, diced
     1   jar (4 ounces) diced pimientos,
         drained
    2/3 cup shredded Parmesan cheese

In a small bowl or jar with a tight-fitting lid, combine oil, vinegar, garlic, salt and pepper; set aside. In a large salad bowl, combine all of the remaining ingredients. Chill until ready to serve. Just before serving, whisk or shake dressing; pour over salad and toss.
Yield: 14 servings.

Italian Bread Salad

(pictured above)
Sandra Castillo, Sun Prairie, Wisconsin
With its delicious pizza flavor, this out-of-the-ordinary salad is always a winner. It's a perfect choice when you're asked to bring a dish to pass.

     1   prebaked Italian bread shell crust
         (14 ounces), cubed
  1-1/2 cups diced fresh tomatoes
    1/2 cup thinly sliced fresh basil
    1/2 cup Italian salad dressing, *divided*
     7   cups ready-to-serve salad greens
     1   small green pepper, julienned
     1   cup sliced pepperoni
     1   cup (4 ounces) shredded part-skim
         mozzarella cheese
    1/2 cup grated Parmesan cheese
    1/2 cup sliced ripe olives

In a large salad bowl, combine bread cubes, tomatoes, basil and 1/4 cup salad dressing; let stand for 5 minutes. Add the salad greens, green pepper, pepperoni, mozzarella cheese, Parmesan cheese and olives. Add remaining salad dressing and toss to coat.
Yield: 8-10 servings.

Potluck Pointer

Try to put finishing touches on green salads once you arrive at the church supper. The longer salad dressings sit over spinach or lettuce, the more the leaves will wilt. Similarly, toss chopped tomatoes, sliced cucumbers and other moist veggies into the salad shortly before serving.

Red Scalloped Potatoes

Clara Honeyager, North Prairie, Wisconsin

Baked in a no-fuss gravy, this is a different way to serve red potatoes. Dill weed and marjoram offer a taste that always seems to appeal to folks.

3 pounds small red potatoes, quartered
2 cans (10-3/4 ounces *each*) condensed cream of mushroom soup, undiluted
2 cups sliced onions
1 cup milk
1/4 cup thinly sliced green onions
1 teaspoon dill weed
1 teaspoon dried marjoram
3/4 teaspoon salt
1/2 teaspoon pepper

Place potatoes in a ungreased 13-in. x 9-in. x 2-in. baking pan. In a large bowl, combine the remaining ingredients; pour over potatoes.

Cover and bake at 350° for 1-1/4 hours. Uncover and bake 10-20 minutes longer or until bubbly and potatoes are tender.

Yield: 10-12 servings.

Vegetable Spiral Sticks

Teri Albrecht, Mt. Airy, Maryland

I love to serve these savory wrapped vegetable sticks for parties or special occasions. They're a simple but stunning contribution.

3 medium carrots
12 fresh asparagus spears, trimmed
1 tube (11 ounces) refrigerated breadsticks
1 egg white, beaten
1/4 cup grated Parmesan cheese
1/2 teaspoon dried oregano

Cut carrots lengthwise into quarters. In a large skillet, bring 2 in. of water to a boil. Add carrots; cook for 3 minutes. Add the asparagus; cook 2-3 minutes longer. Drain and rinse with cold water; pat dry.

Cut each piece of breadstick dough in half. Roll each piece into a 7-in. rope. Wrap one rope in a spiral around each vegetable. Place on a baking sheet coated with nonstick cooking spray; tuck ends of dough under vegetables to secure. Brush with egg white. Combine Parmesan cheese and oregano; sprinkle over sticks. Bake at 375° for 12-14 minutes or until golden brown. Serve warm.

Yield: 2 dozen.

Best-Ever Beans and Sausage

(pictured above)
Robert Saulnier, Clarksburg, Massachusetts
My wife devised this dish, which is extremely popular with our friends. When she asks, "What can I share?", the reply is always, "Bring your beans and sausage...and a couple copies of the recipe."

1-1/2 pounds bulk hot pork sausage
  1 medium green pepper, chopped
  1 medium onion, chopped
  1 can (31 ounces) pork and beans
  1 can (16 ounces) kidney beans, rinsed and drained
  1 can (15-1/2 ounces) great northern beans, rinsed and drained
  1 can (15-1/2 ounces) black-eyed peas, rinsed and drained
  1 can (15 ounces) pinto beans, rinsed and drained
  1 can (15 ounces) garbanzo beans *or* chickpeas, rinsed and drained
1-1/2 cups ketchup
 3/4 cup packed brown sugar
  2 teaspoons ground mustard

In a skillet, cook sausage over medium heat until no longer pink; drain. Add the green pepper and onion; saute until tender.

Drain. Add remaining ingredients; mix well. Pour into a greased 13-in. x 9-in. x 2-in. baking dish.

Cover and bake at 325° for 1 hour. Uncover and bake 20-30 minutes longer or until bubbly.

Yield: 12-16 servings.

Spinach Parmesan Linguine

(pictured below)
Mary Curran, Sandwich, Illinois
If you're looking for a tasty switch from plain, buttered noodles, serve this pleasing pasta toss. Frozen spinach and Parmesan cheese add lively flavor to the linguine.

   1 package (16 ounces) linguine
   1 cup chicken broth
   1 small onion, chopped
   2 garlic cloves, minced
   1 package (10 ounces) frozen chopped spinach, thawed and well drained
1/3 cup milk
   2 tablespoons cream cheese
Salt and pepper to taste
   1 cup (4 ounces) shredded Parmesan cheese
1/2 cup shredded part-skim mozzarella cheese

Cook linguine according to package directions. Meanwhile, in a saucepan over medium-high heat, bring broth to a boil. Add onion and garlic. Reduce heat; cook, uncovered, for 5 minutes. Stir in spinach; cook for 2 minutes.

Add the milk, cream cheese, salt and pepper; stir until cheese is melted. Drain linguine and place in a serving bowl. Add sauce and toss to coat. Sprinkle with Parmesan and mozzarella cheeses; toss to coat.

Yield: 10 servings.

Crumb-Topped Mushrooms

Clara Honeyager, North Prairie, Wisconsin
You can't beat this layered dish when feeding a crowd. The buttery mushrooms go well with beef or most any main course. You'll be asked to share your secret time and again.

  2 packages (12 ounces *each*) butter-flavored crackers, crushed, *divided*
  1 cup butter, melted
4-1/2 pounds fresh mushrooms, thickly sliced
  3 cups heavy whipping cream
  1 teaspoon paprika

In a large bowl, combine 3 cups of cracker crumbs and butter; set aside.

Divide half of the mushrooms between three greased 13-in. x 9-in. x 2-in. baking dishes. Sprinkle with remaining crumbs; top with remaining mushrooms.

Pour cream over all. Sprinkle with buttered crumbs and paprika. Bake, uncovered, at 350° for 30-35 minutes or until golden brown.

Yield: 50-60 servings.

Cheesy Broccoli-Rice Bake

Martha Myers, Ash Grove, Missouri
With low-fat cheese and sour cream, this light casserole is perfect to contribute to a buffet. It's a hearty, rich-tasting accompaniment to any meat.

  1 can (10-3/4 ounces) low-fat condensed cream of broccoli soup, undiluted
  1 can (10-3/4 ounces) low-fat cream of chicken soup, undiluted
  2 cups skim milk
1/2 cup light sour cream
  2 cups (8 ounces) shredded part-skim mozzarella cheese
  1 cup (4 ounces) shredded reduced-fat cheddar cheese
  2 cups uncooked instant rice
  2 cups chopped fresh broccoli
  1 small onion, chopped
  1 teaspoon paprika, *divided*
1/2 teaspoon pepper

In a large bowl, combine soups, milk and sour cream. Stir in cheeses, rice, broccoli, onion, 3/4 teaspoon of paprika and pepper. Transfer to a 13-in. x 9-in. x 2-in. baking dish coated with nonstick cooking spray. Sprinkle with remaining paprika. Cover and bake at 350° for 35 minutes. Uncover; bake 5-10 minutes longer or until rice and broccoli are tender.

Yield: 16 servings.

Potluck Rice Pilaf

(pictured above)
Annette Rodgers, Rosston, Arkansas
A tasty alternative to potatoes, this buttery rice is a popular side dish wherever I take it. I especially like its mild soy sauce flavor, flecks of green onion and toasted slivered almonds.

1/2 cup butter, cubed
  4 cups uncooked long grain rice
  2 quarts water
  2 tablespoons chicken bouillon granules
 10 green onions, thinly sliced
2/3 cup soy sauce
  1 cup slivered almonds, toasted

In a Dutch oven, melt butter. Add rice; cook and stir for 3-5 minutes or until lightly browned. Add water and bouillon; bring to a boil. Reduce heat; cover and simmer for 15-20 minutes or until rice is tender and liquid is absorbed. Remove from the heat; stir in the onions and soy sauce. Cover and let stand for 5 minutes. Stir in almonds.

Yield: 20-22 servings.

Potatoes Supreme

(pictured above)
Mrs. Afton Johnson, Sugar City, Idaho
You need only a handful of ingredients for this satisfying crowd-pleaser. Not only is the cheesy dish a family favorite, but it comes together in a jiffy.

> 8 to 10 medium potatoes, peeled and cubed
> 1 can (10-3/4 ounces) condensed cream of chicken soup, undiluted
> 3 cups (12 ounces) shredded cheddar cheese, *divided*
> 1 cup (8 ounces) sour cream
> 3 green onions, chopped
> Salt and pepper to taste

Place potatoes in a saucepan and cover with water. Bring to a boil; cover and cook until almost tender. Drain and cool.

In a large bowl, combine soup, 1-1/2 cups cheese, sour cream, onions, salt and pepper; stir in potatoes.

Place in a greased 13-in. x 9-in. x 2-in. baking dish. Sprinkle with remaining cheese. Bake, uncovered, at 350° for 25-30 minutes or until heated through.
Yield: 8-10 servings.

Sweet Pineapple Casserole

Mary Ann Marino, West Pittsburgh, Pennsylvania
This hot bake has just the right amount of sweetness, so it's a great accompaniment to meaty entrees. Using canned pineapple makes it a snap to assemble.

> 2 eggs, beaten
> 2 cans (20 ounces *each*) unsweetened crushed pineapple

> 1 cup sugar
> 1/4 cup cornstarch
> 1 teaspoon ground cinnamon
> 1 teaspoon butter

In a large bowl, combine eggs and pineapple. In another bowl, combine sugar, cornstarch and cinnamon. Stir in pineapple mixture.

Transfer to a greased 2-qt. baking dish. Dot with butter. Bake, uncovered, at 350° for 1-1/4 hours or until golden brown.
Yield: 10-12 servings.

Four-Fruit Compote

(pictured below)
Donna Long, Searcy, Arkansas
A beautiful side dish, this compote spotlights winter fruit like bananas, apples, oranges and pineapple. Of course, it can be made any time of year. I'm sure you'll get as many smiles as I do when I bring out this refreshing treat.

> 1 can (20 ounces) pineapple chunks
> 1/2 cup sugar
> 2 tablespoons cornstarch
> 1/3 cup orange juice
> 1 tablespoon lemon juice
> 1 can (11 ounces) mandarin oranges, drained
> 3 to 4 unpeeled apples, chopped
> 2 to 3 bananas, sliced

Drain pineapple, reserving 3/4 cup juice. In a large saucepan, combine sugar and cornstarch. Add pineapple juice, orange juice and lemon juice. Cook and stir over medium heat until thickened and bubbly; cook and stir 1 minute longer. Remove from the heat; set aside.

In a large bowl, combine pineapple chunks, oranges, apples and bananas. Pour warm sauce over the fruit; stir gently to coat. Cover and refrigerate.
Yield: 12-16 servings.

Roasted Vegetables

Cathryn White, Newark, Delaware
Parsnips, turnips, pearl onions, brussels sprouts and a few other vegetables make for a wholesome recipe that I enjoy at fall dinners. Garlic, butter, and thyme nicely complement the flavors of this roasted specialty.

  5 cups cubed unpeeled red potatoes
    (about 1-1/2 pounds)
  7 medium carrots, cut into 1/2-inch slices
  4 medium parsnips, peeled and cut into
    1/2-inch slices
  2 medium turnips, peeled and cut into
    1/2-inch cubes
  1 cup fresh *or* frozen pearl onions
  1 medium red onion, cut into 1/2-inch
    wedges and halved
  3 tablespoons butter, melted
  3 tablespoons olive oil
  1 tablespoon dried thyme
  2 teaspoons salt
1/2 teaspoon pepper
2-1/2 cups brussels sprouts, halved
  3 to 4 garlic cloves, quartered

In a roasting pan, combine the first six ingredients. In a small bowl, combine the butter, oil, thyme, salt and pepper. Drizzle over vegetables; toss to coat. Cover and bake at 425° for 30 minutes. Add brussels sprouts and garlic. Bake, uncovered, for 30-45 minutes or until vegetables are tender, stirring frequently.

Yield: 20 servings.

Caraway Red Cabbage

Rosemarie Kondrk, Old Bridge, New Jersey
My family just adores this fresh-tasting take on red cabbage. It's ideal when the menu includes slices of warm rye bread. Not only is it quick, but it's healthy, too.

1/2 cup chopped onion
  1 tablespoon butter
1/2 cup water
  4 teaspoons white vinegar
3/4 teaspoon caraway seeds
1/2 teaspoon salt
  9 cups shredded red cabbage
Sugar substitute equivalent to 4 teaspoons sugar

In a large saucepan, saute onion in butter until tender. Add water, vinegar, caraway seeds, salt and cabbage. Cover and simmer for 30 minutes, stirring occasionally. Stir in sugar substitute.

Yield: 10 servings.

Editor's Note: This recipe was tested with Splenda No Calorie Sweetener.

Grilled Veggie Mix

(pictured above)
Janet Boulger, Botwood, Newfoundland
This tempting veggie combo is a mouth-watering addition to barbecued fare. To make the recipe even more satisfying, I use my homegrown vegetables and herbs in the mix.

  2 medium zucchini, cut into 1/2-inch slices
  1 large green pepper, cut into
    1/2-inch squares
  1 large sweet red pepper, cut into
    1/2-inch squares
  1 pound fresh mushrooms, halved
  1 large onion, cubed
  6 medium carrots, cut into 1/4-inch slices
  2 cups fresh broccoli florets
  2 cups fresh cauliflowerets
DRESSING:
1/4 cup olive oil
1/4 cup butter, melted
1/4 cup minced fresh parsley
  2 garlic cloves, minced
  1 teaspoon dried basil
1/2 teaspoon dried oregano
1/2 teaspoon salt

Place vegetables in the center of two pieces of double-layered heavy-duty foil (about 18 in. square). Combine dressing ingredients; drizzle over vegetables; toss gently to coat.

Fold foil around mixture and seal tightly. Grill, covered, over medium heat for 30 minutes or until vegetables are tender, turning once.

Yield: 10 servings.

Corn Bread Casserole

(pictured below)
Margaret Mayes, La Mesa, California
We live very close to the Mexican border, so recipes featuring corn and green chilies are popular here. This dish has always been a hit whenever I've taken it to a carry-in dinner.

  2 packages (8-1/2 ounces *each*) corn bread muffin mix
  1 can (15-1/4 ounces) whole kernel corn, drained
  1 can (14-3/4 ounces) cream-style corn
  1 can (4 ounces) chopped green chilies, drained
  1 cup (4 ounces) shredded Monterey Jack cheese

Prepare corn bread mixes according to package directions. Pour half of the batter into a greased 11-in. x 7-in. x 2-in. baking pan. Combine corn and creamed corn; spread over batter. Top with chilies and cheese. Carefully spread with remaining corn bread batter.

Bake, uncovered, at 375° for 25-30 minutes or until a toothpick comes out clean. Serve warm.
Yield: 12 servings.

Spinach Noodle Casserole

Doris Tschorn, Levittown, New York
We enjoyed a similar casserole at a friend's house many years ago. She didn't have a recipe but told me the basic ingredients. I eventually came up with my own version and have shared my secrets many times since. Take a copy of the recipe with you when attending a group supper.

  4 cups uncooked egg noodles
1/4 cup butter, cubed
1/4 cup all-purpose flour
  1 teaspoon salt
1/8 teaspoon pepper
  2 cups milk
  2 packages (10 ounces *each*) frozen chopped spinach, thawed and drained
  2 cups (8 ounces) shredded Swiss cheese
  2 cups (8 ounces) shredded part-skim mozzarella cheese
1/4 cup grated Parmesan cheese
Paprika, optional

Cook noodles according to package directions; drain and rinse in cold water.

Meanwhile, in a large saucepan, melt butter over medium heat. Stir in flour, salt and pepper until smooth. Gradually add milk. Bring to a boil; cook and stir for 2 minutes or until thickened.

Arrange half of the noodles in an ungreased 11-in. x 7-in. x 2-in. baking dish; cover with half of the spinach and half of the Swiss cheese. Spread with half of the white sauce. Repeat layers.

Top with mozzarella and Parmesan cheeses. Sprinkle with paprika if desired.

Cover casserole and bake at 350° for 20 minutes. Uncover; bake 20 minutes longer. Let stand for 15 minutes before cutting.
Yield: 12-14 servings.

Potluck Pointer

When organizing a buffet, most folks stack the plates, eating utensils and napkins at the front of the table. Moving the silverware and napkins to the end of the buffet, however, frees up guests' hands since they only have to balance their plates as they work their way through the line.

Cukes and Carrots

(pictured above)
Karla Hecht, Plymouth, Minnesota
Carrots and green peppers bring extra color and crunch to this garden-fresh cucumber salad. The sweet dressing is a lovely match for the crisp summer produce.

    5 medium cucumbers, thinly sliced
    4 medium carrots, thinly sliced
    1 medium onion, halved and thinly sliced
    1 small green pepper, chopped
    2 teaspoons canning salt
1-1/2 cups sugar
  1/2 cup white vinegar

In a bowl, combine cucumbers, carrots, onion and green pepper. Sprinkle with salt; toss to coat. Cover and refrigerate for 2 hours. Combine sugar and vinegar; pour over vegetables. Cover and refrigerate for at least 1 hour. Serve with a slotted spoon.
Yield: 12 servings.

Sausage Mushroom Dressing

Mary Coleman, Norwood, Massachusetts
Perfect for a large cold-weather or holiday buffet, this dressing is yummy with poultry. Each time I serve it, guests almost pass over the main course in favor of the hearty dressing.

    6 bacon strips, diced
    1 pound fresh mushrooms, sliced
    1 large onion, chopped
    2 celery ribs, chopped
    2 to 3 garlic cloves, minced
  1/2 cup butter, cubed
    1 teaspoon rubbed sage
  1/2 teaspoon salt
  1/4 teaspoon pepper
  28 cups day-old bread cubes (about 3 pounds sliced bread)
    1 pound bulk pork sausage, cooked and drained
2-1/4 to 2-1/2 cups chicken broth

In a large skillet, cook bacon until crisp. Remove to paper towels to drain. Reserve 2 tablespoons drippings. Saute the mushrooms, onion, celery and garlic in the drippings and butter until tender. Stir in the sage, salt and pepper.

    In several large bowls, combine the mushroom mixture, bread cubes, sausage, broth and bacon; toss to coat.

    Transfer to two greased 13-in. x 9-in. x 2-in. baking dishes. Cover and bake at 350° for 45 minutes. Bake, uncovered, 10-15 minutes longer or until lightly browned.
Yield: 2 casseroles (12-16 servings each).

2 cups (8 ounces) shredded cheddar cheese
8 ounces process cheese (Velveeta), sliced
3/4 cup half-and-half cream
3/4 cup seasoned bread crumbs
1/4 cup butter
1/2 cup grated Parmesan cheese

Place broccoli and cauliflower in a steamer basket. Place in a saucepan over 1 in. of water; bring to a boil. Cover and steam for 5-8 minutes or until crisp-tender. Rinse in cold water; drain and set aside. Repeat with carrots and onion, steaming for 4-5 minutes or until tender.

Place vegetables in a bowl; add garlic powder, Italian seasoning, salt and pepper. Stir in macaroni. Spoon half of mixture into a greased 3-qt. baking dish. Sprinkle with half of the mozzarella, cheddar and process cheeses. Repeat layers.

Pour cream over the top. Sprinkle with bread crumbs; dot with butter. Top with Parmesan cheese. Bake, uncovered, at 350° for 30-40 minutes or until bubbly.

Yield: 12-14 servings.

Cheesy Vegetable Medley

(pictured above)
Mary Ulrick, Baconton, Georgia
Can't decide whether to contribute a side dish of vegetables or pasta? Combine them with this medley. It received rave reviews at our volunteer fire department meeting.

3 cups broccoli florets
3 cups cauliflowerets
2 cups julienned carrots
1 small onion, diced
1/2 teaspoon garlic powder
1/2 teaspoon Italian seasoning
1/8 teaspoon salt
1/8 teaspoon pepper
8 ounces elbow macaroni, cooked and drained
2 cups (8 ounces) shredded part-skim mozzarella cheese

Walnut Broccoli Bake

Carolyn Bosetti, LaSalle, Ontario
A friend shared this simple recipe with me years ago and it instantly became a mainstay at my house. When I make it for potluck luncheons, there are no leftovers.

3 packages (10 ounces *each*) frozen chopped broccoli
1/2 cup butter, *divided*
1/4 cup all-purpose flour
4-1/2 teaspoons chicken bouillon granules
2 cups milk
1/2 cup water
4 cups seasoned stuffing croutons
1/2 cup chopped walnuts

Cook broccoli according to package directions; drain and transfer to a greased 3-qt. baking dish. Meanwhile, in a large saucepan, melt 1/4 cup butter. Stir in flour and bouillon. Gradually add milk. Bring to a boil. Reduce heat; cook and stir for 2 minutes or until thickened and bubbly. Pour over broccoli.

In a large saucepan, melt the remaining butter. Add the water, stuffing and walnuts; mix well. Spoon over the broccoli. Bake, uncovered, at 375° for 20-25 minutes or until stuffing is lightly browned.

Yield: 12 servings.

Potluck Pointer

The next time you have to grate a large block of cheese for a church supper specialty, spritz the grater with nonstick cooking spray before you begin. Not only will this help the cheese grate with ease, but you'll find that cleanup is an absolute snap.

Colorful Vegetable Bake

(pictured below)
Betty Brown, Buckley, Washington
My sister gave me the recipe for this side dish years ago, and it's become a staple in our household. Bursting with veggies, it's delicious and feeds a crowd.

    3 cups frozen cut green beans, thawed
      and drained
    2 medium green peppers, chopped
    6 plum tomatoes, chopped and seeded
    2 to 3 cups (8 to 12 ounces) shredded
      cheddar cheese
    3 cups chopped zucchini
    1 cup biscuit/baking mix
  1/2 teaspoon salt
  1/2 teaspoon cayenne pepper
    6 eggs
    1 cup milk

Place beans and peppers in a greased 13-in. x 9-in. x 2-in. baking dish. Top with tomatoes, cheese and zucchini. In a bowl, combine the biscuit mix, salt, cayenne, eggs and milk just until moistened. Pour over the vegetables.

Bake, uncovered, at 350° for 55-60 minutes or until puffed and a knife inserted near the center comes out clean. Let stand for 10 minutes before serving.

Yield: 12 servings.

Hearty Baked Potato Salad

Mary Bengtson-Almquist, Petersburg, Illinois
This warm potato salad is a standout at picnics and other get-togethers. It's great at barbecues or even at large dinner parties.

    8 medium red potatoes, peeled and cut
      into 1-inch chunks
  1/2 cup onion, chopped
    2 tablespoons minced fresh parsley
    1 can (10-3/4 ounces) condensed cheddar
      cheese soup, undiluted
  1/2 cup mayonnaise
  1/2 cup plain yogurt
    4 ounces bacon, cooked, drained and
      crumbled
Paprika

Place potatoes in a large saucepan and cover with water. Bring to a boil. Reduce heat; cover and cook for 15-20 minutes or until tender. Drain.

Spread potatoes evenly over bottom of 13-in. x 9-in. x 2-in. baking pan. Combine onions, parsley, soup, mayonnaise and yogurt; pour over potatoes. Sprinkle with cooked bacon and paprika.

Cover with aluminum foil and bake at 350° for 30 minutes. Uncover; bake 30 minutes longer.

Yield: 10-12 servings.

Loaded Baked Potato Salad

(pictured below)
Jackie Deckard, Solsberry, Indiana
I revamped my mother's potato salad recipe to taste more like baked potatoes with all the fixings I love. When taking it to an event, simply store the creamy dressing separately and combine it with the warm side dish on-site.

        5 pounds small unpeeled red potatoes,
           cubed
        1 teaspoon salt
      1/2 teaspoon pepper
        8 hard-cooked eggs, chopped
        1 pound sliced bacon, cooked and crumbled
        2 cups (8 ounces) shredded cheddar cheese
        1 sweet onion, chopped
        3 dill pickles, chopped
    1-1/2 cups (12 ounces) sour cream
        1 cup mayonnaise
        2 to 3 teaspoons prepared mustard

Place the potatoes in a greased 15-in. x 10-in. x 1-in. baking pan; sprinkle with salt and pepper. Bake, uncovered, at 425° for 40-45 minutes or until tender. Cool in pan on a wire rack.

In a large bowl, combine the potatoes, eggs, bacon, cheese, onion and pickles. In a small bowl, combine the sour cream, mayonnaise and mustard; pour over the potato mixture and toss to coat.

Yield: 20 servings.

Cheesy Zucchini Rice Casserole

(pictured above)
Judy Hudson, Santa Rosa, California
A college roommate gave me this heartwarming recipe a number of years ago, and it still goes over well at potluck dinners today.

        1 cup uncooked long grain rice
        3 medium zucchini, cut into 1/8-inch slices
        1 can (4 ounces) chopped green chilies
        4 cups (16 ounces) shredded Monterey Jack
           cheese, *divided*
        2 cups (16 ounces) sour cream
        2 tablespoons chopped green pepper
        2 tablespoons chopped onion
        1 tablespoon minced fresh parsley
        1 teaspoon salt
        1 teaspoon dried oregano
        1 large tomato, sliced

Cook rice according to package directions. In a saucepan, cook zucchini in 1 in. of water until crisp-tender; drain and set aside. Place rice in a greased shallow 3-qt. baking dish. Layer with chilies and 1-1/2 cups cheese. In a bowl, combine the sour cream, green pepper, onion, parsley, salt and oregano. Spread over cheese. Layer with zucchini and tomato. Sprinkle with remaining cheese.

Cover and bake at 350° for 30 minutes. Uncover; bake 5-10 minutes longer or until heated through and cheese is melted.

Yield: 12 servings.

Thyme Green Beans With Almonds

(pictured below)
Kenna Baber, Rochester, Minnesota
Thyme helps create a nice take on a classic green bean side dish. It's a snap for weeknight meals, yet special enough to take to carry-in suppers.

> 2 pounds fresh green beans, trimmed
> 2 tablespoons butter
> 1 tablespoon minced fresh thyme *or*
>   1 teaspoon dried thyme
> 1/2 teaspoon salt
> 1/2 teaspoon pepper
> 1/3 cup slivered almonds, toasted

Place beans in a steamer basket. Place in a large saucepan over 1 in. of water; bring to a boil. Cover and steam 10-12 minutes or until crisp-tender.

In a large skillet, melt butter; add the beans, thyme, salt and pepper. Cook and stir for 5 minutes or until heated through. Sprinkle with almonds.

Yield: 8 servings.

Cabbage Au Gratin

Linda Funderburke, Brockport, New York
I think this recipe is the perfect example of "Mom's Sunday Best." It was a favorite with me and my 10 brothers and sisters. We thought Mom was the world's best cook and she always outdid herself on Sundays!

> 1 medium head cabbage, shredded
>   (about 8 cups)
> 1 can (10-3/4 ounces) condensed cream
>   of celery soup, undiluted
> 2 tablespoons milk
> 1 cup shredded process cheese (Velveeta)
> 1 cup soft bread crumbs
> 1 tablespoon butter

In a large covered saucepan, cook cabbage in boiling salted water for 5 minutes; drain. Place in a greased 8-in. square baking dish.

In a small saucepan, blend soup and milk; heat well. Add cheese and stir until melted. Pour over cabbage. Saute bread crumbs in butter until golden; sprinkle over cabbage. Bake at 350° for 15-20 minutes or until hot.

Yield: 8-10 servings.

Patchwork Rice Pilaf

(pictured above)
Brenda Scarbeary, Oelwin, Iowa
Very versatile, this side dish always disappears quickly at potlucks, picnics and shared dinners. The apples bring a subtle sweetness to the rice, so the pilaf goes well with a variety of entrees.

    4 celery ribs, chopped
    2 large onions, chopped
    4 medium carrots, chopped
    1 large green pepper, chopped
  1/4 cup butter, cubed
    2 medium tart red apples, chopped
    2 cups sliced fresh mushrooms
    2 packages (6.2 ounces *each*) fast-cooking long grain and wild rice mix
    2 cans (10-1/2 ounces *each*) condensed chicken broth, undiluted
1-1/2 cups water
  1/2 cup slivered almonds

In a large skillet or saucepan, saute the celery, onions, carrots and green pepper in butter until crisp-tender. Add the apples and mushrooms; saute for 2 minutes. Stir in the rice, contents of seasoning packets, broth and water; bring to a boil. Reduce heat; cover and simmer according to rice package directions or until rice is tender and liquid is absorbed. Sprinkle with almonds.
Yield: 12 servings.

Church Supper Potatoes

(pictured below)
Michelle Grigsby, Beavercreek, Ohio
As a pastor's wife, I cook for crowds often. These potatoes are always popular. My own family thinks the spuds are a must with grilled chicken breast.

    3 pounds russet potatoes (about 9 medium), peeled and cut into 1/2-inch cubes
    2 garlic cloves, peeled
    2 packages (3 ounces *each*) cream cheese, softened
    2 tablespoons butter
  1/2 cup sour cream
    2 cups (8 ounces) shredded cheddar cheese, *divided*
    1 teaspoon garlic salt
    1 teaspoon onion salt
    1 package (10 ounces) frozen chopped spinach, thawed and squeezed dry

Place the potatoes and garlic in a large saucepan; cover with water. Cover and bring to a boil; cook for 20-25 minutes or until very tender. Drain well.

In a mixing bowl, mash potatoes and garlic with the cream cheese and butter. Add sour cream, 1 cup of cheddar cheese, garlic salt, onion salt and spinach. Stir just until mixed. Spread into a greased 2-qt. baking dish.

Bake, uncovered, at 350° for 30-35 minutes or until heated through. Top with remaining cheese; bake 5 minutes longer or until cheese is melted.
Yield: 10-12 servings.

Pictured below:
Church Supper Spaghetti (p. 140).

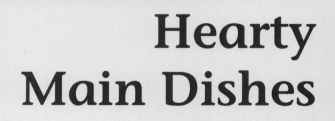

Hearty
Main Dishes

Oven-Barbecue Spareribs

(pictured above)
Lynn Gaston, Selma, Alabama
Folks will go back for seconds once they get a bite of these mildly tangy ribs. That's okay, because the recipe makes a big crowd-pleasing batch. Expect compliments but not any leftovers!

    10 pounds pork spareribs, cut into
        serving-size pieces
     2 large onions, chopped
     1 cup finely chopped celery
     2 cups ketchup
     1 cup apple juice
     1 cup water
    1/2 cup lemon juice
    1/4 cup brown sugar
    1/4 cup ground mustard
    1/4 cup cider vinegar
    1/4 cup Worcestershire sauce
     2 tablespoons paprika
     2 tablespoons prepared horseradish
    1/4 to 1/2 teaspoon cayenne pepper

Place ribs in a single layer in a large baking pans. Bake, uncovered, at 350° for 30 minutes. Drain, reserving 1/4 cup drippings. Turn ribs. Bake 30 minutes longer. Meanwhile, in a saucepan, saute onions and celery in reserved drippings until tender. Stir in the remaining ingredients; bring to a boil.

Drain ribs; pour sauce over ribs. Cover and bake for 15 minutes; turn ribs and baste. Bake 15 minutes longer or until tender.
Yield: 12 servings.

Beef and Pepper Medley

(pictured below)
Dean Schrock, Jacksonville, Florida
For a meaty dish that packs as much a visual punch as it does flavor, try this entree salad. The zesty dressing really marries the flavors of the colorful peppers and warm, tender slices of roasted beef.

     2 tablespoons garlic powder
     2 tablespoons cracked black pepper
     1 eye of round beef roast (about 4 pounds)
     2 large green peppers, julienned
     2 large sweet red peppers, julienned
     2 large sweet onions, cut into thin wedges

DRESSING:
    2/3 teaspoon olive oil
    1/2 cup red wine vinegar
     2 tablespoons Dijon mustard
     2 garlic cloves, minced
    1/2 teaspoon crushed red pepper flakes
    1/2 teaspoon salt

Combine garlic powder and pepper; rub over all sides of roast. Place on a rack in a shallow roasting pan. Preheat oven to 500°.

Place roast in oven and reduce heat to 350°. Bake for 1-1/2 to 2 hours or until meat reaches desired doneness. Chill for 30-40 minutes or until meat is cool enough to handle.

Cut into 3-in. x 1/4-in. x 1/4-in. strips. Place in a large salad bowl; add peppers and onions.

In a jar with tight-fitting lid, combine dressing ingredients; cover and shake well. Pour over salad; toss to coat. Cover and refrigerate overnight. Serve cold.
Yield: 10-12 servings.

Macaroni Chicken Dinner

Zetta Harberts, Beattie, Kansas
You need only about 10 minutes to assemble this potluck staple. It's excellent with hot rolls, mixed fruit and many other items found on a buffet, but my family considers it a complete dinner all by itself!

      2 cans (10-3/4 ounces *each*) condensed
         cream of mushroom soup, undiluted
      1 cup chicken broth
      1 cup milk
    1/2 cup half-and-half cream
  2-1/2 cups cubed cooked chicken
      2 cups uncooked elbow macaroni
      2 cups (8 ounces) shredded cheddar cheese
      2 celery ribs, diced
      4 hard-cooked eggs, chopped
    3/4 cup dry bread crumbs
      2 tablespoons butter, melted

In a large bowl, combine the soup, broth, milk and cream. Stir in the chicken, macaroni, cheese, celery and eggs. Transfer to a greased 3-qt. baking dish.

   Cover and bake at 350° for 30 minutes. Combine bread crumbs and butter; sprinkle over top. Bake, uncovered, 15-20 minutes longer or until macaroni is tender. Let stand for 5 minutes before serving.

Yield: 10-12 servings.

Marinated Turkey Slices

Shavon Hoopes, Vernal, Utah
We love to entertain and found that this summer recipe makes enough for large get-togethers. Marinated and grilled to perfection, the moist turkey breasts are always popular...no matter who we prepare them for.

    1/2 cup soy sauce
    1/2 cup vegetable oil
    1/2 teaspoon prepared horseradish
    1/4 teaspoon garlic powder
      1 cup lemon-lime soda
      3 pounds boneless skinless turkey breast
         halves, cut into 1/4-inch slices

In a blender, combine soy sauce, oil, horseradish and garlic powder; cover and blend on high until smooth. Add soda, cover and blend on high until smooth.

   Pour into several large resealable plastic bags. Add turkey; toss gently to coat. Cover and refrigerate overnight, turning once.

   Drain and discard marinade. Grill turkey, covered, over medium-hot heat for 5-6 minutes or until juices run clear, turning occasionally.

Yield: 12 servings.

Glazed Ham Balls

(pictured above)
Mary Ann Marino, West Pittsburgh, Pennsylvania
My family prefers these to a traditional roasted ham. It seems they gobble them up as soon as I set them out. You can make them ahead and reheat them the next day.

      2 eggs
  1-1/2 cups crushed saltines (about 45 crackers)
      2 pounds ground fully cooked ham
      1 pound ground pork
      2 cups packed brown sugar
      6 tablespoons cider vinegar
      2 teaspoons ground mustard

In a large bowl, combine the eggs and cracker crumbs. Crumble ham and pork over mixture and mix well.

   Shape into 1-1/2-in. balls. Place into two greased 15-in. x 10-in. x 1-in. baking pans. Bake, uncovered, at 350° for 40 minutes or until lightly browned.

   Meanwhile, in a large saucepan, combine the brown sugar, vinegar and mustard. Bring to a boil; cook and stir for 2 minutes or until thickened.

   Drain the ham balls; drizzle with the syrup mixture. Toss to coat. Bake 10 minutes longer or until glazed.

Yield: 4 dozen.

Parmesan Herb Chicken

(pictured above)
Phyllis Joann Schmalz, Kansas City, Kansas
With a golden Parmesan cheese and herb coating, these tender chicken breasts make a tempting and hearty main dish. They're really very little fuss. Just coat them and bake. Their classic flavor suits a wide variety of tastes.

      2 cups grated Parmesan cheese
    1/4 cup minced fresh parsley
      2 tablespoons dried oregano
      2 teaspoons paprika
      1 teaspoon salt
      1 teaspoon pepper
     12 bone-in chicken breast halves
      1 cup butter, melted

In a shallow dish, combine the first six ingredients. Dip chicken in butter, then coat with Parmesan mixture. Place in two greased 15-in. x 10-in. x 1-in. baking pans. Bake, uncovered, at 350° for 40-45 minutes or until the juices run clear.
Yield: 12 servings.

Old-World Kielbasa

Ethel Harrison, North Fort Myers, Florida
Cabbage, stewed tomatoes and caraway seeds turn sliced kielbasa into a traditional dinner that people happily revisit. Best of all, it comes together in one pot!

      1 medium onion, sliced
      2 tablespoons butter
      8 cups shredded cabbage
      1 pound smoked kielbasa, cut into 1/2-inch
         slices
      1 can (14-1/2 ounces) stewed tomatoes
    1/2 cup water
      4 teaspoons caraway seeds
      1 teaspoon paprika

In a Dutch oven, saute onion in butter. Add remaining ingredients; bring to a boil. Reduce heat; cover and simmer for 30 minutes or until cabbage is tender. Serve with a slotted spoon.
Yield: 10 servings.

Mom's Portable Beef

(pictured below)
Lorene Sinclair, Belleville, Ontario
This delicious beef makes great sandwiches for a potluck, picnic or even a camping trip. The dish has a tempting from-scratch flavor that beats cold cuts anytime.

      1 can (14-1/2 ounces) beef broth
      1 medium onion, chopped
      1 cup cider vinegar
      2 tablespoons minced fresh parsley
      1 bay leaf
      1 tablespoon mixed pickling spices
    1/2 teaspoon dried marjoram
    1/2 teaspoon dried savory
    1/2 teaspoon salt
    1/4 teaspoon pepper
      1 beef eye round roast (3 pounds)
     12 to 14 sandwich rolls, split
   Lettuce, tomato and onion, optional

In a Dutch oven, combine the first 10 ingredients; add roast. Cover and bake at 325° for 1-1/2 hours or until meat is tender. Remove the roast and cool completely.

Meanwhile, skim fat and strain cooking juices. Discard bay leaf. Thinly slice the beef. Serve on rolls with warmed juices and lettuce, tomato and onion if desired.
Yield: 12-14 servings.

Bacon Cheeseburger Balls

(pictured above)

Cathy Lendvoy, Boharm, Saskatchewan

When I set these on a buffet table, people are often fooled into thinking they're about to have plain meatballs, until they bite into the crispy coating and the flavorful filling of bacon and cheese.

1 egg
1 envelope onion soup mix
1 pound ground beef
2 tablespoons all-purpose flour
2 tablespoons milk
1 cup (4 ounces) finely shredded cheddar cheese
4 bacon strips, cooked and crumbled

COATING:

2 eggs
1 cup crushed saltines (about 30 crackers)
5 tablespoons vegetable oil

In a bowl, combine egg and soup mix. Crumble beef over mixture and mix well. Divide into 36 portions; set aside. In a bowl, combine the flour and milk until smooth. Add cheese and bacon; mix well. Shape cheese mixture into 36 balls. Shape one beef portion around each cheese ball. In a shallow bowl, beat the eggs. Place cracker crumbs in another bowl. Dip meatballs into egg, then coat with crumbs. In a large skillet over medium heat, cook meatballs in oil for 10-12 minutes or until the meat is no longer pink and coating is golden brown.

Yield: 3 dozen.

Vegetable Ham Stew

Shannon Smith, Mt. Horeb, Wisconsin

I created this thick, heartwarming stew one evening while trying to use up leftover ham. Featuring cabbage, tomatoes, carrots and celery, it became a fast favorite with everyone who tried it.

4 cups water
2 cans (14-1/2 ounces *each*) diced tomatoes, undrained
3 cups shredded cabbage
2 cups diced fully cooked lean ham
3 large carrots, cut into 1-inch pieces
1-1/2 cups chopped celery
3/4 cup chopped onion
1/2 cup chopped green pepper
1 tablespoon sugar
2 teaspoons dried basil
1/2 teaspoon pepper
1/4 teaspoon garlic powder
2 bay leaves
1/4 cup cornstarch
1/4 cup cold water

In a Dutch oven or soup kettle, combine the first 13 ingredients; bring to a boil. Reduce heat; cover and simmer for 1-1/4 hours or until cabbage is tender, stirring occasionally.

Combine cornstarch and cold water until smooth; stir into stew. Bring to a boil; cook and stir for 2 minutes or until thickened. Discard bay leaves before serving.

Yield: 11 servings (2-3/4 quarts).

Shrimp Puffs

(pictured above)
Maudry Ramsey, Sulphur, Louisiana
Shrimp and rice are two foods that are abundant in our area. These shrimp puffs are my family's favorite. In fact, they prefer them to fried shrimp.

2	eggs, *separated*
3/4	cup milk
1	tablespoon vegetable oil
1	cup all-purpose flour
1-1/2	teaspoons baking powder
1-1/2	teaspoons onion powder
1	teaspoon salt
1/2	teaspoon pepper
3	cups cooked rice
1	pound uncooked shrimp, peeled, deveined and chopped *or* 2 cans (4-1/2 ounces *each*) small shrimp, drained
1/4	cup minced fresh parsley
1/2	teaspoon hot pepper sauce

Oil for deep-fat frying

In a large bowl, beat egg yolks, milk and oil. Combine flour, baking powder, onion powder, salt and pepper; add to yolk mixture and mix well. Stir in rice, shrimp, parsley and hot pepper sauce. In a mixing bowl, beat the egg whites until soft peaks form; fold into shrimp mixture. In an electric skillet or deep-fat fryer, heat oil to 350°. Drop batter by tablespoons into hot oil. Fry puffs, a few at a time, for 1-1/2 minutes on each side or until browned and puffy. Drain on paper towels. Serve warm.

Yield: about 4 dozen.

Peppered Rib Roast

(pictured below)
Mary Welch, Sturgeon Bay, Wisconsin
A co-worker shared this restaurant recipe with me when I lived in Minneapolis in the 1970s. The marinade tenderizes the meat, and the drippings make a savory sauce to accompany the beef slices.

1/4	cup coarsely ground pepper
1/2	teaspoon ground cardamom
1	boneless beef rib eye roast (5 to 6 pounds)
1	cup soy sauce
3/4	cup red wine vinegar *or* cider vinegar
1	tablespoon tomato paste
1	teaspoon paprika
1/2	teaspoon garlic powder
1-1/2	teaspoons cornstarch
1/4	cup cold water

Combine the pepper and cardamom; rub over roast. In a gallon-size resealable plastic bag, combine the soy sauce, vinegar, tomato paste, paprika and garlic powder; add the roast. Seal bag and turn to coat; refrigerate overnight.

Drain and discard marinade. Place roast on a rack in a shallow roasting pan. Cover and bake at 350° for 2 to 2-3/4 hours or until meat reaches desired doneness (for medium-rare, a meat thermometer should read 145°; medium, 160°; well-done, 170°). Let stand for 20 minutes before carving.

Meanwhile, for gravy, pour the pan drippings and loosened brown bits into a saucepan; skim fat. Combine cornstarch and cold water until smooth; gradually stir into the drippings. Bring to a boil; cook and stir for 2 minutes or until thickened. Serve with the roast.

Yield: 16-18 servings.

Barbecued Pork Potpie

Joan East, Leawood, Kansas
I cook a roast the day before—or use leftover pork—when I prepare this hearty casserole. A lattice topping made from refrigerated corn bread twists gives it a lovely look.

- 1 cup chopped onion
- 3/4 cup finely chopped celery
- 1 cup chopped sweet red pepper
- 1 large Anaheim pepper, seeded and chopped
- 2 garlic cloves, minced
- 1 tablespoon canola oil
- 1 teaspoon ground cumin
- 1 teaspoon ground coriander
- 1/4 cup white wine vinegar
- 1 can (14-1/2 ounces) reduced-sodium chicken broth
- 1 bottle (12 ounces) chili sauce
- 3 tablespoons brown sugar
- 1 square (1 ounce) unsweetened chocolate, grated
- 1 tablespoon Worcestershire sauce
- 2 tablespoons cornstarch
- 6 cups cubed cooked pork loin roast (2 pounds)
- 1 tube (11-1/2 ounces) refrigerated corn bread twists

In a large nonstick skillet, saute the onion, celery, peppers and garlic in oil until tender. Add cumin and coriander; cook and stir over medium heat for 2 minutes. Add vinegar and cook for 2 minutes.

Set aside 1/2 cup broth. Add the chili sauce, brown sugar, chocolate, Worcestershire sauce and remaining broth to vegetable mixture. Bring to a boil. Reduce heat; simmer, uncovered, for 10-15 minutes, stirring occasionally.

Combine cornstarch and reserved broth until smooth; stir into vegetable mixture. Bring to a boil; cook and stir for 1-2 minutes or until slightly thickened. Stir in pork. Transfer to a 13-in. x 9-in. x 2-in. baking dish coated with nonstick cooking spray.

Roll out corn bread dough and cut into strips; twist and place over filling in a lattice design. Bake, uncovered, at 375° for 10-15 minutes or until golden brown. Let stand for 15 minutes before serving.

Yield: 12 servings.

Editor's Note: When cutting or seeding hot peppers, use rubber or plastic gloves to protect your hands. Avoid touching your face.

Make-Ahead Burritos

(pictured above)
Jennifer Shafer, Durham, North Carolina
Because they're wrapped individually and frozen, you can heat up as many of these comforting burritos as you like. Make a double batch and keep them on hand for last-minute potluck contributions or for speedy meals at home.

- 3 cups shredded cooked chicken *or* beef
- 1 jar (16 ounces) salsa
- 1 can (16 ounces) refried beans
- 1 can (4 ounces) chopped green chilies, drained
- 1 envelope burrito seasoning
- 1/2 cup water
- 16 flour tortillas (8 inches), warmed
- 16 ounces Monterey Jack cheese, cut into 5-inch x 1/2-inch strips

In a large skillet or saucepan, combine meat, salsa, beans, chilies, seasoning and water. Bring to a boil. Reduce heat; simmer, uncovered, for 5 minutes or until heated through.

Spoon about 1/3 cup off-center on each tortilla; top with a cheese strip. Fold edge of tortilla nearest filling over to cover. Fold ends of tortilla over filling and roll up. Wrap individually in aluminum foil. Freeze for up to 2 months.

Yield: 16 burritos.

Mexican Lasagna

(pictured below)
Rose Ann Buhle, Minooka, Illinois
This crowd-pleasing recipe is a keeper. Featuring the south-western tastes people love, the cheesy, layered dish is well-received everywhere I take it.

2 pounds ground beef
1 can (16 ounces) refried beans
1 can (4 ounces) chopped green chilies
1 envelope taco seasoning
2 tablespoons hot salsa
12 ounces uncooked lasagna noodles
4 cups (16 ounces) shredded Colby-
    Monterey Jack cheese, *divided*
1 jar (16 ounces) mild salsa
2 cups water
2 cups (16 ounces) sour cream
1 can (2-1/4 ounces) sliced ripe olives,
    drained
3 green onions, chopped

In a large skillet, cook beef over medium heat until no longer pink; drain. Stir in the beans, chilies, taco seasoning and hot salsa.

In a greased 13-in. x 9-in. x 2-in. baking dish, layer a third of the noodles and meat mixture. Sprinkle with 1 cup of cheese. Repeat layers twice.

Combine mild salsa and water; pour over top. Cover and bake at 350° for 1 hour or until heated through. Top with sour cream, olives, onions and remaining cheese. Bake, uncovered, 5 minutes longer. Let stand 10-15 minutes before cutting.
Yield: 12 servings.

Roast Beef with Onion Au Jus

(pictured below)
Dawn Hembd, Whitehall, Wisconsin
We served this delicious main course to guests after our wedding. Reheated in an electric roaster or slow cooker, it's perfect for carry-in dinners and large get-togethers. You can even serve slices of the tender beef on rolls if you like.

>   2   beef eye round roasts (about 3 pounds *each*)
>   8   garlic cloves, peeled
> 1/4   cup vegetable oil
>   1   envelope onion soup mix
>   2   cups water
> Additional water *or* beef broth
>   1   envelope au jus gravy mix

With a sharp knife, make four slits in the top of each roast and insert garlic cloves into slits. In a Dutch oven over medium-high heat, brown roast on all sides in oil; drain. Rub soup mix over meat. Add water; cover and bake at 325° for 2-1/2 to 3 hours or until tender. Remove meat from cooking liquid; cool meat. Cover and refrigerate overnight. Skim fat from cooking liquid; refrigerate in a covered container.

Slice beef 1/4 in. thick, set aside. Pour cooking liquid into a large measuring cup. If needed, add enough water or beef broth to measure 3 cups.

In a Dutch oven, combine au jus mix and reserved cooking liquid until smooth. Cook and stir over medium heat until mixture comes to a boil. Reduce heat; add sliced beef and reheat on low for 15-20 minutes.

Yield: 18-20 servings.

One-Dish Pork Chop Dinner

(pictured above)
Pat Waymire, Yellow Springs, Ohio
This is a meaty main dish for any affair. Apple juice gives the chops a wonderful flavor, and the cabbage isn't particularly strong so it appeals to a wide variety of tastes.

> 1/3   cup all-purpose flour
>   8   boneless pork loin chops (1/2 inch thick)
> 1/4   cup butter, cubed
> Salt and pepper to taste
>   2   cups apple juice, *divided*
>   2   pounds small red potatoes
>   1   pound *or* 1 jar (16 ounces) small whole onions, drained
>   1   pound carrots, peeled and cut into 3-inch pieces
>   6   to 8 cups shredded cabbage

Place flour in a large resealable plastic bag. Add pork, a few pieces at a time. Seal and toss to coat, reserving remaining flour; set aside.

In a large Dutch oven, melt butter over medium-high heat. Brown chops on both sides. Season with salt and pepper if desired. Remove chops; keep warm and set aside.

Stir reserved flour into pan; cook and stir until a paste forms. Gradually whisk in 1-1/2 cups apple juice; blend until smooth.

Return chops to Dutch oven; cover and bake at 350° for 30 minutes. Add potatoes, onions, carrots and remaining apple juice. Cover and bake 30 minutes longer. Top with cabbage; cover and bake for 1 to 1-1/2 hours or until the pork chops are tender, basting occasionally with juices.

Yield: 8 servings.

Shepherd's Bean Pie

(pictured below)
Karen Cleveland, Spring Valley, Minnesota
This comforting entree is a variation on the traditional English pie. It features cubed ham, fresh green and wax beans, carrots and a handful of crunchy almonds in a creamy Swiss cheese sauce. Topped with mashed potatoes, it's a satisfying dish.

1-1/4 pounds fresh green beans, cut into 2-inch pieces
1-1/4 pounds fresh wax beans, cut into 2-inch pieces
3   medium carrots, cut into 2-inch julienned strips
1/2 small onion, chopped
1   teaspoon butter
1   can (10-3/4 ounces) condensed cream of chicken soup, undiluted
1/2 cup heavy whipping cream
1/2 cup chicken broth
3-1/4 teaspoons dill weed, *divided*
6   ounces cubed fully cooked ham
1-1/2 cups (6 ounces) shredded Swiss cheese, *divided*
1/4 cup slivered almonds
7   cups hot mashed potatoes (with added milk and butter)

Place beans and carrots in a saucepan and cover with water; bring to a boil. Cook, uncovered, for 8-10 minutes or until crisp-tender; drain and set aside. In a small skillet, saute onion in butter for 3-4 minutes or until tender.

In a large bowl, whisk soup, cream, broth and 3 teaspoons of dill. Add the beans, carrots and onion; gently stir to coat. Transfer to a greased shallow 3-qt. baking dish. Top with the ham, 1 cup cheese and almonds. Spread mashed potatoes over the top.

Cover and bake at 350° for 30 minutes. Uncover; sprinkle with remaining cheese and dill. Bake 5-10 minutes longer or until heated through and the cheese is melted.

Yield: 12-15 servings.

Church Supper Spaghetti

(pictured on p. 131)
Verlyn Wilson, Wilkinson, Indiana
Because this sensational recipe feeds so many, I often take it to the church dinners I attend.

1   pound ground beef
1   large onion, chopped
1   medium green pepper, chopped
1   can (14-1/2 ounces) diced tomatoes, undrained
1   cup water
2   tablespoons chili powder
1   package (10 ounces) frozen corn, thawed
1   package (10 ounces) frozen peas, thawed
1   can (4 ounces) mushroom stems and pieces, drained
Salt and pepper to taste
1   package (12 ounces) spaghetti, cooked and drained
2   cups (8 ounces) shredded cheddar cheese, *divided*

In a large skillet, cook beef, onion and green pepper over medium heat until meat is no longer pink. Drain. Add tomatoes, water and chili powder. Cover and simmer for 30 minutes. Add the corn, peas, mushrooms, salt and pepper. Stir in spaghetti.

Layer half of the mixture in a greased 4-qt. baking dish. Sprinkle with 1 cup cheese; repeat layers. Bake, uncovered, at 350° for 20 minutes or until heated through.

Yield: 12 servings.

Church Supper Ham Loaf

Rosemary Smith, Fort Bragg, California
Any leftover holiday ham is ground up and used in this special loaf for a future meal. As the name suggests, it has made more than one appearance on a buffet table after church.

- 1 pound fully cooked ham, ground
- 1 pound lean pork sausage
- 2 cups soft bread crumbs
- 2 eggs
- 1 cup (8 ounces) sour cream
- 1/3 cup chopped onion
- 2 tablespoons lemon juice
- 1 teaspoon curry powder
- 1 teaspoon ground ginger
- 1 teaspoon ground mustard
- 1/8 teaspoon ground nutmeg
- 1/8 teaspoon paprika

SAUCE:
- 1 cup packed brown sugar
- 1/2 cup water
- 1/2 cup cider vinegar
- 1/4 teaspoon pepper

In a large bowl, combine ham, sausage and bread crumbs. In a small bowl, beat eggs; add sour cream, onion, lemon juice and seasonings. Mix well; blend into meat mixture.

Shape into 9-in. x 5-in. x 2-in. loaf in a greased shallow baking pan. Bake, uncovered, at 350° for 30 minutes.

Meanwhile, in a small saucepan, combine sauce ingredients; bring to a boil. Pour over loaf. Bake, uncovered, 20-30 minutes longer or until a meat thermometer reads 160°-170°, basting every 10 minutes. Let stand 10 minutes before slicing.

Yield: 8 servings.

Tenderloin Spinach Spirals

(pictured above)
Marlene Muckenhirn, Delano, Minnesota
These eye-appealing slices are nice for a summer buffet when grilling for a crowd just isn't an option.

- 2 packages (10 ounces *each*) frozen chopped spinach, thawed and squeezed dry
- 2 cups (8 ounces) shredded cheddar cheese
- 1/2 cup raisins, coarsely chopped
- 1/2 cup egg substitute
- 1/4 cup beef broth
- 1/4 cup chopped green onions
- 2 teaspoons salt
- 2 garlic cloves, minced
- 1/4 teaspoon pepper
- 2 whole beef tenderloins (2-1/2 to 3 pounds *each*)
- 2 tablespoons olive oil

In a large bowl, combine the first nine ingredients. Set aside.

Cut each tenderloin horizontally from the long side to within 1/2 in. of opposite side. Open so meat lies flat; cover with plastic wrap. Flatten to 1/2-in. thickness; remove plastic wrap. Spread the spinach mixture over each tenderloin to within 1 in. of edges. Roll up jelly-roll style, starting with a long side; tie at 1-in. intervals with kitchen string.

Place seam side down on a greased rack in a shallow roasting pan; brush with oil. Bake, uncovered, at 425° for 45-60 minutes or until meat reaches desired doneness (for medium-rare, a meat thermometer should read 145°; medium, 160°; well-done, 170°). Let stand for 10 minutes.

Cover and refrigerate until chilled. Discard kitchen string; cut beef into 1/2-in. slices.

Yield: 24 servings.

Potluck Pointer

Bringing a main course to the church supper? Most large cuts of meats need to sit for 10 minutes before they're sliced.

Some potluck goers take their contributions straight from the oven to the event, slicing it once they get there. Others slice the meat at home, arranging it on a platter before they leave the house. In either case, allowing the meat to cool a bit makes slicing much easier and allows for more uniform pieces.

Pizza Meat Loaf Cups

(pictured below)
Susan Wollin, Marshall, Wisconsin
These moist, individual meat loaves are a sure bet for potlucks. Packed with pizza flavor, they're sure to be the talk of the get-together. I even keep them in the freezer for speedy suppers at home.

    1 egg, beaten
  1/2 cup pizza sauce
  1/4 cup seasoned bread crumbs
  1/2 teaspoon Italian seasoning
1-1/2 pounds ground beef
1-1/2 cups (6 ounces) shredded part-skim
      mozzarella cheese
Additional pizza sauce, optional

In a large bowl, combine the egg, pizza sauce, bread crumbs and Italian seasoning. Crumble beef over mixture and mix well. Divide between 12 greased muffin cups; press onto the bottom and up the sides. Fill center with cheese.

    Bake at 375° for 15-18 minutes or until meat is no longer pink. Serve with additional pizza sauce if desired. Or cool, place in freezer bags and freeze for up to 3 months.

Yield: 1 dozen.

Brisket with Chunky Tomato Sauce

(pictured above)
Linda Blaska, Atlanta, Georgia
Treat guests to this impressive brisket, and they'll agree it's the best beef they've ever tasted. A savory tomato sauce adds the finishing touch.

    1 fresh beef brisket (4-1/2 pounds)
    1 teaspoon salt
  1/4 to 1/2 teaspoon pepper
    1 tablespoon olive oil
    3 large onions, chopped
    2 garlic cloves, minced
    1 cup dry red wine *or* beef broth
    1 can (14-1/2 ounces) diced tomatoes,
      undrained
    2 celery ribs with leaves, chopped
  1/2 teaspoon dried thyme
  1/2 teaspoon dried rosemary, crushed
    1 bay leaf
    1 pound carrots, cut into 1/2-inch slices

Season brisket with salt and pepper. In a Dutch oven, brown brisket in oil over medium-high heat. Remove and keep warm. In the same pan, saute onions and garlic until tender. Place brisket over onions. Add the wine or broth, tomatoes, celery, thyme, rosemary and bay leaf.

Cover and bake at 325° for 2 hours, basting occasionally. Add carrots; bake 1 hour longer or until meat is tender. Discard bay leaf. Cool for 1 hour; cover and refrigerate overnight.

Trim visible fat from brisket and skim fat from tomato mixture. Thinly slice beef across the grain. In a saucepan, warm tomato mixture; transfer to a shallow roasting pan. Top with sliced beef. Cover and bake at 325° for 30 minutes or until heated through. Serve sauce over beef.

Yield: 12 servings.

Editor's Note: This is a fresh beef brisket, not corned beef. The meat comes from the first cut of the brisket.

Stick-to-Your-Ribs Supper

Cynthia Chapman, Allendale, South Carolina
This sausage and bean skillet dish appears at Sunday dinners at least once a month. For a little extra zest, add more chili powder and cayenne pepper.

    2 medium green peppers, chopped
    1 large onion, chopped
    1 can (4 ounces) mushroom stems and
       pieces, drained
    2 garlic cloves, minced
    1 tablespoon vegetable oil
    1 pound smoked kielbasa *or* smoked Polish
       sausage, thinly sliced
1-1/2 cups water
    1 can (16 ounces) kidney beans, rinsed and
       drained
    1 can (15 ounces) pinto beans, rinsed and
       drained
    1 can (14-1/2 ounces) diced tomatoes,
       undrained
    2 teaspoons chili powder
    1 teaspoon ground cumin
  1/2 teaspoon salt
  1/8 teaspoon cayenne pepper
  3/4 cup uncooked long grain rice
    1 cup (4 ounces) shredded part-skim
       mozzarella cheese

In a large skillet, saute the green peppers, onion, mushrooms and garlic in oil until tender. Add the sausage, water, beans, tomatoes, chili powder, cumin, salt and cayenne. Bring to a boil. Stir in the rice. Reduce heat; cover and simmer for 20-25 minutes or until rice is tender. Sprinkle with cheese; cover and cook for 5 minutes until cheese is melted.

Yield: 10 servings.

Ground Beef Vermicelli

Diana Holmes, Hubertus, Wisconsin
In this recipe, noodles are first browned to develop a slightly nutty flavor. Then they simmer in a seasoned tomato sauce for a deliciously different dinner contribution.

      8 ounces vermicelli, broken into 2-inch
         pieces
      2 tablespoons butter
      2 pounds lean ground beef
      1 can (15 ounces) tomato sauce
      4 celery ribs, chopped
      2 large onions, finely chopped
      1 can (15-1/4 ounces) whole kernel corn,
         drained
    1/2 cup chopped green pepper
      3 teaspoons garlic powder
      3 teaspoons salt
      1 teaspoon cayenne pepper
      1 teaspoon chili powder
      8 slices process cheese (Velveeta)

In a large skillet, saute vermicelli in butter until browned. Add beef; cook over medium heat until meat is no longer pink. Drain.

Stir in the tomato sauce, celery, onions, corn, green pepper and seasonings; mix well. Cover and simmer for 25 minutes. Arrange cheese slices over the top. Cook, uncovered, until the cheese is melted, about 5 minutes.

Yield: 12 servings.

Apricot Glazed Chicken

Ruby Williams, Bogalusa, Louisiana
Chicken is always a hit, and topped with a sweet glaze, this version has folks lining up for seconds. You'll be surprised at how easy it is to prepare such a large entree.

      9 broiler/fryer chickens (3-1/2 to 4 pounds
         each), quartered
      2 tablespoons dried minced garlic
      2 tablespoons salt
    1-1/2 teaspoons pepper
      1 can (49-1/2 ounces) chicken broth, *divided*
      4 jars (12 ounces *each*) apricot preserves

Place chicken in six greased 13-in. x 9-in. x 2-in. baking dishes. Sprinkle with garlic, salt and pepper.

Pour about 1 cup broth in each dish. Cover and bake at 350° for 30 minutes; drain. Bake, uncovered, for 30-40 minutes.

Combine preserves and remaining broth; spoon over chicken. Bake 9-12 minutes longer or until chicken is golden brown and juices run clear.

Yield: 36 servings.

Broccoli Ham Roll-Ups

(pictured above)
Susan Simmons, Norwalk, Iowa
My mother made these flavorful rolls for me when I came home from the hospital with each of my two children. The roll-ups can be frozen before baking and pulled out of the freezer for a handy potluck dish or a quick meal. They are a wonderful addition to any buffet.

      1 package (10 ounces) frozen chopped
         broccoli
      1 can (10-3/4 ounces) condensed cream of
         mushroom soup, undiluted
      1 cup dry bread crumbs
    1/4 cup shredded cheddar cheese
      1 tablespoon chopped onion
    1-1/2 teaspoons diced pimientos
    1/8 teaspoon rubbed sage
    1/8 teaspoon dried rosemary, crushed
    1/8 teaspoon dried thyme
    Dash pepper
     12 slices fully cooked ham (1/8 inch thick)

Cook broccoli according to package directions; drain. In a bowl, combine the soup, bread crumbs, cheese, onion, pimientos and seasonings. Add broccoli; mix well. Spoon 1/4 cup onto each ham slice and roll up.

Arrange in an ungreased 13-in. x 9-in. x 2-in. baking dish. Cover and bake at 350° for 40 minutes or until heated through.

Yield: 12 servings.

Italian Beef Roll-Ups

(pictured below)

Joanne Gruff, James Creek, Pennsylvania

*I was once asked to make an Italian beef dish but I didn't
have a recipe, so I invented my own. It must have turned
out pretty good, because I've been asked to share the saucy
roll-ups time and again.*

      2 pounds lean ground beef
      2 eggs, lightly beaten
      1 cup Italian-seasoned bread crumbs
  1/2 cup milk
      5 teaspoons dried minced onion
  1-1/2 teaspoons salt
  1/4 teaspoon pepper
      3 to 3-1/2 pounds boneless beef top round
        steak
      2 tablespoons vegetable oil
      4 cups spaghetti sauce, *divided*
Hot cooked spaghetti, optional

In a large bowl, combine the ground beef, eggs,
bread crumbs, milk, onion, salt and pepper; mix
thoroughly. Shape into twelve 3-in. rolls. Cut steak
into twelve 6-1/2-in. x 3-1/2-in. pieces. Wrap each
roll in a piece of steak; secure with toothpicks. In a
large skillet, brown roll-ups in oil over medium
heat.

Spread 2 cups of spaghetti sauce into a 13-in.
x 9-in. x 2-in. baking dish. Place roll-ups over
sauce; cover with remaining sauce. Cover and
bake at 350° for 50-55 minutes or until steak is tender. Remove toothpicks. Serve over pasta if desired.
Yield: 12 servings.

Sweet 'n' Spicy Grilled Pork Chops

(pictured above)

Gladys Peterson, Beaumont, Texas

*This started out as a mild sauce that I decided to "spice
up." You'll find it's easy to adjust the seasonings to suit
your gang's taste. I also like to use the sauce on boneless,
skinless chicken breasts.*

      1 can (14-1/2 ounces) diced tomatoes,
        drained
      1 can (10 ounces) diced tomatoes with
        chilies, undrained
  1/2 cup raisins
  1/4 cup currant jelly
  4-1/2 teaspoons cider vinegar
  1/4 teaspoon *each* garlic powder, salt and
        crushed red pepper flakes
     12 boneless pork chops (3/4 inch thick)

In a blender, combine the tomatoes, raisins, jelly,
vinegar and seasonings; cover and process until
smooth. Pour into a 1-qt. saucepan; bring to a boil.
Reduce heat; simmer, uncovered, for 20 minutes or
until thickened. Set aside 3/4 cup for serving.

Coat grill rack with nonstick cooking spray
before starting grill. Grill pork chops, uncovered,
over medium heat, for 4 minutes. Turn; brush with
sauce. Grill 4-6 minutes longer or until meat juices
run clear. Serve with reserved sauce.
Yield: 12 servings.

Heat 2 tablespoons oil in a large skillet over high. Add asparagus, mushrooms, broccoli, carrots, zucchini, onions and salt. Cook and stir 5 minutes. Remove vegetables from the skillet; set aside.

Add remaining oil to the skillet. Cook chicken, stirring constantly, 5-6 minutes or until it is no longer pink. Return vegetables to the skillet; add peas and cook 3-5 minutes. Set aside.

For sauce, melt butter in a medium saucepan over low heat. Stir in flour to form a smooth paste. Add bouillon cube. Gradually add milk, stirring constantly until sauce is thickened. Season with pepper.

Pour over chicken/vegetable mixture; toss to coat. Serve over spaghetti.

Yield: 8 servings.

Tasty Meat Pie

Cheryl Cattane, Lapeer, Michigan
I work full-time as a nurse, so I like meals that are quick and easy. These comforting, all-in-one pies are filled with ground beef and tender vegetables. At my sister's suggestion, I replaced the prepared gravy I had been using with canned soups for better flavor. Now my husband and teenage son ask for seconds...and thirds.

    1   pound ground beef
    1   small onion, chopped
    1   can (11 ounces) condensed beef with
        vegetables and barley soup, undiluted
    1   can (10-3/4 ounces) condensed golden
        mushroom soup, undiluted
    3   medium uncooked potatoes, cut into
        1/2-inch cubes
    4   medium carrots, sliced 1/8 inch thick
  1/4   teaspoon salt
  1/8   teaspoon pepper
Pastry for double-crust pie (9 inches)

In a skillet, cook beef and onion until meat is no longer pink; drain. Add the soups, potatoes, carrots, salt and pepper; mix well. Divide between two ungreased 9-in. pie plates.

On a floured surface, roll pastry to fit the top of each pie; place over filling. Seal and flute edges; cut slits in top.

Bake at 350° for 45-50 minutes or until golden brown. Let stand on a wire rack for 15 minutes before serving.

Yield: 2 pies (6 servings each).

Chicken Asparagus Pasta Supper

(pictured above)
Ginny Truwe, Mankato, Minnesota
I've used this recipe for years as a contribution to family gatherings and potluck suppers alike. Folks can't seem to get enough of it!

    4   tablespoons vegetable oil, *divided*
  1-1/2 pounds fresh asparagus, cut into 2-inch
        pieces
    8   ounces sliced fresh mushrooms
  1-1/2 cups broccoli florets
    2   carrots, cut into julienne strips
    2   medium zucchini, sliced
    3   green onions, sliced into 1/2-inch pieces
  1/2   teaspoon salt
    4   boneless skinless chicken breasts, cut into
        1-inch pieces
  1/2   cup frozen peas
SAUCE:
    2   tablespoons butter
    2   tablespoons all-purpose flour
    1   chicken bouillon cube
    2   cups milk
  1/4   teaspoon pepper
    1   pound thin spaghetti, cooked and drained

Potluck Mushroom Rice

Yvonne Taylor, Robstown, Texas
Once a week at work, we'd hold a potluck dinner. A co-worker brought this versatile dish, and I left with the recipe.

       3 cups water
 1-1/2 teaspoons beef bouillon granules
 1-1/2 cups uncooked long grain rice
       2 pounds ground beef
       1 large onion, chopped
       1 large green pepper, chopped
       1 jar (6 ounces) whole mushrooms, drained
       1 can (4 ounces) mushroom stems and
            pieces, drained
       1 celery rib, sliced
       1 can (10-3/4 ounces) condensed cream of
            celery soup, undiluted
       1 can (10-3/4 ounces) condensed cream of
            mushroom soup, undiluted
       2 tablespoons Worcestershire sauce
    1/2 teaspoon garlic powder

In a large saucepan, bring water and bouillon to a boil. Add rice. Reduce heat; cover and simmer for 15-20 minutes or until tender.

Meanwhile, in a large skillet, cook beef, onion, green pepper, mushrooms and celery until the meat is no longer pink and the vegetables are tender; drain. Stir in rice, soups, Worcestershire sauce and garlic powder; mix well. Transfer to an ovenproof Dutch oven. Cover and bake at 350° for 30 minutes or until heated through.

Yield: 12-14 servings.

Firemen's Meat Loaf

Peggy Stevens, Rogue River, Oregon
This was voted the best dish in a cooking contest between fire stations in San Bernadino, California. I've used the recipe for years and shared it with many friends. Sliced for guests, it makes a yummy entree at group suppers.

       1 package (6 ounces) crushed corn bread
            stuffing mix
       2 eggs, beaten
       1 can (4 ounces) mushroom stems and
            pieces, drained
       2 teaspoons garlic powder
       3 pounds lean ground beef
       2 cans (4 ounces *each*) chopped green chilies
    1/4 cup shredded cheddar cheese
    1/4 cup salsa

In a large bowl, prepare the corn bread stuffing according to package directions. Add eggs, mushrooms and garlic powder. Crumble beef over mixture and mix well.

Shape into a loaf in a greased 13-in. x 9-in. x 2-in. baking dish. Bake, uncovered, at 350° for 1-1/4 hours; drain. Top with chilies. Cover and bake 20 minutes longer or until meat is no longer pink and a meat thermometer reads 160°.

Sprinkle with cheese and top with salsa. Bake, uncovered, for 5-10 minutes or until the cheese is melted.

Yield: 12 servings.

Potluck Pointer

Not only is it important that everyone has enough to eat at the church supper, but you need to be sure everyone walks away healthy, too.

To keep food safe, hot items must remain hot. Make sure hot dishes are served at 140° or above and you won't have to worry about safety issues. Remember that food will start to cool off on the way to the dinner. Find out if a conventional or microwave oven will be available to reheat your contribution once you arrive at the church supper.

If not, time your dish so it comes out of your kitchen oven as close to the start of the potluck as possible. Wrapping the item in kitchen towels and setting it in an insulated cooler can help keep the food hot as you drive to the get-together. Avoid setting other foods in the cooler.

Keep in mind that while slow cookers and electric roasters do a great job of keeping food hot, it's not recommended that you try re-heating cooled items in them.

Turkey Crescent Wreath

(pictured above)
Jane Jones, Cedar, Minnesota
This savory delight is as pretty to look at as it is to eat! When cooking for a get-together the day after Thanksgiving one year, I prepared it using leftover turkey. Everyone enjoyed slices of the warm, golden wreath and asked for seconds...as well as the recipe.

  2 cups diced cooked turkey breast
  1 cup (4 ounces) shredded reduced-fat
      Swiss cheese
1/2 cup dried cranberries
1/2 cup diced celery
1/2 cup fat-free mayonnaise
1/4 cup chopped walnuts
  3 tablespoons minced fresh parsley
  2 tablespoons honey mustard
1/2 teaspoon pepper
  2 tubes (8 ounces *each*) refrigerated
      reduced-fat crescent rolls
  1 egg white, lightly beaten

In a large bowl, combine the first nine ingredients. Coat a 14-in. pizza pan with nonstick cooking spray.

Separate crescent dough into 16 triangles. Place wide end of one triangle 3 in. from edge of prepared pan with point overhanging edge of pan. Repeat with remaining triangles along outer edge of pan, overlapping the wide ends (dough will look like a sun when complete).

Lightly press wide ends together. Spoon turkey mixture over the wide ends of dough. Fold the points of the triangles over the filling and tuck under wide ends (filling will be visible). Brush with egg white. Bake at 375° for 20-25 minutes or until golden brown.

Yield: 16 servings.

Editor's Note: As a substitute for the honey mustard, combine 1 tablespoon Dijon mustard and 1 tablespoon honey.

Louisiana Jambalaya

Sandra Pichon, Slidell, Louisiana
Nothing jazzes up a food-filled gathering like steaming bowls of jambalaya. This crowd-pleasing variety is chock-full of smoked sausage, ham and shrimp.

1/2 pound smoked sausage, halved and sliced
  2 cups cubed fully cooked ham
1/4 cup vegetable oil
  2 celery ribs, chopped
  1 large onion, chopped
  1 medium green pepper, chopped
  5 green onions, thinly sliced
  2 garlic cloves, minced
  1 can (14-1/2 ounces) diced tomatoes,
      undrained
  1 teaspoon dried thyme
  1 teaspoon salt
1/2 teaspoon pepper
1/4 teaspoon cayenne pepper
  2 cans (14-1/2 ounces *each*) chicken broth
  1 cup uncooked long grain rice
1/3 cup water
4-1/2 teaspoons Worcestershire sauce
  2 pounds cooked shrimp, peeled and
      deveined

In a Dutch oven, saute sausage and ham in oil until lightly browned. Remove and keep warm. In the drippings, saute the celery, onion, green pepper, green onions and garlic until tender. Add tomatoes, thyme, salt, pepper and cayenne; cook 5 minutes longer.

Stir in broth, rice, water and Worcestershire sauce. Bring to a boil. Reduce heat; cover and simmer for 20 minutes or until rice is tender. Stir in sausage mixture and shrimp; heat through.

Yield: 10-12 servings.

Handy Meat Pies

(pictured above)
Amy Stumpf, Hampton, Virginia
These meat-filled pies are as great on a potluck buffet as they are as an appetizer or even a hearty snack.

- 3/4 pound ground beef
- 3/4 pound bulk pork sausage
- 1 medium onion, chopped
- 1/3 cup chopped green onions
- 1 garlic clove, minced
- 2 tablespoons minced fresh parsley
- 1 tablespoon water
- 2 teaspoons all-purpose flour
- 1/2 teaspoon baking powder
- 1/2 teaspoon salt
- 1/4 teaspoon pepper
- 2 tubes (12 ounces *each*) buttermilk biscuits

In a large skillet, brown beef and sausage over medium heat; drain. Add onions and garlic; cook until tender. Stir in parsley, water, flour, baking powder, salt and pepper. Heat through. Cover and refrigerate for at least 1 hour.

On a floured surface, pat 10 biscuits into 4-in. circles. Top each with about 1/3 cup of the meat mixture. Pat remaining biscuits into 5-in. circles and place over filling; seal edges with water. Press edges together with a fork dipped in flour; pierce the top.

Place on an ungreased baking sheet. Bake at 375° for 12-14 minutes or until golden brown and filling is hot.

Yield: 10 servings.

Taco Pasta Shells

Laura Pope, Bloomville, Ohio
Whenever I serve this main course, I tease guests that I have to save leftovers of the dish for my lunch the next day. The creative recipe uses pasta shells, instead of taco shells or tortillas to hold a rich and creamy mixture of beef. Topped with cheese and crushed chips, it's always popular.

- 1-1/2 pounds ground beef
- 1 medium onion, chopped
- 1 package (8 ounces) cream cheese, cubed
- 2 envelopes taco seasoning
- 1 to 2 tablespoons minced chives
- 1 package (12 ounces) jumbo pasta shells, cooked and drained
- 2 cups taco sauce
- 2 cups (8 ounces) shredded plain *or* Mexican-flavored process American cheese
- 1 cup coarsely crushed tortilla chips

In a large skillet, cook beef and onion over medium heat until meat is no longer pink; drain. Stir in cream cheese, taco seasoning and chives; cook until cream cheese is melted. Stuff into pasta shells.

Place in a greased 4-qt. baking dish. Top with taco sauce. Bake, uncovered, at 350° for 20 minutes or until heated through. Sprinkle with cheese and tortilla chips. Bake 5 minutes longer or until the cheese is melted.

Yield: 10-15 servings.

Baked Ziti

(pictured above)
Kim Neer, Mansfield, Ohio
For a comforting Italian dish that is made with ziti pasta and a combination of cheeses and feeds a crowd, give this stick-to-your-ribs casserole a try.

  1 pound lean ground beef
  2 medium onions, chopped
  3 garlic cloves, minced
  1 jar (28 ounces) reduced-sodium meatless spaghetti sauce
  1 can (28 ounces) diced tomatoes, undrained
  1 can (12 ounces) tomato paste
3/4 cup water
  2 tablespoons minced fresh parsley
  1 tablespoon Worcestershire sauce
  2 teaspoons dried basil
1-1/2 teaspoons dried oregano, *divided*
  1 pound uncooked rigatoni *or* medium tube pasta
  1 carton (15 ounces) reduced-fat ricotta cheese
  2 cups (8 ounces) shredded part-skim mozzarella cheese
1/2 cup grated Parmesan cheese, *divided*
1/2 cup egg substitute
1/2 teaspoon salt
1/2 teaspoon pepper

In a large saucepan, cook beef, onions and garlic over medium heat until meat is no longer pink; drain. Stir in spaghetti sauce, tomatoes, tomato paste, water, parsley, Worcestershire sauce, basil and 1 teaspoon oregano. Cover and simmer for 3 hours, stirring occasionally. Cook pasta according to package directions; drain. In a bowl, combine ricotta, mozzarella, 1/4 cup Parmesan cheese, egg substitute, salt and pepper.

In two greased 13-in. x 9-in. x 2-in. baking dishes coated with nonstick cooking spray, spread 1 cup of meat sauce. In each dish, layer a fourth of the pasta, 1 cup meat sauce and a fourth of the cheese mixture. Repeat layers of pasta, sauce and cheese mixture. Top with remaining sauce. Sprinkle with remaining Parmesan cheese and oregano. Cover and bake at 350° for 1 hour or until heated through.
Yield: 2 casseroles.

Hot Dogs with Chili Beans

Joella Bachida, Pflugerville, Texas
This is a recipe my mom used often when I was growing up. The hot dogs are a welcomed attraction at summertime get-togethers alongside bowls of potato salad and chips.

- 1 pound ground beef
- 2 garlic cloves, minced
- 1 cup chopped onions, *divided*
- 1 can (15 ounces) pinto beans, rinsed and drained
- 1 cup water
- 4 teaspoons chili powder
- 1/2 teaspoon salt
- 1/4 teaspoon pepper
- 12 hot dogs, heated
- 12 hot dog buns, split

Shredded Colby *or* cheddar cheese

In a large saucepan, cook beef, garlic and 1/2 cup onion over medium heat until meat is no longer pink; drain. Stir in the beans, water, chili powder, salt and pepper; bring to a boil. Reduce heat; simmer, uncovered, for 30 minutes.

Place hot dogs in buns. Top each with 1/4 cup chili bean mixture. Serve with cheese and remaining onion.

Yield: 12 servings.

Tangy Glazed Ham

Florence McCray, Johnson City, Tennessee
After looking for a glaze recipe, my daughter and I came up with this version. It dresses up any ham.

- 1 boneless fully cooked ham (3 pounds)
- 1/2 cup sweet-and-sour sauce
- 1/4 cup light corn syrup
- 3 tablespoons zesty Italian salad dressing

Place ham in an ungreased 11-in. x 7-in. x 2-in. baking pan. Pour remaining ingredients over ham in the order listed.

Bake, uncovered, at 325°, basting occasionally, for 1-1/4 to 1-1/2 hours or until a meat thermometer reads 140°.

Yield: 12 servings.

Potluck Pointer

Allowing the red sauce in Baked Ziti to simmer 3 hours guarantees maximum flavor. When time's tight, however, you can simmer the sauce for an hour or two with extremely satisfying results.

Herbed Turkey Breast

(pictured below)
Alicia Glovor, Sterling, Alaska
Here's a family favorite that's also perfect when feeding several friends. Lemon juice adds a subtle hint of citrus, while garlic, thyme and rubbed sage create a lovely aroma as the turkey roasts.

- 1 bone-in turkey breast (8-1/2 pounds)
- 3 tablespoons lemon juice, *divided*
- 2 tablespoons olive oil, *divided*
- 2 garlic cloves, minced
- 1-1/2 teaspoons salt
- 1 teaspoon grated lemon peel
- 1 teaspoon dried thyme
- 3/4 teaspoon pepper
- 1/2 teaspoon rubbed sage

Loosen skin from turkey with fingers, leaving skin attached along bottom edges. In a small bowl, combine 1 tablespoon lemon juice, 1 tablespoon oil, garlic and seasonings. Spread under turkey skin.

In a small bowl, combine remaining lemon juice and oil; set aside.

Place turkey on a rack in a shallow roasting pan. Bake, uncovered, at 350° for 2-1/2 to 3 hours or until a meat thermometer reads 170°; basting every 15-20 minutes with lemon mixture. Let stand for 10 minutes. Discard the skin before carving.

Yield: 16 servings.

Overnight Scalloped Chicken Casserole

(pictured above)
Arlyss Gray, Lafayette, Indiana
Don't have much time to spare? Assemble this spirit-warming hot dish the night before. Then, all you have to do is sprinkle the top with the buttered bread crumbs and pop it in the oven an hour before your event.

    2 cans (10-3/4 ounces *each*) condensed
       cream of mushroom soup, undiluted
2-1/2 cups milk
  1/2 pound process cheese (Velveeta)
    4 cups chopped cooked chicken *or* turkey
    1 box (7 ounces) macaroni
    3 hard-cooked eggs, chopped
  1/2 cup butter, melted, *divided*
1-1/2 cups soft bread crumbs

In a large bowl, combine soup, milk, and cheese. Add chicken, macaroni and eggs. Stir in 1/4 cup melted butter.

   Transfer to a greased 13-in. x 9-in. x 2-in. baking dish. Cover and refrigerate for 8 hours or overnight.

   Toss the bread crumbs with remaining butter; sprinkle over casserole. Bake, uncovered, at 350° for 60-65 minutes or until bubbly and golden brown.

Yield: 12 servings.

Glazed Corned Beef

(pictured below)
Perlene Hoekema, Lynden, Washington
I serve this delicious entree at St. Patrick's Day celebrations. The meat is so tender and tasty topped with a simple glaze. Leftovers make excellent Reuben sandwiches.

    1 corned beef brisket (3 to 4 pounds),
       trimmed
    1 medium onion, sliced
    1 celery rib, sliced
  1/4 cup butter
    1 cup packed brown sugar
  2/3 cup ketchup
  1/3 cup white vinegar
    2 tablespoons prepared mustard
    2 teaspoons prepared horseradish

Place corned beef and contents of seasoning packet in a Dutch oven; cover with water. Add onion and celery. Bring to a boil. Reduce heat; cover and simmer for 2-1/2 hours or until meat is tender. Drain and discard liquid and vegetables. Place beef on a rack in a shallow roasting pan; set aside.

   In a saucepan, melt the butter over medium heat. Stir in the remaining ingredients. Cook and stir until sugar is dissolved. Brush over beef. Bake, uncovered, at 350° for 25 minutes. Let stand for 10 minutes before slicing.

Yield: 12 servings.

Pictured below:
Cream of Wild Rice Soup (p. 164).

Soups & Sandwiches

Seafood Gumbo

(pictured below)
Ruth Aubey, San Antonio, Texas
Gumbo is our unofficial state dish! Every Creole cook has a favorite gumbo recipe, and this is mine. Feel free to swap out any of the ingredients, but since gumbo means okra, that item's a must!

1 cup all-purpose flour
1 cup vegetable oil
4 cups chopped onion
2 cups chopped celery
2 cups chopped green pepper
1 cup sliced green onions and tops
4 cups chicken broth
8 cups water
4 cups sliced okra
2 tablespoons paprika
2 tablespoons salt
2 teaspoons oregano
1 teaspoon ground black pepper
6 cups small shrimp, rinsed and drained
1 cup minced parsley
2 tablespoons Cajun seasoning

In a heavy Dutch oven, combine flour and oil until smooth. Cook over medium-high heat for 5 minutes, stirring constantly. Reduce heat to medium. Cook and stir about 10 minutes more, or until mixture is reddish-brown.

Add onion, celery, green pepper and green onions; cook and stir for 5 minutes. Add chicken broth, water, okra, paprika, salt, oregano and pepper. Bring to boil; reduce heat and simmer, covered, for 10 minutes. Add shrimp and parsley. Simmer, uncovered, about 5 minutes more or until seafood is done. Remove from heat; stir in Cajun seasoning.

Yield: about 6 quarts.

Tangy Pork Barbecue

(pictured above)
Carmine Walters, San Jose, California
My neighbor shared this zesty recipe with me in the late '50s, and it's still a hit today. It's the perfect main dish when French fries and coleslaw are also on the menu.

2 tablespoons butter
3 tablespoons all-purpose flour
1 bottle (28 ounces) ketchup
2 cups boiling water
1/4 cup white vinegar
1/4 cup Worcestershire sauce
1 medium onion, chopped
1 garlic clove, minced
2 teaspoons chili powder
1 teaspoon salt, optional
1 teaspoon ground mustard
1/8 teaspoon cayenne pepper
1 boneless pork loin roast (3-1/2 to 4 pounds)
12 sandwich buns, split

In a Dutch oven, melt butter over medium heat. Stir in flour until smooth. Add the next 10 ingredients; bring to a boil. Add roast. Reduce heat; cover and simmer for 3 hours or until meat is tender.

Remove meat; shred with two forks. Skim fat from cooking juices; return meat to juices and heat through. Serve with a slotted spoon on buns.

Yield: 12 servings.

Curried Chicken Pita Pockets

Vicky Whitehead, Norman, Oklahoma
I like to make these sandwiches for special luncheons. Everyone who tries them raves about the refreshing combination of tender chicken, flavorful curry and juicy grapes.

- 3/4 cup mayonnaise
- 1 teaspoon soy sauce
- 1 teaspoon lemon juice
- 1/2 teaspoon curry powder
- 1 small onion, finely chopped
- 2-1/2 cups cubed cooked chicken
- 1-1/2 cups halved seedless green grapes
- 3/4 cup chopped celery
- 1/2 cup sliced almonds
- 10 pita breads, halved

In a large bowl, combine the first five ingredients. Stir in chicken, grapes and celery; refrigerate. Just before serving, add the almonds. Stuff about 1/4 cup into each pita half.

Yield: 10 servings.

Hot 'n' Cheesy Chicken Sandwiches

Nancy Frederiksen, Springfield, Minnesota
These are great sandwiches when you need to feed lots of mouths, such as an entire soccer team. The warm, cheesy filling takes minutes to whip together.

- 6 cups cubed cooked chicken
- 1-1/2 cups chopped celery
- 1 can (10-3/4 ounces) condensed cream of mushroom soup, undiluted
- 3/4 cup mayonnaise
- 3/4 cup chopped green pepper
- 1 teaspoon ground mustard
- 1/2 teaspoon salt
- 1/2 teaspoon pepper
- 3 cups process cheese (Velveeta), cubed
- 24 hamburger buns, split

In a large bowl, combine the first eight ingredients; mix well. Pour into an ungreased 2-1/2-qt. casserole; top with cheese. Cover and bake at 350° for 45 minutes or until bubbly. Let stand for 5 minutes; spoon 1/3 cup onto each bun.

Yield: 24 servings.

Split Pea Soup with Meatballs

(pictured above)
Donna Smith, Grey Cliff, Montana
I like to prepare this for suppers at my church, and I come home with an empty kettle every time. The tender meatballs make a flavorful twist to ordinary split pea soup.

- 1 pound dry green split peas
- 3 medium carrots, sliced 1/2 inch thick
- 3/4 cup diced celery
- 1 medium onion, diced
- 8 cups water
- 3 medium potatoes, cut into 1/2-inch cubes
- 2-1/2 teaspoons salt
- 1/4 teaspoon pepper

MEATBALLS:
- 3/4 cup finely chopped celery
- 1 medium onion, finely chopped
- 4 tablespoons olive oil, *divided*
- 1 pound ground pork
- 1-1/2 cups soft bread crumbs
- 2 tablespoons water
- 1 teaspoon salt
- 1/2 teaspoon dried sage, crushed
- 1 egg

In a Dutch oven or soup kettle, combine peas, carrots, celery, onion and water; bring to a boil over medium heat. Reduce heat; cover and simmer for 1 hour. Add potatoes, salt and pepper; cover and simmer for 30 minutes.

Meanwhile, in a large skillet, saute celery and onion in 2 tablespoons oil until tender; bring to a boil. Add pork, bread crumbs, water, salt, sage and egg; mix well. Form into 3/4-in. balls. In the same skillet, brown meatballs in remaining oil until no longer pink inside. Add to soup; cover and simmer for 15 minutes.

Yield: 10-14 servings (3-1/2 quarts).

Sausage Stromboli

Julie LeBar, Garden Grove, California

This hot, zesty sandwich is the perfect way to feed several hungry mouths at one time. The sour cream and cream cheese layer make this stromboli different from most others.

1 package (1/4 ounce) active dry yeast
1 teaspoon sugar
1 cup warm water (110° to 115°)
1/4 cup olive oil
1/4 teaspoon salt, *divided*
2-1/2 to 3 cups all-purpose flour
3/4 pound bulk pork sausage
1 medium onion, chopped
1 can (8 ounces) tomato sauce
1/2 cup chopped green pepper
1 garlic clove, minced
1-1/2 teaspoons Italian seasoning
Dash pepper
1 cup (8 ounces) sour cream
3 tablespoons whipped chive and onion cream cheese
1 cup (4 ounces) shredded cheddar cheese
1 cup (4 ounces) shredded part-skim mozzarella cheese
1 egg white, lightly beaten
Fennel seed

In a mixing bowl, dissolve yeast and sugar in water; let stand for 5 minutes. Add the oil, 1/8 teaspoon salt and 2 cups flour; beat until smooth. Stir in enough remaining flour to form a soft dough. Turn onto a floured surface; knead until smooth and elastic, about 5 minutes. Place in a greased bowl, turning once to grease top. Cover and let rise in a warm place until doubled, about 1 hour.

Meanwhile, in a skillet, cook sausage and onion over medium heat until meat is no longer pink; drain. Add the tomato sauce, green pepper, garlic, Italian seasoning, pepper and remaining salt; set aside. Punch dough down. On a large greased baking sheet, roll dough into an 18-in. x 12-in. oval. Spread sausage mixture lengthwise down the center.

Combine the sour cream and cream cheese; spread over sausage mixture. Sprinkle with cheeses. Fold one long side of dough over filling. Fold other long side over the top; pinch seam and ends to seal. With a sharp knife, cut slits in top of dough. Cover and let rise until doubled, about 30 minutes.

Brush top with egg white; sprinkle with fennel seed. Bake at 400° for 25-30 minutes or until lightly browned. Let stand for 10 minutes before slicing.

Yield: 12 servings.

Make-Ahead Sloppy Joes

(pictured above)
Alyne Fuller, Odessa, Texas

Having these sandwiches in the freezer is such a time-saver when you're in a bind and need a fast dish to feed a crowd. Wrapped in foil, the sandwiches even stay warm while on a buffet table.

1 pound bulk pork sausage
1 pound ground beef
1 medium onion, chopped
14 to 16 sandwich buns, split
2 cans (8 ounces *each*) tomato sauce
2 tablespoons prepared mustard
1 teaspoon dried parsley flakes
1 teaspoon garlic powder
1 teaspoon salt
1/4 teaspoon pepper
1/4 teaspoon dried oregano

In a skillet, brown sausage, beef and onion. Remove from the heat; drain. Remove the centers from the tops and bottoms of each bun. Tear bread into small pieces; add to skillet. Set buns aside. Stir remaining ingredients into sausage mixture.

Spoon about 1/3 cupful onto the bottom of each bun; replace tops. Wrap individually in heavy-duty foil. Bake at 350° for 20 minutes or until heated through or freeze for up to 3 months.

Yield: 14-16 servings.

Sunday Gumbo

(pictured above)

Debbie Burchette, Summitville, Indiana

With plenty of sausage, chicken and shrimp, plus rice, a medley of vegetables and the "heat" of cayenne, this comforting soup is a great addition to any Sunday get-together. It's also a heartwarming change from chili once the weather turns cold and icy.

1 pound Italian sausage links, cut into
  1/4-inch pieces
1 pound boneless skinless chicken breasts,
  cubed
3 tablespoons vegetable oil
1 medium sweet red pepper, chopped
1 medium onion, chopped
3 celery ribs, chopped
1 teaspoon dried marjoram
1 teaspoon dried thyme
1/2 teaspoon garlic powder
1/2 teaspoon cayenne pepper
3 cans (14-1/2 ounces *each*) chicken broth
2/3 cup uncooked brown rice
1 can (14-1/2 ounces) diced tomatoes,
  undrained
1 pound uncooked medium shrimp, peeled
  and deveined
2 cups frozen sliced okra

In a Dutch oven, brown sausage and chicken in oil. Remove with a slotted spoon and keep warm.

In the drippings, saute red pepper, onion and celery until tender. Stir in the seasonings; cook for 5 minutes.

Stir in the broth, rice and sausage mixture; bring to a boil. Reduce heat; cover and simmer for 20-25 minutes or until rice is tender, sausage is no longer pink and chicken juices run clear.

Stir in the tomatoes, shrimp and okra; cook for 10 minutes or until the shrimp turn pink, stirring occasionally.

Yield: 16 servings (about 4 quarts).

Shaker Bean Soup

(pictured below)
Deborah Amrine, Grand Haven, Michigan
This soup makes a tasty meal-in-one all year long. That's why it's perfect for all of your get-togethers.

- 1 pound dry great northern beans
- 1 meaty ham bone *or* 2 smoked ham hocks
- 1 large onion, chopped
- 3 celery stalks, diced
- 2 carrots, shredded

Salt to taste
- 1/2 teaspoon pepper
- 1/2 teaspoon dried thyme
- 1 can (28 ounces) crushed tomatoes
- 2 tablespoons brown sugar
- 1-1/2 cups finely shredded fresh spinach leaves

Sort and rinse beans. Place in a Dutch oven or soup kettle; cover with water and bring to a boil. Boil 2 minutes. Remove from heat; let stand 1 hour. Drain beans and discard liquid.

In the same kettle, place ham bone, 3 qts. water and beans. Bring to a boil; reduce heat and simmer, covered, 1-1/2 hours or until meat easily falls from the bone. Remove bones from broth and, when cool enough to handle, trim meat. Discard bones. Return ham to kettle. Stir in onion, celery, carrots, salt, pepper and thyme. Simmer, covered, 1 hour or until beans are tender.

Add tomatoes and brown sugar. Cook for 10 minutes. Just before serving, add spinach.

Yield: 20 servings (5 quarts).

Mediterranean Seafood Chowder

Erin Nicole Morris, St. Peters, Missouri
Even those not particularly fond of seafood will enjoy this rich-tasting soup that combines shrimp and cod with long grain rice and delightful herbs.

- 1-1/2 cups chopped sweet yellow *or* red peppers
- 1 large onion, quartered and thinly sliced
- 3 garlic cloves, minced
- 2 tablespoons olive oil
- 1 can (28 ounces) crushed tomatoes
- 2-1/4 cups water
- 1 can (14-1/2 ounces) chicken broth
- 1 cup uncooked long grain rice
- 1/2 cup white wine *or* additional chicken broth
- 1/2 to 1 teaspoon dried thyme
- 1/2 to 1 teaspoon dried basil
- 1/2 teaspoon salt
- 1/8 teaspoon crushed red pepper flakes
- 8 ounces uncooked medium shrimp, peeled and deveined
- 8 ounces cod fillets, cut into pieces

In a large saucepan or Dutch oven, saute the peppers, onion and garlic in oil until tender. Add the tomatoes, water, broth, rice, wine or additional broth and seasonings. Bring to a boil. Reduce heat; cover and simmer for 15-20 minutes or until rice is tender.

Stir in the shrimp and cod; cover and simmer for 2-4 minutes or until shrimp turn pink and fish flakes easily with a fork.

Yield: 10 servings.

Cucumber Party Sandwiches

Veronica Smith, Donnelly, Minnesota
When I serve these refreshing sandwiches at ladies' luncheons, the platter is always emptied. They are so simple to prepare that you'll find yourself making them often.

- 1 package (8 ounces) cream cheese, softened
- 2 teaspoons Italian salad dressing mix
- 1 loaf (16 ounces) snack rye bread
- 1 large cucumber, thinly sliced
- 2 tablespoons minced fresh dill *or* 2 teaspoons dill weed

In a small mixing bowl, beat the cream cheese and salad dressing mix until smooth. Spread on one side of each slice of bread. Top with cucumber slice and sprinkle with dill.

Yield: about 3-1/2 dozen.

Taco Soup

Jane Ficiur, Bow Island, Alberta
I first sampled this soup while camping with friends. After one sip, I just had to have the recipe. It's easy to whip up when you need to feed a crowd or prepare a dish for a group supper but don't have a lot of time.

- 2 pounds ground beef
- 1 medium onion, chopped
- 2 cans (15 ounces *each*) Italian tomato sauce
- 1 can (16 ounces) kidney beans, rinsed and drained
- 1 can (14-1/2 ounces) stewed tomatoes
- 1 can (12 ounces) whole kernel corn, undrained

Shredded cheddar cheese
Tortilla chips

In a large saucepan, cook beef and onion over medium heat until the meat is no longer pink; drain. Add the tomato sauce, beans, tomatoes and corn; bring to a boil. Reduce heat; simmer, uncovered, for 10 minutes. Garnish with cheese. Serve with tortilla chips.
Yield: 10 servings (2-1/2 quarts).

Dressed-Up Dogs

Roseann Loker, Vicksburg, Michigan
Wrapped in a from-scratch dough, these cute hot dogs will be the talk of your next potluck. Leftovers are even good the next day since the sandwiches reheat well in the microwave.

- 2 cups all-purpose flour
- 1 tablespoon baking powder
- 1/2 teaspoon salt
- 1/2 cup shortening
- 3/4 cup milk
- 1 tablespoon butter, melted
- 2 tablespoons grated Parmesan cheese
- 1 tablespoon minced fresh parsley *or* 1 teaspoon dried parsley flakes
- 12 hot dogs

In a bowl, combine flour, baking powder and salt. Cut in shortening until the mixture resembles coarse crumbs. Stir in milk just until moistened. Turn onto a floured surface; knead 10-12 times. Roll into a 13-in. circle. Brush with butter; sprinkle with cheese and parsley. Cut into 12 wedges. Place hot dogs at wide end of wedges and roll up. Place on an ungreased baking sheet with point down. Bake at 425° for 25 minutes or until golden brown.
Yield: 12 servings.

Reuben Deli Sandwiches

(pictured above)
Gigi LaFave Ryan, Longmont, Colorado
Here's a new twist on the classic Reuben sandwich. The filling is easy to prepare and keeps well in the fridge. Served with salads and desserts, these sandwiches make a delicious addition to lunch buffets.

- 3/4 cup mayonnaise
- 1 tablespoon chili sauce
- 1-1/2 teaspoons prepared mustard
- 1/4 teaspoon prepared horseradish
- 1 can (14 ounces) sauerkraut, rinsed and well drained
- 3/4 pound finely chopped corned beef (about 3 cups)
- 2 cups (8 ounces) shredded Swiss cheese
- 30 slices rye bread
- 1/2 cup butter, softened

In a large bowl, combine mayonnaise, chili sauce, mustard and horseradish. Stir in sauerkraut, corned beef and Swiss cheese. Spread 1/3 cup on 15 slices of bread; top with remaining bread. Lightly butter the outsides of bread. Toast sandwiches on a hot griddle for 4-5 minutes per side or until golden brown.
Yield: 15 servings.

Italian Meatball Hoagies

(pictured below)
Anna Collom, Hewitt, Minnesota
Smothered in tomato sauce, these hoagies are winners wherever I take them. The warm sandwiches make welcomed additions to parties.

      4 eggs
    1/2 cup milk
      1 cup grated Parmesan cheese
      2 garlic cloves, minced
      2 tablespoons dried parsley flakes
  1-1/2 teaspoons dried basil
  1-1/2 teaspoons dried oregano
    1/4 teaspoon pepper
      2 pounds ground beef
      2 cups crushed saltines (about 60 crackers)
SAUCE:
      2 cans (15 ounces *each*) tomato sauce
    1/2 cup grated Parmesan cheese
  1-1/2 teaspoons dried oregano
      1 teaspoon dried basil
      1 teaspoon dried parsley flakes
    1/2 teaspoon salt
     12 submarine sandwich buns (about 6 inches), split
Sliced part-skim mozzarella cheese, optional

In a large bowl, combine the first eight ingredients. Crumble beef over mixture and sprinkle with cracker crumbs; mix gently. Shape into 1-in. balls. Place in ungreased 15-in. x 10-in. x 1-in. baking pans. Bake at 350° for 20-25 minutes or until meat is no longer pink. Drain.

In a large saucepan, combine the tomato sauce, Parmesan cheese, oregano, basil, parsley and salt. Bring to a boil over medium heat; add meatballs. Reduce heat; cover and simmer for 20 minutes or until heated through. Serve meatballs and sauce on buns. Top with mozzarella cheese if desired.
Yield: 12 servings.

Pork and Beef Barbecue

Corbin Detgen, Buchanan, Michigan
It's the combination of beef stew meat and pork tenderloin that keeps people asking about these tangy sandwiches. Top them with lettuce and tomatoes for a little variety.

    1 can (6 ounces) tomato paste
  1/2 cup packed brown sugar
  1/4 cup chili powder
  1/4 cup cider vinegar
    2 teaspoons Worcestershire sauce
    1 teaspoon salt
1-1/2 pounds beef stew meat, cut into 3/4-inch cubes
1-1/2 pounds pork tenderloin, cut into 3/4-inch cubes
    3 green peppers, chopped
    2 large onions, chopped
  14 sandwich rolls, split
Lettuce and tomatoes, optional

In a 3-qt. slow cooker, combine the first six ingredients. Stir in beef, pork, green peppers and onions. Cover and cook on high for 6-8 hours or until meat is tender. Shred meat with two forks. Serve on rolls with lettuce and chopped tomatoes if desired.

Yield: 14 servings.

Hamburger Rice Soup

Jean Fisher, Waynesboro, Pennsylvania
The aroma of this soup simmering on the stove makes the kitchen smell so good. The second helping tastes even better than the first! I keep any leftovers in the freezer.

    1 pound ground beef
  1/2 cup chopped onion
3-1/2 quarts water
    1 can (28 ounces) diced tomatoes, undrained
    1 envelope onion soup mix
    3 tablespoons Worcestershire sauce
    1 tablespoon salt
    1 teaspoon brown sugar
    1 teaspoon celery salt
  1/8 teaspoon pepper
  1/2 cup uncooked long grain rice

In a soup kettle or Dutch oven, cook beef and onion over medium heat until meat is no longer pink; drain. Add the water, tomatoes, soup mix, Worcestershire sauce, salt, brown sugar, celery salt and pepper; bring to a boil. Add rice. Reduce heat; cover and simmer for 20-25 minutes or until rice is tender.

Yield: 20 servings (5 quarts).

Tasty Reuben Soup

(pictured above)
Terry Ann Brandt, Tobias, Nebraska
I'm a working mom with limited time to spend in the kitchen, so I'm always looking for quick recipes. With the flavor of a Reuben sandwich, this speedy soup gets compliments from everyone who tries it.

    4 cans (14-1/2 ounces *each*) chicken broth
    4 cups shredded cabbage
    2 cups uncooked medium egg noodles
    1 pound fully cooked kielbasa, halved and cut into 1-inch slices
  1/2 cup chopped onion
    1 teaspoon caraway seeds
  1/4 teaspoon garlic powder
    1 cup (4 ounces) shredded Swiss cheese

In a large saucepan, combine the first seven ingredients; bring to a boil. Reduce heat; cover and simmer for 15 minutes or until cabbage and noodles are tender. Garnish with cheese.

Yield: 10 servings (2-1/2 quarts).

Crab Bisque

(pictured below)
Sherrie Manton, Folsom, Louisiana
This hearty chowder has a rich broth that's swimming with tasty chunks of crab and crunchy corn. It's a special way to celebrate with others.

- 1 celery rib, thinly sliced
- 1 small onion, chopped
- 1/2 cup chopped green pepper
- 3 tablespoons butter
- 2 cans (14-3/4 ounces *each*) cream-style corn
- 2 cans (10-3/4 ounces *each*) condensed cream of potato soup, undiluted
- 1-1/2 cups milk
- 1-1/2 cups half-and-half cream
- 2 bay leaves
- 1 teaspoon dried thyme
- 1/2 teaspoon garlic powder
- 1/4 teaspoon white pepper
- 1/8 teaspoon hot pepper sauce
- 3 cans (6 ounces *each*) crabmeat, drained, flaked and cartilage removed

In a large saucepan or soup kettle, saute celery, onion and green pepper in butter until tender. Add the next nine ingredients; mix well. Stir in crab; heat through. Discard bay leaves.

Yield: 10 servings.

Pepperoni Stromboli

(pictured above)
Shelley Banzhaf, Maywood, Nebraska
I've made these hearty stromboli many times. Prepared with frozen bread dough, the sandwiches satisfy big appetites.

- 2 loaves (1 pound *each*) frozen bread dough, thawed
- 2 eggs, beaten
- 1/3 cup olive oil
- 1/2 teaspoon *each* garlic powder, salt and pepper
- 1/2 teaspoon ground mustard
- 1/2 teaspoon dried oregano
- 1 pound ground beef, cooked and drained
- 1 package (3-1/2 ounces) sliced pepperoni
- 2 cups (8 ounces) shredded part-skim mozzarella cheese
- 1 cup (4 ounces) shredded cheddar cheese
- 1 small onion, chopped

Place each loaf of bread dough in a greased bowl, turning once to grease top. Cover and let rise in a warm place until doubled, about 45 minutes. Punch down. Roll each loaf into a 15-in. x 12-in. rectangle.

In a bowl, combine eggs, oil and seasonings. Brush over dough to within 1/2 in. of edges; set remaining egg mixture aside. Arrange beef, pepperoni, cheeses and onion on dough to within 1/2 in. of edges. Roll up, jelly-roll style, beginning with a long side. Seal the edges well.

Place seam side down on greased baking sheets. Brush with remaining egg mixture. Bake at 375° for 30-35 minutes or until lightly browned. Let stand for 5-10 minutes before cutting.

Yield: about 16 servings.

Oven Cheese Chowder

(pictured below)

Martha Eastham, San Diego, California

This creamy soup deliciously blends zucchini, onion and other vegetables. And even though it uses up a harvest of fresh garden produce, it's terrific any time of the year. Best of all, I prepare it in the oven so I can tend to other things as it simmers.

  1/2 pound zucchini, cut into 1-inch chunks
    2 medium onions, chopped
    1 can (15 ounces) garbanzo beans, rinsed and drained
    1 can (14-1/2 ounces) diced tomatoes, undrained
    1 can (11 ounces) Mexican-style corn, drained
    1 can (14-1/2 ounces) chicken broth
    2 teaspoons salt
  1/4 teaspoon pepper
    1 garlic clove, minced
    1 teaspoon dried basil
    1 bay leaf
    1 cup (4 ounces) shredded Monterey Jack cheese
    1 cup grated Romano cheese
1-1/2 cups half-and-half cream
Additional Monterey Jack cheese, optional

In a 3-qt. baking dish, combine the first 11 ingredients. Cover and bake at 400° for 1 hour, stirring once. Stir in the cheeses and cream. Bake, uncovered, for 10 minutes. Remove bay leaf. Top with additional Monterey Jack if desired.

Yield: 10-12 servings (3 quarts).

Easy Vegetable Soup

(pictured above)

Jan Sharp, Blue Springs, Missouri

Frozen vegetables and canned tomatoes and beans give you a head start when preparing this crowd-pleaser. Set a bowl of tortilla chips next to the soup for a fun alternative to crackers.

    1 pound ground beef
    1 medium onion, chopped
    1 can (28 ounces) diced tomatoes, undrained
    1 package (16 ounces) frozen vegetable blend of your choice
    1 can (16 ounces) kidney beans, undrained
    1 can (14-1/2 ounces) beef broth
    1 envelope taco seasoning
    1 garlic clove, minced
Shredded cheddar cheese, optional

In a large saucepan or Dutch oven, cook beef and onion over medium heat until meat is no longer pink; drain. Add tomatoes, vegetables, beans, broth, taco seasoning and garlic; bring to a boil. Reduce heat; simmer, uncovered, for 10 minutes. Garnish with cheese if desired.

Yield: 10-12 servings (2-3/4 quarts).

Cream of Wild Rice Soup

(pictured on p. 153)
J. Beatrice Hintz, Neenah, Wisconsin
Tender cubes of chicken, fresh vegetables and wild rice make this soup hearty enough for a meal. You can't beat the down-home comfort of a warm bowlful.

  1 large onion, chopped
  1 large carrot, shredded
  1 celery rib, chopped
1/4 cup butter
1/2 cup all-purpose flour
  8 cups chicken broth
  3 cups cooked wild rice
  1 cup cubed cooked chicken breast
1/4 teaspoon salt
1/4 teaspoon pepper
  1 cup fat-free evaporated milk
1/4 cup minced chives

In a large saucepan, saute the onion, carrot and celery in butter until tender. Stir in flour until blended. Gradually add broth. Stir in the rice, chicken, salt and pepper. Bring to a boil over medium heat; cook and stir for 2 minutes or until thickened. Stir in milk; cook 3-5 minutes longer. Garnish with chives.

Yield: 10 servings (2-1/2 quarts).

Baked Ham Hoagies

(pictured above)
Sundra Hauck, Bogalusa, Louisiana
Juicy slices of roasted ham star in these sandwiches. Adding cola to the ham while it bakes guarantees moist, tasty slices that people adore. Top the hoagies with whatever ingredients you'd like.

  1 boneless fully cooked ham (4 to 6 pounds)
1/2 cup water
  1 can (12 ounces) cola
  2 tablespoons brown sugar
15 to 20 hoagie buns, split
Lettuce leaves, sliced Colby-Monterey Jack cheese
  and tomatoes

Place ham in a roasting pan. Score the surface with shallow diagonal cuts, making diamond shapes. Add water to the pan. Cover and bake at 325° for 1-1/4 hours.

Pour cola over ham; sprinkle with brown sugar. Bake, uncovered, 30-45 minutes longer or until a meat thermometer reads 140° and ham is heated through. Let stand for 10 minutes before slicing. Serve on buns with lettuce, cheese and tomatoes.

Yield: 15-20 servings.

Quick Calzones

Clarice Brender, North Liberty, Iowa
These calzones taste delectable with or without the sauce. I prepare half of the calzones with ham and the other half with pepperoni.

  2 cups (8 ounces) shredded part-skim
     mozzarella cheese
  1 carton (15 ounces) ricotta cheese
  6 ounces diced fully cooked ham *or* sliced
     pepperoni
  1 teaspoon garlic powder
  2 loaves (1 pound *each*) frozen bread dough,
     thawed
Warmed spaghetti *or* pizza sauce, optional

In a large bowl, combine the cheeses, ham and garlic powder; mix well. Divide each loaf into eight pieces. On a floured surface, roll each portion into a 5-in. circle. Place filling in the center of each circle. Bring dough over filling; pinch seams to seal.

Place, seam sided down, on greased baking sheets. Bake at 375° for 30-35 minutes or until golden brown. Serve warm with sauce if desired. Refrigerate leftovers.

Yield: 16 servings.

Dorothy's Barbecue

(pictured below)
Virginia Bowser, Palm Springs, California
*A friend shared this recipe with me, and my family loves it!
It's a bit sweeter than most barbecue recipes. It also freezes
well, so I can prepare it ahead of time.*

    1 boneless beef rump roast (5 to 6 pounds)
   12 cups water
    1 bottle (14 ounces) ketchup
    1 cup packed brown sugar
    1 cup hot coffee
    3 tablespoons white vinegar
    2 tablespoons Worcestershire sauce
    1 tablespoon ground mustard
    1 tablespoon prepared horseradish
  1/2 teaspoon celery seed
  1/2 teaspoon garlic powder
  1/2 teaspoon salt
  1/4 teaspoon pepper
  1/8 teaspoon ground allspice
   18 to 20 hamburger buns, split

Place roast and water in a Dutch oven; bring to
a boil. Reduce heat; cover and simmer for 3 to
3-1/2 hours or until meat is tender. Remove heat;
cool. Strain broth; set aside 1-1/2 cups.

In a large saucepan or Dutch oven, combine
ketchup, brown sugar, coffee, vinegar, Worcestershire sauce, mustard, horseradish, seasonings
and reserved broth; bring to a boil. Reduce heat;
simmer, uncovered, for 30 minutes. Thinly slice
or shred roast; add to sauce and heat through.
Serve on buns.

Yield: 18-20 servings.

Pineapple Peach Soup

Teresa Lynn, Kerrville, Texas
I like to take this chilled soup to bring-a-dish events. It is usually different than what other people contribute, and everyone raves about the flavors.

    6 medium fresh peaches, peeled and sliced
    1 can (8 ounces) crushed unsweetened pineapple, undrained
  1/4 cup white grape juice
  1/4 cup lemon juice
    2 tablespoons honey
  3/4 teaspoon ground cinnamon
  1/4 teaspoon ground nutmeg
    1 medium cantaloupe, peeled, seeded and cubed
    1 cup orange juice
Fresh strawberries and whipped cream, optional

In 3-qt. saucepan, combine peaches, pineapple, grape juice, lemon juice, honey, cinnamon and nutmeg; bring to a boil over medium heat. Reduce heat and simmer, uncovered, for 10 minutes. Remove from the heat; cool to room temperature. Stir in three-fourths of the cantaloupe cubes and the orange juice; puree in batches in a blender.

Pour into a large bowl. Add remaining cantaloupe. Cover and refrigerate for at least 3 hours. Garnish with strawberries and whipped cream if desired.

Yield: 8-10 servings (2-1/4 quarts).

Country Cabbage Soup

(pictured above)
Vicky Catullo, Youngstown, Ohio
Here's an old-fashioned favorite that my mother-in-law shared with me. Try stirring in some shredded carrots or frozen mixed vegetables if you like. And if you need to stretch the number of servings a bit, simply add a couple of cups of cooked rice or pasta.

    2 pounds ground beef
    2 cans (28 ounces *each*) stewed tomatoes
    1 medium head cabbage, shredded
    2 large onions, chopped
    6 celery ribs, chopped
Salt and pepper to taste

In a large saucepan or Dutch oven, cook beef over medium heat until no longer pink; drain.

Add the tomatoes, cabbage, onions and celery; bring to a boil. Reduce heat; simmer, uncovered, for 25 minutes or until vegetables are tender. Add salt and pepper.

Yield: 12-14 servings (3-1/4 quarts).

Potluck Pointer

Slow cookers do a great job of keeping soup hot at bring-a-dish events. It's not a good idea to reheat cold soup in a slow cooker, so if you make it in advance, you'll want to reheat it on the stovetop or in the microwave before pouring it into a slow cooker.

Warm sandwiches are also fun potluck contributions. It's best to reheat pre-made sandwiches in the oven as opposed to the microwave. Tightly wrap individual sandwiches in foil to keep them warm on your drive to the dinner. Keep large party subs whole until serving. Then unwrap the foil and slice.

Super Italian Sub

(pictured below)
Patricia Lomp, Middleboro, Massachusetts
I like recipes that can be made ahead of time, and this meaty sandwich offers that convenience. I just wrap the sub tightly in plastic wrap and keep it in the refrigerator. At mealtime, all that's left to do is unwrap it and slice it up.

    1   loaf (1 pound) unsliced Italian bread
  1/3   cup olive oil
  1/4   cup cider vinegar
    8   garlic cloves, minced
    1   teaspoon dried oregano
  1/4   teaspoon pepper
  1/2   pound fully cooked ham, thinly sliced
  1/2   pound thinly sliced cooked turkey
  1/4   pound thinly sliced hard salami
  1/4   pound sliced provolone cheese
  1/4   pound sliced part-skim mozzarella cheese
    1   medium green pepper, thinly sliced into
        rings

Cut bread in half lengthwise; hollow out top and bottom, leaving a 1/2-in. shell (discard removed bread or save for another use). Combine oil, vinegar, garlic, oregano and pepper; brush on cut sides of bread top and bottom. On the bottom half, layer half of the meats, cheeses and green pepper. Repeat layers. Replace bread top. Wrap tightly in plastic wrap; refrigerate for up to 24 hours.
Yield: 10-12 servings.

Beef and Bacon Chowder

(pictured above)
Nancy Schmidt, Center, Colorado
Rave reviews are sure to follow when this creamy chowder appears at your next covered-dish dinner. Bacon makes it a rich and hearty favorite that most folks enjoy.

    1   pound ground beef
    2   cups chopped celery
  1/2   cup chopped onion
    4   cups milk
    3   cups cubed peeled potatoes, cooked
    2   cans (10-3/4 ounces *each*) condensed
        cream of mushroom soup, undiluted
    2   cups chopped carrots, cooked
Salt and pepper to taste
   12   bacon strips, cooked and crumbled

In a soup kettle or Dutch oven, cook beef, celery and onion over medium heat until the meat is no longer pink and the vegetables are tender; drain. Add the milk, potatoes, soup, carrots, salt and pepper; heat through. Stir in the bacon just before serving.
Yield: 12 servings (3 quarts).

Hunter's Chili

(pictured below)
Julie Batterman, Lincoln, Nebraska
Ground beef, bratwurst, veggies, beans and plenty of herbs and seasonings make this a heartwarming addition to any gathering. As soon as hunting season begins, you can find this spicy chili brewing in my kitchen.

- 1 pound uncooked bratwurst
- 1 pound ground beef
- 2 cups chopped onion
- 1 large green pepper, chopped
- 4 cups water
- 1 to 2 garlic cloves, minced
- 1 can (6 ounces) tomato paste
- 1 can (28 ounces) diced tomatoes, undrained
- 1 can (8 ounces) tomato sauce
- 2 cans (16 ounces *each*) kidney beans, rinsed and drained
- 1 can (15-1/4 ounces) whole kernel corn, drained
- 1 can (15 ounces) pinto beans, rinsed and drained
- 2 cans (4 ounces *each*) mushroom stems and pieces, drained
- 3 tablespoons chili powder
- 1 tablespoon paprika
- 1 teaspoon ground cumin
- 1 teaspoon dried oregano
- 1 teaspoon salt
- 1/2 teaspoon pepper
- 1/4 teaspoon cayenne pepper
- 1/4 teaspoon crushed red pepper flakes
- 2 bay leaves

In a 6-qt. Dutch oven or soup kettle over medium heat, brown bratwurst; drain. Remove and thinly slice; return to pan along with beef, onion and green pepper. Cook over medium heat until beef is browned and onion is tender; drain. Add all remaining ingredients. Cover and simmer for 1-2 hours. Remove bay leaves before serving.

Yield: 14-18 servings (4-1/2 quarts).

Chicken Salad Sandwiches

(pictured above)
Judy Kisch-Keuten, Beatrice, Nebraska
I entered this recipe in a contest and it won first place. Celery and toasted almonds add crunch to the filling that's delicious served on English muffins.

- 2 cups cubed cooked chicken
- 2 celery ribs, chopped
- 1/2 cup chopped green pepper
- 1/2 cup mayonnaise
- 1/3 cup slivered almonds, toasted
- 1/4 cup sweet pickle relish
- 1/4 cup sliced pimiento-stuffed olives
- 2 tablespoons chopped onion
- 2 teaspoons prepared mustard
- 3/4 to 1-1/4 teaspoons salt
- 1/4 teaspoon pepper
- 12 English muffins, split and toasted
- 12 lettuce leaves
- 12 thin tomato slices

In a bowl, combine the first 11 ingredients; mix well. Top 12 muffin halves with lettuce leaves; spread with chicken salad. Top with tomato slices and remaining muffin halves.

Yield: 12 servings.

Pictured below:
Cherry Cheese Torte (p. 177).

Delightful
Desserts

Maple-Mocha Brownie Torte

(pictured above)
Amy Flory, Cleveland, Georgia
This gorgeous dessert is at the top of my list of speedy standbys. It's simple because it starts with a brownie mix. The nutty brownie layers are jazzed up with a rich, creamy frosting that boasts an irresistible maple flavor.

   1 package brownie mix (13-inch x 9-inch pan size)
 1/2 cup chopped walnuts
   2 cups heavy whipping cream
   2 teaspoons instant coffee granules
 1/2 cup packed brown sugar
1-1/2 teaspoons maple flavoring
   1 teaspoon vanilla extract
Chocolate curls *or* additional walnuts, optional

Prepare batter for brownie mix according to package directions for cake-like brownies. Stir in walnuts. Pour into two greased 9-in. round baking pans.

Bake at 350° for 20-22 minutes or until a toothpick inserted 2 in. from the edge comes out clean. Cool for 10 minutes before removing from pans to wire racks to cool completely.

In a large mixing bowl, beat cream and coffee granules until stiff peaks form. Gradually beat in brown sugar, maple flavoring and vanilla.

Spread 1-1/2 cups over one brownie layer; top with second layer. Spread remaining cream mixture over top and sides of torte. Garnish with chocolate curls or walnuts if desired. Store in the refrigerator.

Yield: 12 servings.

Honey Bun Cake

Kathy Mayo, Winston-Salem, North Carolina
I take along recipe cards to hand out when I bring this cake to school socials and the like. It always goes quickly.

- 1 package (18-1/4 ounces) yellow *or* white cake mix
- 4 egg whites
- 1 cup (8 ounces) sour cream
- 2/3 cup unsweetened applesauce
- 1/2 cup packed brown sugar
- 2 teaspoons ground cinnamon
- 1-1/2 cups confectioners' sugar
- 2 tablespoons milk
- 1 teaspoon vanilla extract

In a large mixing bowl, combine dry cake mix, egg whites, sour cream and applesauce. Beat on low speed until moistened. Beat on medium for 2 minutes.

Pour half into a greased 13-in. x 9-in. x 2-in. baking pan. Combine brown sugar and cinnamon; sprinkle over batter. Cover with remaining batter; cut through with a knife to swirl. Bake at 325° for 35-40 minutes or until a toothpick inserted near the center comes out clean. Cool on a wire rack.

For glaze, combine confectioners' sugar, milk and vanilla until smooth; drizzle over warm cake.

Yield: 20 servings.

Fruity Angel Food Trifle

Louise Bouvier, Lafleche, Saskatchewan
This summery dessert showcases an attractive assortment of fresh and canned fruit. I refined the original recipe over time to suit our family's tastes.

- 4 cups cold milk
- 2 packages (3.4 ounces *each*) instant vanilla pudding mix
- 1 prepared angel food cake (8 inches)
- 1 carton (8 ounces) frozen whipped topping, thawed
- 1 can (20 ounces) pineapple tidbits, drained
- 1 can (15 ounces) sliced pears, drained
- 1 pint strawberries, sliced
- 4 kiwifruit, peeled, halved and thinly sliced
- 1 cup fresh *or* frozen blueberries, thawed

In a mixing bowl, beat milk and pudding mixes on low speed for 2 minutes; set aside. Split cake horizontally into thirds; place one layer in a 5-qt. serving bowl (about 9-in. diameter). Top with a third of the pudding, whipped topping and fruit. Repeat layers twice. Cover and chill for at least 3 hours.

Yield: 16-20 servings.

Texas Lime Pie

(pictured below)
Diane Bell, Manvel, Texas
With the perfect balance between sweet and tart flavors, this refreshing pie is a great way to beat the heat. Not only does the recipe yield two pies, but it's simple enough for novice bakers who want to contribute a memorable item to a celebration.

- 3 cups graham cracker crumbs
- 1/2 cup packed brown sugar
- 2/3 cup butter, melted
- 3 cans (14 ounces *each*) sweetened condensed milk
- 5 egg yolks
- 2 cups lime juice
- Whipped topping, lime slices and fresh mint, optional

In a large bowl, combine the cracker crumbs, brown sugar and butter until crumbly. Press onto the bottom and up the sides of two greased 9-in. pie plates.

In a large mixing bowl, beat the milk, egg yolks and lime juice on low for 2 minutes or until smooth and slightly thickened.

Pour into prepared crusts. Bake at 350° for 18-22 minutes or until a knife inserted near the center comes out clean. Cool on wire racks for 1 hour. Chill for 6 hours. Garnish with whipped topping, lime and mint if desired.

Yield: 2 pies (6-8 servings each).

Chocolate Cream Cake

(pictured above)
Marge Dellert, Shepherd, Michigan
Whenever I take this moist chocolate cake with butter cream filling to a function, I'm asked for the recipe. My daughter-in-law, Marla, shared it with me.

```
    1  package (18-1/4 ounces) devil's food
       cake mix
  1/2  cup butter, softened
  1/2  cup shortening
1-1/4  cups sugar
  3/4  cup milk
    1  teaspoon vanilla extract
```
GLAZE:
```
    1  cup sugar
  1/3  cup baking cocoa
    3  tablespoons cornstarch
    1  cup cold water
    3  tablespoons butter
    1  teaspoon vanilla extract
```

Prepare and bake cake according to package directions, using a greased and floured 13-in. x 9-in. x 2-in. baking pan. Cool for 10 minutes before inverting onto a wire rack. Cool completely.

For filling, in a large mixing bowl, cream the butter, shortening and sugar until light and fluffy. In a small saucepan, heat milk to 140°; add to the creamed mixture. Beat until sugar is dissolved. Stir in vanilla.

Split cake into two horizontal layers; spread filling over bottom cake layer. Top with remaining cake layer.

For glaze, in a large saucepan, combine the sugar, cocoa and cornstarch. Gradually add water. Bring to a boil; cook and stir for 2 minutes or until thickened.

Remove from the heat; stir in butter and vanilla until glaze is smooth. Cool to lukewarm. Spread over top of the cake. Let stand until set. Refrigerate leftovers.

Yield: 16-20 servings.

Pumpkin Orange Cake

(pictured below)
Shirley Glaab, Hattiesburg, Mississippi
This spice cake is popular at my family gatherings. Not only is it filled with nuts and topped with a unique orange frosting, but I can make it ahead of time.

```
  1/2  cup butter, softened
1-1/4  cups sugar
    2  eggs
    1  cup canned pumpkin
  1/2  cup orange juice
  1/4  cup milk
    1  tablespoon grated orange peel
    2  cups all-purpose flour
    3  teaspoons baking powder
    1  teaspoon ground cinnamon
  1/2  teaspoon baking soda
  1/2  teaspoon salt
  1/2  teaspoon ground ginger
  1/2  teaspoon ground allspice
  1/2  cup chopped walnuts
```
ORANGE FROSTING:
```
  1/3  cup butter, softened
    3  cups confectioners' sugar
    3  tablespoons milk
    2  teaspoons orange juice
4-1/2  teaspoons grated orange peel
```
Candied orange peel, optional

In a large mixing bowl, cream butter and sugar. Add the eggs, one at a time, beating well after each addition. In another mixing bowl, beat pumpkin, orange juice, milk and orange peel. Combine dry ingredients; add to creamed mixture alternately with pumpkin mixture. Fold in nuts.

Pour into a greased 13-in. x 9-in. x 2-in. baking pan. Bake at 350° for 30 minutes or until a toothpick inserted near the center comes out clean. Cool on a wire rack.

For frosting, in a large mixing bowl, beat butter and confectioners' sugar until smooth. Beat in the milk, orange juice and peel. Frost cake. Garnish with candied peel if desired.

Yield: 12 servings.

Sour Cream Cranberry Bars

(pictured above)
Barbara Nowakowski, Mesa, Arizona
An exquisite filling of sour cream, lemon peel and dried cranberries is layered between a buttery crust and a golden crumb topping in these flavorful bars.

    1 cup butter, softened
    1 cup packed brown sugar
    2 cups quick-cooking oats
1-1/2 cups plus 2 tablespoons all-purpose flour,
       divided
    2 cups dried cranberries
    1 cup (8 ounces) sour cream
  3/4 cup sugar
    1 egg, lightly beaten
    1 tablespoon grated lemon peel
    1 teaspoon vanilla extract

In a large mixing bowl, cream the butter and brown sugar. Combine the oats and 1-1/2 cups flour; add to the creamed mixture until blended. Set aside 1-1/2 cups.

Press remaining crumb mixture into an ungreased 13-in. x 9-in. x 2-in. baking pan. Bake at 350° for 10-12 minutes or until lightly browned.

Meanwhile, in a large bowl, combine the cranberries, sour cream, sugar, egg, lemon peel, vanilla and remaining flour.

Spread evenly over crust. Sprinkle with reserved crumb mixture. Bake for 20-25 minutes or until lightly browned. Cool on a wire rack. Refrigerate leftovers.

Yield: about 3 dozen.

Chocolate Bliss Brownies

Juanita Lou Williams, Enid, Oklahoma
I first tried these at a brunch and begged the hostess for the recipe. Sometimes I'll eliminate the frosting and just sprinkle the top with confectioners' sugar.

1/2 cup butter, softened
  1 cup sugar
  4 eggs
  1 can (16 ounces) chocolate syrup
  1 cup all-purpose flour
  1 cup chopped nuts
  1 teaspoon salt
FROSTING:
  6 tablespoons butter, cubed
1-1/2 cups sugar
1/3 cup milk
1/2 cup semisweet chocolate chips

In a large mixing bowl, cream the butter and sugar. Add eggs, one at a time, beating well after each addition. Add chocolate syrup. Beat in flour, nuts and salt until blended.

Pour into a greased 13-in. x 9-in. x 2-in. baking pan. Bake at 350° for 25-30 minutes or until a toothpick inserted near the center comes out clean (brownies may appear moist). Cool on a wire rack.

In a small saucepan, melt butter. Add sugar and milk. Bring to a boil; boil for 30 seconds. Remove from the heat; stir in the chips until melted. Beat until frosting reaches spreading consistency. Frost cooled brownies.

Yield: 4-1/2 dozen.

Streusel Strawberry Pizza

(pictured above)
Karen Ann Bland, Gove, Kansas
This is the best dessert pizza I've ever tasted. It's great for parties where lots of children will be present, although adults snap it up just as quickly.

1	package (18-1/4 ounces) white cake mix
1-1/4	cups quick-cooking oats
1/3	cup butter, softened
1	egg
1	can (21 ounces) strawberry pie filling *or*
	flavor of your choice
1/2	cup chopped nuts
1/4	cup packed brown sugar
1/8	teaspoon ground cinnamon

In a large mixing bowl, combine the dry cake mix, oats and butter until blended; set aside 3/4 cup for topping. Add egg to the remaining crumb mixture and mix well.

Press into a greased 12-in. pizza pan. Build up edges and flute if desired. Bake at 350° for 12 minutes.

Spread pie filling over crust to within 1 in. of edges. Combine the nuts, brown sugar, cinnamon and reserved crumb mixture; sprinkle over filling. Bake for 15-20 minutes or until lightly browned. Cool on a wire rack. Refrigerate leftovers.

Yield: 8-10 servings.

Macaroon Kisses

Angie Lansman, Perry, Iowa
One bite and I think you'll agree this is the best coconut cookie you've ever tasted. Dressed up with chocolate kisses, the treats are always the first to disappear from cookie trays.

1/3	cup butter, softened
1	package (3 ounces) cream cheese, softened
3/4	cup sugar
1	egg yolk
2	teaspoons orange juice
2	teaspoons almond extract
1-1/4	cups all-purpose flour
2	teaspoons baking powder
1/4	teaspoon salt
1	package (14 ounces) flaked coconut, *divided*
1	package (13 ounces) milk chocolate kisses

In a large mixing bowl, cream butter, cream cheese and sugar. Beat in egg yolk, orange juice and extract. Combine flour, baking powder and salt; gradually add to the creamed mixture. Stir in 3-2/3 cups coconut. Cover and refrigerate for 30 minutes or until easy to handle.

Roll into 1-in. balls, then roll in remaining coconut. Place 1 in. apart on ungreased baking sheets. Bake at 350° for 12-15 minutes or until the edges are lightly browned. Immediately press a chocolate kiss into the center of each cookie. Cool for 1 minute before removing to wire racks.

Yield: about 4-1/2 dozen.

Deep-Dish Cherry Pie

(pictured below)
Lillian Heston, Warren, New Jersey
Who can resist a cherry pie featuring a flaky homemade crust? This scrumptious version is easier than two-crust pies, and you can use fresh or frozen cherries with equally tasty results.

  6 cups pitted tart red cherries
3/4 cup sugar
3/4 cup packed brown sugar
  3 tablespoons cornstarch
  1 teaspoon almond extract
  2 to 3 drops food coloring, optional
Dash salt
  3 to 4 tablespoons butter

CRUST:
1-1/2 cups all-purpose flour
  1 tablespoon sugar
1/2 teaspoon salt
1/2 teaspoon ground nutmeg
1/2 cup plus 2 tablespoons shortening
  4 to 5 tablespoons ice water
Milk *or* heavy whipping cream
Additional sugar

In a large mixing bowl, combine cherries, sugars, cornstarch, extract, food coloring and salt. Place in a greased 1-1/2-qt. to 2-qt. casserole. Dot with butter. Set aside.

For crust, in a large bowl, combine the flour, sugar, salt and nutmeg. Cut in shortening. Add water, a little at a time, until a dough forms. Do not overmix. Roll out on a floured surface to fit the top of the casserole. Place on top of the cherries, pressing against the sides of the dish. Cut decorative designs or slits in center of crust.

Brush with milk or cream and sprinkle with sugar. Bake at 350° for 1 hour or until crust is golden brown. Cool at least 15 minutes before serving.

Yield: 8-10 servings.

Blond Toffee Brownies

(pictured above)
Mary Williams, Lancaster, California
Whenever a friend brought these brownies to bake sales, they sold in minutes. After getting the recipe from her, I was happy to discover how quickly they could be thrown together. I was even more excited when my family said that the thin, chewy bars are the best they've ever tasted.

        1/2 cup butter, softened
          1 cup sugar
        1/2 cup packed brown sugar
          2 eggs
          1 teaspoon vanilla extract
    1-1/2 cups all-purpose flour
          2 teaspoons baking powder
        1/4 teaspoon salt
          1 cup English toffee bits *or* almond brickle
              bits

In a large mixing bowl, cream butter and sugars. Add eggs, one at a time, beating well after each addition. Beat in vanilla. Combine the flour, baking powder and salt; gradually add to creamed mixture. Stir in toffee bits.

Spread into a greased 13-in. x 9-in. x 2-in. baking pan. Bake at 350° for 35-40 minutes or until a toothpick inserted near the center comes out clean. Cool on a wire rack. Cut into bars.

Yield: 1-1/2 dozen.

Potluck Pointer

Potlucks are a great time to customize favorite recipes. For instance, replace half of the toffee bits in Blond Toffee Brownies with chopped nuts. Drizzle some melted white chocolate over the brownies or use a cookie cutter to cut them into fun shapes.

Cookie Sheet Apple Pie

(pictured below)
Bertha Jeffries, Great Falls, Montana
I belong to several volunteer service groups, and this old-fashioned dessert has been a real time-saver when there's a large crowd to feed. It serves far more than an ordinary pie with about the same amount of effort.

    3-3/4 cups all-purpose flour
    1-1/2 teaspoons salt
        3/4 cup shortening
          3 eggs, lightly beaten
        1/3 cup milk
          8 cups sliced peeled tart baking apples
    1-1/2 cups sugar
          1 teaspoon ground cinnamon
        1/2 teaspoon ground nutmeg
          1 cup crushed cornflakes
          1 egg white, beaten

In a large bowl, combine flour and salt. Cut in shortening until mixture resembles coarse crumbs. Add eggs and milk; mix to form dough. Chill for 20 minutes.

Divide dough in half; roll one half to fit the bottom and sides of a greased 15-in. x 10-in. x 1-in. baking pan. Arrange apples over crust. Combine sugar, cinnamon, nutmeg and cornflakes; sprinkle over apples. Roll remaining dough to fit top of pan and place over apples. Seal edges; cut slits in top.

Brush with egg white. Bake at 400° for 15 minutes. Reduce heat to 350°; bake for 25-30 minutes or until golden brown.

Yield: 16-20 servings.

Easy Rhubarb Dessert

(pictured above)
Mildred Mesick, Richmond, New York
Here's a memorable and attractive dessert, particularly when it's served warm with ice cream. It takes only a few moments to slice the rhubarb, then just combine it with five other ingredients and pop it all in the oven.

> 4 cups sliced fresh *or* frozen rhubarb
> 1 package (3 ounces) raspberry gelatin
> 1/3 cup sugar
> 1 package (18-1/4 ounces) yellow *or* white cake mix
> 1 cup water
> 1/3 cup butter, melted
> Ice cream, optional

Place rhubarb in a greased 13-in. x 9-in. x 2-in. baking dish. Sprinkle with the gelatin, sugar and cake mix. Pour water evenly over dry ingredients; drizzle with butter.

Bake at 350° for 1 hour or until rhubarb is tender. Serve with ice cream if desired.
Yield: 16-20 servings.

Editor's Note: If using frozen rhubarb, measure rhubarb while still frozen, then thaw completely. Drain in a colander, but do not press liquid out.

Cherry Cheese Torte

(pictured below)
Lisa Radelet, Boulder, Colorado
You can't help but impress people when you set out this lovely torte. It makes any occasion feel a bit more special.

> 2 packages (3 ounces *each*) ladyfingers
> 1 package (8 ounces) cream cheese, softened
> 1 cup plus 1 teaspoon sugar, *divided*
> 2 teaspoon vanilla extract, *divided*
> 2 teaspoons lemon juice
> 1 teaspoon grated lemon peel
> 2 cups heavy whipping cream
> 1 can (21 ounces) cherry *or* blueberry pie filling

Place a layer of ladyfingers on the bottom and around the sides of an ungreased 9-in. springform pan. In a large mixing bowl, beat the cream cheese, 1 cup sugar and 1 teaspoon vanilla until smooth. Add lemon juice and peel; mix well.

In small mixing bowl, beat cream until it begins to thicken. Add remaining sugar and vanilla; beat until stiff peaks form. Fold into cream cheese mixture. Spread half over crust. Arrange remaining ladyfingers in a spoke pattern over top. Evenly spread with the remaining cream cheese mixture. Top with pie filling. Cover and refrigerate overnight. Remove sides of pan just before serving.
Yield: 12 servings.

Chocolate Cheesecake Bars

Louise Good, Flemington, New Jersey
When you don't have time to bake a real cheesecake, reach for this tasty recipe. A thick, tender crust is covered with a creamy chocolate filling and then sprinkled with a crumb topping.

- 1 cup butter, softened
- 1-1/2 cups sugar
- 2 eggs
- 1/2 teaspoon almond extract
- 3 cups all-purpose flour
- 1 teaspoon baking powder
- 1/2 teaspoon salt

FILLING:
- 2 cups (12 ounces) semisweet chocolate chips
- 1 package (8 ounces) cream cheese
- 1 can (5 ounces) evaporated milk
- 1 cup chopped walnuts
- 1/2 teaspoon almond extract

In a large mixing bowl, cream butter and sugar. Add eggs, one at a time, beating well after each addition. Beat in extract. Combine flour, baking powder and salt; gradually add to the creamed mixture until mixture resembles coarse crumbs (do not overmix). Set aside half for topping. Press the remaining crumb mixture into a greased 13-in. x 9-in. x 2-in. baking pan.

For filling, in a large saucepan, combine the chocolate chips, cream cheese and milk. Cook over low heat until chips are melted; stir until smooth and blended. Remove from the heat; stir in walnuts and extract.

Spread over crust; sprinkle with reserved crumb mixture. Bake at 375° for 35-40 minutes or until golden brown. Cool on a wire rack. Cut into bars. Store in the refrigerator.

Yield: 4 dozen.

Potluck Pointer

Lightly spraying plastic wrap with nonstick cooking spray can help prevent the frosting from lifting off of your covered cakes and cupcakes. Give it a try the next time you attend a church supper.

And if you're whipping up bars or brownies for a charity bake sale, why not tape a copy of the recipe to the outside of the plastic wrap? The buyer is sure to appreciate your thoughtfulness.

Apple Pear Cake

(pictured below)
Mary Ann Lees, Centreville, Alabama
When my sister made this apple cake for me, I had to ask for the recipe because it was so moist and yummy.

- 2 cups shredded peeled tart apple
- 2 cups shredded peeled pears
- 2 cups sugar
- 1-1/4 cups vegetable oil
- 1 cup raisins
- 1 cup chopped pecans
- 2 eggs, beaten
- 1 teaspoon vanilla extract
- 3 cups all-purpose flour
- 2 teaspoons baking soda
- 2 teaspoons ground cinnamon
- 1/2 teaspoon ground nutmeg
- 1/2 teaspoon salt

CREAM CHEESE FROSTING:
- 1 package (3 ounces) cream cheese, softened
- 3 cups confectioners' sugar
- 1/4 cup butter, softened
- 2 tablespoons milk
- 1/2 teaspoon vanilla extract

In a large bowl, combine the first eight ingredients. Combine dry ingredients; stir into the fruit mixture.

Pour into a greased 13-in. x 9-in. x 2-in. baking pan. Bake at 325° for 1 hour or until a toothpick inserted near the center comes out clean. Cool on a wire rack.

For the frosting, in a large mixing bowl, beat the cream cheese, confectioners' sugar and butter until smooth. Beat in the milk and vanilla; frost cake. Store in the refrigerator.

Yield: 12-15 servings.

Creamy Banana Pie

(pictured above)
Rita Pribyl, Indianapolis, Indiana
When friends ask if I know of any good banana dishes, I instantly pass along this dessert. Everyone who tastes a slice enjoys its delicious, old-fashioned flavor.

      1 envelope unflavored gelatin
  1/4 cup cold water
  3/4 cup sugar
  1/4 cup cornstarch
  1/2 teaspoon salt
2-3/4 cups milk
      4 egg yolks, beaten
      2 tablespoons butter
      1 tablespoon vanilla extract
      4 medium firm bananas, *divided*
      1 cup heavy whipping cream, whipped
      1 pastry shell (10 inches), baked
Juice and grated peel of 1 lemon
  1/2 cup apple jelly

Soften gelatin in cold water; set aside. In a saucepan, combine the sugar, cornstarch and salt. Whisk in the milk until smooth. Cook and stir over medium-high heat until thickened and bubbly. Reduce heat; cook and stir 2 minutes longer. Remove from the heat. Stir a small amount of hot filling into yolks. Return all to the pan, stirring constantly. Bring to a gentle boil. Cook and stir 2 minutes longer. Remove from the heat; stir in softened gelatin until dissolved. Stir in butter and vanilla. Cover the surface of custard with plastic wrap and chill until no longer warm.

Slice three bananas; fold into custard along with whipped cream. Spoon into pie shell. Cover and refrigerate until set, about 4-5 hours.

Just before serving, place lemon juice in a small bowl and slice the remaining banana into it. Melt jelly in a saucepan over low heat. Drain banana; pat dry and arrange over filling. Lightly brush banana with the jelly. Sprinkle with grated lemon peel. Refrigerate leftovers.

Yield: 8 servings.

Cherry Kringle

(pictured above)
Mary Christianson, Carmel, Indiana
This soft yeast dough bakes into a golden, tender pastry that surrounds a luscious cherry center. Since the recipe makes four kringles, there's plenty to share with others. You can also freeze one or two for future use.

  1 package (1/4 ounce) active dry yeast
  1 cup warm milk (110° to 115°)
  4 cups bread flour
  2 tablespoons sugar
  1 teaspoon salt
1/2 cup cold butter
1/2 cup shortening
  2 eggs, lightly beaten
  4 cups cherry pie filling

ICING:
  2 cups confectioners' sugar
  2 to 3 tablespoons milk

In a large mixing bowl, dissolve yeast in warm milk. In another bowl, combine flour, sugar and salt; cut in butter and shortening until crumbly. Add to yeast mixture. Add eggs; beat to form a very soft dough (do not knead). Cover and refrigerate for at least 8 hours.

Turn dough onto a lightly floured surface; divide into fourths. Roll each portion into a 14-in. x 11-in. rectangle; spread cherry pie filling down the center third of each rectangle. Starting at a long side, fold a third of the dough over filling; fold other third over top. Pinch to seal; pinch ends and tuck under. Place 2 in. apart on greased baking sheets.

Bake at 350° for 25 minutes or until golden brown. Remove from pans to wire racks to cool completely. Combine icing ingredients; drizzle over kringles.

Yield: 4 loaves.

Banana Snack Cake

(pictured below)
Dawn Fagerstrom, Warren, Minnesota
I make this moist banana cake for birthday parties and other get-togethers, but I also use the recipe for cupcakes. They taste great even without the frosting.

1/2 cup shortening
3/4 cup packed brown sugar
1/2 cup sugar
  2 eggs
  1 cup mashed ripe bananas (2 to 3 medium)
  1 teaspoon vanilla extract
  2 cups all-purpose *or* whole wheat flour
  1 teaspoon baking soda
  1 teaspoon salt
1/2 cup buttermilk
1/2 cup chopped nuts

FROSTING:
1/2 cup packed brown sugar
1/4 cup butter, softened
  6 tablespoons milk
2-1/2 to 3 cups confectioners' sugar

In a large mixing bowl, cream shortening and sugars. Add eggs, one at a time, beating well after each addition. Beat in bananas and vanilla. Combine flour, baking soda and salt; add to the creamed mixture alternately with buttermilk. Stir in nuts.

Pour into a greased 13-in. x 9-in. x 2-in. baking pan. Bake at 350° for 25-30 minutes or until a toothpick inserted near the center comes out clean. Cool on a wire rack.

For frosting, combine brown sugar, butter and milk in a large saucepan. Bring to a boil over medium heat; boil and stir for 2 minutes. Remove from the heat; cool to lukewarm.

Gradually beat in confectioners' sugar until frosting reaches spreading consistency. Frost the cake.

Yield: 12 servings.

Peanut Butter Brownies

(pictured above)
Margaret McNeil, Memphis, Tennessee
The combination of chocolate and peanut butter makes these marbled brownies a real crowd-pleaser. They're so good, they once won a ribbon at our local fair.

>   3 eggs
>   1 cup butter, melted
>   2 teaspoons vanilla extract
>   2 cups sugar
> 1-1/4 cups all-purpose flour
>   3/4 cup baking cocoa
>   1/2 teaspoon baking powder
>   1/4 teaspoon salt
>   1 cup milk chocolate chips

FILLING:
>   2 packages (8 ounces *each*) cream cheese, softened
>   1/2 cup creamy peanut butter
>   1/4 cup sugar
>   1 egg
>   2 tablespoons milk

In a large mixing bowl, combine eggs, butter and vanilla. Combine dry ingredients; add to egg mixture and mix well. Stir in chocolate chips. Set aside 1 cup for topping. Spread remaining batter into a greased 13-in. x 9-in. x 2-in. baking pan.

In a small mixing bowl, beat cream cheese, peanut butter and sugar until smooth. Add egg and milk, beating on low just until combined. Carefully spread over batter. Drop reserved batter by tablespoonfuls over filling. Cut through batter with a knife to swirl.

Bake at 350° for 35-40 minutes or until a toothpick inserted near the center comes out clean. Cool on a wire rack before cutting. Refrigerate until serving.
Yield: 3 dozen.

Butterscotch Muffins

(pictured below)
Jill Hazelton, Hamlet, Indiana
Butterscotch pudding gives a distinctive flavor to these muffins topped with brown sugar and nuts. My son made them for a 4-H competition, and they won first place.

>   2 cups all-purpose flour
>   1 cup sugar
>   1 package (3.4 ounces) instant vanilla pudding mix
>   1 package (3.4 ounces) instant butterscotch pudding mix
>   2 teaspoons baking powder
>   1 teaspoon salt
>   1 cup water
>   4 eggs
>   3/4 cup vegetable oil
>   1 teaspoon vanilla extract

TOPPING:
>   2/3 cup packed brown sugar
>   1/2 cup chopped pecans
>   2 teaspoons ground cinnamon

In a large bowl, combine the flour, sugar, pudding mixes, baking powder and salt. Combine the water, eggs, oil and vanilla; stir into the dry ingredients just until moistened. Fill greased or paper-lined muffin cups two-thirds full.

Combine the topping ingredients; sprinkle over batter. Bake at 350° for 15-20 minutes or until a toothpick comes out clean. Cool for 5 minutes before removing from pans to wire racks.
Yield: about 1-1/2 dozen.

Cranberry Meringue Pie

(pictured at top right)
Tina Dierking, Showhegan, Maine
This sweet-tart cranberry pie is simply mouth-watering and a nice change at autumn coffee socials from the typical apple and pumpkin pies.

- 1 package (12 ounces) fresh *or* frozen cranberries, thawed
- 1 cup orange juice
- 3/4 cup water
- 3/4 cup sugar
- Sugar substitute equivalent to 3/4 cup sugar
- 1/3 cup quick-cooking tapioca
- 2 teaspoons grated orange peel
- 1/4 teaspoon salt

MERINGUE:
- 4 egg whites
- 1/4 teaspoon cream of tartar
- 1/2 cup sugar
- 1 pastry shell (9 inches), baked

Place cranberries in a food processor; cover and pulse until coarsely chopped.

In a large saucepan, combine the cranberries, orange juice, water, sugar, sugar substitute, tapioca, orange peel and salt. Let stand for 5 minutes. Bring to a boil over medium heat, stirring constantly. Reduce heat; simmer for 10 minutes, stirring constantly. Keep warm.

In a large mixing bowl, beat egg whites until foamy. Add cream of tartar; beat on medium speed until soft peaks form. Gradually beat in sugar, 1 tablespoon at a time, beating until stiff peaks form. Spoon warm filling into pastry shell.

Spread meringue evenly over filling, sealing to crust. Bake at 350° for 18-22 minutes or until golden brown. Cool for 1 hour. Chill, covered, for at least 4 hours.

Yield: 8 servings.

Editor's Note: This recipe was tested with Splenda No Calorie Sweetener.

Lemon Cheese Pie

(pictured at bottom right)
Dorothy Dombrowski, Milwaukee, Wisconsin
A sheet of refrigerated pie pastry makes this church-supper staple easy to prepare. It's the heavenly filling, however, that keeps folks lining up for seconds.

- 1 sheet refrigerated pie pastry
- 1 cup sugar
- 1/4 cup plus 2 teaspoons cornstarch
- 1/2 teaspoon salt
- 1 cup water
- 2 tablespoons butter
- 2 teaspoons grated lemon peel
- 3 to 4 drops yellow food coloring, optional
- 1/2 cup plus 1 teaspoon lemon juice, *divided*
- 1 package (8 ounces) fat-free cream cheese
- 1/2 cup confectioners' sugar
- 1 cup reduced-fat whipped topping

Lightly roll out pastry into a 12-in. circle; transfer to a 9-in. pie plate. Trim pastry to 1/2 in. beyond edge of plate, reserving scraps for garnish. Flute edges. Line unpricked pastry shell with a double thickness of heavy-duty foil. Bake at 450° for 8 minutes. Remove foil; bake 5 minutes longer. Cool on a wire rack.

Roll out pastry scraps to 1/8-in. thickness. Cut out star shapes with 1-1/2-in. cookie cutters. Place on a baking sheet. Bake at 450° for 8 minutes or until golden brown. Cool on a wire rack.

In a large saucepan, combine the sugar, cornstarch and salt. Stir in water until blended. Bring to a boil; cook and stir for 2 minutes or until very thick. Remove from the heat; stir in butter, lemon peel and food coloring if desired. Gently stir in 1/2 cup lemon juice. Cool to room temperature, about 1 hour.

In a large mixing bowl, beat cream cheese and confectioners' sugar until smooth. Fold in whipped topping and remaining lemon juice. Spread into crust; top with lemon filling. Refrigerate for 6 hours or until the top is set. Garnish with pastry stars.

Yield: 10 servings.

Potluck Pointer

Pies are an ideal item to bring to a church supper, picnic or other carry-in event. Whether featuring apples, cherries, lemon or pumpkin, these classic desserts are proven to tickle the sweet tooth of anyone who approaches the dessert table.

In addition, the goodies usually don't need to be reheated or kept particularly cold so food safety isn't often an issue. Best of all...they travel well.

To make sure pies arrive in good condition, turn a foil pie plate upside down, and set it over the dessert. Use a rubber band or two to keep the plate in place.

Favorite Chocolate Sheet Cake

(pictured below)
Mary Lewis, Escondido, California
My mother adapted this family pleaser from a recipe for vanilla cake that was in a church cookbook. The cake is so flavorful that it doesn't really need frosting...but I always feel you can never have enough chocolate!

    1   cup butter, softened
    2   cups sugar
    4   eggs
    2   teaspoons vanilla extract
2-1/4   cups cake flour
    1   teaspoon baking soda
    1   teaspoon salt
    1   cup buttermilk
    3   squares (1 ounce *each*) bittersweet
        chocolate, melted

FROSTING:
  1/4   cup baking cocoa
  1/3   cup milk
  1/2   cup butter, cubed
    1   teaspoon vanilla extract
3-1/2   cups confectioners' sugar

In a large mixing bowl, cream butter and sugar. Add eggs, one at a time, beating well after each addition. Beat in vanilla. Combine the flour, baking soda and salt; add to creamed mixture alternately with buttermilk. Beat in chocolate until combined.

Pour into a greased 15-in. x 10-in. x 1-in. baking pan. Bake at 350° for 23-27 minutes or until a toothpick inserted near the center comes out clean. Cool on a wire rack.

For frosting, in a small saucepan, bring cocoa and milk to a boil over medium heat, stirring constantly. Remove from the heat; stir in butter and vanilla until butter is melted. Whisk in confectioners' sugar until smooth. Drizzle over cake and spread quickly. Let stand until set.

Yield: 24 servings.

Lemon Poppy Seed Cake

(pictured above)
Betty Bjarnason, Egbert, Ontario
I complete this luscious cake by brushing on sweetened lemon juice and dusting it with confectioners' sugar. No one guesses it's made with a convenient packaged cake mix.

    1   package (18-1/4 ounces) lemon cake mix
    1   package (3.4 ounces) instant lemon
        pudding mix
  3/4   cup warm water
  1/2   cup vegetable oil
    4   eggs
    1   teaspoon lemon extract
    1   teaspoon almond extract
  1/3   cup poppy seeds
  1/2   cup confectioners' sugar
Juice of 1 lemon
Additional confectioners' sugar, optional

In a mixing bowl, combine cake and pudding mixes. Add the water, oil, eggs and extracts. Beat for 30 seconds on low speed. Beat for 3 minutes on medium speed. Stir in poppy seeds. Pour into a greased and floured 12-cup fluted tube pan.

Bake at 350° for 50-60 minutes or until a toothpick inserted near the center comes out clean. Cool in pan 10 minutes before inverting onto a serving plate. Combine confectioners' sugar and lemon juice; brush over the warm cake. Cool. Dust with additional confectioners' sugar if desired.

Yield: 12-16 servings.

Pretzel Dessert

(pictured below)
Rita Winterberger, Huson, Montana
The next time you're invited to a bring-a-dish event, consider this cherry-topped treat. Everyone will be talking about the pretzel crust and asking for the secret to the tasty, vanilla filling.

  2 cups crushed pretzels
3/4 cup sugar
3/4 cup butter, melted
  2 envelopes whipped topping mix
  1 cup cold milk
  1 teaspoon vanilla extract
  1 package (8 ounces) cream cheese, cubed
  1 cup confectioners' sugar
  1 can (21 ounces) cherry pie filling

In a bowl, combine pretzels, sugar and butter; set aside 1/2 cup for topping. Press the remaining mixture into an ungreased 13-in. x 9-in. x 2-in. dish.

In a mixing bowl, beat whipped topping mix, milk and vanilla on high speed for 4 minutes or until soft peaks form. Add cream cheese and confectioners' sugar; beat until smooth. Spread half over crust. Top with the pie filling and remaining cream cheese mixture. Sprinkle with reserved pretzel mixture. Refrigerate overnight.
Yield: 16 servings.

Lemon Ladyfinger Dessert

(pictured above)
Katherine Buch, Waterford, New Jersey
I have many fond memories of watching my mother-in-law assemble this no-bake dessert for parties. It looks so impressive and time-consuming but actually comes together quite easily. It's lovely for spring functions.

    1 package (3 ounces) lemon gelatin
    1 cup confectioners' sugar
    2 cups boiling water
    2 cups heavy whipping cream
  1/2 teaspoon almond extract
    1 teaspoon grated lemon peel
    1 package (3 ounces) ladyfingers
Lemon peel strips, optional

In a large mixing bowl, dissolve gelatin and sugar in water; stir until completely dissolved. Refrigerate until slightly thickened, about 45 minutes.

Beat in cream and extract until cream mixture mounds slightly, about 10 minutes. Fold in lemon peel. Split ladyfingers and arrange upright around the edge of a 2-1/2-qt. serving bowl (about 8-in. diameter). Set aside any unused ladyfingers for garnish or another use.

Pour cream mixture into bowl. Garnish with remaining ladyfingers and lemon peel strips if desired. Cover and refrigerate for 2-3 hours.
Yield: 8-10 servings.

Coconut Pecan Cookies

(pictured below)
Diane Selich, Vassar, Michigan
With chocolate chips and coconut in the batter and a yummy pecan-coconut frosting, these cookies will remind you of German chocolate cake. A drizzle of chocolate tops them off nicely.

- 1 egg, lightly beaten
- 1 can (5 ounces) evaporated milk
- 2/3 cup sugar
- 1/4 cup butter, cubed
- 1-1/4 cups flaked coconut
- 1/2 cup chopped pecans

COOKIE DOUGH:
- 1 cup butter, softened
- 3/4 cup sugar
- 3/4 cup packed brown sugar
- 2 eggs
- 1 teaspoon vanilla extract
- 2-1/4 cups all-purpose flour
- 1 teaspoon baking soda
- 1 teaspoon salt
- 4 cups (24 ounces) semisweet chocolate chips, *divided*
- 1/4 cup flaked coconut

For frosting, in a large saucepan, combine the egg, milk, sugar and butter. Cook and stir over medium-low heat for 10-12 minutes or until slightly thickened and mixture reaches 160°. Stir in coconut and pecans. Set aside.

In a large mixing bowl, cream butter and sugars. Add eggs, one at a time, beating well after each addition. Beat in vanilla. Combine the flour, baking soda and salt; gradually add to creamed mixture. Stir in 2 cups chips and coconut.

Drop by tablespoonfuls 2 in. apart onto ungreased baking sheets. Bake at 350° for 8-10 minutes or until lightly browned. Cool for 10 minutes before removing to wire racks to cool completely.

In a microwave, melt the remaining chocolate chips; stir until smooth. Frost cooled cookies; drizzle with melted chocolate.

Yield: 6-1/2 dozen.

Chocolate Raspberry Bars

Diana Olmstead, Yelm, Washington
A boxed cake mix simplifies the assembly of these treats. The bars are rich, so I cut them into small pieces.

- 1 package (18-1/4 ounces) devil's food cake mix
- 1 egg
- 1/3 cup butter, softened
- 1 jar (12 ounces) seedless raspberry jam

TOPPING:
- 1 package (10 to 12 ounces) vanilla *or* white chips
- 1 package (8 ounces) cream cheese, softened
- 2 tablespoons milk
- 1/2 cup semisweet chocolate chips
- 2 tablespoons butter

In a bowl, combine cake mix, egg and butter until crumbly. Press into a greased 15-in. x 10-in. x 1-in. baking pan. Bake at 350° for 8-10 minutes or until a toothpick inserted near the center comes out clean (crust will appear puffy and dry). Cool on a wire rack. Spread jam over the crust.

In a microwave or heavy saucepan, melt vanilla chips; stir until smooth. In a mixing bowl, beat cream cheese and milk until smooth. Add melted chips; mix well. Carefully spread over jam. Melt chocolate chips and butter; stir until smooth. Drizzle or pipe over the cream cheese layer. Refrigerate before cutting.

Yield: about 6 dozen.

Rasberry Peach Delight

(pictured above)
Alice Reed, Penfield, New York
This no-bake specialty is a snap to toss together with a pre-pared angel food cake. I sometimes layer it in a glass trifle bowl and top it with fresh raspberries for an elegant pres-entation that really stands out on a dessert table. Best of all, nobody guessed it's been "lightened" up!

  1 prepared angel food cake (8 inches), cut into 1-inch cubes
  1 package (.3 ounce) sugar-free raspberry gelatin
  1 cup boiling water
  1 cup cold water
  1 can (16 ounces) reduced-sugar sliced peaches, drained and halved
  3 cups cold fat-free milk
  1 package (1.5 ounces) sugar-free instant vanilla pudding mix
  1 carton (8 ounces) frozen reduced-fat whipped topping, thawed

Arrange cake cubes in a 13-in. x 9-in. x 2-in. dish. In a small bowl, dissolve gelatin in boiling wa-ter; stir in cold water. Pour over cake. Arrange peaches over gelatin.

In a large bowl, whisk milk and pudding mix for 2 minutes. Let stand for 2 minutes or until soft set. Spoon over peaches. Top with whipped top-ping. Cover and refrigerate for at least 2 hours before cutting.

Yield: 15 servings.

Peaches 'n' Cream Pie

Dana Tittle, Forest City, Alaska
A layer of fresh peaches helps the silky filling of this crustless pie stand out on a dessert buffet. A sprinkling of cinnamon-sugar makes it extra special.

3/4 cup all-purpose flour
  1 package (3 ounces) cook-and-serve vanilla pudding mix
1/2 cup milk
  1 egg
  1 teaspoon baking powder
1/4 teaspoon salt
  4 large fresh peaches, peeled and sliced
  1 package (8 ounces) cream cheese, softened
1/2 cup sugar

TOPPING:
  2 teaspoons sugar
1/8 to 1/4 teaspoon ground cinnamon

In a large mixing bowl, combine the first six in-gredients; beat for 2 minutes. Spread into a greased 9-in. pie plate. Arrange peaches over batter to within 1/2 in. of edge.

In a small mixing bowl, beat cream cheese and sugar until smooth; spoon over peaches. Combine sugar and cinnamon; sprinkle over the top. Bake at 350° for 35 minutes golden brown around the edge and a toothpick inserted in edge of pie comes out clean. Cool on a wire rack. Refrigerate leftovers.

Yield: 8 servings.

Georgia Pecan Cake

(pictured above)
Carolyn Griffin, Macon, Georgia
With its hint of lemon and crunchy nuts, this cake is an instant classic no matter where you serve it. One taste and you'll see why!

>   1 cup butter, softened
>   2 cups sugar
>   4 eggs
>   1 teaspoon vanilla extract
> 1/2 teaspoon lemon extract
>   3 cups all-purpose flour
> 3/4 teaspoon salt
> 1/2 teaspoon baking powder
> 1/2 teaspoon baking soda
>   1 cup buttermilk
>   1 cup chopped pecans

In a large mixing bowl, cream butter and sugar until light and fluffy. Add the eggs, one at a time, beating well after each addition. Beat in extracts. Combine the flour, salt, baking powder and baking soda; set 1/4 cup aside. Add the remaining flour mixture to the creamed mixture alternately with buttermilk. Toss pecans with the reserved flour mixture; fold into batter.

Pour into a greased and floured 10-in. tube pan. Bake at 325° for 60-70 minutes or until a toothpick inserted near the center comes out clean. Cool for 10 minutes before removing from pan to a wire rack to cool.

Yield: 12-16 servings.

Chocolate-Caramel Supreme Pie

(pictured below)
Diana Stewart, Oelwein, Iowa
At a church fund-raiser, I purchased a pie-a-month package furnished by a local family. From among all the varieties they made, this one was the best, with its chocolate crust, creamy caramel filling and fluffy topping.

> 30 caramels
>   3 tablespoons butter, melted
>   2 tablespoons water
>   1 chocolate crumb crust (9 inches)
> 1/2 cup chopped pecans, toasted
>   1 package (3 ounces) cream cheese, softened
> 1/3 cup confectioners' sugar
> 3/4 cup milk chocolate chips
>   3 tablespoons hot water
>   1 carton (8 ounces) frozen whipped topping, thawed
> Chocolate curls, optional

In a large saucepan, add the caramels, butter and water. Cook and stir over medium heat until caramels are melted. Spread over crust; sprinkle with pecans. Refrigerate for 1 hour.

In a large mixing bowl, beat cream cheese and sugar until smooth; spread over caramel layer. Refrigerate.

In a large saucepan, melt chocolate chips with hot water over low heat; stir until smooth. Cool slightly.

Fold in whipped topping. Spread over cream cheese layer. Garnish with chocolate curls if desired. Chill until serving. Refrigerate leftovers.

Yield: 8 servings.

Black Forest Trifle

(pictured above)
Peggy Linton, Cobourg, Ontario
When I want a dessert that's fit for a feast, I turn to this trifle. The recipe calls for a convenient brownie mix, so it's simple to make.

- 1 package brownie mix (13-inch x 9-inch pan size)
- 2 packages (2.8 ounces *each*) chocolate mousse mix
- 1 can (21 ounces) cherry pie filling
- 1 carton (16 ounces) frozen whipped topping, thawed
- 4 Skor candy bars, crushed

Prepare and bake brownies according to package directions; cool completely on a wire rack. Meanwhile prepare mousse according to package directions.

Crumble brownies; sprinkle half into a 4-qt. trifle dish or glass bowl. Top with half of the pie filling, mousse, whipped topping and candy bars. Repeat layers. Cover and refrigerate for 8 hours or overnight.

Yield: 16 servings.

Hawaiian Cake

(pictured below)
Estella Traeger, Milwaukee, Wisconsin
For a dessert that suits any occasion, I dress up a boxed cake mix with pineapple, coconut and a combination of instant pudding, cream cheese and whipped topping. Try it once and you're sure to make it again.

- 1 package (18-1/4 ounces) yellow cake mix
- 2 cups cold milk
- 2 packages (3.4 ounces *each*) instant vanilla pudding mix
- 1 package (8 ounces) cream cheese, softened
- 1 carton (8 ounces) frozen whipped topping, thawed
- 1 can (20 ounces) crushed pineapple, drained
- 1/2 cup chopped maraschino cherries, drained
- 1/2 cup flaked coconut
- 1/2 cup chopped walnuts

Prepare cake mix according to package directions. Pour into a greased 15-in. x 10-in. x 1-in. baking pan. Bake at 350° for 20-25 minutes or until a toothpick inserted near the center comes out clean; cool completely.

In a large mixing bowl, combine milk and pudding mixes; beat in cream cheese until smooth. Fold in whipped topping. Spread over cooled cake. Top with remaining ingredients. Refrigerate until serving.

Yield: 16-20 servings.

Blueberry Lattice Bars

(pictured below)
Debbie Ayers, Baileyville, Maine
Since our area has an annual blueberry festival, my daughters and I are always looking for ideas to enter in the recipe contest. These lovely bars won a blue ribbon one year.

```
  1     cup butter, softened
1/2     cup sugar
  1     egg
2-3/4   cups all-purpose flour
1/2     teaspoon vanilla extract
1/4     teaspoon salt
```

FILLING:
```
  3     cups fresh or frozen blueberries
  1     cup sugar
  3     tablespoons cornstarch
```

In a large mixing bowl, cream butter and sugar. Add the egg, flour, vanilla and salt; mix well. Cover and refrigerate for 2 hours.

Meanwhile, in a saucepan, bring the blueberries, sugar and cornstarch to a boil. Cook and stir for 2 minutes or until thickened.

Roll two-thirds of the dough into a 14-in. x 10-in. rectangle. Place in a greased 13-in. x 9-in. x 2-in. baking dish. Top with filling. Roll out remaining dough to 1/4-in. thickness. Cut into 1/2-in.-wide strips; make a lattice crust over filling.

Bake at 375° for 30-35 minutes or until top is golden brown. Cool on a wire rack. Cut into bars. **Yield:** 2 dozen.

Golden Raisin Oatmeal Cookies

(pictured above)
Marion Lowery, Medford, Oregon
For a slightly different twist on a traditional favorite, try these crisp, chewy cookies. With golden raisins and a mild orange tang, they're a staple at the picnics I attend.

```
3/4     cup butter, softened
  1     cup packed brown sugar
1/2     cup sugar
  1     egg
  2     tablespoons water
  1     teaspoon vanilla extract
  3     cups quick-cooking oats
2/3     cup all-purpose flour
  2     tablespoons grated orange peel
  1     teaspoon ground cinnamon
1/2     teaspoon baking soda
2/3     cup golden raisins
```

In a large mixing bowl, cream butter and sugars until light and fluffy. Beat in egg, water and vanilla. Combine the oats, flour, orange peel, cinnamon and baking soda; gradually add to the creamed mixture. Stir in the raisins (dough will be stiff).

Drop by level tablespoonfuls 2 in. apart onto ungreased baking sheets. Bake at 350° for 12-15 minutes or until the edges are lightly browned. Remove to wire racks to cool. **Yield:** 4 dozen.

Apple Bundt Cake

(pictured below)
Virginia Horst, Mesa, Washington
I love this recipe because the cake has a thin, crunchy crust and a soft, delicious inside. With the butter cream sauce, it's almost like eating candy.

    2 eggs
    2 cups sugar
1-1/2 cups vegetable oil
    3 cups all-purpose flour
    1 teaspoon baking soda
    1 teaspoon ground cinnamon
  1/2 teaspoon salt
    3 cups diced peeled apples
    1 cup chopped pecans

BUTTER CREAM SAUCE:
  1/2 cup butter
    1 cup sugar
  1/2 cup heavy whipping cream
    1 teaspoon vanilla extract

In a large mixing bowl, beat the eggs, sugar and oil. Combine the flour, baking soda, cinnamon and salt; gradually add to batter (batter will be very stiff). Fold in apples and pecans. Pour into a greased and floured 10-in. fluted tube pan. Bake at 325° for 1-1/4 to 1-1/2 hours or until a toothpick inserted near the center comes out clean. Cool for 10 minutes before removing to a wire rack.

For sauce, melt butter in a small saucepan. Add the sugar, cream and vanilla. Cook and stir over low heat until sugar is dissolved and sauce is heated through. Slice cake; serve with warm sauce. Refrigerate leftover sauce.

Yield: 12-16 servings.

Chewy Pecan Pie Bars

(pictured above)
Judy Taylor, Shreveport, Louisiana
This is one of my husband's favorite recipes. It offers all of the goodness of pecan pie in easy-to-serve bars. I like to dust them with confectioners' sugar.

  1/4 cup butter, melted
    2 cups packed brown sugar
  2/3 cup all-purpose flour
    4 eggs
    2 teaspoons vanilla extract
  1/4 teaspoon baking soda
  1/4 teaspoon salt
    2 cups chopped pecans
Confectioners' sugar

Pour butter into a 13-in. x 9-in. x 2-in. baking pan; set aside. In a large mixing bowl, combine brown sugar, flour, eggs, vanilla, baking soda and salt; mix well. Stir in pecans. Spread over butter.

Bake at 350° for 30-35 minutes. Remove from the oven; immediately dust with confectioners' sugar. Cool before cutting.

Yield: about 2 dozen.

Potluck Pointer

Measuring with a ruler before cutting a pan of bars helps create even servings. Use a sharp knife when cutting bars, and be sure to slice all the way through to the bottom of the pan. Consider cutting your bars into diamond shapes to help them stand out on a dessert buffet.

Chocolate Mint Brownies

(pictured above)
Helen Baines, Elkton, Maryland
One of the best things about these treats is that they get more moist if left in the refrigerator for a day or two. The problem at our house is no one can leave them alone before I need to take them to an event.

 1/2 cup butter, softened
   4 eggs
   1 can (16 ounces) chocolate syrup
   1 teaspoon vanilla extract
   1 cup all-purpose flour
 1/2 teaspoon salt
   1 cup sugar
FILLING:
 1/2 cup butter, softened
   2 cups confectioners' sugar
   1 tablespoon water
 1/2 teaspoon mint extract
   3 drops green food coloring
TOPPING:
   1 package (10 ounces) mint chocolate chips
 1/2 cup plus 1 tablespoon butter, cubed

In a large mixing bowl, combine the first seven ingredients. Beat at medium speed for 3 minutes. Pour batter into a greased 13-in. x 9-in. x 2-in. baking pan. Bake at 350° for 30 minutes (top of brownies will still appear wet). Cool completely on a wire rack.

In a mixing bowl, combine the filling ingredients until creamy. Spread over cooled brownies. Refrigerate until set.

For the topping, melt chocolate chips and butter. Let cool for 30 minutes, stirring occasionally. Spread over filling. Chill. Cut into squares. Store in the refrigerator.

Yield: 5-6 dozen.

Cherry Cheese Delight

(pictured below)
Kathy Branch, West Palm Beach, Florida
You couldn't ask for anything more than a nutty crust topped with a smooth cream cheese mixture and sweet cherries. Since this dessert is made the night before, you don't have to worry about last-minute fuss.

   1 cup all-purpose flour
   1 cup chopped pecans
 1/2 cup packed brown sugar
 1/2 cup butter, softened
FILLING:
   2 packages (8 ounces *each*) cream cheese, softened
 1/2 cup confectioners' sugar
   1 teaspoon vanilla extract
   1 carton (12 ounces) frozen whipped topping, thawed
   2 cans (21 ounces *each*) cherry pie filling

In a bowl, combine flour, pecans and brown sugar. With a fork, stir in butter until crumbly. Lightly pat into an ungreased 13-in. x 9-in. x 2-in. baking dish. Bake at 350° for 18-20 minutes or until golden brown. Cool completely.

For filling, in a mixing bowl, beat the cream cheese, confectioners' sugar and vanilla until smooth. Fold in whipped topping. Carefully spread over crust. Top with pie filling. Cover and refrigerate for at least 2 hours.

Yield: 12-15 servings.

Pictured below: Yankee-Doodle Sirloin Roast (p. 206), Red, White 'n' Blue Salad (p. 206), Liberty Sauerkraut Salad (p. 206), Patriotic Pasta (p. 207) and Stars and Stripes Torte (p. 207).

Seasonal Fare

Holiday Ham

(pictured above)
Betty Butler, Union Bridge, Maryland
When I was a young girl, ham made appearances at all of our holiday dinners. The old-fashioned flavor of this version reminds folks of their Grandma's kitchen and is always a success.

1	can (20 ounces) sliced pineapple
1/2	spiral-sliced fully cooked bone-in ham (8 to 10 pounds)
2/3	cup maraschino cherries
1-1/2	cups packed brown sugar
1/2	teaspoon seasoned salt

Drain pineapple, reserving juice. Place ham on a rack in a shallow roasting pan. Secure pineapple and cherries to ham with toothpicks. Combine brown sugar and seasoned salt; rub over ham. Gently pour pineapple juice over ham.

Bake, uncovered, at 325° for 1-1/2 to 2 hours or until a meat thermometer reads 140° and ham is heated through. Baste frequently with brown sugar mixture.

Yield: 18-20 servings.

Daffodillies

(pictured below)
Earleen Lillegard, Prescott, Arizona
Filled with dill-flavored cream cheese, these cute biscuits are an adorable accompaniment to any spring meal. I've been baking the savory flowers for over 25 years, and they're always a hit...whether I take them to church gatherings or make them for my grandchildren.

1	tube (12 ounces) refrigerated buttermilk biscuits
1	package (8 ounces) cream cheese, softened
2	tablespoons butter, softened
1	teaspoon dill weed
1	teaspoon prepared mustard

Dash salt
Dash white pepper

Separate each biscuit into three equal layers. Place 1 in. apart on greased baking sheets. With a kitchen shears or sharp knife, cut eight slits a third of the way toward center to form petals. Make a deep thumbprint in the center of each.

In a small mixing bowl, combine remaining ingredients. Place heaping teaspoonfuls of cream cheese mixture in the center of each biscuit. Bake at 375° for 8-10 minutes or until golden brown. Serve warm or at room temperature.

Yield: 2-1/2 dozen.

Pizza Dip in a Pumpkin

Laurene Hunsicker, Canton, Pennsylvania
I make this dip in the fall when entertaining friends.
Everyone enjoys the pizza flavor and fun presentation.

    1 small pie pumpkin (about 2-1/2 pounds)
  1/2 cup finely chopped onion
  1/4 cup finely chopped green pepper
    1 tablespoon butter
2-1/2 cups pizza sauce
    1 cup (4 ounces) shredded part-skim
       mozzarella cheese
  1/2 cup finely chopped pepperoni
  1/2 cup grated Parmesan cheese
    1 teaspoon Italian seasoning
Breadsticks

Cut top off of pumpkin; scoop out seeds and fibers.
Replace top; place pumpkin on an ungreased baking sheet. Bake at 350° for 20-25 minutes or until
hot.

Meanwhile, in a small saucepan, saute onion
and green pepper in butter until tender. Stir in
the pizza sauce, mozzarella cheese, pepperoni,
Parmesan cheese and Italian seasoning. Cook and
stir over medium heat until dip is heated through
and cheese is melted. Pour into hot pumpkin.
Serve with breadsticks.

Yield: 3 cups.

Wild Rice Turkey Dish

Clara Sawlaw, Paris, Illinois
This comforting casserole has been one of my favorite
meals to serve company, particularly in the fall. Made in
one easy step, the satisfying main course is a time-saver
that people can't seem to get enough of.

    6 cups cooked wild rice
    3 cups cubed cooked turkey
    1 can (10-3/4 ounces) condensed cream of
       mushroom soup, undiluted
    3 celery ribs, sliced
1-1/3 cups sliced fresh mushrooms
    1 medium onion, chopped
    1 cup (8 ounces) sour cream
  1/2 cup butter, melted
    1 teaspoon salt
  1/4 teaspoon pepper

In a large bowl, combine all of the ingredients.
Pour into a greased 13-in. x 9-in. x 2-in. baking
dish. Cover and bake at 350° for 45 minutes. Uncover and bake 15 minutes longer or until lightly
browned.

Yield: 10 servings.

Holiday Green Salad

(pictured above)
Rita Farmer, Houston, Texas
This combination of crisp greens, a well-seasoned dressing
and dried cranberries can't be beat. It's the ideal salad to
bring to a luncheon or an evening social.

    6 cups torn iceberg lettuce
    6 cups torn romaine
    3 green onions, thinly sliced
    1 celery rib, thinly sliced
  1/4 cup vegetable oil
  1/4 cup white vinegar
  1/4 cup sugar
    1 tablespoon minced fresh parsley
  1/2 to 1 teaspoon hot pepper sauce
  1/4 teaspoon salt
  3/4 to 1 cup dried cranberries
  1/4 cup sliced almonds, toasted

In a large bowl, combine greens, onions and celery. In a small bowl, combine the oil, vinegar, sugar, parsley, hot pepper sauce and salt; mix well.
Pour over salad; toss to coat. Add cranberries and
almonds.

Yield: 10-12 servings.

Potluck Pointer

Are you organizing a seasonal gathering? It's easy to
add a touch of festive flair to church halls when
buffets are topped with brightly colored, disposable
table coverings. Greeting card outlets and party sup-
ply stores often carry rolls of the plastic coverings at
discount prices.

If your parish operates in conjunction with a grade
school, find out if an art class can help create whim-
sical decorations that fit the season or holiday.

Hearty Lasagna

(pictured above)
Marcy Cella, L'Anse, Michigan
Featuring a cute, heart-shaped cutout, this fetching dish is perfect to share around Valentine's Day. Best of all, you can make the lasagna ahead of time!

1-1/2 pounds ground beef
　1　medium onion, chopped
　1　garlic clove, minced
　3　tablespoons olive oil
　1　can (28 ounces) Italian diced tomatoes, undrained
　1　can (8 ounces) tomato sauce
　1　can (6 ounces) tomato paste
　1　teaspoon dried oregano
　1　teaspoon sugar
　1　teaspoon salt
1/4　teaspoon pepper
　2　carrots, halved
　2　celery ribs, halved
　12　ounces lasagna noodles
　1　carton (15 ounces) ricotta cheese
　2　cups (8 ounces) shredded part-skim mozzarella cheese
1/2　cup grated Parmesan cheese

In a large skillet, cook beef, onion and garlic in oil until meat is no longer pink and onion is tender; drain. Stir in tomatoes, tomato sauce, tomato paste, oregano, sugar, salt and pepper. Place carrots and celery in sauce. Simmer, uncovered, for 1-1/2 hours, stirring occasionally.

Meanwhile, cook lasagna noodles according to package directions. Drain; rinse in cold water. Remove and discard carrots and celery.

In a greased 13-in. x 9-in. x 2-in. baking dish, layer one-third of the noodles, one-third of the meat sauce, one-third of the ricotta, one-third of the mozzarella and one-third of the Parmesan. Repeat layers once. Top with remaining noodles and meat sauce.

Cut a heart out of aluminum foil and center on top of sauce. Dollop and spread remaining ricotta round heart. Sprinkle with remaining mozzarella and Parmesan. Bake, uncovered, at 350° for 45 minutes. Remove and discard foil heart. Let stand 10-15 minutes before cutting.

Yield: 12 servings.

Cranberry Salad

Nell Bass, Macon, Georgia
This attractive gelatin salad is an eye-appealing way to serve bright cranberries.

    1 cup sugar
    1 cup water
    1 package (6 ounces) lemon gelatin
    4 cups fresh cranberries, finely chopped
    2 large unpeeled apples, cored and finely chopped
    1 unpeeled orange, seeded and finely chopped
 1/2 cup chopped pecans
Lettuce leaves, optional
Mayonnaise, optional

In a saucepan, bring sugar and water to a boil, stirring constantly. Remove from heat; immediately stir in gelatin until dissolved. Chill until mixture is the consistency of unbeaten egg whites.

Fold in the cranberries, apples, orange and pecans. Spoon into a 6-1/2-cup ring mold or an 11-in. x 7-in. x 2-in. dish. Chill until firm. If desired, serve on lettuce leaves and top with a dollop of mayonnaise.

Yield: 12-15 servings.

Winter Squash Casserole

Glendora Hauger, Siren, Wisconsin
Years ago, my dad stored our bounty of garden-fresh squash in the coldest part of the basement. In winter, the squash was so hard, Mother sometimes used an ax to cut it into pieces for cooking. Her hard work was worth it, because we really enjoyed this satisfying casserole.

    6 cups mashed winter squash
 1/2 cup butter, melted
    6 eggs, beaten
    1 cup sugar
 1/2 teaspoon salt

TOPPING:
    1 cup packed brown sugar
 1/2 cup butter, softened
 1/4 cup all-purpose flour
 1/2 cup slivered almonds

In a large bowl, combine the first five ingredients. Pour into an ungreased 13-in. x 9-in. x 2-in. baking dish.

Combine topping ingredients and crumble over the top. Bake, uncovered, at 350° for 45 minutes or until a knife inserted near the center comes out clean.

Yield: 12 servings.

New Year's Oyster Stew

(pictured below)
Christa Scott, Santa Fe, New Mexico
My husband is a former member of the Air Force's Thunderbird team, and I developed this recipe after he unexpectedly invited the whole team for dinner. Not only was it ready in 30 minutes, but it turned out to be the best oyster stew I'd ever made.

 1/4 cup butter, cubed
    3 leeks, white part only, chopped
    2 potatoes, peeled and diced
    2 cups water
    3 chicken bouillon cubes
    2 cups milk
    2 cups half-and-half cream
 1/4 teaspoon cayenne pepper
    4 cans (16 ounces *each*) oysters, drained
Salt and pepper to taste
Fresh chopped parsley

In a large soup kettle or Dutch oven, melt butter and saute leeks until tender, about 10 minutes. Add potatoes, water and bouillon cubes; cover and simmer 20 minutes or until potatoes are tender. Cool.

Transfer to a blender. Cover and process on high until blended. Return to kettle; add all remaining ingredients. Cook on low until heated through (do not boil).

Yield: 12 servings.

Vegetable Wreath with Dip

(pictured above)
Edna Hoffman, Hebron, Indiana
Veggies and dip are a mainstay at most covered-dish suppers. I like to dress up this appetizer by cutting vegetables into festive shapes and arranging them as a wreath during the holidays. It's a nice conversation piece or even a centerpiece on a buffet table.

        1   package (8 ounces) cream cheese,
               softened
    1/4   cup mayonnaise
    1/2   teaspoon chili powder
    1/2   teaspoon dill weed
    1/4   teaspoon garlic powder
    1/4   cup sliced green onions
    1/4   cup chopped ripe olives, well drained
        4   cups fresh broccoli florets
        1   medium green pepper, cut into strips
        8   cherry tomatoes
        1   medium jicama, sliced
        1   medium sweet red pepper

In a small mixing bowl, combine the first five ingredients; mix well. Stir in onions and olives. Cover and refrigerate for at least 2 hours.

Transfer dip to a serving bowl; place in the center of a 12-in. round serving plate. Arrange broccoli, green pepper and tomatoes in a wreath shape around the dip.

Using a small star cookie cutter, cut out stars from jicama slices; place over wreath. Cut red pepper into five pieces that form the shape of a bow; position on wreath.

Yield: 12 servings.

Christmas Fruit Salad

(pictured below)
Ina Vickers, Dumas, Arkansas
I like to share this delightful salad, which is a staple at holiday potlucks. My mother-in-law served it at the very first Thanksgiving I spent with my husband's family.

        3   egg yolks, beaten
        3   tablespoons water
        3   tablespoons white vinegar
    1/2   teaspoon salt
        2   cups heavy whipping cream, whipped
        3   cups miniature marshmallows
        2   cups halved green grapes
        1   can (20 ounces) pineapple tidbits, drained
        1   can (11 ounces) mandarin oranges,
               drained
        1   jar (10 ounces) red maraschino cherries,
               drained and sliced
        1   cup chopped pecans
        3   tablespoons lemon juice

In a large saucepan, combine egg yolks, water, vinegar and salt. Cook over medium heat, stirring constantly, until mixture thickens and reaches 160°. Remove from the heat and cool; fold in whipped cream.

In a large bowl, combine remaining ingredients. Add dressing; toss to coat. Cover and refrigerate for 24 hours.

Yield: 12-14 servings.

After-Thanksgiving Turkey Soup

Valorie Walker, Bradley, South Carolina
As much as my family loves Thanksgiving, we all look forward to this cream soup that uses leftover turkey. It makes a big batch.

    1 leftover turkey carcass (from a 12- to
       14-pound turkey)
    3 medium onions, chopped
    2 large carrots, diced
    2 celery ribs, diced
    1 cup butter, cubed
    1 cup all-purpose flour
    2 cups half-and-half cream
    1 cup uncooked long grain rice
    2 teaspoons salt
    1 teaspoon chicken bouillon granules
  3/4 teaspoon pepper

Place turkey carcass in a soup kettle or Dutch oven and cover with water. Bring to a boil. Reduce heat; cover and simmer for 1 hour. Remove carcass; cool. Set aside 3 qt. of broth. Remove turkey from bones and cut into bite-size pieces; set aside.

In a soup kettle or Dutch oven, saute the onions, carrots and celery in butter until tender. Reduce heat; stir in flour until blended. Gradually add 1 qt. of reserved broth. Bring to a boil; cook and stir for 2 minutes or until thickened.

Add cream, rice, salt, bouillon, pepper, remaining broth and reserved turkey. Reduce heat; cover and simmer for 30-35 minutes or until the rice is tender.

Yield: 16 servings (about 4 quarts).

Lemon Cider

Annette Engelbert, Bruce Crossing, Michigan
As a warm addition to a chilly autumn gathering, this three-ingredient cider can't be beat. But it's also popular when served over ice as a punch. I got the idea from my sister, who runs an apple orchard with her husband.

    1 gallon apple cider
    1 can (12 ounces) frozen lemonade
       concentrate, thawed
    1 lemon, thinly sliced *or* cinnamon sticks

In a punch bowl, combine cider and lemonade. Float lemon slices on top. To serve warm, heat cider and lemonade; garnish individual servings with a cinnamon stick.

Yield: 4-1/2 quarts.

Hugs 'n' Kisses Brownie

(pictured above)
Kristi Van Batavia, Kansas City, Missouri
When I needed a dessert in a hurry, I dressed up a brownie mix with on-hand ingredients to come up with this impressive, heart-shaped treat.

      1 package fudge brownie mix (8-inch square
         pan size)
      1 egg
    1/4 cup vegetable oil
    1/4 cup water
  1-1/2 cups vanilla *or* white chips, *divided*
     14 to 16 milk chocolate kisses
     14 to 16 striped chocolate kisses
  1-1/2 teaspoons shortening

In a large bowl, stir brownie mix, egg, oil and water until well blended. Fold in 1 cup vanilla chips.

Pour into a greased 9-in. heart-shaped or round springform pan. Bake at 350° for 35-40 minutes or until a toothpick inserted 2 in. from the side of pan comes out clean.

Let stand for 10 minutes; alternate milk chocolate and striped kisses around edge of pan with points toward center. Melt shortening and remaining vanilla chips; stir until smooth. Drizzle over brownie. Cool completely. Remove sides of springform pan.

Yield: 10-12 servings.

Touchdown Cookies

(pictured below)
Sister Judith LaBrozzi, Canton, Ohio
It's easy to dress up dessert for a Sunday dinner after a big game. With some sweet touches, you can transform regular sugar cookies into these special treats for football fans.

> 1 cup butter, softened
> 1 cup sugar
> 2 eggs
> 1 teaspoon vanilla extract
> 3 cups all-purpose flour
> 2 teaspoons cream of tartar
> 1 teaspoon baking soda

GLAZE:
> 2 cups confectioners' sugar
> 4 to 5 tablespoons hot water
> 3 to 4 teaspoons baking cocoa

In a large mixing bowl, cream butter and sugar. Add eggs, one at a time, beating well after each addition. Beat in vanilla. Combine the flour, cream of tartar and baking soda; gradually add to creamed mixture. Cover and refrigerate for 3 hours or until easy to handle.

On a lightly floured surface, roll out dough to 1/8-in. thickness. Cut with a football-shaped cookie cutter. Place 2 in. apart on ungreased baking sheets. Bake at 350° for 8-10 minutes or until lightly browned. Remove to wire racks to cool.

In a large mixing bowl, combine confectioners' sugar and enough hot water to achieve spreading consistency; beat until smooth. Place 3 tablespoons glaze in a small bowl; set aside.

Add cocoa to remaining glaze; stir until smooth. Spread brown glaze over cookies. Pipe white glaze onto cookies to form football laces.
Yield: 4-1/2 dozen.

Pigskin Sandwiches

(pictured above)
Sister Judith LaBrozzi, Canton, Ohio
Guests won't need much coaching to run for sandwiches when they're served on tasty football buns, like those I baked for a theme party. They were part of a sporty dinner I planned for residents at a nursing home, where I head the food staff.

> 1 package (1/4 ounce) active dry yeast
> 1/2 cup sugar, *divided*
> 2 cups warm water (110° to 115°), *divided*
> 1/2 cup plus 2 tablespoons butter, softened, *divided*
> 1-1/2 teaspoons salt
> 1 egg, beaten
> 6-1/2 to 7 cups all-purpose flour
> Mayonnaise *or* mustard, optional
> Lettuce leaves and sliced tomatoes
> 18 slices process American cheese
> 2-1/2 pounds sliced deli ham
> 4 ounces cream cheese, softened

In a large mixing bowl, dissolve yeast and 2 teaspoons sugar in 1/4 cup warm water. Let stand for 5 minutes. Add 1/2 cup butter, salt, egg and remaining sugar and water. Beat in 4 cups flour until smooth. Stir in enough remaining flour to form a soft dough.

Turn onto a floured surface; knead until smooth and elastic, about 6-8 minutes. Place in a greased bowl, turning once to grease top. Cover and let rise in a warm place until doubled, about 1 hour.

Punch dough down. Turn onto a lightly floured surface; divide into 18 pieces. Shape into ovals; place 2 in. apart on greased baking sheets. Cover and let rise until doubled, about 30 minutes.

Bake at 350° for 18-23 minutes or until golden.

Melt remaining butter; brush over buns. Remove from pans to wire racks to cool.

Split buns. Spread with mayonnaise or mustard if desired. Top with lettuce, tomato, cheese and ham. Replace tops. Place cream cheese in a plastic bag; cut a small hole in the corner of the bag. Pipe football laces on sandwiches.

Yield: 18 servings.

Summer Spinach Salad

(pictured below)
Callie Berger, Diamond Springs, California
Tossed with ripe banana chunks, fresh strawberries and toasted almonds, this warm-weather salad looks and tastes extra special. The tangy poppy seed dressing is a snap to combine in the blender.

- 1/2 cup vegetable oil
- 1/4 cup chopped onion
- 2 tablespoons plus 2 teaspoons red wine vinegar
- 2 tablespoons plus 2 teaspoons sugar
- 1-1/2 teaspoons ground mustard
- 1/2 teaspoon salt
- 1-1/2 teaspoons poppy seeds
- 8 cups torn fresh spinach
- 3 green onions, sliced
- 2 pints fresh strawberries, sliced
- 3 large ripe bananas, cut into 1/2-inch slices
- 1/2 cup slivered almonds, toasted

Place the first six ingredients in a blender or food processor; cover and process until the sugar is dissolved. Add the poppy seeds; process just until blended.

In a salad bowl, combine the remaining ingredients. Drizzle with dressing; toss to coat.

Yield: 14 servings.

St. Patrick's Day Cupcakes

(pictured above)
Kathy Meyer, Almond, Wisconsin
Stir-and-bake cupcakes go together super quick, and this variety is no exception. Pistachio pudding mix gives the goodies a mild flavor and pretty pastel color that makes them perfect for St. Patrick's Day.

- 1-3/4 cups all-purpose flour
- 2/3 cup sugar
- 1 package (3.4 ounces) instant pistachio pudding mix
- 2 teaspoons baking powder
- 1/2 teaspoon salt
- 2 eggs
- 1-1/4 cups milk
- 1/2 cup vegetable oil
- 1 teaspoon vanilla extract

Green food coloring, optional
Cream cheese frosting

In a large bowl, combine the dry ingredients. In another bowl, beat eggs, milk, oil and vanilla; add to dry ingredients and mix until blended.

Fill paper-lined muffin cups three-fourths full. Bake at 375° for 18-22 minutes or until a toothpick inserted in the center comes out clean. Cool on a wire rack. Add food coloring to frosting if desired. Frost cupcakes.

Yield: 1 dozen.

Chocolate Mint Creams

(pictured above)
Beverly Fehner, Gladstone, Missouri
This recipe came from an old family friend and is always high on everyone's cookie request list. I make at least six batches during the holidays to take to various functions.

    1   cup butter, softened
1-1/2   cups confectioners' sugar
    2   squares (1 ounce *each*) unsweetened
        chocolate, melted and cooled
    1   egg
    1   teaspoon vanilla extract
2-1/2   cups all-purpose flour
    1   teaspoon baking soda
    1   teaspoon cream of tartar
  1/4   teaspoon salt

FROSTING:
  1/4   cup butter, softened
    2   cups confectioners' sugar
    2   tablespoons milk
  1/2   teaspoon peppermint extract
Green food coloring, optional

In a large mixing bowl, cream butter and confectioners' sugar. Add the chocolate, egg and vanilla; mix well. Combine the dry ingredients; gradually add to creamed mixture, beating well. Shape dough into a 2-in.-diameter roll; wrap in plastic wrap. Refrigerate for 1 hour or until firm.

Unwrap dough and cut into 1/8-in. slices. Place 2 in. apart on ungreased baking sheets. Bake at 400° for 7-8 minutes or until edges are firm. Remove to wire racks to cool. In a small mixing bowl, combine frosting ingredients. Frost cookies. Store in airtight containers.

Yield: about 6 dozen.

Roasted Root Vegetables

(pictured below)
Cathryn White, Newark, Delaware
This side dish's deep harvest colors make it any eye-catching addition to a fall dinner spread. It's a fix-it-and-forget-it favorite of mine.

    2   cups pearl onions
    2   pounds red potatoes, cut into 1/2-inch
        pieces
    1   large rutabaga, peeled and cut into
        1/2-inch pieces
    1   pound parsnips, peeled and cut into
        1/2-inch pieces
    1   pound carrots, cut into 1/2-inch pieces
    3   tablespoons butter, melted
    3   tablespoons olive oil
4-1/2   teaspoons dried thyme
1-1/2   teaspoons salt
  3/4   teaspoon coarsely ground pepper
    2   packages (10 ounces *each*) frozen brussels
        sprouts, thawed
    3   to 4 garlic cloves, minced

In a Dutch oven or large kettle, bring 6 cups water to a boil. Add the pearl onions; boil for 3 minutes. Drain and rinse with cold water; peel.

In a large roasting pan, combine the onions, potatoes, rutabaga, parsnips and carrots. Drizzle with butter and oil. Sprinkle with thyme, salt and pepper; toss to coat.

Cover and bake at 425° for 30 minutes. Uncover; stir in brussels sprouts and garlic. Bake, uncovered, for 50-60 minutes or until vegetables are tender and begin to brown, stirring occasionally.

Yield: 16-18 servings.

Independence Day Delight

Linnea Tucker, Dolores, Colorado
Lovely and delightful, this layered treat rounds out any meal. The recipe came from my grandmother.

    2 packages (3 ounces *each*) raspberry gelatin,
         divided
    2 cups boiling water, *divided*
1-1/2 cups cold water, *divided*
    1 envelope unflavored gelatin
    1 cup half-and-half cream
  3/4 to 1 cup sugar
    1 package (8 ounces) cream cheese, cubed
  1/2 cup chopped pecans
    1 teaspoon vanilla extract
    1 can (15 ounces) blueberries in syrup,
         undrained

In a large bowl, dissolve one package of raspberry gelatin in 1 cup boiling water. Stir in 1 cup cold water. Pour into a 13-in. x 9-in. x 2-in. dish; chill until set. In a small bowl, soften unflavored gelatin in the remaining cold water; set aside.

In a large saucepan, combine cream and sugar; whisk over medium heat until sugar is dissolved. Add cream cheese and softened unflavored gelatin; cook and stir until smooth. Cool. Stir in pecans and vanilla. Spoon over raspberry gelatin. Refrigerate until completely set.

In a large bowl, dissolve second package of raspberry gelatin in remaining boiling water. Stir in blueberries. Carefully spoon over cream cheese layer. Chill several hours or overnight.

Yield: 12-16 servings.

Snowball Peaches

Renae Moncur, Burley, Idaho
Peach halves took on a festive look when I planned single-serving salads for a winter brunch.

    2 packages (3 ounces *each*) cream cheese,
         softened
    2 tablespoons apricot preserves
    1 cup pineapple tidbits, drained
    3 cans (15-1/4 ounces *each*) peach halves,
         drained
Leaf lettuce
Fresh mint, optional

In a small mixing bowl, beat the cream cheese and preserves until blended. Stir in pineapple. Place peaches cut side up on a lettuce-lined serving platter; fill with cream cheese mixture. Garnish with mint if desired.

Yield: 15 servings.

Rainbow Angel Food Cake

(pictured above)
Pat Habiger, Spearville, Kansas
This sunny striped cake with a light glaze can brighten a number of special occasions—from Easter gatherings to potlucks to baby and bridal showers.

    1 cup cake flour
1-1/2 cups sugar, *divided*
1-1/2 cups egg whites
1-1/2 teaspoons cream of tartar
1-1/2 teaspoons vanilla extract
  1/2 teaspoon almond extract
  1/4 teaspoon salt
Red, yellow and green food coloring
1-1/2 cups confectioners' sugar
    2 to 3 tablespoons milk

Sift flour and 3/4 cup sugar four times; set aside. In a large mixing bowl, beat egg whites, cream of tartar, extracts and salt on high speed until soft peaks form but mixture is still moist and glossy. Add remaining sugar, 2 tablespoons at a time, beating well after each addition.

Sift flour mixture, a fourth at a time, over egg white mixture; fold gently, using about 15 strokes for each addition. Divide batter into three bowls. To the first bowl, add 1 drop red and 1 drop yellow food coloring. To the second bowl, add 2 drops yellow food coloring. To the third bowl, add 2 drops green food coloring. Fold food coloring into each.

Spoon orange batter into an ungreased 10-in. tube pan; carefully spread to cover bottom. Spoon yellow batter over orange layer (do not mix). Spoon green batter over yellow layer. Bake at 375° for 30-36 minutes or until top crust is golden and cracks feel dry. Immediately invert cake in pan to cool completely. Loosen sides of cake from pan and remove.

In a small bowl, combine confectioners' sugar and milk until smooth; drizzle over cake.

Yield: 16 servings.

Yankee-Doodle Sirloin Roast

(pictured above)

Laurie Neverman, Green Bay, Wisconsin

In the spirit of July Fourth, my sister and I planned a theme menu that included Liberty Sauerkraut Salad, Patriotic Pasta, Stars and Stripes Torte, and Red, White 'n' Blue Salad as well as this delectable roast. Marinating the meat overnight boosted the flavor and helped make it a nice change from burgers and hot dogs.

- 1/2 cup beef broth
- 1/2 cup teriyaki *or* soy sauce
- 1/4 cup vegetable oil
- 2 tablespoons brown sugar
- 2 tablespoons finely chopped onion
- 3 garlic cloves, minced
- 1 teaspoon Worcestershire sauce
- 1/2 teaspoon hot pepper sauce
- 1 boneless beef sirloin tip roast (about 4 pounds)

In a large resealable plastic bag, combine the first eight ingredients; add roast. Seal bag and turn to coat; refrigerate overnight. Drain and discard marinade. Place roast on a rack in a shallow roasting pan. Bake, uncovered, at 350° for 1-1/2 to 2-1/4 hours or until meat reaches desired doneness (for medium-rare, a meat thermometer should read 145°; medium, 160°; well-done, 170°). Let stand for 10-15 minutes before slicing.

Yield: 12-14 servings.

Red, White 'n' Blue Salad

(pictured on p. 193)

Laurie Neverman

A star design made with fresh berries gave this gelatin salad a patriotic personality at our parade of holiday foods! Everyone loved the creamy filling and fruity flavors.

- 1 package (3 ounces) berry blue gelatin
- 2 cups boiling water, *divided*
- 2-1/2 cups cold water, *divided*
- 1 cup fresh blueberries
- 1 envelope unflavored gelatin
- 1 cup heavy whipping cream
- 6 tablespoons sugar
- 2 cups (16 ounces) sour cream
- 1 teaspoon vanilla extract
- 1 package (3 ounces) raspberry gelatin
- 1 cup fresh raspberries

Whipped topping and additional berries, optional

In a large bowl, dissolve berry blue gelatin in 1 cup boiling water; stir in 1 cup cold water. Add blueberries. Pour into a 3-qt. serving bowl. Refrigerate until firm, about 1 hour.

Meanwhile, in a saucepan, sprinkle unflavored gelatin over 1/2 cup cold water; let stand for 1 minute. Add the cream and sugar; cook and stir over low heat until gelatin and sugar are completely dissolved. Cool to room temperature. Whisk in sour cream and vanilla. Spoon over the blue layer. Refrigerate until firm.

In a large bowl, dissolve raspberry gelatin in remaining hot water; stir in remaining cold water. Add raspberries. Spoon over cream layer. Chill until set. Garnish with whipped topping and additional berries if desired.

Yield: 14-16 servings.

Liberty Sauerkraut Salad

(pictured on p. 193)

Laurie Neverman

If there are grilled items at your get-together, consider bringing this tangy, no-stress salad.

- 1 can (14 ounces) sauerkraut, rinsed and drained
- 1 medium green pepper, diced
- 1 cup diced celery
- 1 medium onion, diced
- 3/4 to 1 cup sugar
- 1/2 cup cider vinegar
- 1 jar (2 ounces) diced pimientos, drained

In a 1-qt. serving bowl, combine all of the ingredients. Cover and refrigerate overnight. Serve with a slotted spoon.

Yield: 8 servings.

Patriotic Pasta

(pictured above)
Laurie Neverman
A popular side dish on our Independence Day menu, this hearty pasta salad fit our theme with bright red cherry tomatoes, white cauliflower plus blue cheese.

DRESSING:
- 1/4 cup mayonnaise
- 1/4 cup sour cream
- 1/4 cup crumbled blue cheese
- 1-1/2 teaspoons milk
- 1/2 teaspoon *each* salt and white vinegar
- 1/4 teaspoon garlic powder
- 1/4 teaspoon pepper
- 1/2 teaspoon honey mustard
- 1/8 teaspoon cayenne pepper

SALAD:
- 2-1/2 cups uncooked penne pasta
- 1 garlic clove, minced
- 3/4 teaspoon minced fresh basil *or* 1/4 teaspoon dried basil
- 2 tablespoons olive oil
- 1-1/2 cups fresh cauliflowerets
- 1 cup cherry tomatoes, halved
- 3 green onions, chopped
- 1/4 cup chopped sweet red pepper
- 4 ounces part-skim mozzarella cheese, cut into 1-inch strips
- 2 tablespoons grated Parmesan cheese

In a small bowl, combine the dressing ingredients; set aside. Meanwhile, cook pasta according to package directions; rinse in cold water and drain. Transfer to a large bowl.

In a large skillet, saute garlic and basil in oil until garlic is tender. Pour over pasta. Add the cauliflower, tomatoes, green onions, red pepper, cheese and dressing; toss to coat. Cover and refrigerate until serving.

Yield: 12-14 servings.

Editor's Note: As a substitute for honey mustard, combine 1/4 teaspoon Dijon mustard and 1/4 teaspoon honey.

Stars and Stripes Torte

(pictured below)
Laurie Neverman
Everyone loved the silky filling and familiar fruit flavors in this after-dinner specialty. It's impressive-looking but not difficult to make.

- 1 package (18-1/4 ounces) white cake mix
- 1-1/2 cups cold milk
- 1 package (3.3 ounces) instant white chocolate pudding mix
- 1/2 teaspoon almond extract
- 1 cup heavy whipping cream, whipped
- 1-2/3 cups raspberry pie filling
- 1-2/3 cups blueberry pie filling
- Fresh blueberries and raspberries, optional

Prepare and bake cake according to package directions, using two greased 9-in. round baking pans. Cool for 10 minutes before removing from pans to wire racks to cool completely.

In a small mixing bowl, beat milk and pudding mix on low speed for 2 minutes. Beat in extract. Cover and refrigerate for 10 minutes. Fold in whipped cream.

Split each cake into two horizontal layers. Place bottom layer on a cake plate; spread with raspberry pie filling. Top with second cake layer; spread with 1-2/3 cups of pudding mixture. Top with third cake layer; spread with blueberry pie filling. Top with remaining cake layer and pudding mixture.

Place the blueberries around the top edge of cake and form a star with the blueberries and raspberries if desired.

Yield: 10-14 servings.

Peanut Butter Eggs

(pictured above)
Ethel Charles, Elizabethtown, Pennsylvania
These easy-to-make confections are a must at Easter. Have youngsters help you shape the eggs, then reward them with some of the chocolaty candies.

    1 package (8 ounces) cream cheese,
       softened
1/2 cup butter, softened
    1 jar (17.3 ounces) creamy peanut butter
    1 teaspoon vanilla extract
    1 package (2 pounds) confectioners' sugar
    2 cups flaked coconut, optional
    6 cups (36 ounces) semisweet chocolate
       chips
1/3 cup shortening

In a large mixing bowl, beat cream cheese, butter, peanut butter and vanilla until smooth. Beat in sugar. Stir in coconut if desired. Form rounded tablespoonfuls into egg shapes. Place on waxed paper-lined baking sheets. Chill for 30 minutes.

In a microwave-safe bowl or heavy saucepan, melt chocolate chips and shortening; stir until smooth. Dip eggs until coated; place on waxed paper to harden.

For more decorative eggs, place about 1/4 cup melted chocolate in a small plastic bag. Cut a hole in the corner of the bag; pipe chocolate over tops of eggs. Store in the refrigerator.

Yield: about 5-1/2 dozen.

Easter Bunny Bread

(pictured at right)
Taste of Home Test Kitchen
Grab a couple loaves of frozen bread dough and a few other items, and you'll have this cute bunny hopping into the hearts of everyone at your church supper. Offering guests the veggies of your choice and a prepared dip, he's sure to steal the spotlight at any get-together.

    2 loaves (1 pound *each*) frozen bread dough,
       thawed
    2 raisins
    2 sliced almonds
    1 egg, lightly beaten
Lettuce leaves
Dip of your choice
Assorted vegetables

Cut a fourth off of one loaf of dough; shape into a pear to form head. For body, flatten remaining portion into a 7-in. x 6-in. oval; place on a greased baking sheet. Place head above body. Make narrow cuts, about 3/4 in. deep, on each side of head for whiskers.

Cut second loaf into four equal portions. For ears, shape two portions into 16-in. ropes; fold ropes in half. Arrange ears with open ends touching head. Cut a third portion of dough in half; shape each into a 3-1/2-in. oval for back paws. Cut two 1-in. slits on top edge for toes. Position on each side of body.

Divide the fourth portion of dough into three pieces. Shape two pieces into 2-1/2-in. balls for front paws; shape the remaining piece into two 1-in. balls for cheeks and one 1/2-in. ball for nose. Place paws on each side of body; cut two 1-in. slits for toes. Place cheeks and nose on face. Add raisins for eyes and almonds for teeth.

Brush dough with egg. Cover and let rise in a warm place until doubled, about 30-45 minutes. Bake at 350° for 25-30 minutes or until golden brown. Remove to a wire rack to cool.

Place bread on a lettuce-lined 16-in. x 13-in. serving tray. Cut a 5-in. x 4-in. oval in center of body. Hollow out bread, leaving a 1/2-in. shell (discard removed bread or save for another use). Line with lettuce and fill with dip. Serve with assorted vegetables.

Yield: 1 loaf.

Trick-or-Treat Brownies

(pictured above)
Flo Burtnett, Gage, Oklahoma
Attending an October potluck? Use a cookie cutter to easily turn homemade chocolate brownies into friendly pumpkin shapes. It's a snap to jazz them up with orange frosting. Children think they're great!

```
1-1/2  cups sugar
  3/4  cup butter, melted
1-1/2  teaspoons vanilla extract
    3  eggs
  3/4  cup all-purpose flour
  1/2  cup baking cocoa
  1/2  teaspoon baking powder
  1/4  teaspoon salt
    1  can (16 ounces) vanilla frosting
```
Orange paste food coloring
Green and black decorating gel
Candy corn and milk chocolate M&M's, optional

In a large mixing bowl, beat the sugar, butter and vanilla until light and fluffy. Beat in the eggs until well blended. Combine the flour, cocoa, baking powder and salt; gradually add to sugar mixture.

Line a greased 13-in. x 9-in. x 2-in. baking pan with waxed paper; grease the paper. Spread batter evenly in pan. Bake at 350° for 18-22 minutes or until brownies begin to pull away from sides of pan. Cool on a wire rack.

Run a knife around edge of pan. Invert brownies onto a work surface and remove waxed paper.

Cut brownies with a 3-in. pumpkin cookie cutter, leaving at least 1/8 in. between each shape. (Discard scraps or save for another use.) Tint frosting with orange food coloring; frost brownies. Use green gel to create the pumpkin stems and black gel and candy corn and M&M's if desired to decorate the faces.

Yield: about 1 dozen.

Pistachio Mallow Salad

Pattie Ann Forssberg, Logan, Kansas
This fluffy salad is a real treat since it's creamy but not overly sweet. It's easy to mix up, and the flavor gets better the longer it stands. It's perfect for St. Patrick's Day, served in a green bowl.

```
    1  carton (16 ounces) frozen whipped
       topping, thawed
    1  package (3.4 ounces) instant pistachio
       pudding mix
    6  to 7 drops green food coloring, optional
    3  cups miniature marshmallows
    1  can (20 ounces) crushed pineapple,
       undrained
  1/2  cup chopped pistachios or walnuts
```

In a large bowl, combine whipped topping, pudding mix and food coloring if desired. Fold in the marshmallows and pineapple. Cover and refrigerate for at least 2 hours. Just before serving, sprinkle with nuts.

Yield: 12 servings.

Poinsettia Cookies

(pictured below)

Helen Burch, Jamestown, New York

These sugar-sprinkled treats are as pretty to look at as they are to eat! They're beautiful on a cookie tray at home or a dessert table at a get-together.

- 1 cup butter, softened
- 1 cup confectioners' sugar
- 1 egg
- 1-1/2 teaspoons almond extract
- 1 teaspoon vanilla extract
- 2-1/2 cups all-purpose flour
- 1 teaspoon salt

Red decorator's sugar

Red and green candied cherries, quartered

In a large mixing bowl, cream butter and sugar. Add egg and extracts; mix well. Combine flour and salt; gradually add to creamed mixture. Divide dough in half; wrap in plastic wrap. Chill overnight or until firm.

On a lightly floured surface, roll out one portion of dough to a 12-in. x 10-in. rectangle approximately 1/8 in. thick. Cut into 2-in. squares. In each square, make 1-in. slits in each corner. Bring every other corner up into center to form a pinwheel; press lightly. Sprinkle cookies with red sugar and press a candied cherry piece into the center of each.

Place 1 in. apart on ungreased baking sheets. Bake at 350° for 8-10 minutes. Cool 1-2 minutes before removing to a wire rack.

Yield: about 4 dozen.

Jingle Bell Spread

(pictured above)

Karen Balistrieri, Oconomowoc, Wisconsin

No need to ring this "dinner bell" to summon guests—the sight of it's enough to make folks come running. The creamy spread gets a festive look from red pepper, pimientos and parsley. If you like, you can mold the mix into a Christmas tree, star, candy cane or any other appealing shape.

- 2 packages (8 ounces *each*) cream cheese, softened
- 1/2 cup mayonnaise
- 1/3 cup grated Parmesan cheese
- 10 bacon strips, cooked and crumbled
- 1/4 cup sliced green onions
- 1/2 cup minced fresh parsley
- 1 jar (2 ounces) diced pimientos, drained

Sweet red pepper strips, optional

Assorted crackers

In a large mixing bowl, beat cream cheese until smooth. Stir in mayonnaise, Parmesan cheese, bacon and onions.

Drop by spoonfuls onto a serving platter in the shape of a bell; carefully spread with an icing knife to fill in the bell. Sprinkle with parsley and pimientos. Add red pepper strips across bell if desired. Serve with crackers.

Yield: 3 cups.

Easter Egg Bread

(pictured above)
Heather Durante, Wellsburg, Virginia
I've made this Easter treat for over 20 years. Colored hard-cooked eggs baked in the dough give the sweet bread such a festive look. The filling loaf is wonderful with baked ham.

       6 to 6-1/2 cups all-purpose flour
    1/2 cup sugar
       2 packages (1/4 ounce *each*) active dry yeast
       1 to 2 teaspoons ground cardamom
       1 teaspoon salt
   1-1/2 cups milk
       6 tablespoons butter, cubed
       4 eggs
       3 to 6 hard-cooked eggs
   Vegetable oil
       2 tablespoons cold water

In a large mixing bowl, combine 2 cups flour, sugar, yeast, cardamom and salt. In a saucepan, heat milk and butter to 120°-130°. Add to dry ingredients; beat just until moistened. Add 3 eggs; beat until smooth. Stir in enough remaining flour to form a soft dough.

Turn onto a floured surface; knead until smooth and elastic, about 6-8 minutes. Place in a greased bowl, turning once to grease top. Cover and let rise in a warm place until doubled, about 45 minutes.

Dye hard-cooked eggs; lightly rub with oil. Punch dough down. Turn onto a lightly floured surface; divide dough into thirds. Shape each portion into a 24-in. rope.

Place ropes on a greased baking sheet and braid; bring ends together to form a ring. Pinch ends to seal. Gently separate braided ropes and tuck dyed eggs into openings. Cover and let rise until doubled, about 20 minutes.

Beat water and remaining egg; gently brush over dough. Bake at 375° for 28-32 minutes or until golden brown. Remove from pan to a wire rack to cool. Refrigerate leftovers.
Yield: 1 loaf.

Jack-o'-Lantern Burgers

(pictured below)
Vicki Schlechter, Davis, California
It's fun to set smiling faces on these nicely seasoned burgers I serve at fall parties. Hungry guests welcome the sandwiches…and they're a can't-miss entree for a casual get-together.

       1 envelope onion soup mix
    1/4 cup ketchup
       2 tablespoons brown sugar
       2 teaspoons prepared horseradish
       2 teaspoons chili powder
   2-1/2 pounds ground beef
      10 slices process American cheese
      10 hamburger buns, split

In a large bowl, combine soup mix, ketchup, brown sugar, horseradish and chili powder. Crumble beef over mixture; mix well. Shape into 10 patties. Grill, broil or pan-fry until the meat is no longer pink.

Cut eyes, nose and mouth out of each cheese slice to create a jack-o'-lantern. Place cheese on burgers; cook until cheese is slightly melted, about 1 minute. Serve on buns.

Yield: 10 servings.

Pumpkin-Pecan Cake Roll

(pictured above)
Nell Bass, Macon, Georgia
I made this cake roll one Thanksgiving as a tasty change of pace from pumpkin pie. The moist spice cake and creamy filling made it a much-loved dessert at many functions since then.

   3 eggs
   1 cup sugar
  3/4 cup all-purpose flour
  3/4 cup canned pumpkin
1-1/2 teaspoons ground cinnamon
   1 teaspoon baking powder
   1 teaspoon ground ginger
  1/2 teaspoon salt
  1/2 teaspoon ground nutmeg
   1 teaspoon lemon juice
   1 cup finely chopped pecans
Confectioners' sugar

FILLING:
   2 packages (3 ounces *each*) cream cheese, softened
  1/4 cup butter, softened
   1 cup confectioners' sugar
  1/2 teaspoon vanilla extract

Line a greased 15-in. x 10-in. x 1-in. baking pan with waxed paper and grease the paper; set aside. In a mixing bowl, beat eggs for 5 minutes. Add the sugar, flour, pumpkin, cinnamon, baking powder, ginger, salt and nutmeg; mix well. Add lemon juice. Spread batter evenly in prepared pan; sprinkle with pecans.

Bake at 375° for 15 minutes or until cake springs back when lightly touched. Cool for 5 minutes. Turn cake onto a kitchen towel dusted with confectioners' sugar. Gently peel off waxed paper. Roll up cake in towel jelly-roll style, starting with a short side. Cool completely on a wire rack.

In a large mixing bowl, combine the filing ingredients; beat until smooth. Unroll cake; spread filling over cake to within 1/2 in. of edges. Roll up again; place seam side down on a serving platter. Cover and refrigerate for at least 1 hour before serving.

Yield: 12 servings.

Christmas Chicken

Marcia Larson, Batavia, Illinois
I've been fixing this delectable entree at Christmas for over 10 years, but you don't have to wait for the holidays to serve it. The chicken breasts marinate overnight for easy preparation, then simply coat with crumbs and bake.

```
 16  boneless skinless chicken breast halves
  2  cups (16 ounces) sour cream
1/4  cup lemon juice
  4  teaspoons Worcestershire sauce
  2  teaspoons celery salt
  2  teaspoons pepper
  2  teaspoons paprika
  1  teaspoon seasoned salt
  1  teaspoon garlic salt
1-1/2 to 2 cups crushed butter-flavored crackers
1/2  cup vegetable oil
1/2  cup butter, melted
```

Place the chicken in two large resealable plastic bags. In a bowl, combine the sour cream, lemon juice, Worcestershire sauce and seasonings. Pour over chicken; seal bags and toss to coat. Refrigerate overnight.

Drain and discard marinade. Coat chicken with cracker crumbs; place in two greased 13-in. x 9-in. x 2-in. baking dishes. Combine oil and butter; drizzle over chicken. Bake, uncovered, at 350° for 50-60 minutes or until juices run clear.
Yield: 16 servings.

Eggnog Dip

Sharon MacDonnell, Lantzville, British Columbia
I put together a cookbook of my grandma's Christmas recipes that includes this classic appetizer. Serve it as a dip with fresh fruit or drizzle it over cake for dessert.

```
1-1/2 cups eggnog
  2  tablespoons cornstarch
1/2  cup sour cream
1/2  cup heavy whipping cream
  1  tablespoon sugar
1/2  teaspoon rum extract, optional
```
Assorted fruit and pound cake cubes

In a saucepan, combine the eggnog and cornstarch until smooth. Bring to a boil; boil and stir for 2 minutes. Remove from the heat; stir in sour cream. Cool completely.

In a large mixing bowl, beat whipping cream and sugar until stiff peaks form. Fold into eggnog mixture with extract if desired. Cover and refrigerate overnight. Serve with fruit and cake cubes.
Yield: about 2-1/2 cups.

Editor's Note: This recipe was tested with commercially prepared eggnog.

Christmas Glow Punch

(pictured below)
Marge Hodel, Roanoke, Illinois
With a pretty crimson color, this sweet tropical beverage is perfect for the holidays. Have the punch base chilling in the refrigerator, then add the chilled ginger ale and sherbet just before serving.

```
4-1/2 cups tropical punch
  1  cup cranberry juice
  1  can (6 ounces) pineapple juice
1/3  cup lemon juice
  2  to 3 cups chilled ginger ale
  1  pint raspberry sherbet
```

In a 2-qt. container, combine the punch and juices. Cover and refrigerate until chilled. Just before serving, transfer to a small punch bowl. Stir in ginger ale; top with scoops of sherbet.
Yield: about 2 quarts.

Pictured below:
Blueberry Angel Dessert (p. 227).

Quick & Easy

Haystack Supper

(pictured above)
Jill Steiner, Hancock, Minnesota
Featured on a buffet table at our family reunion, this taco-style dish was a true crowd-pleaser. Folks were pleasantly surprised to find a layer of rice, and everyone enjoyed the cheesy sauce. Best of all, it came together in about 30 minutes!

1-3/4   cups crushed saltines (about 40 crackers)
2   cups cooked rice
3   pounds ground beef
1   large onion, chopped
1-1/2   cups tomato juice
3/4   cup water
3   tablespoons taco seasoning mix
Seasoned salt, salt and pepper to taste
4   cups shredded lettuce
3   medium tomatoes, diced
1/2   cup butter, cubed
1/2   cup all-purpose flour
4   cups milk
1   pound process American cheese, cubed
3   cups (12 ounces) shredded sharp cheddar cheese
1   jar (10 ounces) pimiento-stuffed olives
1   package (14-1/2 ounces) tortilla chips

Divide crackers between two ungreased 13-in. x 9-in. x 2-in. baking dishes. Top with rice.

In a large skillet, cook beef and onion until meat is no longer pink; drain. Add the tomato juice, water and seasonings; simmer for 15-20 minutes. Spoon over rice. Sprinkle with lettuce and tomatoes.

In a large saucepan, melt butter. Stir in flour until smooth. Gradually add milk. Bring to a boil; cook and stir for 2 minutes or until thickened. Re-

duce heat; stir in American cheese until melted.

Pour over the tomatoes. Top with cheddar cheese and olives. Serve with chips. Refrigerate any leftovers.

Yield: 10-12 servings.

Spicy Party Mix

(pictured below)
June Mullins, Livonia, Missouri
When you can't think of what to bring to a get-together, consider this simple party mix. Sesame seeds are a fun addition to the crispy combo of ingredients that both children and adults go for. Chili powder, cumin and curry powder lend a bit of a kick.

10   cups Crispix
2   cups salted peanuts
1-1/2   cups pretzel sticks
1/2   cup sesame seeds, toasted
1/2   cup vegetable oil
2   tablespoons lemon juice
1   tablespoon chili powder
1   tablespoon curry powder
1   teaspoon garlic salt
1   teaspoon onion salt
1/2   teaspoon ground cumin

In a large bowl, combine the cereal, peanuts, pretzels and sesame seeds. In a saucepan, combine the remaining ingredients; bring to a boil. Pour over the cereal mixture and stir to coat. Spread in a greased 15-in. x 10-in. x 1-in. baking pan.

Bake at 250° for 10 minutes or until golden brown, stirring once. Cool completely. Store in an airtight container.

Yield: 4 quarts.

Cheesy Wild Rice

Lisa Hofer, Hitchcock, South Dakota
I rely on easy-to-make soups when there's not a lot of time to cook. I replaced the wild rice requested in the original recipe with a boxed rice mix. This creamy concoction is now requested regularly.

  1 package (6.2 ounces) fast-cooking long grain and wild rice mix
  4 cups milk
  1 can (10-3/4 ounces) condensed cream of potato soup, undiluted
  8 ounces process cheese (Velveeta), cubed
1/2 pound sliced bacon, cooked and crumbled

In a large saucepan, prepare rice according to package directions. Stir in the milk, soup and cheese. Cook and stir until cheese is melted. Garnish with bacon.
Yield: 8 servings.

Cream Cheese Cupcakes

Nancy Reichert, Thomasville, Georgia
It's hard to believe these cupcakes can taste so delicious, yet be so easy. Frost them if you wish, but they're just as good plain, which is great news when you're short on time.

  1 package (3 ounces) cream cheese, softened
  1 package (18-1/4 ounces) yellow cake mix
1-1/4 cups water
1/2 cup butter, melted
  3 eggs
Chocolate frosting, optional

In a large mixing bowl, beat cream cheese until smooth. Beat in cake mix, water, butter and eggs.
  Spoon batter by 1/4 cupfuls into paper-lined muffin cups. Bake at 350° for 25 minutes or until golden brown. Remove to a wire rack to cool completely. Frost if desired.
Yield: 2 dozen.

Potluck Pointer

As seen with Cream Cheese Cupcakes, cake mixes are an invaluable time-saver. When you don't have a moment to spare, disguise a cake mix by replacing the water called for with coffee or even a carbonated beverage. Or you can stir a little citrus peel, cinnamon or flaked coconut into the batter to give the dessert a homemade appeal.

Fluffy Pistachio Dessert

(pictured above)
Christine Strouf, St. Nazianz, Wisconsin
This creamy torte is one of my family's favorites, even with the low-fat, low-sugar ingredients.

1/2 cup reduced-fat margarine (70% vegetable oil spread), softened
  1 cup all-purpose flour
1/2 cup confectioners' sugar
1/2 cup chopped walnuts

FIRST LAYER:
  1 package (8 ounces) fat-free cream cheese, softened
  1 cup (8 ounces) nonfat sour cream
  1 carton (8 ounces) frozen light whipped topping, thawed

SECOND LAYER:
  3 cups cold fat-free milk
  2 packages (1 ounce *each*) sugar-free fat-free instant pistachio pudding mix

TOPPING:
  1 carton (8 ounces) frozen light whipped topping, thawed
  2 tablespoons ground walnuts

In a mixing bowl, cream the margarine. Add flour and sugar; blend until crumbly. Stir in walnuts. Press onto the bottom of a 13-in. x 9-in. x 2-in. baking dish coated with nonstick cooking spray. Bake at 375° for 10-12 minutes or until set. Cool.
  In a mixing bowl, beat cream cheese and sour cream. Fold in whipped topping. Spread over the crust. In another mixing bowl, combine milk and pudding mixes; beat on low speed for 2 minutes. Spread over first layer. Carefully spread whipped topping over second layer. Sprinkle with walnuts. Chill at least 1 hour.
Yield: 24 servings.

Coconut Cream Pie

(pictured above)
Jerraine Barlow, Colorado City, Arizona
This recipe yields two luscious desserts to bring to carry-in dinners or even to serve guests at home. Sprinkled with toasted coconut, the pies use ready-made graham cracker crusts and require only a few other ingredients for the creamy filling.

    1-1/2 cups cold milk
        1 package (3.4 ounces) instant coconut
           cream pudding mix
        1 package (8 ounces) cream cheese,
           softened
        1 carton (8 ounces) frozen whipped
           topping, thawed
        2 graham cracker crusts (9 inches *each*)
      1/2 cup flaked coconut, toasted

In a large mixing bowl, beat milk and pudding mix on low speed for 2 minutes or until thickened.

In another bowl, beat cream cheese. Add to pudding and mix well. Fold in whipped topping. Spoon into the crusts; sprinkle with coconut. Refrigerate until serving.

Yield: 2 pies (6-8 servings each).

Pumpkin Cookie Dip

Gloria Kirchman, Eden Prairie, Minnesota
A few moments are all you need for this autumnal dip, which goes perfect with store-bought gingersnaps.

        1 package (8 ounces) cream cheese,
           softened
        2 jars (7 ounces *each*) marshmallow creme

        1 can (15 ounces) solid-pack pumpkin
        1 teaspoon ground cinnamon
        1 teaspoon grated orange peel
Gingersnaps *or* vanilla wafers

In a large mixing bowl, beat the cream cheese and marshmallow creme until smooth. Stir in pumpkin, cinnamon and orange peel. Serve with cookies. Store leftovers in the refrigerator.

Yield: 4 cups.

Graham Cracker Brownies

(pictured below)
Cathy Guffey, Towanda, Pennsylvania
I enjoy making these brownies for last-minute bake sales and family gatherings alike. My grandmother first baked them nearly 50 years ago, and they're as popular today as they were then!

        2 cups graham cracker crumbs (about 32
           squares)
        1 cup (6 ounces) semisweet chocolate chips
        1 teaspoon baking powder
Pinch salt
        1 can (14 ounces) sweetened condensed milk

In a large bowl, combine all ingredients. Spread into a greased 8-in. square baking pan.

Bake at 350° for 30-35 minutes or until a toothpick inserted near the center comes out clean. Cool on a wire rack.

Yield: 1-1/2 dozen.

Fresh Broccoli Salad

(pictured above)
Marilyn Fields, Groveland, California
Thanks to bottled salad dressing and the pre-cut vegetables found in today's produce department, you can toss this refreshing salad together in a matter of minutes.

    2 pounds fresh broccoli, cut into bite-size
       pieces
    1 package (12 ounces) fresh mushrooms,
       sliced
    2 small red onions, thinly sliced into rings
    1 can (2-1/4 ounces) sliced ripe olives,
       drained
 1-1/2 cups prepared Italian salad dressing
   1/3 cup shredded Parmesan cheese

In a large bowl combine all ingredients; toss to coat. Cover and chill for at least 2 hours.
Yield: 12 servings.

Potluck Pointer

Skillet Zucchini can be prepared the day before serving. Simply cook the zucchini for 3 to 4 minutes, then cover and refrigerate the mixture overnight. Reheat it in a large kettle before serving.

Skillet Zucchini

Linda Fabian, Wheatland, Wyoming
Simply made on the stovetop, this savory combination of sausage, onion, peppers and zucchini in a tomato-based sauce was a hit at our potluck wedding dinner.

    1 pound fully cooked kielbasa *or* Polish
       sausage links, cut into 1/4-inch slices
  1/4 cup vegetable oil
    2 medium green peppers, chopped
    2 cups sliced celery
    1 large onion, chopped
    2 garlic cloves, minced
    8 to 10 medium zucchini, cut into
       1/4-inch slices
    2 cans (28 ounces *each*) diced tomatoes,
       undrained
    2 teaspoons dried oregano
    2 teaspoons salt
    1 teaspoon pepper

In a Dutch oven, cook sausage in oil over medium heat until browned. Add the peppers, celery, onion and garlic; saute for 5 minutes or until vegetables are crisp-tender. Stir in the zucchini, tomatoes, oregano, salt and pepper. Bring to a boil. Reduce heat; cover and simmer for 6-8 minutes until zucchini is tender.
Yield: 24-26 servings.

Refreshing Lemon-Lime Drink

(pictured below)
Lisa Castillo, Bourbonnais, Illinois
Here is a version of the famous margarita that doesn't include any alcohol. Bursting with lemon and lime flavors, it's perfect for get-togethers on hot summer days or on a buffet of Mexican favorites.

> 1 can (12 ounces) frozen limeade
>   concentrate, thawed
> 2/3 cup frozen lemonade concentrate, thawed
> 1 teaspoon orange extract
> 1-1/2 cups water
> 6 cups chilled lemon-lime soda
> 1 medium lemon, sliced
> 1 medium lime, sliced

In a large container, combine the limeade and lemonade concentrates and orange extract. Stir in water.

Just before serving, stir in lemon-lime soda. Serve over ice. Garnish with lemon and lime slices.

Yield: 12 servings (3 quarts).

Crunchy Asparagus Medley

(pictured above)
Mary Gaylord, Balsam Lake, Wisconsin
Celery, water chestnuts and toasted almonds help this recipe live up to its "crunchy" name. I've prepared the warm side dish for many events, including a Hawaiian-theme dinner I once hosted.

> 1-1/2 pounds fresh asparagus, cut into
>   2-inch pieces
> 1 cup thinly sliced celery
> 2 cans (8 ounces *each*) sliced water
>   chestnuts, drained
> 1/4 cup slivered almonds, toasted
> 2 tablespoons soy sauce
> 2 tablespoons butter

In a large saucepan, cook the asparagus and celery in 1/2 in. of water for 3-5 minutes or until crisp-tender; drain. Stir in the water chestnuts, almonds, soy sauce and butter; heat through.

Yield: 8-10 servings.

Pennsylvania Dutch Coleslaw

Deb Darr, Falls City, Oregon
With all of the cabbage that is grown here in the Northwest, this recipe is a real natural for us! My mother used to make this refreshing salad on holidays to celebrate with friends and family.

> 1 medium head green cabbage, shredded
>   (about 8 cups)
> 1 cup shredded red cabbage
> 4 to 5 carrots, shredded
> 1 cup mayonnaise
> 2 tablespoons cider vinegar
> 1/2 cup sugar
> 1 teaspoon salt
> 1/4 teaspoon pepper

In a large bowl, combine cabbage and carrots; set aside. In a small bowl, combine all remaining ingredients; pour over cabbage mixture. Toss well and refrigerate overnight.

Yield: 12-16 servings.

Quick Garlic Toast

Teresa Ingebrand, Perham, Minnesota
Mom knew how to easily round out a meal with these crisp and cheesy garlic toasts. They're yummy alongside a slaw or salad, and they are excellent for soaking up gravy from a stew. Consider them the next time you attend a spaghetti dinner or another bring-a-dish supper.

- 1/3 cup butter, softened
- 12 slices bread
- 1/2 teaspoon garlic salt
- 3 tablespoons grated Parmesan cheese

Spread butter on one side of each slice of bread. Cut each slice in half; place plain side down on a baking sheet. Sprinkle with garlic salt and Parmesan cheese.

Broil 4 in. from the heat for 1-2 minutes or until lightly browned.

Yield: 12 slices.

Corn Pasta Salad

Bernice Morris, Marshfield, Missouri
After tasting this chilled salad at a family reunion, I immediately asked for the recipe. The tricolor pasta, crunchy corn, red onion and green pepper give the zesty salad plenty of appeal.

- 2 cups cooked tricolor spiral pasta
- 1 package (16 ounces) frozen corn, thawed
- 1 cup chopped celery
- 1 medium green pepper, chopped
- 1 cup chopped seeded tomatoes
- 1/2 cup diced pimientos
- 1/2 cup chopped red onion
- 1 cup picante sauce
- 2 tablespoons vegetable oil
- 1 tablespoon lemon juice
- 1 garlic clove, minced
- 1 tablespoon sugar
- 1/2 teaspoon salt

In a large bowl, combine the first seven ingredients. In a jar with a tight-fitting lid, combine the picante sauce, oil, lemon juice, garlic, sugar and salt; shake well.

Pour over pasta mixture and toss to coat. Cover and refrigerate overnight.

Yield: 10 servings.

Cappuccino Mousse Trifle

(pictured above)
Tracy Bergland, Prior Lake, Minnesota
This is the easiest trifle I've ever made, yet it looks and tastes like I spent hours on it. I pipe whipped topping around the edge of the bowl, grate chocolate in the center and sprinkle with cinnamon.

- 2-1/2 cups cold milk
- 1/3 cup instant coffee granules
- 2 packages (3.4 ounces *each*) instant vanilla pudding mix
- 1 carton (16 ounces) frozen whipped topping, thawed, *divided*
- 2 loaves (10-3/4 ounces *each*) frozen pound cake, thawed and cubed
- 1 square (1 ounce) semisweet chocolate, grated
- 1/4 teaspoon ground cinnamon

In a large mixing bowl, stir milk and coffee granules until dissolved; remove 1 cup and set aside. Add pudding mixes to the remaining milk mixture; beat on low speed for 2 minutes or until thickened. Fold in half of the whipped topping.

Place a third of the cake cubes in a 4-qt. serving or trifle bowl. Layer with a third of the reserved milk mixture and pudding mixture and a fourth of the grated chocolate. Repeat layers twice. Garnish with remaining whipped topping and chocolate. Sprinkle with cinnamon. Cover and refrigerate until serving.

Yield: 16-20 servings.

Taco Dip Platter

(pictured below)

Marieann Johansen, Desert Hot Springs, California

To make this zesty appetizer, you simply layer beans, salsa, cheese and other taco-like ingredients onto a platter. I like to call it a walking dip, because you can scoop some on a plate with a few tortilla chips, then take it with you as you stroll around and talk with friends.

- 1 can (15 ounces) refried beans
- 1 cup chunky salsa
- 1 cup guacamole
- 2 cups (16 ounces) sour cream
- 1 can (4 ounces) chopped green chilies
- 1 can (2-1/4 ounces) sliced ripe olives, drained
- 1/2 cup finely shredded cheddar cheese
- 1/2 cup finely shredded Monterey Jack cheese

Tortilla chips

Spread beans on a 12-in. serving plate. Layer salsa, guacamole and sour cream over beans, leaving a 1-in. edge around each layer. Sprinkle with chilies, olives and cheeses. Refrigerate until ready to serve. Serve with tortilla chips.

Yield: 16-20 servings.

10-Minute Taco Salad

Cindy Stephan, Owosso, Michigan

Mom often made this hearty main-dish salad for my three brothers and me when we were growing up. Now it's one of my husband's favorite meals—and one I frequently fix for weekend guests.

- 2 cans (16 ounces *each*) chili beans, undrained
- 1 package (10-1/2 ounces) corn chips
- 2 cups (8 ounces) shredded cheddar cheese
- 4 cups chopped lettuce
- 2 small tomatoes, chopped
- 1 small onion, chopped
- 1 can (2-1/4 ounces) sliced ripe olives, drained
- 1-1/4 cups salsa
- 1/2 cup sour cream

In a saucepan or microwave-safe bowl, heat the beans. Place corn chips on a large platter. Top with beans, cheese, lettuce, tomatoes, onion, olives, salsa and sour cream.

Yield: 8 servings.

Banana Blueberry Pie

Priscilla Weaver, Hagerstown, Maryland
It takes just moments to assemble two of these fruity pies. You could even take one to your event and enjoy the second at home with your family the next day.

    1 package (8 ounces) cream cheese,
          softened
  3/4 cup sugar
    2 cups whipped topping
    4 medium firm bananas, sliced
    2 pastry shells (9 inches), baked
    1 can (21 ounces) blueberry pie filling
Fresh blueberries and mint and additional sliced
    bananas, optional

In a mixing bowl, beat cream cheese and sugar until smooth. Fold in whipped topping and bananas. Pour into pastry shells. Spread with pie filling. Refrigerate for at least 30 minutes. Just before serving, garnish with blueberries, mint and bananas if desired.

Yield: 2 pies (6-8 servings each).

Pepper Parmesan Beans

Marian Platt, Sequim, Washington
A colorful mixture of peppers and green beans get an Italian treatment with basil and Parmesan cheese in this delightful vegetable dish.

    1 large sweet red pepper, diced
    1 small green pepper, diced
  1/4 cup chopped onion
    1 garlic clove, minced
  1/4 cup olive oil
1-1/2 pounds fresh green beans, cut into 2-inch
          pieces
    1 tablespoon minced fresh basil *or* 1
          teaspoon dried basil
    1 teaspoon salt
  1/3 to 1/2 cup shredded Parmesan cheese

In a large skillet, saute the peppers, onion and garlic in oil until the vegetables are tender, about 3 minutes. Add the beans, basil and salt; toss to coat. Cover and cook over medium-low heat for 7-8 minutes or until beans are crisp-tender. Stir in cheese.

Yield: 8 servings.

Taco Stovetop Supper

(pictured above)
Barbara Ingils, Addy, Washington
Green chilies, Mexicorn and taco seasoning add south-of-the-border flair to this quick skillet dish. The recipe makes a lot. It's perfect for potluck guests to spoon into tortillas, topping everything off with shredded cheese, chopped onion and other garnishes.

    2 pounds ground beef
    2 cans (15-1/2 ounces *each*) hot chili beans
    2 cans (10 ounces *each*) diced tomatoes and
          green chilies
    1 can (11-1/2 ounces) picante V8 juice
    1 can (11 ounces) Mexicorn, drained
    2 envelopes taco seasoning
Optional garnishes: tortillas, shredded cheddar
    cheese, chopped onion, shredded lettuce
    and/or taco sauce

In a Dutch oven, cook beef over medium heat until no longer pink; drain. Stir in beans, tomatoes, V8 juice, corn and taco seasoning. Simmer, uncovered, for 15-20 minutes or until heated through. Garnish as desired.

Yield: 10-12 servings.

Southwestern Bean Soup

(pictured below)
Jackie Hacker, Seville, Ohio
You can stir up a large kettle of this chunky soup in no time at all. Offer tortilla chips, shredded cheese and sour cream alongside the pot for garnish. Adjust the pepper sauce to your liking, or reduce the broth for a thicker batch.

    1   large onion, chopped
    1   teaspoon vegetable oil
    2   cans (15 ounces *each*) black beans, rinsed
        and drained
    2   cans (14-1/2 ounces *each*) diced tomatoes
        with garlic and onion
    2   cans (14-1/2 ounces *each*) chicken broth
    1   can (16 ounces) kidney beans, rinsed and
        drained
    1   can (15 ounces) cannellini *or* white kidney
        beans, rinsed and drained
1-1/2   cups fresh *or* frozen corn
    4   garlic cloves, minced
1-1/2   teaspoons ground cumin
1-1/2   teaspoons chili powder
  1/8   to 1/4 teaspoon hot pepper sauce

In a Dutch oven or soup kettle, saute the onion in oil until tender. Stir in the remaining ingredients; bring to a boil. Reduce heat; simmer, uncovered, for 5 minutes or until heated through.

Yield: 12 servings (3 quarts).

Herbed Tossed Salad

(pictured above)
Margery Bryan, Moses Lake, Washington
Ten minutes are all you need to toss together this green salad. The homemade dressing features garlic, oregano and basil, and appeals to most tastes.

      1   cup vegetable oil
    1/3   cup tarragon vinegar
      1   garlic clove, minced
      2   teaspoons minced fresh oregano *or* 1/2
          teaspoon dried oregano
      1   teaspoon salt
  3/4   to 1 teaspoon minced fresh basil *or* 1/4
          teaspoon dried basil
    1/2   teaspoon minced fresh parsley
Mixed salad greens
Sliced cucumber and sweet red pepper

In a jar with tight-fitting lid, combine the first seven ingredients; shake well. In a large salad bowl, combine greens, cucumber and red pepper. Drizzle with dressing and toss to coat.

Yield: about 1-1/3 cups dressing.

Tomato Crouton Casserole

(pictured below)
Norma Nelson, Punta Gorda, Florida
This baked dish uses lots of brilliant tomatoes and seasonings that give it an Italian twist. Every time it's part of a buffet, someone asks for the recipe.

- 8 medium tomatoes, peeled and cut into wedges
- 8 slices bread, crusts removed and cubed
- 1/2 cup plus 2 tablespoons butter, melted
- 1 teaspoon salt
- 1 teaspoon dried basil
- 1 teaspoon dried thyme
- 3/4 cup grated Parmesan cheese

Arrange tomatoes in a greased 13-in. x 9-in. x 2-in. baking dish. Top with bread cubes. Combine butter, salt, basil and thyme; drizzle over bread and tomatoes. Sprinkle with cheese. Bake, uncovered, at 350° for 30-35 minutes or until tomatoes are tender.
Yield: 8-10 servings.

French Peas

Pat Walter, Pine Island, Minnesota
A friend shared this tasty way to present peas. Bright green and festive, this side dish has a slightly sweet flavor that takes less than 30 minutes to prepare.

- 2 cans (8 ounces *each*) sliced water chestnuts, drained
- 2 tablespoons chopped onion
- 1/4 cup butter, cubed
- 2 teaspoons all-purpose flour
- 1/2 teaspoon sugar
- 1/2 teaspoon salt
- 1/2 cup milk
- 8 cups frozen peas, thawed
- 2 cups shredded lettuce

In a large saucepan, saute water chestnuts and onion in butter until onion is tender. Stir in the flour, sugar and salt until blended. Gradually add milk; stir in peas. Bring to a boil. Reduce heat; cover and cook for 3-5 minutes or until peas are tender and sauce is slightly thickened. Add lettuce; cook until lettuce is wilted.
Yield: 12-14 servings.

Melon Cucumber Medley

(pictured above)
Edie DeSpain, Logan, Utah
A light, lemony dressing complements a beautiful mixture of melons and sliced cucumbers. This delightful summer salad is especially good served at a brunch or luncheon.

    1/2 cup vegetable oil
    1/4 cup lemon juice
      1 teaspoon sugar
    1/2 teaspoon salt
Dash pepper
      6 cups melon balls *or* cubes (cantaloupe,
         honeydew *and/or* watermelon)
      3 medium cucumbers, thinly sliced
Lettuce leaves, optional

In a jar with a tight-fitting lid, combine the oil, lemon juice, sugar, salt and pepper; shake until sugar is dissolved.

   In a bowl, combine melon and cucumbers; drizzle with dressing. Cover and refrigerate for at least 1 hour. Serve in a lettuce-lined bowl if desired.
Yield: 12 servings.

1-2-3 Barbecue Sausage

Clara Johnson, Eldorado, Ohio
Ten minutes are all you need to whip up these saucy bites. They make wonderful appetizers for a party.

      6 pounds smoked sausage, cut into
         2-inch pieces
      2 bottles (18 ounces *each*) barbecue sauce
      2 cups packed brown sugar

Divide sausages between two ungreased 13-in. x 9-in. x 2-in. baking dishes. Combine barbecue sauce and brown sugar; pour over sausages and toss to coat.

   Bake, uncovered, at 350° for 35-40 minutes or until sauce is thickened, stirring once.
Yield: about 24 servings.

Snappy Peas 'n' Mushrooms

(pictured below)
Laura Mahaffey, Annapolis, Maryland
Seasoned with dill, this versatile side dish can be on the buffet table in mere minutes. Just wrap the fresh vegetables in foil, seal tightly and grill until tender. It's that easy!

      1 pound fresh sugar snap *or* snow peas
    1/2 cup sliced fresh mushrooms
      2 tablespoons sliced green onions
      1 tablespoon snipped fresh dill *or*
         1 teaspoon dill weed
      2 tablespoons butter
Salt and pepper to taste

Place peas and mushrooms on a piece of double-layer heavy-duty foil (about 18 in. square). Sprinkle with onions and dill; dot with butter. Fold foil around the mixture and seal tightly. Grill, covered, over medium-hot heat for 5 minutes. Turn; grill 5-8 minutes longer or until the vegetables are tender. Season with salt and pepper.
Yield: 8-10 servings.

Teriyaki Chicken

(pictured above)
Edna Luce, Kearney, Nebraska
When my granddaughter was married, we served this savory chicken over rice at the reception. It requires very little fuss and is so tasty.

    3/4 cup vegetable oil
    3/4 cup soy sauce
    1/3 cup chili sauce
      3 tablespoons sesame seeds
      3 tablespoons white vinegar
      6 garlic cloves, minced
  1-1/2 teaspoons sugar
    3/4 teaspoon ground ginger
    3/4 teaspoon pepper
     24 boneless skinless chicken breast halves
        (about 6 ounces *each*)
Toasted sesame seeds

In a large bowl, combine the first nine ingredients. Pour 3/4 cup marinade into each of three large resealable plastic bags. Add eight chicken breasts to each bag; seal bags and turn to coat. Refrigerate for 6 hours or overnight, turning once.

   Discard marinade. Transfer chicken to two greased 15-in. x 10-in. x 1-in. baking pans. Bake, uncovered, at 350° for 10-13 minutes on each side or until chicken juices run clear.

   To grill, cook, uncovered, over medium-hot heat for 5-7 minutes on each side or until chicken juices run clear. Sprinkle with sesame seeds before serving.

Yield: 24 servings.

Blueberry Angel Dessert

(pictured on p. 215)
Carol Johnson, Tyler, Texas
Make the most of angel food cake, pie filling and whipped topping by preparing this light dessert that won't keep you in the kitchen for hours. It's the perfect way to end a big summer meal. It's also ideal for a potluck.

    1 package (8 ounces) cream cheese, softened
    1 cup confectioners' sugar
    1 carton (8 ounces) frozen whipped
      topping, thawed
    1 prepared angel food cake (16 ounces), cut
      into 1-inch pieces
    2 cans (21 ounces *each*) blueberry pie filling

In a large mixing bowl, beat cream cheese and sugar until smooth; fold in whipped topping and cake cubes. Spread evenly into an ungreased 13-in. x 9-in. x 2-in. dish; top with pie filling. Cover and refrigerate for at least 2 hours before cutting into squares.

Yield: 12-15 servings.

Potluck Pointer

Keep Teriyaki Chicken hot in an electric roaster set on low. A bit of beef broth will keep it tender.

Shrimp Appetizer Spread

(pictured above)
Brenda Buhler, Abbotsford, British Columbia
There's no secret to this creamy seafood dish; it's simply delicious! I first tasted it at a friend's house and liked it so much, I requested the recipe. I love how it dresses up an appetizer table.

> 1 package (8 ounces) cream cheese, softened
> 1/2 cup sour cream
> 1/4 cup mayonnaise
> 3 packages (5 ounces *each*) frozen cooked salad shrimp, thawed
> 1 cup seafood sauce
> 2 cups (8 ounces) shredded part-skim mozzarella cheese
> 1 medium green pepper, chopped
> 1 small tomato, chopped
> 3 green onions with tops, sliced
> Assorted crackers

In a large mixing bowl, beat the cream cheese, sour cream and mayonnaise until smooth.

Spread mixture on a round 12-in. serving platter. Sprinkle with shrimp. Top with seafood sauce. Sprinkle with mozzarella cheese, green pepper, tomato and onions. Cover and refrigerate. Serve with crackers.

Yield: 20 servings.

Butter-Dipped Biscuit Squares

Rebekah DeWitt, Star City, Arkansas
You can bake up these buttery biscuits in less than a half hour. Not only are they the easiest and best biscuits I've ever had, but they go well with virtually any meal, making them a welcomed contribution to covered-dish events.

> 2 cups self-rising flour
> 2 tablespoons sugar
> 1 cup milk
> 1/2 cup butter, melted
> All-purpose flour

In a bowl, combine the self-rising flour, sugar and milk; mix well. Turn onto a floured surface; sprinkle with all-purpose flour. Pat dough to 1/2-in. thickness. With a sharp knife dipped in flour, cut into 3-in. x 2-in. pieces.

Pour butter into an ungreased 13-in. x 9-in. x 2-in. baking pan. Dip one side of each piece into melted butter. Carefully turn to coat. Bake, uncovered, at 450° for 10 minutes or until golden brown.

Yield: 15 biscuits.

Editor's Note: As a substitute for each cup of self-rising flour, place 1-1/2 teaspoons baking powder and 1/2 teaspoon salt in a measuring cup. Add all-purpose flour to measure 1 cup.

Spaghetti Salad

(pictured below)
Kali Berry, Shawnee, Oklahoma
My family loves this salad, especially during the hot summer months. With fresh ingredients from our garden, it looks terrific on a salad buffet.

    12   ounces thin spaghetti
     1   cup (4 ounces) shredded part-skim
         mozzarella cheese
    1/2 cup diced pepperoni
    1/2 cup diced fully cooked ham
    1/2 cup chopped green pepper
    1/2 cup diced tomato
    1/2 cup chopped onion
    1/2 cup chopped cucumber
    1/4 cup sliced ripe olives
     1   avocado, peeled and diced, optional
     1   bottle (8 ounces) Italian salad dressing

In a large saucepan, cook spaghetti according to package directions. Meanwhile in a large salad bowl, add the cheese, pepperoni, ham, green pepper, tomato, onion, cucumber and olives. Add avocado if desired.

Rinse pasta with cold water; drain well. Place on top of salad ingredients. Drizzle with salad dressing; toss lightly to coat. Chill until serving.
Yield: 15-20 servings.

Nutty Broccoli Slaw

(pictured above)
Dora Mae Clapsaddle, Kensington, Ohio
A sweet dressing nicely coats a crisp blend of broccoli slaw mix, carrots, onions, almonds and sunflower kernels in this no-fuss recipe. Crushed ramen noodles provide even more crunch, making it a smash hit everywhere I take it.

        1   package (3 ounces) chicken ramen noodles
        1   package (16 ounces) broccoli coleslaw mix
        2   cups sliced green onions (about 2
             bunches)
    1-1/2   cups broccoli florets
        1   can (6 ounces) ripe olives, drained and
             halved
        1   cup sunflower kernels, toasted
      1/2   cup slivered almonds, toasted
      1/2   cup sugar
      1/2   cup cider vinegar
      1/2   cup olive oil

Set aside the noodle seasoning packet; crush the noodles and place in a large bowl. Add the slaw mix, onions, broccoli, olives, sunflower kernels and almonds.

In a jar with a tight-fitting lid, combine the sugar, vinegar, oil and contents of noodle seasoning packet; shake well. Drizzle over salad and toss to coat.
Yield: 16 servings.

Four-Pasta Beef Bake

(pictured above)
Harriet Stichter, Milford, Indiana
This hearty casserole looks and tastes a lot like lasagna, but it's quicker to prepare since you don't have to layer the ingredients. Have fun with selecting the shapes of pasta you'd like to use!

    8 cups uncooked pasta (four different
       shapes)
    2 pounds ground beef
    2 medium green peppers, chopped
    2 medium onions, chopped
    2 cups sliced fresh mushrooms
    4 jars (26 ounces *each*) meatless spaghetti
       sauce
    2 eggs, lightly beaten
    4 cups (16 ounces) shredded part-skim
       mozzarella cheese

Cook pasta according to package directions. Meanwhile, in a large skillet, cook the beef, green peppers, onions and mushrooms over medium heat until meat is no longer pink; drain.

Drain pasta and place in a large bowl; stir in the beef mixture, two jars of spaghetti sauce and eggs.

Transfer to two greased 13-in. x 9-in. x 2-in. baking dishes. Top with remaining sauce; sprinkle with cheese. Bake, uncovered, at 350° for 25-30 minutes or until heated through.

Yield: 2 casseroles (8-10 servings each).

Bohemian Kolaches

(pictured below)
Maxine Hron, Quincy, Illinois
This recipe was given to me by my mother-in-law, who received it from her mother. It was a standard treat in their family, made nearly every week. Now I make these little yeast breads for special occasions.

    2 packages (1/4 ounce *each*) active dry yeast
  1/2 cup sugar, *divided*
    2 cups warm milk (110° to 115°)
    4 cups all-purpose flour, *divided*
    4 egg yolks
    1 teaspoon salt
  1/4 cup butter, softened
    2 cups canned prune, poppy seed, cherry *or*
       lemon pie filling
    1 egg white, beaten

In a small bowl, dissolve yeast and 1 tablespoon sugar in warm milk; let stand 10 minutes. In large mixing bowl, combine 2 cups flour, remaining sugar, egg yolks, salt, butter and yeast/milk mixture. Mix until smooth. Add enough remaining flour to make a stiff dough. Turn out onto a floured surface and knead until smooth and elastic, about 6-8 minutes. Add additional flour, if necessary. Place dough in greased bowl, turning once to grease top. Cover; let rise in a warm place until doubled in bulk, about 1 hour.

Punch dough down and allow to rise again. Roll out on floured surface to 1/2-in. thickness. Cut with large glass or 2-1/2-in. cutter. Place on greased baking sheets; let rise until doubled, about 45 minutes. Firmly press indentation in center and fill each roll with a heaping tablespoon of filling. Brush dough with egg white. Bake at 350° for 10-15 minutes or until rolls are light golden brown.

Yield: about 28 rolls.

Au Gratin Potatoes and Ham

Evie Pond, Ipswich, South Dakota
Reach for this comforting sensation when there are more than 100 people hoping to enjoy a plate of food at your event. Creamy, hearty and comforting, it's one dish that everyone will enjoy.

20 pounds red potatoes
8 pounds fully cooked ham, cubed
4 cans (10-3/4 ounces *each*) condensed cream of celery soup, undiluted
8 cups milk
1/2 cup all-purpose flour
6 pounds process cheese (Velveeta), cubed
2 teaspoons pepper
2 teaspoons paprika

Place potatoes in several Dutch ovens or soup kettles and cover with water. Bring to a boil. Reduce heat; cover and cook for 15-20 minutes or until tender. Drain.

Peel if desired and cut into cubes. Place about 6 cups of potatoes each in eight greased 13-in. x 9-in. x 2-in. baking pans. Add about 3-1/2 cups of cubed ham to each pan.

In the same Dutch ovens, combine soup, milk and flour over medium heat. Bring to a boil; cook and stir for 2 minutes or until thickened. Add cheese, pepper and paprika. Reduce heat and cook until the cheese is melted.

Pour about 2-1/4 cups of sauce into each pan. Cover and bake at 350° for 40 minutes. Uncover and bake 5-10 minutes longer or until bubbly.
Yield: 140 servings.

Big-Batch Burgers

Kay Kendrick, Ruffin, North Carolina
We had these juicy hamburgers while attending a family picnic. Everyone loved them so much we all had to have a copy of the recipe.

1-1/2 cups crushed butter-flavored crackers (about 38 crackers)
1 cup applesauce
1 envelope onion soup mix
2 tablespoons Worcestershire sauce
1 tablespoon hot pepper sauce
2-1/2 teaspoons seasoned salt
5 pounds ground beef
20 hamburger buns, split

In a several large bowls, combine the first six ingredients. Crumble beef over mixture and mix well. Shape into 20 patties. Broil, grill or pan-fry until no longer pink. Serve on buns.
Yield: 20 servings.

Pumpkin Chocolate Loaf

(pictured above)
Kathy Gardner, Rockville, Maryland
These fudgy loaves, with a hint of pumpkin and spice, have been a favorite for years. They can be sliced to serve with morning coffee or as an after-dinner treat.

3-1/2 cups sugar
1-1/4 cups vegetable oil
3 eggs
1 can (29 ounces) solid-pack pumpkin
3 squares (1 ounce *each*) unsweetened chocolate, melted and cooled
1-1/2 teaspoons vanilla extract
3-3/4 cups all-purpose flour
1-1/2 teaspoons salt
1-1/2 teaspoons baking powder
1-1/4 teaspoons baking soda
1-1/4 teaspoons ground cinnamon
1 to 1-1/4 teaspoons ground cloves
1/2 teaspoon ground nutmeg
2 cups (12 ounces) semisweet chocolate chips

In a large bowl, combine sugar and oil. Add eggs; mix well. Stir in the pumpkin, chocolate and vanilla; mix well. Combine the dry ingredients; stir into pumpkin mixture just until blended. Stir in chips.

Transfer to three greased 9-in. x 5-in. x 3-in. loaf pans. Bake at 350° for 55-65 minutes or until a toothpick inserted near the center comes out clean. Cool for 10 minutes before removing from pans to wire racks. Wrap and freeze for up to 6 months.
Yield: 3 loaves.

Watermelon Boat

(pictured above)
Ruth Seitz, Columbus Junction, Iowa
"Wow!" is what folks will say when they dig into this lovely fruit salad piled high in an eye-catching display.

- 1 cup lemon juice
- 3/4 cup sugar
- 2 teaspoons all-purpose flour
- 2 eggs, beaten
- 1 cup heavy whipping cream
- 1 large watermelon
- 1 large honeydew, cut into cubes *or* balls
- 1 large cantaloupe, cut into cubes *or* balls
- 2 pints fresh strawberries, sliced
- 1/2 pound green grapes

Combine lemon juice, sugar and flour in a saucepan; bring to a boil. Reduce heat to low. Stir 1/4 cup into eggs; return all to pan. Cook and stir for 15 minutes or until mixture coats a spoon (do not boil). Cool. Fold in whipped cream; cover and chill until serving.

For watermelon boat, cut a thin slice from bottom of melon with a sharp knife to allow it to sit flat. Mark a horizontal cutting line 2 in. above center of melon. With a long sharp knife, cut into melon along cutting line, making sure to cut all the way through. Gently pull off the top section of the rind.

Remove fruit from both sections and cut into cubes or balls; set aside. To cut decorative edge, place melon on its side. Position a 2-1/2-in. star cookie cutter against inside edge of melon, allowing only half of star to cut through rind. Use a mallet if necessary to help push cookie cutter through melon.

Insert a toothpick into flat edge of removed piece. Attach piece onto melon edge where last cut ends. Repeat cutting and attaching pieces until entire melon edge is completed.

In a large bowl, combine honeydew, cantaloupe, strawberries, grapes and watermelon; spoon into boat. Serve with dressing.

Yield: 32-36 servings (about 2 cups dressing).

Seafood Soup

Victor Miller, Levittown, Pennsylvania
Sea scallops and shrimp are the starring attractions in this popular cream soup. Imitation crabmeat and a hint of thyme round out comforting bowlfuls.

4-1/2 quarts chicken broth
   10 packages (8 ounces *each*) imitation crabmeat
    2 medium onions, diced
1-1/2 cups butter, cubed
  1/4 cup all-purpose flour
    5 pounds sea scallops
    3 pounds cooked medium shrimp, peeled and deveined
1-1/4 teaspoons dried thyme
    1 teaspoon dried parsley
    4 cups heavy whipping cream
Salt and pepper to taste

In a large kettle, bring broth and crab to a boil. Reduce heat; cover and simmer for 20 minutes or until crab breaks into pieces when stirred. Meanwhile, in several large skillets, saute onions in butter until tender. Stir in flour until blended. Stir into crab mixture; return to a simmer.

    Add scallops, shrimp, thyme and parsley. Simmer, uncovered, for 5-7 minutes or until scallops turn opaque. Add the cream, salt and pepper; cook and stir until heated through (do not boil).
Yield: 48 servings (12 quarts).

Smoky Spareribs

Lornetta Kaminski, St. Benedict, Saskatchewan
Feeding a big crowd is never easier than when these finger-licking spareribs are on the menu. There's really nothing to the lip-smacking main course.

 100 pounds pork spareribs, cut into serving-size pieces
    8 bottles (42 ounces *each*) barbecue sauce
    4 cans (20 ounces *each*) crushed pineapple, undrained
    5 pounds brown sugar
    1 to 2 bottles (4 ounces *each*) Liquid Smoke, optional

Place ribs in large roasting pans. Cover and bake at 350° for 1 hour; drain. Bake 15-20 minutes longer or until almost tender.

    Meanwhile, in a kettle, combine barbecue sauce, pineapple, brown sugar and Liquid Smoke if desired; cook and stir until sugar is dissolved. Drain ribs; pour sauce over ribs. Bake, uncovered, for 15-20 minutes or until the meat is tender.
Yield: 100 servings.

Reunion BBQ'S

(pictured below)
Margery Bryan, Royal City, Washington
Here's a favorite I rely on when I need to make a lot of sandwiches. The tangy mixture takes advantage of quick-cooking oats to help feed a bunch.

    5 pounds ground beef
    2 cups chopped onion
    3 cups water
    2 tablespoons ketchup
    2 to 3 tablespoons chili powder
    2 tablespoons salt
    1 tablespoon pepper
    1 teaspoon ground mustard
    1 cup quick-cooking oats
  24 hamburger buns, split

In a several large saucepans or Dutch ovens, brown beef and onion over medium heat; drain. Add water, ketchup, chili powder, salt, pepper and mustard; bring to a boil. Stir in oats. Reduce heat; cover and simmer for 30 minutes. Serve on buns.
Yield: 24 servings.

BLT Dip

Emalee Payne, Eau Claire, Wisconsin
Fans of bacon, lettuce and tomato sandwiches will fall for this savory dip. It's easy to transport to different functions and always draws recipe requests.

- 2 cups (16 ounces) sour cream
- 2 cups mayonnaise
- 2 pounds sliced bacon, cooked and crumbled
- 6 plum tomatoes, chopped
- 3 green onions, chopped

Assorted crackers *or* chips

In a large bowl, combine the sour cream, mayonnaise, bacon, tomatoes and onions. Refrigerate until serving. Serve with crackers or chips.
Yield: 6 cups.

All-Occasion Punch

(pictured below)
Carol Van Sickle, Versailles, Kentucky
People are surprised when they discover how simple this thirst-quenching beverage is. The pretty pink color is especially nice for baby or bridal showers, but the punch disappears no matter when it's served.

- 8 cups cold water
- 3 cans (6 ounces *each*) frozen lemonade concentrate, thawed
- 2 liters ginger ale, chilled
- 1 liter cherry lemon-lime soda, chilled

Ice ring, optional

In a large punch bowl, combine water and lemonade. Stir in ginger ale and soda. Top with an ice ring if desired.
Yield: 5-1/2 quarts.

Reunion Meatballs

Toni King, London, Kentucky
Whenever we attend a picnic or family get-together, people expect me to bring these saucy meatballs and copies of the recipe. My aunt passed the recipe on to me years ago.

- 1/2 cup milk
- 1 egg
- 1 medium onion, chopped
- 3 bacon strips, cooked and crumbled
- 1/2 cup crushed saltines (about 15 crackers)
- 2 teaspoons salt
- 1-1/2 pounds lean ground beef
- 1/2 pound bulk pork sausage

SAUCE:
- 1 bottle (14 ounces) ketchup
- 1-1/4 cups water
- 1/2 cup white vinegar
- 1/2 cup packed brown sugar
- 1 medium onion, chopped
- 1 tablespoon chili powder
- 1-1/2 teaspoons Worcestershire sauce

Dash salt

In a large bowl, combine the first six ingredients. Crumble beef and sausage over mixture and mix well. Shape into 1-1/2-in. balls. Place in a greased 13-in. x 9-in. x 2-in. baking dish.

In a saucepan, mix sauce ingredients. Bring to a boil; reduce heat. Simmer, uncovered, for 5 minutes. Pour over meatballs. Bake, uncovered, at 350° for 1-1/2 hours or until meat is no longer pink.
Yield: 40 meatballs.

Super Pasta Salad

Ken Churches, San Andreas, California
I've been making meals for large groups for years, and this noodle salad is a favorite. Using bottled Italian dressing makes the specialty a breeze to prepare.

- 15 pounds spaghetti (broken into 2-1/2-inch pieces), cooked and drained
- 16 cups Italian salad dressing
- 5 bottles (2.62 ounces *each*) Salad Supreme Seasoning
- 3 bunches celery, diced
- 12 medium green peppers, diced
- 12 medium onions, diced
- 6 pounds cheddar cheese, cut into 1/4-inch cubes
- 12 pounds tomatoes, seeded and diced

In a several large containers, combine all ingredients; toss to coat. Chill overnight.
Yield: 150 servings.

Cherry Bars

(pictured above)

Jane Kamp, Grand Rapids, Michigan

Want something simple to satisfy a large group? Try these festive, fruit-filled bars. With plenty of color from cherry pie filling and a subtle almond flavor, they're destined to become one of your most requested goodies.

1	cup butter, softened
2	cups sugar
4	eggs
1	teaspoon vanilla extract
1/4	teaspoon almond extract
3	cups all-purpose flour
1	teaspoon salt
2	cans (21 ounces *each*) cherry pie filling

GLAZE:

1	cup confectioners' sugar
1/2	teaspoon vanilla extract
1/2	teaspoon almond extract
2	to 3 tablespoons milk

In a large mixing bowl, cream butter and sugar. Add eggs, one at a time, beating well after each addition. Beat in the extracts. Combine flour and salt; add to the creamed mixture. Mix just until combined.

Spread 3 cups batter into a greased 15-in. x 10-in. x 1-in. baking pan. Spread with pie filling. Drop the remaining batter by teaspoonfuls over filling.

Bake at 350° for 30-35 minutes or until a toothpick comes out clean. Cool on a wire rack. Combine the glaze ingredients; drizzle over bars.

Yield: 5 dozen.

Beef Stew for a Crowd

Jackie Holland, Gillette, Wyoming

When it comes to feeding a large group, it's smart to serve a meal-in-one such as this chunky stew. Simply toss together a great big salad and some sliced loaves of bread and dinner is ready.

2-1/2	pounds beef stew meat, cut into 1/2-inch cubes
3	tablespoons vegetable oil
12	cups water
2	cans (15 ounces *each*) tomato sauce
1/4	cup beef bouillon granules
1	teaspoon salt, optional
1/2	teaspoon pepper
3-1/2	pounds potatoes, peeled and cubed
4	medium carrots, sliced
3	celery ribs, sliced
2	medium onions, coarsely chopped
3/4	cup all-purpose flour
1-1/2	cups cold water

In a soup kettle, brown beef in oil; drain. Stir in the water, tomato sauce, bouillon, salt if desired and pepper. Bring to a boil. Reduce heat; cover and simmer 1-1/2 hours or until the meat is tender.

Add the potatoes, carrots, celery and onions. Return to a boil. Reduce heat; cover and simmer 25-30 minutes or until the vegetables are tender.

Combine flour and cold water until smooth; gradually stir into stew. Bring to a boil; cook and stir for 2 minutes or until thickened.

Yield: 22 servings (5-1/2 quarts).

Asparagus in Puff Pastry

(pictured below)
Dianne Werdegar, Naperville, Illinois
This is one of my all-time favorite appetizers. Fast and easy, the golden bites are always a huge hit. I make and freeze batches of them during asparagus season for parties throughout the year.

      2 cups water
    24 fresh asparagus spears (about 1 pound), trimmed
      1 package (8 ounces) cream cheese
  1/2 teaspoon salt
      1 package (17-1/4 ounces) frozen puff pastry dough, thawed
  1/4 cup egg substitute

In a large nonstick skillet, bring water to a boil. Add asparagus; cover and cook for 3 minutes. Drain asparagus and immediately place in ice water; drain and pat dry. In a mixing bowl, beat cream cheese and salt until smooth; set aside.

Unfold the dough on a lightly floured surface. Cut each sheet in half widthwise. For each rectangle, spread cream cheese mixture lengthwise over half of the dough to within 1/2 in. of edges. Arrange two rows of three asparagus spears lengthwise in a single layer over cream cheese.

Brush edges of dough with some of the egg substitute; fold dough over filling and press edges together to seal. Cover and refrigerate for 1 hour.

Cut widthwise into 1-1/4-in. pieces. Place 1 in. apart on a baking sheet coated with nonstick cooking spray. Brush with remaining egg substitute. Bake at 425° for 8-12 minutes or until golden. Serve warm.

Yield: 28 servings.

Crunchy Potato Balls

(pictured above)
Nancy Eash, Gambier, Ohio
These potato balls make a good side dish or even an appetizer. In addition, they are a delicious way to use up leftovers. I have even substituted ground-up hot dogs or sausage for the ham.

        2 cups very stiff mashed potatoes
        2 cups finely chopped fully cooked ham
        1 cup (4 ounces) shredded cheddar *or* Swiss cheese
    1/3 cup mayonnaise
        1 egg, beaten
        1 teaspoon prepared mustard
    1/4 teaspoon pepper
        2 to 4 tablespoons all-purpose flour
  1-3/4 cups crushed cornflakes

In a bowl, combine the potatoes, ham, cheese, mayonnaise, egg, mustard and pepper; mix well. Add enough of the flour to make a stiff mixture. Chill. Shape into 1-in. balls; roll in cornflakes. Place on a greased baking sheet. Bake at 350° for 25 to 30 minutes. Serve warm.

Yield: about 6 dozen.

Potluck Fruit Salad

Fran Du Bay, Corrales, New Mexico
Here's a colorful combination of pineapple, strawberries and kiwifruit that serves 30. A citrus dressing and whipped topping make it extra special.

- 1 can (20 ounces) pineapple chunks
- 2/3 cup sugar
- 2 tablespoons all-purpose flour
- 1/4 cup orange juice
- 2 tablespoons lemon juice
- 2 eggs, lightly beaten
- 2 cups whipped topping
- 3 pints fresh strawberries, sliced
- 6 cups green grapes
- 6 medium firm bananas, cut into 1/2-inch slices
- 6 kiwifruit, peeled, halved and sliced

Drain pineapple, reserving juice; set pineapple aside. In a saucepan, combine sugar and flour. Stir in orange, lemon and reserved pineapple juices. Bring to a boil. Remove from heat. Stir a small amount of hot mixture into eggs; return all to pan, stirring constantly. Bring to a boil; cook and stir for 2 minutes or until thickened.

Cool to room temperature, stirring several times, about 20 minutes. Fold in whipped topping. In a large bowl, combine strawberries, grapes, bananas, kiwi and pineapple. Add dressing; toss.
Yield: 30 servings.

Spicy Chicken Wings

Gay Avery, Massena, New York
These wings may be a bit hot, but soy sauce and ground ginger offer a terrific Asian flair that people can't get enough of.

- 32 pounds chicken wings
- 8 cups soy sauce
- 1/2 to 2 cups hot pepper sauce
- 2 cups water
- 2 cups vegetable oil
- 3/4 cup cornstarch
- 8 teaspoons ground ginger
- 2 garlic cloves, minced

Place wings on greased baking sheets. Bake at 375° for 40-50 minutes or until juices run clear; drain. Meanwhile, combine remaining ingredients in a saucepan; bring to a boil, stirring occasionally. Boil for 2 minutes or until thickened.

Transfer wings to large roasting pans. Top with sauce. Bake, uncovered, for 60-70 minutes, stirring occasionally or until heated through.
Yield: about 240 appetizers.

Tangy Fruit Punch

(pictured above)
Ann Cousin, New Braunfels, Texas
A variety of fruity flavors mingle in this rosy punch. It's a popular beverage for a brunch since its versatile, sweet-tart taste goes great with all kinds of foods…from scrambled eggs to sliced ham.

- 1 can (46 ounces) pineapple juice
- 1 can (12 ounces) frozen orange juice concentrate, thawed
- 3/4 cup lemonade concentrate
- 1 cup water, *divided*
- 1/2 cup sugar
- 2 large ripe bananas
- 1 package (20 ounces) frozen unsweetened whole strawberries, thawed
- 2 liters ginger ale, chilled

In a punch bowl or large container, combine pineapple juice, orange juice concentrate, lemonade concentrate, 1/2 cup water and sugar.

Place bananas, strawberries and remaining water in a blender; cover and process until smooth. Stir into the juice mixture. Cover and refrigerate. Just before serving, stir in ginger ale.
Yield: 25-30 servings (about 5 quarts).

Zesty Sloppy Joes

(pictured above)
Sandy Abrams, Greenville, New York
A fantastic blend of seasonings means no one can eat just one of these sandwiches which are always a hit at gatherings. I have never served them without getting recipe requests.

   4 pounds ground beef
   1 cup chopped onion
   1 cup finely chopped green pepper
   2 cans (10-3/4 ounces *each*) condensed tomato soup, undiluted
   1 can (15 ounces) thick and zesty tomato sauce
   1 can (8 ounces) tomato sauce
 3/4 cup packed brown sugar
 1/4 cup ketchup
   3 tablespoons Worcestershire sauce
   1 tablespoon prepared mustard
   1 tablespoon ground mustard
   1 teaspoon chili powder
   1 teaspoon garlic salt
  20 to 25 hamburger buns

In a large saucepan or Dutch oven, cook beef and onion over medium heat until meat is no longer pink. Add green pepper. Cook and stir for 5 minutes; drain. Add the next 10 ingredients; bring to a boil. Reduce heat; cover and simmer for 1 hour, stirring occasionally. Serve on buns.
Yield: 20-25 servings.

Crab-Salad Jumbo Shells

(pictured below)
Jo Anne Anderson, Knoxville, Iowa
A friend gave me the idea for these delightful stuffed shells. I've kept adjusting the ingredients to suit my family's tastes, and I've been making this refreshing version for a long time.

  30 uncooked jumbo pasta shells
   1 cup finely chopped fresh broccoli florets
   1 garlic clove, minced
   2 packages (8 ounces *each*) imitation crabmeat, chopped
   1 cup (8 ounces) sour cream
 1/2 cup mayonnaise
 1/4 cup finely shredded carrot
 1/4 cup diced seeded peeled cucumber
   1 tablespoon chopped green onion
   1 teaspoon dill weed

Cook pasta according to package directions; rinse in cold water and drain well.

Meanwhile, in a microwave-safe bowl, combine the broccoli and garlic. Cover and microwave on high for 1 minute or until crisp-tender.

Transfer to a large bowl; stir in the remaining ingredients. Stuff into pasta shells. Cover and refrigerate overnight.
Yield: 30 stuffed shells.

Chicken Church Casserole

Charlotte Pizio, Bryn Mawr, Pennsylvania
This chicken-pasta hot dish is a down-home treasure that's become a staple at my church's luncheons. Try it the next time you're cooking for a big crowd.

- 20 cups cubed cooked chicken
- 1 package (2 pounds) elbow macaroni, cooked and drained
- 6 jars (6 ounces *each*) sliced mushrooms, drained
- 2 jars (4 ounces *each*) diced pimientos, drained
- 2 large green peppers, chopped
- 2 large onions, chopped
- 4 cans (10-3/4 ounces *each*) condensed cream of celery soup, undiluted
- 4 cans (10-3/4 ounces *each*) condensed cream of mushroom soup, undiluted
- 2 pounds process cheese (Velveeta), cubed
- 1-1/3 cups milk
- 4 teaspoons dried basil
- 2 teaspoons lemon-pepper seasoning
- 2 cups crushed cornflakes
- 1/4 cup butter, melted

In several large bowls, combine the chicken, macaroni, mushrooms, pimientos, peppers and onions. In several other large bowls, combine the soups, cheese, milk, basil and lemon-pepper; add to chicken mixture. Pour about 12 cups each into four greased 13-in. x 9-in. x 2-in. baking pans. Cover and refrigerate overnight. Remove from refrigerator 30 minutes before baking.

Combine cornflakes and butter; sprinkle over the casseroles. Cover and bake at 350° for 45 minutes. Uncover and bake 15-20 minutes longer or until bubbly.

Yield: 45-50 servings.

Turkey Nachos

Gayle Lewis, Winston, Oregon
Chunks of leftover turkey are a tasty addition to this thick, cheesy dip which starts with just three basic items.

- 1 can (10-3/4 ounces) condensed cheddar cheese soup, undiluted
- 3/4 cup salsa
- 1 cup cubed cooked turkey *or* chicken

Tortilla chips

Combine soup and salsa in a saucepan or microwave-safe bowl. Stir in turkey; cook until heated through. Serve warm with tortilla chips.

Yield: About 2 cups.

Combine oil and garlic; brush inside bread shells. Sprinkle with 1 teaspoon Italian seasoning. Layer bottom of each loaf with a fourth of the roast beef, mozzarella, basil, tomatoes, salami, artichokes, salad greens, chicken and onion. Repeat layers. Season with salt, pepper and remaining Italian seasoning.

Drizzle with remaining oil mixture if desired. Replace bread tops; wrap tightly in plastic wrap. Refrigerate for at least 1 hour before slicing.

Yield: 2 loaves (12 servings each).

Macaroni Salad

(pictured below)
LaVerna Mjones, Moorhead, Minnesota
This hearty pasta salad is sure to please a wide variety of tastes and appetites...and it serves a lot of folks!

    2 pounds uncooked elbow macaroni
   12 hard-cooked eggs, chopped
2-1/2 pounds fully cooked ham, cubed
    1 package (16 ounces) frozen peas, thawed
    3 cups sliced celery
    1 large green pepper, chopped
  1/2 cup chopped onion
    1 jar (4 ounces) diced pimientos, drained
    4 cups mayonnaise

Cook macaroni according to package directions. Rinse in cold water; drain and cool completely. Place in a large bowl. Stir in remaining ingredients. Cover and refrigerate for at least 3 hours.

Yield: 34 servings.

Layered Picnic Loaves

(pictured above)
Marion Lowery, Medford, Oregon
This sandwich is inspired by one I tried in New York. Made ahead of time, it's easily carted to gatherings, and guests say it's super.

    2 unsliced loaves (1 pound *each*) Italian
      bread
  1/4 cup olive oil
    3 garlic cloves, minced
    2 teaspoons Italian seasoning, *divided*
  1/2 pound deli roast beef
  3/4 pound sliced part-skim mozzarella cheese
   16 fresh basil leaves
    3 medium tomatoes, thinly sliced
  1/4 pound thinly sliced salami
    1 jar (6-1/2 ounces) marinated artichoke
      hearts, rinsed, drained and sliced
    1 package (10 ounces) ready-to-serve salad
      greens
    8 ounces thinly sliced deli chicken
    1 medium onion, thinly sliced
  1/4 teaspoon salt
  1/8 teaspoon pepper

Cut loaves in half horizontally; hollow out tops and bottoms, leaving 1/2-in. shells (discard removed bread or save for another use).

Tomato-Onion Phyllo Pizza

(pictured at left)
Neta Cohen, Bedford, Virginia

With a delicate crust and lots of lovely tomatoes on top, this dish is a special one to serve to guests. I make it often when fresh garden tomatoes are in season. It freezes well unbaked, so I can keep one on hand to pop in the oven for a quick dinner.

>   5 tablespoons butter, melted
>   7 sheets sheets phyllo dough
>   (18 inches x 14 inches)
>   7 tablespoons grated Parmesan cheese, *divided*
>   1 cup (4 ounces) shredded part-skim
>   mozzarella cheese
>   1 cup thinly sliced onion
>   7 to 9 plum tomatoes (about 1-1/4
>   pounds), sliced
> 1-1/2 teaspoons minced fresh oregano *or*
>   1/2 teaspoon dried oregano
>   1 teaspoon minced fresh thyme *or* 1/4
>   teaspoon dried thyme

Salt and pepper to taste

Brush a 15-in. x 10-in. x 1-in. baking pan with some of the melted butter. Lay a sheet of phyllo in pan, folding edges in to fit (keep remaining dough covered with waxed paper to avoid drying out). Brush dough with butter and sprinkle with 1 tablespoon Parmesan cheese. Repeat layers five times, folding edges for each layer.

Top with remaining dough, folding edges to fit pan; brush with remaining butter. Sprinkle with mozzarella cheese; arrange onion and tomatoes over the cheese. Sprinkle with oregano, thyme, salt, pepper and remaining Parmesan. Bake at 375° for 20-25 minutes or until edges are golden brown.

Yield: 28 slices.

Cheeseburger Mini Muffins

(pictured below right)
Teresa Kraus, Cortez, Colorado

I invented these cute little muffins so I could enjoy the flavor of cheeseburgers without resorting to fast food. I often freeze a batch and reheat however many I need. They're also great as appetizers.

>   1/2 pound ground beef
>   1 small onion, finely chopped
> 2-1/2 cups all-purpose flour
>   1 tablespoon sugar
>   2 teaspoons baking powder
>   1 teaspoon salt
>   3/4 cup ketchup
>   3/4 cup milk
>   1/2 cup butter, melted
>   2 eggs
>   1 teaspoon prepared mustard
>   2 cups (8 ounces) shredded cheddar cheese

In a skillet, cook beef and onion over medium heat until meat is no longer pink; drain. In a bowl, combine the flour, sugar, baking powder and salt. In another bowl, combine the ketchup, milk, butter, eggs and mustard; stir into the dry ingredients just until moistened. Fold in the beef mixture and cheese. Fill greased miniature muffin cups three-fourths full.

Bake at 425° for 15-18 minutes or until a toothpick comes out clean. Cool for 5 minutes before removing from pans to wire racks. Refrigerate leftovers.

Yield: 5 dozen.

Cajun Pork Sandwiches

(pictured above)
Mae Kruse, Monee, Illinois
This recipe's specially seasoned rub adds a little spice to tender, juicy slices of pork. You'll watch in delight as these open-faced sandwiches disappear from the buffet table!

      2 pork tenderloins (1 pound *each*), trimmed
      2 teaspoons vegetable oil
      3 tablespoons paprika
      2 teaspoons dried oregano
      2 teaspoons dried thyme
1-1/2 teaspoons garlic powder
   1/2 teaspoon pepper
   1/2 teaspoon salt, optional
   1/2 teaspoon ground cumin
   1/4 teaspoon ground nutmeg
   1/4 teaspoon cayenne pepper
    36 French bread slices *or* mini buns
Butter *or* mayonnaise
Lettuce leaves
Thin slivers of green and sweet red pepper

Place tenderloins in a greased 13-in. x 9-in. x 2-in. baking pan. Rub each with oil.

In a large bowl, combine the paprika, oregano, thyme, garlic powder, pepper, salt if desired, cumin, nutmeg and cayenne; pat over tenderloins. Cover and refrigerate overnight.

Bake at 425° for 25-30 minutes or until a meat thermometer reads 160°-170°. Let stand for 10 minutes; thinly slice. Spread bread or buns with butter or mayonnaise; top with lettuce, pork and green and red pepper.

Yield: 3 dozen.

Potluck Pointer

When organizing a large, covered-dish get-together, consider the following:

Ask everyone to bring their contribution in a disposable container. This will make cleaning up a snap.

Purchase some resealable storage bags that guests can use to take home leftovers. This way you won't be swamped with lots of extra food.

Ask everyone to bring a few copies of their recipe so they can share it with others.

Sausage Swirls

(pictured below)

Gail Guild, Rome, New York

My husband is a chaplain, so our lives are a whirlwind of potluck brunches, lunches and dinners. These delicious swirls truly complement scrambled eggs and fresh fruit.

      4 cups all-purpose flour
  1/4 cup cornmeal
      2 tablespoons sugar
      2 teaspoons baking powder
      1 teaspoon salt
  2/3 cup vegetable oil
  3/4 to 1 cup milk
      2 pounds uncooked bulk pork sausage

In a large bowl, combine the flour, cornmeal, sugar, baking powder and salt. Stir in oil until the mixture resembles coarse crumbs. Gradually stir in enough milk to form a soft dough.

Turn onto a floured surface; knead lightly for 30 seconds. Roll into two 16-in. x 10-in. rectangles. Crumble uncooked sausage over dough to within 1/2 in. on all sides. Carefully roll up from 16-in. end. Wrap in foil; chill for at least 1 hour.

Cut into 1/2-in. slices; place 1 in. apart on ungreased baking sheets. Bake at 400° for 15-20 minutes or until lightly browned. Serve warm or cold. Store in the refrigerator.

Yield: about 4 dozen.

Parmesan Knots

(pictured above)

Cathy Adams, Parkersburg, West Virginia

Refrigerated biscuits make these buttery snacks a snap. They're handy to make ahead of time and keep in the freezer. Simply reheat the knots on the day of your event.

  1/2 cup vegetable oil
  1/4 cup grated Parmesan cheese
  1-1/2 teaspoons dried parsley flakes
  1-1/2 teaspoons dried oregano
      1 teaspoon garlic powder
Dash pepper
      3 cans (12 ounces *each*) refrigerated
          buttermilk biscuits

In a small bowl, combine oil, cheese, parsley, oregano, garlic powder and pepper; set aside.

Cut each biscuit in half. Roll each portion into a 6-in. rope; tie in a loose knot. Place on greased baking sheets.

Bake at 450° for 6-8 minutes or until golden brown; immediately brush with the Parmesan mixture. Serve warm or freeze for up to 2 months.

Yield: 5 dozen.

Editor's Note: To use frozen biscuits, bake according to package directions.

Home-Style Meat Loaf

Allison Craig, Ormstown, Quebec
Down-home meat loaf is hard to resist, and with this recipe I can make sure that lots of friends get a chance to enjoy such a specialty. Guests seem to like the fact that this version uses both ground beef and ground pork.

    5 eggs
    4 cups milk
    4 cups dry bread crumbs
2-1/2 cups shredded carrots
1-1/4 cups chopped onions
    5 teaspoons salt
    4 teaspoons pepper
  10 pounds ground beef
    5 pounds ground pork

In five large bowls, combine the first seven ingredients. Crumble meat over top; mix well.

Shape into five loaves; place each in an ungreased 13-in. x 9-in. x 2-in. baking dish. Bake, uncovered, at 350° for 75-85 minutes or until meat is no longer pink and a meat thermometer reads 160°. Drain; let stand for 10 minutes before cutting.

Yield: 5 meat loaves (12 servings each).

Church Supper Chili

Vera Tollefsen, Whitefish Bay, Wisconsin
There's nothing to satisfying a huge group of hungry people with this recipe at your fingertips. Because it relies on so many canned items, it stirs up without much of a time commitment.

  21 pounds ground beef, browned and drained
    9 cans (15-3/4 ounces *each*) pork and beans
    9 cans (16 ounces *each*) kidney beans, rinsed and drained
    9 cans (28 ounces *each*) diced tomatoes, undrained
    9 cans (29 ounces *each*) tomato sauce
    3 pounds onions, finely chopped
7-1/2 cups finely chopped celery with leaves
    9 large green peppers, finely chopped
    9 bay leaves
    2 tablespoons salt
    5 tablespoons chili powder
    1 tablespoon paprika
    1 tablespoon pepper
    1 tablespoon ground cumin
    1 tablespoon cayenne pepper

Combine all of the ingredients in three large kettles. Cover and cook over medium heat for 2-3 hours. Discard bay leaves.

Yield: 100 servings (25 quarts).

Block-Party Beans

(pictured above)
LaDonna Daley, Elyria, Ohio
A variety of canned beans makes this tangy side dish as simple as it is taste tempting. Loaded with ground beef and chopped onion, the barbecue staple feeds lots of friendly faces.

    2 pounds ground beef
    2 cups chopped onion
    1 cup chopped celery
    1 can (10-3/4 ounces) cream of tomato soup, undiluted
    1 can (6 ounces) tomato paste
1/2 cup ketchup
    1 can (14-1/2 ounces) cut green beans, drained
    1 can (15-1/4 ounces) lima beans, drained
    1 can (15-1/2 ounces) wax beans, drained
    1 can (15-1/2 ounces) chili beans, undrained
    1 can (16 ounces) pork and beans, undrained
1/2 cup packed brown sugar
    2 tablespoons prepared mustard

In a large Dutch oven, brown beef over medium-high heat; drain. Add onion and celery; cook, uncovered, until tender. Stir in soup, tomato paste and ketchup; simmer, uncovered, 15-20 minutes.

Spoon into a large roaster. Stir in all the beans, brown sugar and mustard. Bake, uncovered, at 350° for 1 hour.

Yield: 25 servings.

General Recipe Index

This handy index lists every recipe by food category, major ingredient and/or cooking method, so you can easily locate recipes to suit your needs.

APPETIZERS & SNACKS
Cold Appetizers
Antipasto Platter, 32
Best Deviled Eggs, 13
Cheesy Onion Roll-Ups, 31
Fruit Kabobs, 30
Party Pitas, 25
Roast Beef Roll-Ups, 38
Sweet-Sour Deviled Eggs, 34
Tangy Mozzarella Bites, 37
Tortellini Nibblers, 39
Zippy Cheese Logs, 36

Dips
Baked Crab Dip, 31
BLT Dip, 238
Eggnog Dip, 214
Hot Bacon Cheese Dip, 74
Hot Crab Dip, 73
Pizza Dip in a Pumpkin, 195
Pumpkin Cookie Dip, 218
Ricotta Pepperoni Dip, 29
Slow Cooker Cheese Dip, 78
Strawberry Fruit Dip, 94
Taco Dip Platter, 222
Vegetable Wreath with Dip, 198
Zesty Vegetable Dip, 40

Hot Appetizers
Asparagus Snack Squares, 25
Baked Sausage Wontons, 26
Barbecue Sausage Bites, 65
Beef Stew for a Crowd, 239
Broccoli-Chicken Cups, 36
Chicken-Pesto Pan Pizza, 28
Chicken Wings with Apricot Sauce, 230
Crispy Cheese Twists, 29
Crispy Onion Wings, 33
Garden Focaccia, 27
Garlic Cheese Biscuits, 39
Golden Chicken Nuggets, 35
Ham and Cheese Puffs, 31
Hawaiian Roll-Ups, 26
Herbed Cheese Wafers, 29
Italian Bread Wedges, 37
Mini Chicken Turnovers, 24
Olive Cheese Bread, 36
1-2-3 Barbecue Sausage, 226
Sausage Sandwich Squares, 33
Spicy Chicken Wings, 241
Spinach Phyllo Bundles, 34
Spinach Squares, 35
Sunshine Chicken Wings, 38
Turkey Nachos, 243
Wontons with Sweet-Sour Sauce, 40

Snacks
Candy Snack Mix, 19
Fried Cinnamon Strips, 26
Rainbow Gelatin Cubes, 25
Spicy Party Mix, 216

Spreads
Colorful Crab Appetizer Pizza, 24
Hot Artichoke Spread, 32
Jingle Bell Spread, 211
Reuben Spread, 78
Seafood Delight, 6
Sesame Cheese Ball, 39
Shrimp Appetizer Spread, 228

APPLES
Apple Broccoli Salad, 19
Apple Bundt Cake, 191
Apple Cherry Cobbler, 14
Apple Pear Cake, 178
Apple Walnut Crescents, 93
Cookie Sheet Apple Pie, 176
Meaty Apple Skillet, 102

APRICOTS
Apricot Barley Casserole, 56
Apricot Glazed Chicken, 144
Chicken Wings with Apricot Sauce, 230

ARTICHOKES
Artichoke-Red Pepper Tossed Salad, 109
Hot Artichoke Spread, 32

ASPARAGUS
Asparagus Pasta Salad, 107
Asparagus Snack Squares, 25
Chicken Asparagus Pasta Supper, 146
Crunchy Asparagus Medley, 220

BACON
Amish Breakfast Casserole, 101
Bacon 'n' Egg Lasagna, 95
Bacon Cheddar Pinwheels, 94
Bacon Cheeseburger Balls, 135
Bacon Wild Rice Bake, 125
Beef and Bacon Chowder, 167
BLT Dip, 238
Glazed Bacon, 99
Smoky Bacon Wraps, 86
Two-Pot Dinner, 77

BANANAS
Banana Blueberry Pie, 223
Banana Snack Cake, 180
Creamy Banana Pie, 179

BARLEY (see Rice & Barley)

BARS & BROWNIES
Bars
Almond Fruit Squares, 98
Blueberry Lattice Bars, 190
Cherry Bars, 239
Chewy Pecan Pie Bars, 191
Chocolate Cheesecake Bars, 178
Chocolate-Covered Crispies, 17
Chocolate Raspberry Ears, 186
Double Chip Bars, 8
Sour Cream Cranberry Bars, 173

Brownies
Blond Toffee Brownies, 176
Brownies in a Cone, 21
Chocolate Bliss Brownies, 173
Chocolate Mint Brownies, 192
Double-Decker Brownies, 22
Graham Cracker Brownies, 218
Hugs 'n' Kisses Brownie, 199
Peanut Butter Brownies, 181
Trick-or-Treat Brownies, 210

BEANS
Beans 'n' Greens, 104
Best-Ever Beans and Sausage, 118
Black Bean Tortilla Casserole, 48

Block-Party Beans, 248
Four Bean Salad, 113
Green Bean Casserole, 12
Ground Beef Baked Beans, 55
Hot Dogs 'n' Beans, 80
Hot Dogs with Chili Beans, 151
Pepper Parmesan Beans, 223
Shaker Bean Soup, 158
Shepherd's Bean Pie, 140
Slow-Simmered Kidney Beans, 64
Southwestern Bean Soup, 224
Three-Bean Casserole, 12
Thyme Green Beans with Almonds, 129

BEEF (also see Ground Beef)
Appetizers
Reuben Spread, 78
Roast Beef Roll-Ups, 38

Main Dishes
Autumn Pot Roast, 202
Beef and Pepper Medley, 132
Beef Stew for a Crowd, 239
Brisket with Chunky Tomato Sauce, 142
Busy Day Beef Stew, 76
Flavorful Beef in Gravy, 79
Glazed Corned Beef, 152
Italian Beef Roll-Ups, 145
Marinated Pot Roast, 79
Old-World Sauerbraten, 72
Peppered Rib Roast, 136
Roast Beef with Onion Au Jus, 139
Slow-Cooked Short Ribs, 68
Tangy Beef and Vegetable Stew, 70
Tenderloin Spinach Spirals, 141
Yankee-Doodle Sirloin Roast, 206

Sandwiches
Beef and Bacon Chowder, 167
Beef Barbecue, 81
Brisket for a Bunch, 82
Dorothy's Barbecue, 165
Layered Picnic Loaves, 244
Mom's Portable Beef, 134
Pork and Beef Barbecue, 161
Reuben Deli Sandwiches, 159
Shredded Beef Sandwiches, 75

Soup
Tasty Reuben Soup, 161

BEVERAGES
All-Occasion Punch, 238
Christmas Glow Punch, 214
Citrus Grove Punch, 97
Cranberry Apple Cider, 66
Lemon Cider, 199
Orange Lemonade, 20
Refreshing Lemon-Lime Drink, 220
Spice Coffee, 66
Tangy Fruit Punch, 241

BLUEBERRIES
Banana Blueberry Pie, 223
Blueberry Angel Dessert, 227
Blueberry Kuchen, 95
Blueberry Lattice Bars, 190
Blueberry Oat Muffins, 96
Independence Day Delight, 205
Stars and Stripes Torte, 207

SAUSAGE (continued)
Main Dishes
Old-World Kielbasa, 134
Penne Sausage Bake, 59
Pepperoni Pizzazz, 45
Sausage Spaghetti Spirals, 57
Stick-to-Your-Ribs Supper, 143
Taco Pasta Shells, 149
Salads & Side Dishes
Best-Ever Beans and Sausage, 118
Kielbasa Summer Salad, 108
Sausage Mushroom Dressing, 123
Sandwiches
Bandito Chili Dogs, 72
Dressed-Up Dogs, 159
Make-Ahead Sloppy Joes, 156
Pepperoni Stromboli, 162
Sausage Stromboli, 156
Super Italian Sub, 167

SEAFOOD (see Fish & Seafood)

SIDE DISHES (also see Casseroles)
Potatoes
Crunchy Potato Balls, 240
Rice
Patchwork Rice Pilaf, 130
Potluck Mushroom Rice, 147
Potluck Rice Pilaf, 119
Vegetables
Block-Party Beans, 248
Braised Brussels Sprouts, 125
Caraway Red Cabbage, 121
Crunchy Asparagus Medley, 220
French Peas, 225
Grilled Veggie Mix 121
Herb-Buttered Corn, 6
Roasted Vegetables, 121
Snappy Peas 'n' Mushrooms, 226
Thyme Green Beans with Almonds, 129
Vegetable Spiral Sticks, 117

SLOW COOKER RECIPES
Appetizers
Barbecue Sausage Bites, 65
Hot Bacon Cheese Dip, 74
Hot Crab Dip, 73
Reuben Spread, 78
Slow Cooker Cheese Dip, 78
Beverages
Cranberry Apple Cider, 66
Spice Coffee, 66
Desserts
Chocolate-Raspberry Fondue, 73
Minister's Delight, 65
Main Dishes
Bandito Chili Dogs, 72
Beef and Barley, 76
Brisket for a Bunch, 82
Busy Day Beef Stew, 76
Chicken Stew, 74
Chili Mac, 66
Easy Chow Mein, 80
Easy-Does-It Spaghetti, 83
Egg Noodle Lasagna, 74
Flavorful Beef in Gravy, 79
Ground Beef Stew, 73
Ham with Cherry Sauce, 71
Hot Dogs 'n' Beans, 80
Marinated Pot Roast, 79
No-Fuss Pork and Sauerkraut, 77
Old-World Sauerbraten, 72

Pizza Casserole, 65
Slow-Cooked Chicken and Stuffing, 69
Slow-Cooked Short Ribs, 68
Slow-Cooked Spaghetti and Meatballs, 13
Tangy Beef and Vegetable Stew, 70
Turkey with Cranberry Sauce, 69
Two-Pot Dinner, 77
Sandwiches
Beef Barbecue, 81
Hot Ham Sandwiches, 68
Italian Turkey Sandwiches, 71
Shredded Beef Sandwiches, 75
Side Dishes
Cheesy Creamed Corn, 82
Creamy Hash Browns, 84
Fruit Salsa, 84
Hearty Wild Rice, 79
Hot Fruit Salad, 71
Moist Poultry Dressing, 64
Slow-Cooked Broccoli, 67
Slow Cooker Mashed Potatoes, 69
Slow-Simmered Kidney Beans, 64
Soups
Pork Chili, 81
Potato Chowder, 75

SOUPS
After-Thanksgiving Turkey Soup, 199
Beef and Bacon Chowder, 167
Chunky Beef Chili, 16
Church Supper Chili, 248
Country Cabbage Soup, 166
Crab Bisque, 162
Cream of Wild Rice Soup, 164
Creamy Carrot Soup, 203
Easy Vegetable Soup, 163
Hamburger Rice Soup, 161
Hearty Chicken Vegetable Soup, 15
Hunter's Chili, 168
Mediterranean Seafood Chowder, 158
Oven-Baked Bean Soup, 55
Oven Cheese Chowder, 163
Pineapple Peach Soup, 166
Pork Chili, 81
Potato Chowder, 75
Seafood Gumbo, 154
Seafood Soup, 235
Shaker Bean Soup, 158
Southwestern Bean Soup, 224
Split Pea Soup with Meatballs, 155
Sunday Gumbo, 157
Taco Soup, 159
Tasty Reuben Soup, 161

SPAGHETTI
Church Supper Spaghetti, 140
Confetti Spaghetti, 61
Easy-Does-It Spaghetti, 83
Garden-Fresh Spaghetti, 237
Slow-Cooked Spaghetti and Meatballs, 13
Spaghetti Goulash, 46

SPINACH
Layered Spinach Salad, 113
Spinach Noodle Casserole, 122
Spinach Parmesan Linguine, 118
Spinach Phyllo Bundles, 34
Spinach Squares, 35
Summer Spinach Salad, 201
Tenderloin Spinach Spirals, 141
Tossed Spinach Salad, 105

SQUASH & ZUCCHINI
Butternut Squash Casserole, 62
Cheesy Zucchini Bake, 58

Cheesy Zucchini Rice Casserole, 128
Skillet Zucchini, 219
Summer Squash Casserole, 237
Winter Squash Casserole, 197
Zucchini Ricotta Bake, 50

STEWS
Beef Stew for a Crowd, 239
Brunswick Stew, 236
Busy Day Beef Stew, 76
Chicken Stew, 74
Louisiana Jambalaya, 148
New Year's Oyster Stew, 197
Oven Jambalaya, 61
Tangy Beef and Vegetable Stew, 70
Vegetable Ham Stew, 135

STRAWBERRIES
Brunch Berry Pizza, 100
Potluck Strawberry Trifle, 17
Strawberry Fruit Dip, 94
Strawberry Yogurt Crunch, 91
Streusel Strawberry Pizza, 174

STUFFING & DRESSING
Chicken 'n' Corn Bread Dressing, 53
Moist Poultry Dressing, 64
Sausage Mushroom Dressing, 123
Slow-Cooked Chicken and Stuffing, 69

TOMATOES
Tomato Crouton Casserole, 225
Tomato-Onion Phyllo Dough Pizza, 245
Tomato Parmesan Salad, 116

TURKEY
After-Thanksgiving Turkey Soup, 199
Corn Bread Turkey Casserole, 61
Ham & Turkey Pasta Salad, 109
Herbed Turkey Breast, 151
Italian Turkey Sandwiches, 71
Marinated Turkey Slices, 133
Turkey Crescent Wreath, 148
Turkey Nachos, 243
Turkey Noodle Casserole, 56
Turkey with Cranberry Sauce, 69
Wild Rice Turkey Dish, 195

VEGETABLES (also see specific kinds)
Almond Celery Bake, 42
Black-Eyed Pea Casserole, 52
Braised Brussels Sprouts, 125
Cheesy Vegetable Medley, 126
Colorful Vegetable Bake, 127
Colorful Veggie Bake, 47
Crumb-Topped Mushrooms, 119
Easy Vegetable Soup, 163
Garden-Fresh Spaghetti, 237
Grilled Veggie Mix, 121
Herbed Vegetable Medley, 51
Marinated Vegetable Salad, 18
Marinated Veggie Salad, 114
Mostaccioli Veggie Salad, 115
Roasted Root Vegetables, 204
Roasted Vegetables, 121
Sally's Vegetable Salad, 112
Snappy Peas 'n' Mushrooms, 226
Tangy Beef and Vegetable Stew, 70
Vegetable Bake, 46
Vegetable Ham Stew, 135
Vegetable Spiral Sticks, 117
Vegetable Wreath with Dip, 198
Veggie Noodle Ham Casserole, 51
Veggie-Packed Strata, 88

Alphabetical Index

A

After-Thanksgiving Turkey
  Soup, 199
All-Occasion Punch, 238
Almond Celery Bake, 42
Almond Fruit Squares, 98
Almond Mandarin Salad, 108
Amish Breakfast Casserole, 101
Angel Rolls, 19
Antipasto Platter, 32
Apple Broccoli Salad, 19
Apple Bundt Cake, 191
Apple Cherry Cobbler, 14
Apple Pear Cake, 178
Apple Walnut Crescents, 93
Apricot Barley Casserole, 56
Apricot Glazed Chicken, 144
Artichoke-Red Pepper Tossed
  Salad, 109
Asparagus in Puff Pastry, 240
Asparagus Pasta Salad, 107
Asparagus Snack Squares, 25
Au Gratin Potatoes and Ham, 233
Autumn Pot Roast, 202

B

Bacon 'n' Egg Lasagna, 95
Bacon Cheddar Pinwheels, 94
Bacon Cheeseburger Balls, 135
Bacon Swiss Squares, 91
Bacon Wild Rice Bake, 125
Baked Crab Dip, 31
Baked Ham Hoagies, 164
Baked Sausage Wontons, 26
Baked Ziti, 150
Banana Blueberry Pie, 223
Banana Snack Cake, 180
Bandito Chili Dogs, 72
Barbecue Sausage Bites, 65
Barbecued Pork Potpie, 137
Beans 'n' Greens, 104
Beef and Bacon Chowder, 167
Beef and Barley, 76
Beef and Pepper Medley, 132
Beef Barbecue, 81
Beef Stew for a Crowd, 239
Beefy Biscuit Cups, 230
Best Deviled Eggs, 13
Best-Ever Beans and Sausage, 118
Big-Batch Burgers, 233
Black Bean Tortilla Casserole, 48
Black-Eyed Pea Casserole, 52
Black Forest Crepes, 101
Black Forest Trifle, 189
Black Hills Golden Egg Bake, 90
Block-Party Beans, 248
Blond Toffee Brownies, 176
BLT Dip, 238
Blueberry Angel Dessert, 227
Blueberry Kuchen, 95
Blueberry Lattice Bars, 190
Blueberry Oat Muffins, 96
Bohemian Kolaches, 232
Braised Brussels Sprouts, 125
Brisket for a Bunch, 82
Brisket with Chunky Tomato
  Sauce, 142
Broccoli-Chicken Cups, 36
Broccoli Ham Roll-Ups, 144

Broccoli Quiche Muffins, 91
Brownies in a Cone, 21
Brunch Berry Pizza, 100
Brunch Enchiladas, 90
Brunch Fruit Salad, 92
Brunswick Stew, 236
Busy Day Beef Stew, 76
Butter-Dipped Biscuit Squares, 228
Butternut Squash Casserole, 62
Butterscotch Muffins, 181

C

Cabbage au Gratin, 129
Cajun Pork Sandwiches, 246
Calico Potato Salad, 106
California Pasta Salad, 114
Candy Snack Mix, 19
Cappuccino Mousse Trifle, 221
Caraway Red Cabbage, 121
Carrot Coin Casserole, 44
Cheeseburger Mini Muffins, 245
Cheesy Broccoli-Rice Bake, 119
Cheesy Broccoli Rigatoni, 124
Cheesy Creamed Corn, 82
Cheesy Egg Puffs, 97
Cheesy Onion Roll-Ups, 31
Cheesy Shell Lasagna, 60
Cheesy Vegetable Medley, 126
Cheesy Wild Rice, 217
Cheesy Zucchini Bake, 58
Cheesy Zucchini Rice Casserole, 128
Cherry Bars, 239
Cherry Cheese Delight, 192
Cherry Cheese Torte, 177
Cherry Danish, 230
Cherry Kringle, 180
Chewy Pecan Pie Bars, 191
Chicken 'n' Corn Bread Dressing, 53
Chicken Asparagus Pasta
  Supper, 146
Chicken Church Casserole, 243
Chicken-Pesto Pan Pizza, 28
Chicken Salad Sandwiches, 168
Chicken Stew, 74
Chicken Wings with Apricot
  Sauce, 230
Chili-Cheese Spoon Bread, 52
Chili Mac, 66
Chive-Cheese Corn Bread, 29
Chocolate Bliss Brownies, 173
Chocolate-Caramel Supreme
  Pie, 188
Chocolate Cheesecake Bars, 178
Chocolate-Covered Crispies, 17
Chocolate Cream Cake, 172
Chocolate Mint Brownies, 192
Chocolate Mint Creams, 204
Chocolate Peanut Butter
  Cookies, 236
Chocolate Raspberry Bars, 186
Chocolate-Raspberry Fondue, 73
Christmas Chicken, 214
Christmas Fruit Salad, 198
Christmas Glow Punch, 214
Chunky Beef Chili, 16
Church Coleslaw, 7
Church Supper Chili, 248
Church Supper Ham Loaf, 141
Church Supper Potatoes, 130

Church Supper Sloppy Joes, 21
Church Supper Spaghetti, 140
Citrus Grove Punch, 97
Coconut Cream Pie, 218
Coconut Pecan Cookies, 186
Colorful Crab Appetizer Pizza, 24
Colorful Vegetable Bake, 127
Colorful Veggie Bake, 47
Confetti Spaghetti, 61
Cookie Sheet Apple Pie, 176
Corn Bread Casserole, 122
Corn Bread Turkey Casserole, 61
Corn Pasta Salad, 221
Country Cabbage Soup, 166
Country Rice Salad, 106
Crab Bisque, 162
Crab-Salad Jumbo Shells, 242
Cranberry Apple Cider, 66
Cranberry Meringue Pie, 182
Cranberry Salad, 197
Cream Cheese Cupcakes, 217
Cream of Wild Rice Soup, 164
Cream-Topped Grapes, 99
Creamy Banana Pie, 179
Creamy Carrot Casserole, 60
Creamy Carrot Soup, 203
Creamy Hash Brown Bake, 17
Creamy Hash Browns, 84
Crispy Cheese Twists, 29
Crispy Fried Chicken, 6
Crispy Onion Wings, 33
Crumb-Topped Mushrooms, 119
Crunchy Asparagus Medley, 220
Crunchy Corn Medley, 111
Crunchy Potato Balls, 240
Cucumber Party Sandwiches, 158
Cukes and Carrots, 123
Curried Chicken Pita Pockets, 155

D

Daffodillies, 194
Deep-Dish Cherry Pie, 175
Deli-Style Pasta Salad, 11
Deluxe German Potato Salad, 124
Deluxe Macaroni 'n' Cheese, 13
Deluxe Potato Ham Bake, 47
Do-Ahead Brunch Bake, 89
Dorothy's Barbecue, 165
Double Chip Bars, 8
Double-Decker Brownies, 22
Dressed-Up Dogs, 159
Easter Bunny Bread, 208
Easter Egg Bread, 212
Easy Chow Mein, 80
Easy-Does-It Spaghetti, 83
Easy Rhubarb Dessert, 177
Easy Vegetable Soup, 163
Egg Noodle Lasagna, 74
Eggnog Dip, 214

F

Favorite Chocolate Sheet Cake, 184
Firecracker Casserole, 62
Firemen's Meat Loaf, 147
Flavorful Beef in Gravy, 79
Fluffy Fruit Salad 109
Fluffy Pineapple Dessert, 217
Four Bean Salad, 113
Four-Cheese Bow Ties, 43
Four-Fruit Compote, 120

Four-Pasta Beef Bake, 232
French Country Casserole, 48
French Peas, 225
Fresh Broccoli Salad, 219
Fried Cinnamon Strips, 26
Fruit Kabobs, 30
Fruit Salsa, 84
Fruity Angel Food Trifle, 171

G

Garden Bean Salad, 115
Garden Focaccia, 27
Garden-Fresh Spaghetti, 237
Garlic Cheese Biscuits, 39
Georgia Pecan Cake, 188
Glazed Bacon, 99
Glazed Corned Beef, 152
Glazed Ham Balls, 133
Golden Chicken Nuggets, 35
Golden Raisin Oatmeal
  Cookies, 190
Graham Cracker Brownies, 218
Greek Pasta and Beef, 44
Green Bean Casserole, 12
Grilled Cheese in a Pan, 62
Grilled Picnic Chicken, 9
Grilled Veggie Mix, 121
Grits 'n' Sausage Casserole, 93
Ground Beef Baked Beans, 55
Ground Beef Stew, 73
Ground Beef Vermicelli, 144

H

Ham 'n' Cheese Omelet Roll, 87
Ham 'n' Cheese Potato Bake, 10
Ham 'n' Cheese Potato Salad, 110
Ham and Cheese Puffs, 31
Ham 'n' Cheese Strata, 100
Ham 'n' Tater Bake, 49
Ham & Turkey Pasta Salad, 109
Ham with Cherry Sauce, 71
Hamburger Casserole, 43
Hamburger Noodles, 47
Hamburger Rice Soup, 161
Ham-Swiss Strudel, 94
Handy Meat Pies, 149
Hawaiian Cake, 189
Hawaiian Roll-Ups, 26
Haystack Supper, 216
Hearty Baked Potato Salad, 127
Hearty Chicken Vegetable
  Soup, 15
Hearty French Toast, 102
Hearty Hotcakes, 98
Hearty Lasagna, 196
Hearty Rice Casserole, 54
Hearty Wild Rice, 79
Herb-Buttered Corn, 6
Herbed Cheese Wafers, 29
Herbed Tossed Salad, 224
Herbed Turkey Breast, 151
Herbed Vegetable Medley, 51
Holiday Green Salad, 195
Holiday Ham, 194
Home-Style Meat Loaf, 248
Homemade Sage Sausage
  Patties, 98
Honey Bun Cake, 171
Hot 'n' Cheesy Chicken
  Sandwiches, 155

Hot Artichoke Spread, 32
Hot Bacon Cheese Dip, 74
Hot Crab Dip, 73
Hot Dogs 'n' Beans, 80
Hot Dogs with Chili Beans, 151
Hot Fruit Salad, 71
Hot Ham Sandwiches, 68
Hugs 'n' Kisses Brownie, 199
Hunter's Chili, 168

I

Independence Day Delight, 205
Italian Beef Roll-Ups, 145
Italian Bread Salad, 116
Italian Bread Wedges, 37
Italian Meatball Hoagies, 160
Italian Potato Salad, 105
Italian Turkey Sandwiches, 71

J

Jack-o'-Lantern Burgers, 212
Jingle Bell Spread, 211

K

Kielbasa Summer Salad, 108

L

Layered Fresh Fruit Salad, 110
Layered Picnic Loaves, 244
Layered Spinach Salad, 113
Lemon Cheese Pie, 182
Lemon Cider, 199
Lemon Ladyfinger Dessert, 185
Lemon Poppy Seed Bread, 87
Lemon Poppy Seed Cake, 184
Liberty Sauerkraut Salad, 206
Loaded Baked Potato Salad, 128
Louisiana Jambalaya, 148

M

Macaroni Chicken Dinner, 133
Macaroni Salad, 244
Macaroon Kisses, 174
Make-Ahead Burritos, 137
Make-Ahead Sloppy Joes, 156
Maple-Mocha Brownie Torte, 170
Marinated Pot Roast, 79
Marinated Turkey Slices, 133
Marinated Vegetable Salad, 18
Marinated Veggie Salad, 114
Meaty Apple Skillet, 102
Meaty Spinach Manicotti, 55
Mediterranean Seafood
   Chowder, 158
Melon Cucumber Medley, 226
Melon Fruit Bowl, 93
Mexican Lasagna, 138
Mini Chicken Turnovers, 24
Mini Ham Quiches, 88
Mini Sausage Pizzas, 97
Minister's Delight, 65
Moist Poultry Dressing, 64
Mom's Portable Beef, 134
Mostaccioli, 22
Mostaccioli Veggie Salad, 115

N

Neptune's Lasagna, 59
New Year's Oyster Stew, 197
No-Fuss Pork and Sauerkraut, 77
Nutty Broccoli Slaw, 229

O

Oktoberfest Roast Pork, 202
Old-World Kielbasa, 134
Old-World Sauerbraten, 72

Olive Cheese Bread, 36
One-Dish Pork Chop Dinner, 139
1-2-3 Barbecue Sausage, 226
Orange Lemonade, 20
Oven-Barbecue Spareribs, 132
Oven Cheese Chowder, 163
Oven Jambalaya, 61
Overnight Coleslaw, 111
Overnight Pancakes, 89
Overnight Scalloped Chicken
   Casserole, 152

P

Parmesan Herb Chicken, 134
Parmesan Knots, 247
Parsley Tortellini Toss, 113
Party Pitas, 25
Pasta Crab Salad, 111
Patchwork Rice Pilaf, 130
Patriotic Pasta, 207
Peaches 'n' Cream Pie, 187
Peanut Butter Brownies, 181
Peanut Butter Eggs, 208
Pecan-Filled Coffee Rings, 18
Penne Sausage Bake, 59
Pennsylvania Dutch Coleslaw, 220
Pepper Parmesan Beans, 223
Peppered Rib Roast, 136
Pepperoni Pizzazz, 45
Pepperoni Stromboli, 162
Pierogi Casserole, 55
Pigskin Sandwiches, 200
Pineapple Ham Bake, 42
Pineapple Peach Soup, 166
Pistachio Mallow Salad, 210
Pizza by the Yard, 14
Pizza Casserole, 65
Pizza Dip in a Pumpkin, 195
Pizza Meat Loaf Cups, 142
Pizza Pasta Casserole, 49
Pizza Salad, 105
Plum Sausage Bites, 88
Poinsettia Cookies, 211
Popular Potluck Casserole, 42
Pork and Beef Barbecue, 161
Pork Chili, 81
Pork Noodle Casserole, 58
Potato Chowder, 75
Potatoes Supreme, 120
Potluck Chicken Casserole, 15
Potluck Fruit Salad, 241
Potluck Hot Dish, 50
Potluck Mushroom Rice, 147
Potluck Rice Pilaf, 119
Potluck Strawberry Trifle, 17
Pretzel Dessert, 185
Pumpkin Chocolate Loaf, 233
Pumpkin Cookie Dip, 218
Pumpkin Orange Cake, 172
Pumpkin-Pecan Cake Roll, 213

Q

Quick Calzones, 164
Quick Garlic Toast, 221

R

Rainbow Angel Food Cake, 205
Rainbow Gelatin Cubes, 25
Raspberry Cream Cheese Coffee
   Cake, 92
Raspberry Peach Delight, 187
Red Scalloped Potatoes, 117
Red, White 'n' Blue Salad, 206

Refreshing Lemon-Lime
   Drink, 220
Reuben Deli Sandwiches, 159
Reuben Spread, 78
Reunion BBQ's, 235
Reunion Meatballs, 238
Rhubarb Berry Delight Salad, 104
Ricotta Pepperoni Dip, 29
Roast Beef Roll-Ups, 38
Roast Beef with Onion Au Jus, 139
Roasted Root Vegetables, 204
Roasted Vegetables, 121
Root Beer Cookies, 20

S

St. Patrick's Day Cupcakes, 201
Sally's Vegetable Salad, 112
Sausage Hash Brown Bake, 86
Sausage Mushroom Dressing, 123
Sausage Sandwich Squares, 33
Sausage Spaghetti Spirals, 57
Sausage Stromboli, 156
Sausage Swirls, 247
Scrambled Egg Muffins, 99
Seafood Delight, 6
Seafood Gumbo, 154
Seafood Lasagna, 57
Seafood Soup, 235
Sesame Cheese Ball, 39
Seven-Fruit Salad, 7
Shaker Bean Soup, 158
Shepherd's Bean Pie, 140
Shredded Beef Sandwiches, 75
Shrimp Appetizer Spread, 228
Shrimp Pasta Salad, 116
Shrimp Puffs, 136
Skillet Zucchini, 219
Slow-Cooked Broccoli, 67
Slow-Cooked Chicken and
   Stuffing, 69
Slow-Cooked Short Ribs, 68
Slow-Cooked Spaghetti and
   Meatballs, 13
Slow Cooker Cheese Dip, 78
Slow Cooker Mashed Potatoes, 69
Slow-Simmered Kidney
   Beans, 74
Smoky Bacon Wraps, 86
Smoky Spareribs, 235
Snappy Peas 'n' Mushrooms, 226
Snowball Peaches, 205
Sour Cream Cranberry Bars, 173
Southwest Sausage Bake, 96
Southwestern Bean Soup, 224
Southwestern Pasta Salad, 8
Southwestern Salad, 114
Spaghetti Goulash, 46
Spaghetti Squash, 229
Spice Coffee, 66
Spicy Chicken Wings, 241
Spicy Party Mix, 216
Spinach Noodle Casserole, 122
Spinach Parmesan Linguine, 118
Spinach Phyllo Bundles, 34
Spinach Squares, 35
Split Pea Soup with Meatballs, 155
Stars and Stripes Torte, 207
Stick-to-Your-Ribs Supper, 143
Strawberry Fruit Dip, 94
Strawberry Yogurt Crunch, 91
Streusel Strawberry Pizza, 174
Summer Spinach Salad, 201

Summer Squash Casserole, 237
Summer Sub Sandwich, 10
Sunday Gumbo, 157
Sunshine Chicken Wings, 38
Super Italian Sub, 167
Super Pasta Salad, 238
Sweet 'n' Spicy Grilled Pork
   Chops, 145
Sweet Pineapple Casserole, 120
Sweet-Sour Deviled Eggs, 34
Swiss 'n' Crab Supper Pie, 53

T

Taco Dip Platter, 222
Taco Pasta Shells, 149
Taco Soup, 159
Taco Stovetop Supper, 223
Tangy Beef and Vegetable Stew, 70
Tangy Cauliflower Salad, 106
Tangy Fruit Punch, 241
Tangy Glazed Ham, 151
Tangy Mozzarella Bites, 37
Tangy Pork Barbecue, 154
Tasty Meat Pie, 146
Tasty Reuben Soup, 161
10-Minute Taco Salad, 222
Tenderloin Spinach Spirals, 141
Teriyaki Chicken, 227
Texas Lime Pie, 171
Three-Bean Casserole, 12
Thyme Green Beans with
   Almonds, 129
Tomato Crouton Casserole, 225
Tomato-Onion Phyllo Dough
   Pizza, 245
Tomato Parmesan Salad, 116
Tortellini Nibblers, 39
Tossed Spinach Salad, 105
Touchdown Cookies, 200
Trick-or-Treat Brownies, 210
Tropical Sweet Potatoes, 125
Tuna Noodle Cups, 49
Turkey Crescent Wreath, 148
Turkey Nachos, 243
Turkey Noodle Casserole, 56
Turkey with Cranberry Sauce, 69
Two-Pot Dinner, 77

V

Vegetable Bake, 46
Vegetable Ham Stew, 135
Vegetable Spiral Sticks, 117
Vegetable Wreath with Dip, 198
Veggie Noodle Ham Casserole, 51
Veggie-Packed Strata, 88

W

Walnut Broccoli Bake, 126
Watermelon Boat, 234
Wild Rice Harvest Casserole, 54
Wild Rice Turkey Dish, 195
Winter Cabbage Salad, 203
Winter Squash Casserole, 197
Wontons with Sweet-Sour
   Sauce, 40

Y

Yankee-Doodle Sirloin Roast, 206

Z

Zesty Sloppy Joes, 242
Zesty Vegetable Dip, 40
Zippy Cheese Logs, 36
Zucchini Ricotta Bake, 50